Samuel Hibbert-Ware

A Description of the Shetland Islands

Comprising an account of their, Scenery, Antiqities, and Superstitions

Samuel Hibbert-Ware

A Description of the Shetland Islands

Comprising an account of their, Scenery, Antiqities, and Superstitions

ISBN/EAN: 9783744717106

Printed in Europe, USA, Canada, Australia, Japan

Cover: Foto ©Andreas Hilbeck / pixelio.de

More available books at **www.hansebooks.com**

A

DESCRIPTION

OF THE

SHETLAND ISLANDS,

COMPRISING AN ACCOUNT OF THEIR

SCENERY, ANTIQUITIES, AND SUPERSTITIONS,

BY

SAMUEL HIBBERT, M.D., F.R.S.E., &c.

"*Dispecta est et Thule.*"—TACITUS.

PRINTED FOR ARCHIBALD CONSTABLE AND CO. EDINBURGH;
AND HURST, ROBINSON AND CO. LONDON.
Edinburgh, 1822.

REPRINTED BY T. & J. MANSON,
Lerwick, 1891.

TO THE

WERNERIAN SOCIETY

OF EDINBURGH

THE PRESENT VOLUME IS, WITH MUCH RESPECT,

INSCRIBED,

AS AN ACKNOWLEDGMENT OF THE HIGH ESTIMATION

ENTERTAINED BY THE WRITER REGARDING THE OBJECTS OF

THAT INSTITUTION

AND THE ZEAL OF ITS MEMBERS IN ILLUSTRATING

THE

NATURAL HISTORY

OF THE

BRITISH ISLANDS.

PREFACE TO THE REPRINT.

H IBBERT'S valuable work on Shetland having become very scarce, and accessible only to a limited few, the more interesting parts of the book, (the geological section being omitted), were reprinted in the "Shetland News" in the course of 1890-91. A very general desire was expressed, when the proposal to reprint the work in the newspaper was announced, that at the same time an opportunity should be afforded to the public of procuring it in book form. Hence the issue of this volume. As it was not intended to reproduce the book in an expensive form, arrangements were not made for including the plates and maps which are given in the original, but as a specimen of the former, one page of the engravings has been reproduced in fac simile ; and the music of two native airs has been added. The spelling of the original has been adhered to throughout, and in other respects every effort has been made to reproduce an accurate reprint of the original volume.

T. & J. MANSON.

CONTENTS.

ITINERARY THROUGH THE ISLES OF SHETLAND.

ITER I.

	PAGE
LEITH TO DUNROSSNESS IN SHETLAND .	1-27

Distant View of Fair Isle, 4. Traditionary Narrative of the Shipwreck of the Spanish Armada in 1588, 4.—Approach to Dunrossness, 8.—Grutness Voe to Quendal, 12.—Remarks on the Dark Period of the History of Shetland and Orkney, 13.—Quendal Bay, 19.

NOTES TO ITER I.   27-31

ITER II.

SOUTH-EAST DISTRICT OF SHETLAND   33-118

History of the Udallers of Shetland, 34.—Appendix to the History, 65.—Holms of Quendal Bay, 69.—Fitfiel Head, 70.—Garthsness, 72.—Sumburgh, 73. Sumburgh to Sandwick, 81.—Ancient Weapons of War discovered in Shetland, 82.—Burgh of Mousa, 86.—Burroland, 89.—Sandlodge, 90.—Coningsburgh, 91.—Fladibister to Scalloway, 92.—Scalloway, 93.—Tingwall, 98. -Ancient State of the Jurisdiction of Shetland, 99.—Tingwall to Lerwick, 106.—Lerwick, 107.—Islands of Bressay and Noss, 109.—Lerwick to Catfirth, 111.—Eswick to Lunna, 114.—Island of Whalsey and the Out-Skerries, 116.
Illustrations of the Law of Udal Succession, 119.—Illustrations of the Feudal Tenures of Shetland, 132.—Ancient Rental of Shetland, 133.

NOTES TO ITER II. .   138-146

ITER III.

NORTH ISLES OF SHETLAND, MID DISTRICT OF MAINLAND, ISLES IN
BAY OF SCALLOWAY 147-279

Island of Fetlar, 148.—Account of David Gilbert Tait, a lad born deaf and blind, 151.—Belmont to Woodwick, 155.—Kirk of Baliasta, 157.—Hermananess to Haroldswick, 158.—Crucifield, 160.—Balta Sound, 163.—Castle of Mounces, 164.—Uyea Sound, 165.—Uyea Sound to the

Island of Hascosea, 167.—Island of Yell, 169.—Yell Sound, 172.—Lunna to Aithsvoe, 175.—Ancient and Present State of Sheep Pastures, 182.—Trolhouland, 189.—Cullswick to the Voo of Sand, 195.—Bay of Scalloway, 196.—Scalloway to Bigsetter Voe, 200.

NOTES TO ITER III. 209-210

ITER IV.

WEST OF SHETLAND 213-276

Island of Meikle Roe, 213.—Dutch Herring Fishery of Shetland, 214.—Mavis Grind to Feideland, 216.—The Haaf, 221.—Sand Voe to Roeness Voe, 224.—Fishing Tenures of Shetland, 226.—Hillswick, 228.—Regents' Fishing Bank, 230.—Helga Water, 232.—Tangwick to Roeness Voe, 234.—Hillswick to Mavis Grind, 238.—Aithsvoe to Clousetter, 241.—Onzie Firth to Norbay, 243. Papa Stour, 249. Festivities of Shetland, 252.—Sword Dance, &c., ib.—Ve Skerries, 260. Sandness to Vailey, 264.—Witchcraft, 265.—Island of Foula, 274.—Foula to Bressay Sound, 276.

NOTES TO ITER IV. 280-288

GENERAL APPENDIX.

Bressay, Coalfish, Whales, Population, &c., 289-290.—Music of Shetland, with Specimens, 291.

INDEX TO THE ITINERARIES 292-294

PREFACE

THE general plan of this work is by no means what was at first intended; without, therefore, this explanation, it may be liable to animadversion. My original object was to publish nothing more than the result of certain geological researches conducted in Shetland, with an Essay on Stratification, illustrative of the views on which an explanation of the complicated distribution of the rocks of these islands would be attempted. Under this arrangement, many pages had been printed off, when, on the supposition that a work of this kind, purely mineralogical, could only bear reference to a very limited class of readers, it was recommended to me to extend my plan, by including a popular account of the Scenery and Manners of the country, and a particular notice of its Antiquities. I was eventually induced to comply with this request, notwithstanding the peculiar awkwardness of allowing matter of a lighter kind to mingle with investigations purely scientific; but in order to obviate, in some degree, the inconvenience of the arrangement that resulted from an altered system, the miscellaneous account of the country is printed in a larger type, and being completely separated from the Geology, each department of the book may be easily read as a detached work.

Respecting the various subjects treated of, a few words may be said. Of the Antiquities which were to be investigated, none are so singular as those that relate to the Udal System, and to the process of Feudalization which took place in Shetland and Orkney. Into this curious research I inadvertently plunged, and the task of reconciling opposite statements, and of arranging the materials that came into my possession, has been infinitely beyond what could be calculated upon, having been such as to induce a consumption of time, that, being totally out of the sphere of my proper pursuits, nothing can repay. I may, indeed, truly state my case to be that of an illustrious townsman of my own, who, in a work executed with a learning to which I can have no pretensions, however great may have been my trouble, has remarked, that, "had he foreseen the full extent of his scheme at first, he should never have had the hardiness to form it; had he foreseen in any part of the execution the time and the labour which the rest would have cost him, he had certainly shrunk back from the attempt, and had closed the whole work immediately; but he proceeded on the model before him, ever flattering himself, that a few months more would dismiss him from the employ, and remit him again to those professional studies which he had very unwittingly deserted."*

With the exception of my account of the Geology of Shetland, and the ancient Udal System of the country, all the other matter may be considered as of a popular character. A view is given of the manners and state of a country, which, in their simplicity, do not a little resemble what the most improved districts of England and Scotland must have been many centuries ago. Thus, in respect to the Agriculture of these islands, I have rather dwelt upon the curious features attending it, than imitated prior visitors by pointing out all the improvements of which it is susceptible. The natives, indeed, as husbandmen, differ little from that humble state of advancement, which has been so well described in a Teutonic poem of the eighth century, the original of which, along with a Latin translation, appears in a recent work, illustrative of ancient Scandinavian manners.

Baurn ôlu thau   "Suis rebus contenti
Biuggu oc undu, —   Domos edificarunt et liberos genuerunt,—
lögdu garda   Sæpibus segetes cingebant,
akra toddu   Agros oblimabant,
unnu at svinum   Sues nutriebant,
geita gættu   Capras custodiebant,
oc grófu torf.   Et cespites effodiebant."

Song of King Eric.†

There has, in fact, been scarcely any exertion made until very recently, to improve the condition of the country. It is true, that, in the year 1742, the Earl of MORTON had interest sufficient to bring in a bill, whereby he obtained a discharge of the reversion of Orkney and Shetland to the Crown, for the sum on account of which he held them in pledge, pleading that the emoluments were not sufficient to pay the interest of the mortgage, and promising to ameliorate the state of these islands, by draining lochs, and establishing fisheries and manufactories. These chimerical schemes, however, it is needless to add, were never put into execution. But about seven years ago, the Agricultural Society of Shetland was formed, the institution of which ought deservedly to be considered as an epoch in the annals of this country. The effect of a number of well-educated individuals of rank and property meeting together to consult on the state and circumstances of the several districts in which they reside, cannot but be favourable to the interest of the whole of the community. At the same time, the introduction of a better state of husbandry, which is connected with many complicated relations under which the landholders stand, not only to the Superior of the country, but to the Government of Great Britain, must necessarily be a very slow process. Yet, under all these untoward circumstances, the industry evinced by the Society is scarcely less than that which has

---

* Mr Whittaker of Manchester, in the Preface to his History, &c., 4to, vol. i.
† Illustrations of Northern Antiquities, printed at Edinburgh, A.D. 1814, p. 449.

been attributed to an early civilizer of the Northmen a thousand years ago:

öxn nam at temia	Boves didicit mansuefacere,
ardr at giorva	Aratra fabricare,
hús at timbra	domos ædificare,
hladur at smida	horrea struere,
karta at giorfa	currus parare,
oc keyra plóg.	et aratro terram vertere.

Song of King Eric.

Respecting the Fisheries of Shetland, little more than a popular view is given of them: but to the Superstitions of the country, a greater degree of importance has been attached than may be conceived necessary; the motive for which has been to preserve opinions, that in this sequestered group of islands seem to approach much nearer to the original Pagan tenets of the Scandinavians, than are to be found in several districts of Norway itself.

The subjects to which I have little adverted are connected with Zoology. This omission has been chiefly owing to the unexpected extent to which other matter treated of has swelled the volume. For the same reason, no account is given of the Botany and Meteorology of the country.

The Geology of Shetland cost me great pains to draw up; my labour was also much impeded, by the wretched charts of these islands that have been published, so that I was obliged, with the aid of nothing more than a pocket compass, to climb almost every point of high land in the country, in order to obtain a new draught fit for my purpose. The map, therefore, that is now produced, appears so totally different to any that has ever been before engraved, as to have every claim to the title of a New Survey. That it contains many imperfections is to be expected, but I believe they do not affect it in the least, in a geological point of view.*

It is to myself a source of regret, that my investigations have been confined to a class of rocks (the primitive), of which WERNER appears to have entertained very imperfect notions. But that no erroneous view may be entertained of what I have said with regard to this truly great naturalist, I shall state my conviction, that although his system is, in several respects, open to many strictures, yet, *taken as a whole*, there has been nothing proposed by any other theorist, that has comprehended so many inductions that appear perfectly unobjectionable; and the mode of prosecuting the study of rocks that he first taught, has given to the history of geological science a new era.

An abstract of that part of the present work, which relates to the distribution of the rocks of Shetland was first read to the Wernerian Natural History Society, and it was to their active President, Professor JAMESON, that I produced, as the fruits of my

---

* The rocks of Shetland, which I have undertaken to illustrate, were first examined partially by Professor Jameson, and the work he produced is a highly creditable memorial of the early attention that he paid to Geology. Since this Gentleman's visit, Dr Traill and Dr Fleming have visited the country, each of whom has given a very good description of the districts which he examined. I have made several allusions to their researches, whenever I had no opportunity of directing my own personal observations to the objects that attracted their attention; and have mentioned, in a particular manner, the more important remarks that they made. Professor Jameson's account of Shetland, was published above twenty years ago, being afterwards reprinted in his Mineralogical Travels through Scotland. Dr Traill's short notice of Shetland will be found in Mr Neill's Tour, and Dr Fleming's in Mr Shirreff's Agricultural Survey of Shetland, and in the paper on the Rocks of Papa Stour, given in vol. i. of the Wernerian Transactions.

voyage to Shetland, Chromate of Iron. This result of my first journey having been communicated to one who was well able to judge of its importance, he was, upon examining the metal, so struck with the quality and magnitude of the masses which I had brought over with me, that, at his earnest request, I consented to undertake a second voyage to Shetland, for the purpose of rendering the discovery conducive to its interests, and, at the same time, of completing a Geological Survey of that country. In the history, then, of my labours, I have no slight mention to make of the encouragement that they met with from Professor JAMESON, who, in constantly stimulating his pupils to persevere in investigating the Mineralogy of Scotland, shews in all such instances a zeal that is well calculated to prove the National utility of the Science that he teaches with such success.

I may now, perhaps, be allowed to remark, that I had long, for several reasons, abandoned the idea of giving any farther account of my investigations in Shetland, than were made public through the means of a Scientific Journal ; but the honorary token of approbation that I received from the Society of Arts and Commerce in London, as a reward of my discovery of the Chromate of Iron, urged me to offer to the public the details of all my researches, to which the circumstance that they were pleased to stamp with their approval, was merely incidental. Accordingly, the present volume comprehends the account of an arduous examination of the nature and distribution of the rocks of Shetland, carried on in the autumn of the year 1817, and continued in the ensuing summer, during a period of six months, the chief obstacle to it arising from the imperfect maps that have hitherto been rendered of the country. In the process of such a minute survey, it can rarely fail to happen that some contribution to the resources of the country should not follow ; and it is a pleasing reflection, that a truly patriotic Society exists, whose approbation is the best stimulus that can be given to the renewal of exertions, the object of which is to encrease our knowledge of the mineralogical productions of the British kingdom.

During the progress of this work, I have felt particularly obliged to Dr BREWSTER for the ready assistance that he has always afforded me, whenever, from the uncertainty that too frequently prevails in identifying minerals from their external characters alone, I should have been unable to discover their nature without a chemical analysis. It is, indeed, from optical researches such as those which he is now pursuing, that we must expect to see mineralogy advanced to a rank among the sciences that it has hitherto failed in attaining.

As a considerable part of this work is historical, it was necessary to consult many scarce works, for the loan of several of which, I have been greatly indebted to Mr DAVID LAING of Edinburgh. Much information has been given me by the gentlemen of Shetland, particularly by WILLIAM HENDERSON, Esq. of Bardister, to whom I would return my warmest acknowledgments for the interest and zeal he has taken in procuring me materials for this work. From his superior intelligence, relative to the earlier manners of the country, I have derived much valuable information. So many, indeed, have been my obligations to this gentleman, that I should be ungrateful in not mentioning them in a particular manner.

The attentions paid me during my visit to Shetland, I shall often feel myself called upon to acknowledge. I may indeed safely aver, that the grateful sense I entertained of them after a first visit to this country, had no small share in influencing all my conduct subsequent to my discovery of the chromate of iron. Upon the result of my journey being published, several inquiries were made after this mineral on views of speculation; but as its site was known to no one but myself, I was unwilling to afford any clue to the knowledge of it, until the proprietors of the ground, whoever they might be, had been apprised of an event so important to their interests. This was the object of my second visit to Shetland; and in communicating every instruction in my power relative to the nature and value of the ore that was diffused in large masses throughout the hills near Balta Sound, as well as in urging the importance of a minute examination of the rocks in which it abounded, I sought for nothing more than to leave behind me some memorial of the visit of a stranger, happy to acknowledge the hospitality of this remote extremity of the British Islands.

NOTICE.

On account of this publication swelling to a size far beyond what I could have anticipated, in consequence of its enlarged plan, I have been obliged, for this reason alone, to withhold, under the form of notes, many references and authorities, and, in a few instances, the acknowledgments due to authors from whom I have derived assistance in my descriptions. I may therefore now observe, that the modern statistical accounts which I have chiefly consulted, in order to correct my observations on the subject of the husbandry and fisheries of the country, have been those written by THOMAS MOUAT, Esq., and by the Reverend Messrs MORRISON and BARCLAY; having availed myself more particularly of their remarks in my description of some of the implements and operations of agriculture. I have also examined the observations on general subjects which are to be found in Mr NEILL's Tour, in Dr EDMONSTONE's History of Shetland, and in Mr SHIRREFF's Agricultural Survey. In reverting to the earlier state of manners in Shetland, the ancient Country Acts published by Mr LEISK of Uyea have suggested many inquiries.

Much information on the superstitions of the country, I obtained while rambling among the wild, sequestered districts of the west of Shetland; and many of them have, since my return to Scotland, been communicated to me by some of my friends.

I shall lastly observe, that a volume of Mr Low's MS. Tour having fallen into my possession, it will be found that I have frequently adverted to it. The work was drawn up with great care, but from some unexplained cause, was never published, while the most important observations were selected from it (evidently with the author's consent), and appeared in Mr PENNANT's Arctic Zoology. After poor Low's MSS. had been thus freely drawn upon, little more remained meriting a distinct publication, and the Tour, along with the author's Fauna Orcadensis, eventually fell into the hands of his friend Mr PATON, when they were again, by other writers, more or less ransacked for information. On the occasion of Mr PATON's decease, Mr Low's MSS. were brought to the hammer, when the Fauna Orcadensis fortunately came into the possession of Dr LEACH, who published it, with a well deserved tribute to the author's memory. The

Tour afterwards appeared in the sale catalogue of Mr LAING of Edinburgh, when it was purchased by myself; but there was little matter left that had not, in some shape or other, been long before the public, the drawings being the most valuable part of the whole. Some information, however, respecting the earlier customs of Shetland, still remained that had escaped the notice of those who had seen the work, and it is now for the first time, presented to the public; and if I have been more particular in referring to any one individual that has been consulted than to another, it has been to this excellent yet unfortunate author, having indeed no other wish than to render every tribute in my power to departed merit.

The numerous plates that are given in the body of the work, were for the most part from slight sketches that I made, which were not originally intended for the public eye, otherwise they would have been produced with more care and selection. New drawings, however, were made from these, while I was in England, by an ingenious young artist of Manchester, Mr PARRY. For an original view I am indebted to a friend, and I have been favoured with another by a gentleman of Edinburgh. A small view of Foula, and a figure of the Torsk fish, are by Mr Low, and three sketches, viz., of the Cradle of Noss, the Fort of Lerwick, and the Burgh of Culswick, have before appeared in a Magazine of the present publishers.

It ought to be particularly remarked, that, on account of the necessity of observing a certain order in the geological description of the various places examined, I found it impossible, in describing an itinerary through Shetland, conducted with the view of noticing the miscellaneous objects occurring in each successive district, to regulate it by the strict rules that a regular diary of my travels might demand. But having visited almost every corner of Shetland, I am perhaps entitled, for this reason only, to assume the functions of a guide, and to lead the reader through the country in the route that is most convenient for examination, rather than in the order in which I passed through it myself. In pursuance of this plan, the Itinerary is divided into distinct Iters,—*a word lately Anglicised, and in common acceptation among antiquaries, to express a district through which a gradual progress has been made. In this sense it has been used by many authors, among whom is* Mr FENTON, *in his Historical Tour through Pembrokeshire.*

I may also be permitted to observe, that while this Work was in the press, a new novel by the " Great Unknown" was announced, with the notice that the scene was laid in Shetland. Among the many reasons that I have had for regretting the present publication, in its enlarged plan, it is assuredly not the least of them, that this volume must appear cotemporaneous with THE PIRATE; *for, in adverting to the scenery and manners of this country, I am sensible that I cannot fail to provoke a comparison which must be highly to my disadvantage. Still, we owe so many obligations to the Author of Waverley, for the pleasure he has afforded us in perusing his works, that an author ought not to complain if he has incautiously brought himself into such a dilemma as to stand as a mere foil to the greatest of all modern masters of description.*

ITINERARY

THROUGH THE

ISLES OF SHETLAND.

Iter I.

LEITH TO DUNROSSNESS IN SHETLAND.

> "Ponti profundis clausa recessibus,
> Strepens procellis, rupibus obsita,
> Quam grata defesso virentem,"
> [Thule] "sinum nebulosa pandis?"
>
> JOHNSON, *De Skia Insula.*

THE cluster of Islands and Rocks, which, under the name of SHETLAND, form the northern barrier of the British Kingdom, are, with the exception of two of them only, contiguous to each other. If these be excluded from the number, the rest may be placed between 59° 48' 30", and 60° 52' North latitude, and between 52' and 1° 57' of West longitude from London. The two remote islands are named Fair Isle and Foula. Fair Isle is situated about twenty-four miles to the south of the Mainland in Shetland, and Foula about twenty miles to the west.—See Note I.

The principal communication that Shetland has with Scotland is maintained by the Port of Leith, from which it is distant about 96 leagues. During the summer season, one or more vessels go and return from this harbour very frequently;

fishing materials, grain, woollen and linen goods, and spirits, are sent from Scotland, whilst this country receives in return dried fish, hosiery, oil, and some little kelp. In one of these vessels, a convenient passage is afforded for the Shetland Archipelago.

These islands, in a Geological point of view, afford, perhaps, one of the best specimens that can be found in any country of a Primitive district, all the known mountain-masses peculiar to it being present. A few rocks also occur of a newer kind, consisting of Werner's oldest Sandstone, associated with secondary Porphyries.

To the Naturalist, therefore, who may be induced to follow the route I am now taking, in order to investigate the relations of a class of rocks that are too little known, I would offer the experience of a summer's itinerary among these islands, in the hopes that, as a guide through the country, it may prove of some assistance to his future researches.

He, also, to whom the study of Geology is yet new, may be informed, that there is, perhaps, no greater advantage to be derived than from tracing, in their actual progress, the researches which are pursued in order to decide the Geological character of a district. There is, likewise, no incipient object to which the attention of the Student can be more profitably directed, than to the examination of the nature and relative position of Primitive Rocks, for which the strata of England and Wales present inferior opportunities. To facilitate, therefore, the studies of the aspirant, I shall occasionally dwell much longer, than may by some be deemed necessary, on circumstances that are perfectly familiar to the adept.

It is to be confessed, however, that Geology would be a pursuit of inferior attraction, if it did not involve a tolerable share of hypothesis, without which, as I have heard it seriously contended, the character of the Geologist would be reduced to that of the most inferior menial of Science, and, in comparision with the undaunted theorist, whose vivid imagination can readily apply the facts collected by others to the explanation of the Earth's structure, he would become a mere hewer of wood and drawer of water. These sentiments ought not, perhaps, to be admitted without considerable qualification; and yet in endeavouring to estimate the character of a mere collector of mineralogical specimens, or of a mere topographical recorder of the names of rocks, it is scarcely possible to descend much lower in the scale of scientific contributors. It is true that we continue to hear the fastidious Naturalist rail against Theory; but it may be fairly questioned, if, amidst this prudish declamation, there does not still remain some lurking hypothesis or other, that imparts to him the ardour with which he is observed to scale the precipitous cliff; for it is difficult to suppose that such an uncommon alacrity can have been excited by no other motive than that of being the humble recorder of some few external characters of Nature. Far be it, then, from the candid Geologist, to disown the importance and influence of theory; and with regard to the distribution of the strata of Shetland, there is every necessity for incorporating as much of hypothesis in our researches, as may be necessary for wielding with vigour the heavy hammer that is directed to the resolution of primitive rocks. But what particular views to adopt for the purpose is a distinct question: so many reveries of Cosmogony succeed to each other, that it is difficult to state precisely in what particular opinions consists the Petromania of the day.

But, notwithstanding the bold and poetical flights of imagination by which the study of rocks may be enlivened, it is still not sufficient of itself to protect a long journey, which is exclusively geognostical, from insufferable tædium. The attention cannot be always confined to the relations of stratified and unstratified rocks; and in courting some relief from a diversification of objects, the attention of the Shetland visitor may be occasionally directed to the incalculable riches of the Northern Seas; these are tardily resigned for the use of the British nation, whose tutelary saint was never yet the anxious guardian of its Fisheries.

If, also, the spirit of Petromania has not rendered the mind of the Geognost insensible to every other impression, but that which results from the external characters of minerals, he may surely devote some portion of his time to examine the simple manners of a race of People, who have as good a claim to the title of PRIMITIVE as the rocks among which they dwell. He may, for a time, lay down the ponderous hammer with which he is caparisoned, for the purpose of tracing, in the language, domestic habits, or agriculture of this people, some tokens of their early emigration from the shores of ancient Scandinavia. He may relinquish his labours for a short period, to contemplate the simple architecture of the defensive Burgh; or, when with infinite toil, he has ascended a peak that overlooks all other hills, he may pause, for a few moments, to inspect the lonely Watch-tower that crowns its summit. With these combined inducements, then, for our voyage, we will now set sail, invoking, at the same time, in the set form of the English Poet Drayton, the local genius of the Shetland Archipelago, whom Scandinavian writers, "prisco sermone," were wont to name Hialtlandia. By her benignant influence may we be conducted safely amidst the sounds and creeks of Hyperborean Seas!

> "Go thou before us still thy circling shores about,
> And, in this wandering maze, help to conduct us out,—
> Wise Genius! by thy help, that so we may descry
> How thy fair mountains stand, and how thy vallies lie."
>
> DRAYTON'S *Poly-olbion.*

The vessels which regularly trade between Leith and Shetland present humble cabin accommodations; but in the Lerwick Packet these were wholly overlooked in the national welcome with which the worthy master, Captain Simpson, appeared to meet his passengers as they came on board, and in the unremitting attention which he paid to their comfort during the whole of their voyage. With a favourable wind, the passage to Shetland is made in about fifty hours, but too frequently vessels are compelled, from contrary winds, to put into some harbour on the eastern coast of Scotland.

The sail along the Scottish coast possesses much interest; it is enlivened by the numerous towns which diversify the coasts of Fife, and, on leaving the Frith of Forth, by the noble light-house similar to that of Eddiston, the erection of which has been completed by the ingenuity of Mr Stevenson;—afterwards appear in succession Montrose, Aberdeen, and Peterhead. On passing Kinnaird's Head, leaving in course of time the counties of Banff and Moray to the south-west, and the coasts of Caithness and Orkney remotely to the west, we lose all sight of land for several hours.

DISTANT VIEW OF FAIR-ISLE.

The earliest intimation of our approach to Shetland is afforded by the distant appearance of Fair-Isle, which, in our direct course, we leave to the westward a few leagues. This is a small island, said to be composed of sandstone, which presents in its elevation something of an ellipitical outline. It is scarcely more than two miles in length, and perhaps one in breadth, being situated about twenty-five miles SSW. from the southern extremity of Mainland, the largest of the Shetland Islands.—See Note, No. 2.

TRADITIONARY NARRATIVE OF THE SHIPWRECK OF THE DUKE DE MEDINA SIDONIA, COMMANDER OF THE SPANISH ARMADA, IN THE YEAR 1588.

Fair Isle is, to an Englishman, associated with an event of no common interest in the annals of his country, since it is connected with the personal disaster of the Commander himself of the Invincible Armada of Spain.

When, by the valour of the English Navy, in the memorable year 1588, the Spanish fleet had been dispersed with incalculable loss, the Duke de Medina Sidonia, to whom the command of the Armada had been intrusted, resolved to sail northward, and, by making the tour of the British Islands, to reach the Spanish harbours of the Western Ocean. He was pursued by the English Admiral as far north as the Frith of Forth, when, owing to bad weather, and an ill supply of provisions, the chace was given up. Meanwhile the Armada, in its northern destination, had passed the Orkneys; it was then overtaken by a violent tempest. Of the ships which had been engaged with the English Navy, many had lost their anchors, and these, for the most part, perished in their endeavours to keep out at sea. The galleons, which composed two-thirds of the Spanish fleet, were, from their unwieldy size, left to the mercy of an ocean over which they had little or no controul, whence numerous wrecks of them took place on the shores of Scotland and Ireland. Thus, of an armada conceived to be Invincible, which had consisted of 150 sail, carrying 2600 brass guns, and 30,000 soldiers, marines and slaves, scarcely one-half returned to the haughty monarch of Spain with the disastrous news, that the sceptre of England was still unwrested from the Protestant grasp. While General History is, however, silent regarding the personal adventures of the Duke de Medina, which befel him in the Scottish seas, the deficiency is amply supplied by traditionary accounts yet extant among the isles of Shetland.

In the tempest which completed the discomfiture of the Spanish Navy, the Admiral saw his own vessel driving fast to the precipitous rocks of Fair-Isle: he was successful in making for a small creek on the eastern side of the island, when his unwieldy, anchorless ship struck and went to pieces, the commander and 200 of his men effecting a landing in their boats with the greatest difficulty.

The Duke now found himself inclosed in a small island, the extent and fertility of which could afford little more support than was necessary for the few families which were accustomed to derive from it a precarious subsistence; whilst the population of the place was, by the addition of his shipwrecked crew, considerably more than doubled. The autumnal gales had also set in, which, by keeping the fishermen on shore, threatened to cut off all supplies of food from the sea: from the same cause, also, the light boats of the island were precluded from crossing a dangerous channel of nearly nine leagues, ever disturbed by impetuous currents and tides, for the purpose of procuring from the Mainland of Shetland a vessel, in which the Spanish soldiers might be either conveyed to a place capable of affording adequate provisions, or might be transported early in the spring to some friendly port on the Continent. It also appears, that the Duke had long hesitated whether he should make any entreaty whatever for succour to the inhabitants of Shetland, being doubtful of the reception he should find among them. He was not ignorant that these islands were under the direct influence of a Protestant king, whose sentiments on the subject of the Spanish invasion of England were far from ambiguous. The Scottish Monarch had indeed considered, that the danger which so lately threatened England, had also threatened Scotland, and the sentiments he was known to utter were the echo of Elizabeth's caution, That if the Spanish enterprise had succeeded, he could have only hoped for the indulgence which Polyphemus had promised Ulysses,— To be the last devoured.

Whilst meditating on what measures ought to be adopted, it does not appear that the Duke had availed himself, so soon as he ought to have done, of the means in his power to extricate himself from an island, the scanty resources of which menaced his soldiers with all the horrors of a winter's famine. But, if the alarming prospect was late in making any forcible impression on the mind of the Spanish Commander, it was instantly seen by the natives of Fair-Isle in all its hideous colouring; and they, therefore, became anxious to secure for the use of themselves and their own families the scanty stock of provisions and cattle which remained in the island. An ample opportunity was now given to the Duke for shewing to a defenceless people, whose compliance with his requisition for provisions he could have easily commanded by force, that generous spirit inseparable from true chivalry, which had long tempered with some of the most amiable feelings of human nature, the military habits of southern Europe: for he gave the strictest orders to his soldiers, and in these he was supported by his officers, that no provisions should be received from the inhabitants of Fair-Isle, without a bountiful pecuniary remuneration. Accordingly, the voice of tradition still reports. that the unfortunate visitors of Fair-Isle paid nobly in Spanish ryalls for the provisions which they might so easily have obtained without the least compensation.

The Spaniards had consumed nearly all the victuals of the island; they had eaten up everything they could collect, such as horned cattle, sheep, fish, fowl, and even horses, when the natives were tempted, in self-defence, to evade the delivery of any farther contribution. To avoid, however, the least appearance of hostility to their visitors, they availed themselves of the darkness of the night, for the purpose of secreting among the recesses of the cliffs known only to themselves, the provisions which appeared indispensable for their own existence.

All the horrors of famine now began to rage in the island. Many of the Spaniards had providentially saved from the wreck a reserve of bread; to which was added fish-oil, in which it was dipped. But others who were destitute of this coarse nourishment, perished for hunger.

It would have been well for the memory of the transactions of Fair-Isle, that the same voice of tradition which has recorded in honourable terms the magnanimity of the wretched Spaniards, should, at the same time, have suppressed a recital of the treachery of the natives among whom they had been thrown. The Spaniards were suppliants for the food which, from their superior force, they might have commanded; but the beings to whom this concession was made, only returned the obligation by an over-anxiety for self-preservation, and by a desire to rid the island, in the basest mode, of the unfortunate causes of the famine. When any Spaniards, debilitated by hunger, were found to be detached from the rest of their companions, the barbarous islanders are said to have availed themselves of this incapacity to resistance, by secretly throwing them over the banks into the sea. It is even said, that the roofs of the houses used in the island for drying fish, were so contrived as to be let fall upon the unsuspecting strangers, who were for this purpose invited to seek beneath them a shelter from the weather.*

At length, all sustenance appeared to fail, not only the Spaniards, but the natives of Fair-Isle themselves; and the Duke was determined to encounter every risk of hostility from the neighbouring islands, which he knew to be under the government of a Protestant king, by sending out a boat or yawl to make known his situation, and to implore that a suitable vessel might be provided to release his famished crew from the horrors which they were then suffering.

The boat was dispatched in the first place to Andrew Umphrey of Berry, who was then said to have farmed the isle. It is not added, at the same time, whether the appeal was made to one who was within or without the pale of the Romish Church; but of this fact we may be assured, that the instantaneous relief which the case required was neither converted into a Catholic nor a Protestant question.

Andrew Umphrey set off for Fair-Isle with all dispatch, and in the approach of a sail to the island, the imagination may, without any assistance from tradition, truly paint to itself the anxious faces of the Spaniards, exhibiting alternate emotions of hope and fear, as they conceived the visit to be friendly or hostile.

The mission was, however, soon declared to be propitious, and the famished Spaniards being assisted on board, were cheered with the immediate hopes of food, with the further assurance that their sufferings would obtain for them, every where throughout Shetland, the most hospitable reception,—with the promise, that the ship which now bore them should attempt their escape to some convenient port on the Continent, from whence they might

---

* Sherriff's Agricultural Survey of Shetland, p. 7.

once more hope to embrace the friends they had left in the fertile valleys of Old Spain.
   The vessel appears to have touched at Quendal Bay, the nearest point in the Mainland of Shetland. This was with a view to the superior accommodation due to the illustrious rank of the Duke, which the house of a worthy Scottish gentleman afforded, of the name of Malcolm Sinclair.
   The Duke de Medina landed in the complete costume of a Spanish nobleman, with a view to impress on the simple islanders some notion of the rank which he held in his own country. On being introduced to his host, he was received with the unfeigned welcome that was due to an illustrious and an unfortunate stranger. This feeling was not, however, wholly unmixed with Malcolm's conscientious disapproval of the cause which led eventually to the Duke's disaster, though he wished, at the same time, that emotions of this nature should intrude themselves as little as possible, so as to interfere with the rites of hospitality. An intention so laudable was soon put to a trial,—particularly when the Duke, in order to satisfy himself of the imposing effect which his appearance might have caused in the country, bade his interpreter inquire, If his host had seen before a person of his rank and mien. Malcolm Sinclair, who, in estimating the consequence of his guest had ever considered him as the redoubted champion of Great Babylon, bluntly replied in broad Scots, " Farcie in that face! I have seen many prettier men hanging on the ' Burrow-Muir.' " * It was well for the feelings of the Spanish Commander, that his interpreter's knowledge of the English tongue had not yet extended to its provincialities, and that it was impossible to translate this coarse reply.
   The Duke de Medina is said to have lingered at Quendal, as the guest of Malcolm Sinclair, until the vessel could be equipped in a manner sufficiently effective for the conveyance of himself and his party to the Continent. Meanwhile the Spaniards, in order to remain near the person of their commander, had entrenched themselves in the vicinity. The walls and earthworks which they hastily constructed may be yet traced, along with the foundations of temporary buildings.
   There is, besides, a small fortification to be seen, about thirty miles to the north of Quendal, in the small islet of Kirkholm, which is also ascribed to the Spaniards ; but this is satisfactorily explained by the tradition, that there was another unfortunate galleon belonging to the Armada, which suffered shipwreck on the coast of Shetland ; and that the crew were long detained in this more northerly part of the country, until they could be conveyed to their distant homes. The mural defence which this second party threw up, to add security to their insular position, may be still detected, together with a well of water for the use of the small garrison. Not far remote from Kirkholm may be likewise seen the ruins of a neat chapel, dedicated to the Holy Virgin : it was erected by the same grateful strangers, to beguile their vacant hours, in memory of their preservation on the hospitable shores of Shetland.
   · A month or more had elapsed ere the equipment of the vessel destined to transport the Duke de Medina's party was completed. At length the foreign guests took a final leave of

---

   * Sir Robert Sibbald's Account of Shetland.—" *Farcie* in that face," i.e., " *unsightliness* is in that face, or, it is an *ill-favoured* face,"—an uncouth term of opprobium, very properly obsolete.—" *Burrow-Muir,*" the ancient Tyburn of Edinburgh.

the islanders among whom they had last resided. In a few days the Spanish Commander was landed safely at the Port of Dunkirk, for which service he rewarded his deliverer with a present of three thousand marks.

Such are the traditions relating to the tempest of the Scottish seas, incidental to the history of the leader himself of the celebrated Armada of Spain. The passing traveller, to whom the rocks of Fair-Isle approach in view, and to whom may be narrated the interesting events with which they are associated, may possibly belong to that country where religious freedom has long been secured against the invasion of

" Banditti saints disturbing distant lands."

Is he then authorised to suppose that special interpositions of Providence have averted the danger which threatened to blast the hopes of English Protestantism? Is he allowed to imagine, as others have done before him, that the remains of the powerful fleet which had eluded the thunder of English guns, were only preserved in their flight for the purpose of being nobler victims of the more powerful artillery of the skies, which was heard in the northern seas? Is he justified in presuming, that the escape of the infatuated slaves of Spain, who had eluded the vigilance of their Protestant foes, was only permitted, in order that a signal occasion might be afforded for the unequivocal voice of Heaven itself in its denunciation of the unhallowed cause of the Spanish crusade? Be it so. But there are events now transacting in the civil and religious communities of the world, which lead to a less contracted view of the laws of the Divine Government. These events are far from instructing us, that such laws, when directed against superstition, armed with political authority, are manifested by the contingencies of atmospheric phenomena, or by the incidents of war. No. These decrees of Heaven are more silently revealed in a process that is moral; in a process that is corrective, not vindictive; in a process that is slow, yet universal in its extent, and influencing as well the victims as the agents of persecution. Already are we presented with the sublime spectacle of the lineal descendents of those ancient foes of the Reformed Religion of Europe, that in days of yore would have lighted on English ground the torch of infuriated bigotry, employed on their own soil in its final extinction; in repairing on Iberian land the desolations which its flames had spread, and in erecting on the fertile banks of the Guadelquiver, the peaceful standard of civil and religious liberty.--Note III.

APPROACH TO DUNROSSNESS IN SHETLAND.

No sooner do the rocks of Fair-Isle recede from observation, than Fitfiel Head, a considerable hill to the south of the Mainland, first rises to view. In the ancient northern language of the country, Fitfiel is said to signify the *White Mountain**. To this promontory succeeds a contiguous one to the east of it, less elevated, but stretching more to the south; this is named Sumburgh Head.

As we approach towards the shores of Dunrossness in Shetland, the general features of

---

* See Chalmers's *Caledonia*, vol. i., p. 262.

a large tract of the principal island, named the Mainland, are gradually developed in perspective. The country seems to be characterised rather by the number than by the height of its hills : but the nakedness of their surface, which not a tree or shrub interposes to conceal, recalls every chilling idea that may have been preconceived in the mind of Hyperborean desolation. The stranger can scarcely avoid contrasting the sterility that appears before his eyes, with the richness of the valleys that he may have so lately quitted on the banks of the Forth. Shetland truly appears to be what was long ago said of it by a Stirlingshire visitor, " the skeleton of a departed country."*

Our proximity to land is announced, in good weather, by the appearance of numerous boats, fishing by means of hand-lines for seethe and cod. The Scandinavian character of the natives first becomes evident in the form and lightness of their boats or yawls, the planks of which are still imported from Norway, so modelled by the hands of the carpenter, that, when they arrive in Shetland, little more labour is required than to put them together. These boats are generally about eighteen feet in keel, and about six in beam ; they carry six oars, and are furnished with a square-sail. Their extreme buoyancy, and the ease with which they cut the waves, are the circumstances insisted upon by the fishermen, as rendering their construction particularly adapted to the stormy seas upon which they are launched. Many of the boats are, however, less in size, being adapted only for four oars.

The boat-dress of the fishermen is in many respects striking. A worsted covering for the head, similar in form to the common English or Scotch nightcap, is dyed with so many colours, that its bold tints are recognised at a considerable distance, like the stripes of a signal flag. The boatmen are also invested, as with a coat of mail, by a surtout of tanned sheep skin, which covers their arms, and descends from below their chin to their knees : † whilst, like an apron or kilt, it overlaps their woollen *femoralia* ; for with the latter article, it is needless to observe, the Shetlander is better provided than the Gaelic Highlander. This sheepskin garb has generally an exquisite finish given to it by boots of neat-skin materials, not sparing in width, reaching up to the knees, and, altogether, vying in their ample dimensions with the notable leather galligaskins, with which painters have long been wont to encompass the royal calves of Charles XII. when they have represented him as planning the trenches of Fredericshal. A nobleman, who visited Shetland a few years ago, was, indeed, so struck with the fishing-garb of the natives of the place, that he took away with him a perfect specimen of the same, for the special purpose of assigning to it a place in his museum, at no remote distance from kindred illustrations of the habits of the Esquimaux or of the New Zealanders.

To antiquarian eyes, however, the trim of the Shetland boat-dress may present no inaccurate model of the calfskin costume of the ancient English mummers, who looked so fierce in their guise, that one of the personæ of an old drama was made to say,

"I'll wrap me in a rousing calf-skin suit,
And come like some hobgoblin."
Old Play of " *Wily Beguiled.*"

---

* Neill's *Tour through Orkney and Shetland*, p. 159.

† This dress has been described by Dr Kemp as put on with the *woollen side inwards*. Does the expression imply that the wool is preserved ? I have not myself seen it retained.

In allusion also to these welcome promoters of the sports of Christmas, who may, in the honest boatmen of Shetland, find parallel representatives in every thing save wit, Constance and Faulconbridge, in Shakespeare's Play of King John, most pointedly *"smoke the skin-coat"* of the Archduke of Austria :

" Thou wear'st a lion's hide ! doff it for shame,
And hang a calf-skin on those recreant limbs."
King JOHN, *Act 3. Scene 1.*

There can be no doubt that the leathern dress of Shetland is of Scandinavian origin ; a similar one is still worn in the Isles of Faroe, and Bishop Pontoppidan describes the same as being common in his time among the peasantry of Norway. It must also be of great antiquity, but whether the name of Lodbrog was added to the titles of the Danish King Regner, from some important improvement on this garb, by which they were converted into regular *Braccae*, I shall leave for antiquaries, deeper versed than myself in Scandinavian lore, to determine. " Methinks," says that paragon of Archaiologists, Aylett Sammes of Christ's College in Cambridge, " I see the Danish King Lothbrock, in his *fur-leather breeches*, (for so his name importeth,) in as good verses as ale could inspire, hugging himself in the hopes of full pots in the world to come :

" We have stood true to snick and snee,
And now I laugh to think,
In Woden's Hall there benches be,
Where we may sit and drink.
There we shall tope our bellies full
Of nappy ale in full-brimm'd skull."
See a free translation from the Runic of Regner Lothbrock's well-known Death Song, in Aylett Sammes's Britannica Edition 1676, page 436.

But of this enough :— The true antique cut of the Shetland boat-dress requires no ornament that any superfluous hemmings or fringes can give it, under the learned name of " Annotations " and " Postils." I may briefly add, that the weight of this coreaceous garb, which is almost as ponderous as the chain-armour, that, in the niche of some sacred fane, invests the limbs of the bold crusader, is often disdained by the younger natives, who leave the warmth which it yields to be enjoyed by those who are more advanced in years. They themselves are contented with a common seaman's jacket and trowsers of the usual form, and, in the place of the worsted cap, with a plain hat of straw.

Here it may be proper to observe, that the Packet which conveys passengers from Leith to Shetland is generally destined to Lerwick,—nearly thirty miles distant from the most southerly point of the Mainland. For reasons, therefore, that will be explained on a future occasion, it will be of considerable advantage, that our geological researches should commence either from the most southerly or northerly extremity of the country ; and if the weather permit, it will be advisable to be put on shore at the nearest point of Dunrossness.

Taking leave of our attentive master of the Lerwick Packet, and entering a Shetland fishing boat, we are now introduced to the inhabitants of the country. The first question that will be asked a stranger, preceding even the usual interrogatories of name, country, occupation, destination, and so forth, will be the price of meal in Leith, with which, it is expected, that he should be as much interested as they themselves. This is very natural: the poor natives are, by the uncertainty of their climate, furnished with precarious crops, not generally adequate to the requisition of their families, and, in a scarce season, the slender remuneration for their labour, which altogether precludes an indulgence in such a luxury as meal, obliges them to live almost wholly on fish.

In the discourse of the Shetlanders, which the stranger may now, perhaps, for the first time, hear, he can scarcely fail to be struck with their accent, which certainly partakes much more of the English than of the Scottish manner. When Orkney and Shetland were transferred from the government of Norway to that of Scotland, in payment of part of the portion of Margaret, daughter of the King of that country, to James the Third, the Scandinavian natives of these islands gradually abandoned the Norse language in consequence of their encreased intercourse with the nation to which they were annexed: but they still retain many Norwegian terms, and, along with these, their own national accent. We, therefore, now find, that there is an acuteness of tone and an elevation of voice, that impart to the discourse of the Shetlanders much of the spirit of the English mode of utterance; whilst not unfrequently their pronunciation partakes of the still more modulated and impassioned tones of the Irish: but among none of the natives is to be found the Scotch peculiarity of expression, which is less diversified by alternations of grave and acute accents, since all the effects of emphasis is intended to be conveyed in the prolonged measure with which particular words or syllables are pronounced.

An amusing altercation took place about twelve years ago, in a paper-war, which was carried on between a Shetland and a Scotch gentleman, respecting the peculiarity of their respective accents. "The English language," remarked Dr Kemp of Edinburgh, "is spoken by all the natives of Shetland, but with such a rapidity, (at least it appears so to strangers,) and such a sharpness of accent, together with a kind of lisp and guttural sound, that it requires no little attention to understand them." This observation drew from the late Mr Mouat of Belmont a retort courteous on the Scotch mode of pronunciation*: "Most people," remarked the Shetland gentleman, "in characterising the dialect of others, understand their own to be the standard or criterion, and, on that principle, the Shetlander is entitled to retort the Doctor's observations: He speaks the English language, but drawls out his words so slowly, and with such an obtuse accent, that it requires no little attention to understand him." Mr Mouat then added, that "it was at St James's only the preference could be determined." This was a proper reply: for the notion of a standard of accent or language will ever involve an association of the rank of the individuals by whose influence particular dialects first became objects of imitation. It has thus been justly remarked, that if the Court of Great Britain had, since the union of England and Scotland, been held at Holyrood instead of St James's, the fashionable dialect of this kingdom might have been

---

* See Pamphlets, entitled "*Observations on the Islands of Shetland,*" &c. Printed by Order of the Highland Society, 1801, and Letter in reply, " By the Landholders of Shetland," 1802.

found in the Lowland Pastorals of Allan Ramsay.

It is, however, a separate object of inquiry, if the accent of a country bear any corresponding relation to its national character. Spurzheim, when in Edinburgh, took some pains to prove to his pupils, that the organ of Cautiousness was a general developement of the Scottish cerebrum. Yet it is perhaps questionable, if, from less ambiguous sources some happier manifestation might not have been derived. Why not, in estimating national character, extend the fashionable lucubrations of Phrenology to the lingual as well as to the cerebral organs? The less varied and measured accents of Caledonia's sons, which appear to be in unison with "a mien more grave," offer a striking contrast

"To the blunt speech which bursts without a pause,"

or to the acuteness and rapidity of English utterance,—or to the still more impassioned articulations of the Green Isle of the Ocean,—or to the milder, yet equally modulated accents of neglected Hialtlandia.

GRUTNESS VOE TO QUENDAL, DUNROSSNESS.

As our boat draws near to the shore, a landing-place appears a little to the north of the steep cliffs of Sumburgh-Head. The first prospect that encounters the attention of the traveller is dreary enough. An immense accumulation of blowing-sand appears before him, which has ravaged one of the most fertile estates of the island. It is well known, that when very small breaches are made in the superficial turf that covers an extensive deposit of fine sand, an escape of the levigated particles of the subsoil immediately takes place, and all the ravages of a sand-flood ensue. Professor Jameson, in his visit many years ago to Shetland, judiciously recommended, for the recovery of the land, the growth of such plants as the Galium cruciatum and verum, the Elymus arenarius, the Triticum junceum, or the Arundo arenaria. But this advice has long passed by unheeded; and the latest visitor, Dr Fleming, found, that the seeds which grew among the sand were, for the laudable purpose of making besoms, still dug up by the roots,—that numerous herds of swine were still allowed to roam at large and dig in the sand, and that rabbits even appeared to meet with a hospitable protection.*

A sandy tract leads to Quendal Bay, where, for some little distance, the eye obtains no relief from an extensive waste of sand, save from small insulated tufts of verdure, that are idly supposed to mock, rather than to encourage, the redeeming hopes of the husbandman. The view, is, indeed, as unvaried as that which Sister Anne saw when, from the loftiest turret of Blue-Beard's gloomy mansion, she anxiously looked out for the expected horsemen; and, with a slight deviation from the text of this delightful tale of our infancy, the disappointed traveller may exclaim, "I see nothing but the sand blowing, and the grass growing!"

---

* Jameson's Mineralogy of the Scottish Isles, vol. ii., p. 199. App. to Shirreff's Agriculture of Orkney and Shetland, p. 434.

REMARKS ON THE DARK PERIOD OF THE HISTORY OF SHETLAND AND ORKNEY, SUGGESTED BY THE DISCOVERY OF ROMAN RELICS IN THE PARISH OF DUNROSSNESS.

The dreariness of the scene is soon interrupted by a fertile green sward, studded with cottages, that is continued to West Voe and Sumburgh Head, which we leave to the south. This ground is rendered somewhat interesting by the evidence which it has afforded of a Roman visit to Shetland. About forty years ago, a copper medal of Vespasian, the reverse Iudæa Victa, is recorded to have been turned up by the plough. I have examined several of the coins that are said to have been found in different parts of Shetland, which were those of Galba, Ælius Cæsar and Trajan. In one district, Northmavine, a Pugio was reported to have been discovered. There are also small fortifications, occurring in different parts of the country, that will be noticed in the course of this itinerary, which manifest striking marks of a Roman construction. —See Note IV.

The presence of remains like these found in the parish of Dunrossness* and elsewhere, may excite some little curiosity to learn the occasions which might have induced the Romans to visit the seas to the north of Scotland, as well as to know the race of people by whom Shetland might have been inhabited during so remote a period. This inquiry is, at the same time, so connected with the earliest state of Orkney as well as of Shetland, that it will be impossible to investigate the history of the one country to the exclusion of the earliest annals of the other.

Agricola visited Orkney in the eighty-fourth year of the Christian Era. But this group of islands seems to have been known to the ancients before this period, since Diodorus Siculus alludes to a promontory in the north of Scotland, supposed to be some headland in the Pentland Firth, under the name of Cape Orcas, whilst Pomponius Mela states the number of the islands of Orkney to be about thirty.

But, if the situation of Orkney was known to the ancients before the time of Agricola, Shetland was much less distinctly recognised, unless under the vague name of Thule, it was occasionally glanced at by Pomponius Mela or Pliny.† Thule was long a term of general application, to denote a place either in Britain, Ireland, the north of Scotland, or in regions even still farther north, which was supposed to be involved in darkness, whilst its shores were washed by a boisterous ocean ; its situation, therefore, always varied with the uncertain geographical information Roman writers possessed of the British or Caledonian Seas. It is, however, certain, that Shetland was the Thule which was actually seen by Agricola, in his circumnavigation of the British Islands.

---

* I find that the proper name of Dunrossness, as it appears in Norwegian annals, is *Dynraust* Ness, so named from *raust*, *roost*, or conflict of tide off Sumburgh Head, which, in the year 1242, proved fatal to King Harold, of the Isle of Man, in sailing to Norway. " Interea nuptiæ Regis Haraldi, cum filia Regis [Norvegiæ] insigni apparatu confectæ, inde Rex ad conventum cum Sveciæ Rege institutum magna classe comitatuq ; profectus, in Elldeyar Sunda, seu sinu Elldeyensi Jonem Dungadi fillium Regem pronunciavit, qvi tanto honore auctus, in aqvilonares Norvegiæ partes Dugale comitante rediit, uterq ; in Hæbudas Manniæ Regi Haraldo, itineris socii futuri, verum proposito desistentes Jon Bergis, Dugall ad Regem Haconem in austris morantem profectus hiemavit, Rex autem Haraldus cum uxore, splendidoque comitatu, unica nave Bergis solvit, inque itinere cum omnibus vectoribus vecturaque periit in vortice *Dynraust*, qvi Hialtlandiam ab austro spectat, ut vulgo conjectant, eo qvod fragmenta navis, in australis istius insulæ partes æstus devexerit."—Torfæus, p. 164.

† For a compendious view of the various opinions of the ancients on the situation of Thule, see Sir Robert Sibbald's "Thule of the Ancients," as given in Gibson's Camden, page 1089 to 1100 ; and particularly " An Inquiry into the Original Inhabitants of Britain," by Sir James Foulis, in the Transactions of the Society of the Antiquaries of Scotland, Vol. i., page 155 to 169.

When Agricola, in the year 84, visited Orkney, he is said not only to have discovered, but to have subjugated these islands. Hence the important inference, that they were at so early a period actually inhabited. The expression of Tacitus is, "invenit *domuit*que." It is, consequently, with much surprise, that I have seen a supposition lately hazarded, in a volume of Scottish Antiquities, that Orkney was in the time of Agricola unpeopled. It is, indeed, possible to conceive, that when Agricola is said to have subdued the Orkneys, his biographer meant no more than that he was victorious in the sense in which Dryden applied the term to the hero of one of his Tragedies;

"Almanzer is victorious without fight;"

Or in which Fielding's no less triumphant hero Lord Grizzle, with equal felicity, enlarged upon the idea :

"Thus far our arms with victory are crown'd ;
For, though we have not fought, yet we have found
No enemy to fight withal."
Life and Death of Tom Thumb the Great, Act iii. Scene 7.

It is to be remarked, that two of the islands of Shetland, Foula and Fair-Isle, are to be seen from Orkney; accordingly, it has been with every reason supposed, that the Thule which Agricola saw from thence could be no other country than Shetland. "Dispecta est et Thule quam hactenus nix et hiems abdebat."

Thus, it would appear, that in the time of Agricola, whilst Shetland was only distantly observed, and was unexplored, Orkney was actually inhabited. The next question is, Of what race were descended the Aborigines of Orkney; or as the Archæologists of a century ago were wont to express themselves, From what fountain and original source was derived unto us these puissant Orcadians? Seeing, therefore, that all good historiographers have thus handled their chronicles, an inquiry into national descent will be our first object; for this is no less expedient in treating of humble provincial annals, than a lineal pedigree is to the consequence of some homely country gentleman, who, deprived of its emblazoning support, might never have been recorded in any other terms, than that he was "a marvellous good neighbour, in sooth, and a very good bowler."* For very sufficient reasons, therefore, the aboriginal inhabitants of Orkney may be announced as having been derived from a Celtic stock; as having been descended from a people who have been traced from the Euxine to the Atlantic, occupying at one time the whole of Europe, south of the Baltic, and probably even farther north; whose tribes were subsequently limited to the west of Europe, who, from four to five centuries before the Christian era, seized the country on the Po, settled in Germany, overran, under Brennus and Camillus, the whole of Italy,—their last depredations being committed in Greece, and even in Asia. Most of the Celtic tribes appear to have been lost in their intermixture with the inhabitants of the countries which, from predatory motives, they had visited, whilst the remainder were eventually compelled to

---

* Love's Labour Lost, act v.

confine themselves to the country of Gaul, in which was comprised, during the time of Cæsar, France, part of Germany, and the British Islands.

But the Celtic Emigration from the Euxine to Britain is more distinctly (I dare not add more authentically) described in the ancient Triades of Wales, and in the curious comments upon them which are to be found in the oldest manuscripts of that country. "Of the three pillars of the Island of Britain, the first is Hu Gadarn, who first brought the race of the Cymry into the Island of Britain; and they came from the land of Hav called Defrobani, *(where Constantinople stands,* says the ancient commentator,) and they passed over Môr Tawch *(the German Ocean,)* to the Island of Britain, to Llydan *(the coast of Gaul,)* where they remained." The Celtic race of Scotland is again referable to the tribes who are said to have "come into the Island of Britain by the consent of the nation of the Cymry, without weapon and without assault." Of these, one was the tribe of the Caledonians, and another was the Gwyddelian race in Alban (Scotland.)*

The Celtic tribe of the Caledonians might probably have inhabited, during the campaigns of Cæsar, certain woods near the banks of the Thames †, exchanging soon afterwards the rich plains of the south of England for the more inaccessible regions of the north, where, amidst wilds and natural fastnesses, they might more successfully resist the Roman eagle. ‡

The Gwyddelian race in Alban (Scotland,) are the proper Aborigines of North Britain: and they have been for centuries described by Welch bards, and other writers of that country, under the name of Gwyddyl, Pichti, or Fichti, the (P) of the British being frequently changed to (F.) The term Pichti denotes a tribe of the *open country*, or of *the waste or desart*§; and it may be identified with the name Picti, which was used by the Romans to denote the same Celtic people who inhabited Scotland. The near resemblance in sound of the Celtic Pichti to the Latin expression for a painted people, caused the Romans to associate under this appellation the well known habit of *tattooing,* to which the Aborigines of Britain, like the savage American tribes of the present day, were originally addicted. ‖ The use, therefore, of the term Picti became particularly significant in its perverted acceptation, of the wild hordes of ancient Caledonia, who could not be prevailed upon to renounce the habit of painting their bodies, in favour of the refinements of civilization which the Romans had early introduced among the Britons of the south.

It is now time to avail ourselves of these preliminary remarks in the hypothesis we may entertain regarding the first peopling of Orkney, and in the ultimate conjectures of a similar nature which we may form regarding Shetland.

On the assumption, then, that the expression of Tacitus, relating to Agricola's visit to Orkney, "invenit *domuit*que," naturally implies that the islands were then inhabited, the

---

* Davies's Celtic Researches, pages 154 and 155.
† "Eosdem rursus Britannos sequtus in Caledonias sylvas." L. Annæ Flori epitome, Rer., Rom., lib. iii., cap. 10.
‡ I am aware, that an opinion very different to this is usually entertained by antiquaries.
§ Chalmers's *Caledonia*, vol. i., p. 204.
‖ "*Nec falso nomine Pictos edomuit.*" *Cl. Claudiani de III. Cons. Hon. Aug. Paneg.*

Aborigines must have been Celtic, since the Gothic tribes, who succeeded to the Celts in the possession of Europe, are not recorded as encroaching so far westward as the British Island until the 4th century.

On the natural probability, also, that the first peopling of Orkney took place from the contiguous shores of the north of Scotland, the Aborigines of these islands must have been Pictish in the Latin, rather than in the Celtic sense of the term ; for with the Romans the designation was generic, and not only included the proper Celtic Pichti, as well as the Caledonians, who had migrated from the south, but every other contemporary tribe, under whatever name it might be specifically distinguished, that inhabited the northern wilds of Britain. In this comprehensive sense Eumenes the Orator applies the word Picti in the 4th century: "Non dico Caledonum aliorumque Pictorum." Thus also Ammianus Marcellinus: "Picti in duas gentes divisi Dicaledones et Vecturiones."*

Most probably, then, a Celtic race, known at a later period of the Roman campaigns in Britain, under the generic name of Picts, were the Aborigines of Orkney. There is, however, another circumstance to be taken into consideration. The language that is common to Celtic tribes is well known to have been transmitted to modern times in the Cymraeg or Welch tongue, in the Armorican, the Irish, and the Scoto-Irish or Gaelic of the Scotch Highlands. Orkney itself is recorded in the Triades of Wales, as one of the principal islands of Great Britain ; and the most satisfactory etymology of the name is referable to the Celtic word ore, signifying what is *outward, extreme or bordering*, and ynis, enis, and inis, expressive of an *island*. But to the notion that a Celtic race originally inhabited Orkney, this derivation imparts a feeble degree of support. A conclusion to this effect would have been much more satisfactorily deduced from the knowledge, that Celtic names are still applied to the specific localities of the country : that Celtic names are still retained in describing the islands, hills, valleys, lakes or bays by which this territory is diversified. Such evidence, however, is totally withheld from us ; for without a single exception, all the topographical names, of Orkney as well as of Shetland, are preserved in the Scandinavian tongue. No hypothesis, therefore, of the first peopling of either country by a Celtic race can be defended, that does not, at the same time, admit from subsequent causes, so complete a removal of the aboriginal colonists, as to imply, that the first appellations which had been imposed upon the localities of the country, must have become irrecoverably lost. Let us then endeavour to ascertain, if such an admission meet with any sanction from the testimony of Roman writers.

For about a century and a half subsequent to Agricola's circumnavigation around Britain, there is not to be obtained, from any authentic source, the least intimation regarding the state of Orkney. This silence is at length broken, by the short, yet empathic

---

* This is the only occasion in the course of the present itinerary, in which I shall involve myself in the Pictish question, with the exception, perhaps, of a few brief remarks, that may be made in treating of the Scandinavian Burgh,—improperly enough named Pictish. From the numerous disquisitions to which the Pictish inquiry has given rise, it is now become the stalest and most tedious of Antiquarian subjects. I consider that the very best view that has yet been taken of the question, is to be found in the First Volume of Dr Chalmers's Caledonia, under the head of the Pictish Period of North-Britain. A summary of the classical authorities from which the opinions that had been given in this work are chiefly derived, may be found in an excellent paper of Sir James Foulis, published in the Antiquarian Transactions of Scotland, vol. i., p. 155, &c. See also Whittaker's History of Manchester, 4to, vol. i., p. 415 and 416.

intelligence on the subject that is communicated to us by Solinus: "Numero tres, vacant homine, non habent silvas, tantum junceis herbis inhorrescunt, cætera earum nudæ arenæ et rupes tenent." This information must have been procured about the middle of the third century; and, really, little is wanting to complete the chilling picture it presents of arctic solitude: Orkney was seen,—but no human inhabitants,—no trees; no objects visible but marshes, steril sands and rocks. Solinus has inaccurately computed these islands at no more than three ;—a possible error. In order to determine their real number, Orcadian sounds and creeks must be explored. But what inducement could there be for the visitors of this deserted Archipelago to undertake a research so devoid of interest,— so fruitless in its ultimate object ?

Since the period when Orkney was pronounced to be uninhabited, more than a century had elapsed ere this country came again to be recorded in Roman annals. A Gothic or Teutonic people, of a very different origin to that of the Celts, may be regarded as the second description of colonists, by whom Orkney was peopled. The language which they spoke is perpetuated in such dialects as the English of the present day, the Lowland-Scotch, the Belgic or Low-Dutch proper, the German, the Norwegian, the Danish, the Swedish, and several others. With great probability, it has been supposed, that the Goths, the Getæ of Thrace and the Scythians of Little Tartary, were of the same race of people. The Goths appear to have been long settled near the northern embouchure of the Danube ; and at the Christian Era, a few of these tribes were scantily interspersed among the Celtic Aborigines, dwelling between the Euxine and the Atlantic. About the third century, the Goths first became formidable to Europe ; they ravaged Mœsia, and destroyed the city of Istropolis, returning from their predatory excursion beyond the Danube. They afterwards extended the conquests in various directions ; but their encroachments on the Roman boundaries were first felt in the fourth century. It was then that the Saxon rovers, who were of Gothic descent, proved of considerable annoyance to navigation, and that the coasts and islands of the northern seas were conveniently resorted to in the course of their piratical excursions. So audacious, at length, became their depredations, that the Romans found it necessary to exert themselves in a special manner against these marauders. It was on this occasion, therefore, that Theodosius chased them into their most secret and remote haunts, and that Orkney, and probably Shetland also, were bedewed with Saxon blood :

" —————— Maduerunt Saxone fuso
    Orcades."

CLAUD. *Carm. De 3 Consul. Honorii.*

This signal chastisement was only of temporary advantage. The power of the Gothic tribes still gradually increased, and when the declining government of Italy was obliged, for the defence of its own immediate frontiers, to recall its troops from every distant province, a Saxon sceptre succeeded to the Roman eagle in the sovereignty of Britain.

Subsequent to the visit of Theodosius to the Orcades, all accounts of this country, from the testimony of Latin authors, are found to cease ; and, until its Scandinavian history commences, the vacancy is only supplied by Monkish fables, to which it is not necessary for a moment to advert.

By ancient Scandinavia, from which country the progenitors of the present race of inhabitants in Orkney and Shetland were originally derived, may be understood the territories lying to the north of the Baltic Sea, namely, Denmark, Norway, Sweden, Lapland and Finland. Antiquaries are disposed to believe that a Scandinavian people occupied Orkney before the sixth century ; founding their opinion on the credited history of Columba, the Christian Missionary, who, in the year 565, met at the residence of Bridei, the Pictish King, a Scandinavian chief of Orkney.*

We have at length endeavoured, from the testimony of authentic writers, to render probable the supposition, that the successive colonists of Orkney were composed of Celtic, Saxon, and Scandinavian tribes. But it may be now asked, Are we, from the same description of evidence, entitled to infer, that similar tribes succeeded in like manner to the possession of the contiguous islands of Shetland? Certainly not. That the same people who inhabited Orkney might have passed over into the adjoining islands more northerly situated, is a very probable circumstance. An encouragement is, therefore, given to the inquiry, Whether certain ancient relics or monuments generally ascribed to the Celtæ, Saxons, or early Scandinavians, are not to be found as abundant in Orkney as in Shetland? This investigation will be prosecuted in the course of our itinerary.

Such are the few occasional glimpses of light which shed their dim lustre over the early annals of Orkney and Shetland, rendering, in the words of Milton, "darkness visible." As the general result, however, of this research, three periods in the history of these islands may be kept in view.

In the first period, when Agricola visited Orkney, a Celtic race very probably inhabited the country, who appear to have completely forsaken it a century and a half afterwards, since it was described by Solinus in the middle of the third century as a complete desart.

In the second period, Orkney, and probably Shetland also, were infested by a Gothic tribe of Saxon rovers : these were routed A.D. 368, by Theodosius.

In the third period, probably at or before the sixth century, succeeded in the possession of these islands the Scandinavians, who were the progenitors of the present race of inhabitants in Orkney and Shetland.

Incidental to this investigation, we may now advert to the Roman coins which were found at Dunrossness, and elsewhere in Shetland. The date of one of them is of the reign of Adrian, or a few years previous to the Lieutenantship of the intelligent Lollius Urbicus, by whom North Brtiain was well explored,—by whom new roads were constructed, new stations were fixed, and new iters were settled. Did this active governor, then, explore the coasts and islands of Caledonia, as far north as the Ultima Thule, which was seen by Agricola from the shores of Orkney? Or are the Roman coins found in Shetland, to be rather considered as having been left by the soldiers of Theodosius, when chacing the Saxon pirates to their remotest and most secret haunts ? A reply to these questions must,

---

* See Chalmers's *Caledonia*, vol. i., p. 262.

of necessity, be the vainest of conjectures. Let us, therefore, be content with the mere indication afforded by the discovery of certain vestiges of antiquity, that the Roman eagle did once condescend to visit the distant shores of ancient Hialtlandia. But in the attempt to speculate on the occasion of these visits, a heavy censure hangs fearfully over the head of the too daring archæologist. "As the final cause of the principle of curiosity," say certain critics, "is the acquisition of knowledge, it is a perversion much to be lamented, that it should so often be found to fasten most keenly on those objects, about which little or nothing can be known. A mere scrap of something, between knowledge and conjecture, if it be but obtained with sufficient difficulty, appears far more valuable to persons of this description, than abundance of real information, if easily acquired, and if as easily gained by others as themselves.*— See Note V.

QUENDAL BAY.

The shores of Quendal conclude our short walk from the landing place whence we set out on the east of Dunrossness.

Quendal Bay is an open inlet of the Sea, extending due north about two miles into the land, from the surface of which appear a few small holms, that afford a pasture for cattle. East of the Bay, and at the head of it, dreary tracts of blowing sand are to be seen, where may be still detected the ruins of scattered buildings, that have long since yielded to the removal of the light sand which laid bare their foundation. Here was the ancient estate of Brow, worth, before it was destroyed, 3000 merks a-year, nearly equivalent to £200 Sterling,—a considerable rental for Shetland fifty or sixty years ago. These barren sandhills are agreeably contrasted on the opposite side of the bay, with the green verdure of Garthsness and Quendal, which slope gradually towards the water's edge, whilst the remoter cliffs of Fitfiel Head, or *the white mountain*, towering above the whole, majestically close the perspective. Quendal forms the north-west angle of the bay, characterised by a neat white farm-house, productive fields of corn, not unworthy the rich district of the Lothians, while, in the same direction, signs of an encreased population appear in the numerous cottages by which the distant landscape is diversified. Nothing is indeed wanting but a few trees to complete this picture of fertility; and it is contemplated with encreased relief to the mind, when opposed to the depressing sandy desart to which it is contiguous. So abrupt, indeed, is the transition from the excess of fecundity to complete barrenness, that the plain line of demarcation between the two extremes, might, in days of dark superstition, have been supposed to describe the exact site over which some balefull spell had heavily hung, so as to blast for ever the productive hopes of the husbandman. The interest of the scene is not a little encreased, when the traveller recalls to his memory the events of "olden time," with which the shores of Quendal are associated. His imagination may paint to itself the shipwrecked crew which had belonged to the flag-ship of the Spanish Armada, transported from the fatal rocks of Fair-Isle in a small trading vessel, and anchoring in the bay

---

* See Quotation from the Monthly Review in Ledwich's Antiquities of Ireland, p. 155.

which now arrests his attention;—in completing the ideal picture, he may conceive of the Commander himself in the act of landing, attired in the costly and imposing dress of the Spanish nobleman, followed in the rear by the remains of his famished soldiers, whilst to greet their arrival, a numerous concourse of simple islanders, headed by the hospitable Malcolm Sinclair, are collected on the beach, expressing in their silent countenances the mixed feelings of awe and commiseration.

Thus engaged, the deep tracts of sand which impede the course of the traveller occasion little or no fatigue. At the head of the Bay, the slight remains of a wall, together with two or three erect monuments, proclaim the site of the ancient church of Quendal, which, about half a century ago, was one of the neatest religious edifices in the country. The ravages of the blowing sand had then commenced, and whenever the wind came from the sea, the sand was dislodged, and an inundation took place presenting in miniature the appearance of an Arabian desart. Then might the pious natives of Dunrossness be observed in their weekly pilgrimage to the parish-kirk, to pursue a toilsome peregrination through deep lodgements of sand, overwhelmed, at the same time, in clouds of drifted particles that obscured the horizon, through which horsemen and footmen were dimly descried at a distance, like the ghosts of Ossian through the dun clouds of rocky Morven. Even when included within the precincts of the church, its sanctuary could afford little shelter from the general pervasion of the sand-shower, the fine ingredients of which easily insinuated themselves through the minutest crannies, and were diffused over all the pews.*
At length, the walls were no longer able to resist the causes, which, in removing the sand to a distance, undermined their foundations; melancholy exposures, at the same time, took place of the bodies of the recent dead, the remembrance of which event is still perpetuated by numerous skulls and other relics of mortality, which being left to bleach upon the sandy plain, have acquired a whiteness so incomparable, as to arrest the attention of the most heedless passenger. The erection of a new parish church was eventually found necessary, in a situation secure from the agency of similar causes of destruction.

The monuments of the old kirk of Quendal which still remain, belong to the Scottish families of Sinclair, Stewart, and Bruce, which settled in Dunrossness about two centuries ago. The inscriptions upon them are very plain, not materially differing from multitudes of a similar date, to be found in North Britain, where they were doubtless carved, and from thence imported.

The white farm-house which, with its fertile corn-fields and pastures, so enlivens the westerly view of Quendal, is tenanted by Mr Ogilvie, to whose hospitality, whilst remaining in this country, I was much indebted. This gentleman is well acquainted with the farming-improvements of North Britain, and he has meritoriously introduced as many of them as were applicable to the more uncertain climate of the British Thule. Turnips, bear or big, clover and oats, are raised in regular rotations. He has reclaimed some part of the sandy waste, immediately contiguous to his farm, by planting potatoes upon it, which was not taken up for the first year, but suffered to rot among the soil, so as to form a tenacious

---

* Low's MS. Tour through Shetland, A.D. 1774.

medium for the blowing-sand, by which means, in a subsequent year, it was rendered capable of yielding a crop of oats, or fit for the reception of proper grass seeds. The sand-inundations of Dunrossness are, however, evidently on the decline, since their origin was less referable to repeated accumulations of sand thrown up by the sea during heavy gales, and afterwards dispersed, than to the existing nature of the subsoil of the country, which, by improvident removals of the binding herbage that had long restrained its escape, was allowed to devastate all the estates to which it was blown in any considerable quantity.

Mr Ogilvie's excellent management of his farm has had a powerful effect among the smaller tenants, in stimulating them to similar exertions. In the year 1818, when the Agricultural Society of Shetland offered to three parishes a premium for sowing turnips, all the competitors were of Dunrossness. One small tenant had a fifth of an acre of good turnips, drilled and very well cleaned; another had a full quarter of an acre covered in the same manner, the ground having been thrice ploughed over; but the crop of the third competitor failed. Several small patches of ground, belonging to individuals who had not contended for the prize, attracted the particular attention of the Committee who adjudged the rewards.

The numerous cottages occurring in the vicinity of Quendal are of a better construction than is to be generally found in Shetland, although they still retain much of their ancient Scandinavian character. The oldest Shetland dwellings are built of rude stones, with a cement of clay, or they are still more coarsely formed of stones and clods. After the wooden rafters have been laid, they are roofed with what are provincially called *flaas*, or, in the absence of these, with *pones*. *Flaas* are compact vegetable layers, consisting of the short fibres of mossy or heathy roots closely interwoven with each other. The removal of a layer of this description from the surface of dry moss land, is never accomplished by cutting, but by tearing away; and this manual operation is so like what Dean Swift, in his description of the mode of collecting *Irish scraws*, calls " Flaying off the green surface of the ground," that it is probably to the Scandinavian word *flaa* or *flae*, we must look for the etymology of the Shetland word *flaas*.* When layers composed of flaas are doubled, they are considered to be impervious to rain, and in this state are placed upon the rafters of the houses. It has been also remarked, that, instead of flaas, the Shetlanders frequently substitute what they call *pones*. These last mentioned materials for roofing are nothing more than swards of earth cut very thin, upon the surface of which grows a short grass. They differ from another species of turf, recognised in Shetland as well as in Scotland, under the name of Fails, in the following respect: Fails are the thickest portions of turf that are cut, being used for the construction of walls and dikes: Pones have always a covering of grass; they are thinner than fails, and they are never used for the construction of dikes, but for the sole purpose of roofing.† A roof formed of thin turf has long been considered as

---

* See Johnson's Dictionary for the word *Flay.*

† *Fails* is said to be a Suio-Gothic word, signifying a *sward*, (solum herbidum). The derivation of *Pones* is obscure; it does not occur in Dr Jamieson's Etymological Dictionary; but this learned antiquary defines a *Poiner* (Q. dealer in *Poins* or *Pones* ?) to be " one who gains a livelihood by digging *feal, divots* or *clay*, and selling them for *covering houses* and other purposes." It is needless to observe, that the true Shetland or Scandinavian word *Flaas* can scarcely be confounded with the Scotch *Flaw* or *Flow peat*, as described by Dr Jamieson, the distinction between them being so very evident.

the peculiar characteristic of the Scandinavian cottage. Bishop Pontoppidan says, that the Norwegian peasants lay over the rafters of their dwellings the sappy bark of birch trees, which they cover again with turf three or four inches in width. Probably, then, in a country destitute of wood, like Shetland, the natives might have been first induced, in the place of a supply of other materials for roofing, to have adopted the Scotch method of thatching; but they appear to have still retained the use of pones or flaas, since over these they lay the straw, and afterwards secure the whole with *simmonds* or bands formed also of straw. In most of the Shetland cottages the fire-place is in the middle of the room, and the smoke ascends through a large aperture in the roof, after the usual manner of the hovels of the Scotch Highlands. Windows are become much more general than they were some years ago; for, among some of the oldest habitations, no other light is received than through the aperture which allows an egress to the smoke. To this opening is given the Scottish name of *lumb*, but in the obsolete language of Shetland, it was called the *livra*,—a word resembling the ancient *liuren* or light-hole of the Norwegians. Yet many old Shetland houses are not destitute of that notable improvement of domestic architecture known by the name of chimney; for by the Scandinavians its invention was ascribed to royalty itself, which had previously condescended to hold its courts within the sable, fuliginous walls of Rog-Stuerne, or smoke rooms. It is recorded in Norwegian annals, that so early as the eleventh century, King Oluf Kyrre was the first who removed fire-places from the middle of rooms, and ordered chimneys and stoves to be erected.* The byre or cow-house generally adjoins the dwelling, and is frequently entered by a common door, that introduces the stranger first to the cattle, and afterwards to the apartment devoted to the use of the family. In most of the Shetland habitations a partition of turf runs across the room, which is occasionally carried up to the height of the house, being intended as well for the purpose of storing up victuals as for a separate dormitory. But generally the beds, which consist of a few coarse blankets or straw, are placed in any convenient angle of the cottage. One or two cumbrous wooden chairs, designed for the heads of the family, with the addition of a few benches constitute the heavy part of the furniture.— Such is a specimen of the ancient cottage of Shetland; but in the vicinity of Quendal dwellings of this kind are more rarely found than in other parts of the country; and the antiquary will be often chagrined in observing such provoking modern improvements as slate roofs, regular windows, and detached cowhouses, all of which have been introduced into the country by that foe to archæological sources of pleasure, ever stimulating to innovation,— a sense and desire of encreased comfort. Quitting, therefore, for the present, the habitations of the Shetland peasants, we may briefly glance at the numerous rude dykes which are constructed around them :—These observe great irregularity in their direction, sometimes inclosing only one cottage, and sometimes uniting many which are distant from each other.

Such are the general remarks, that may suffice for the present, regarding the humble dwellings of these islanders: ample opportunities will be afforded in the course of this

---

* See Pontoppidan's " History of Norway, *Translation*," vol. ii., p. 278.

itinerary, for examining more in detail their rural economy. Our attention may now be turned from the contemplation of Shetland cottages to the inhabitants within them, whose general physiognomy may by this time have become sufficiently familiar to us.

The natives of these islands are rarely very tall; they are of the middle size, remarkably well proportioned, light and nimble. It is true, that all these characters are less observable among the females of the country; for the male sex, in relinquishing most species of domestic drudgery for the adventurous occupation of fishing, cause a more than ordinary portion of labour, fatal to the preservation of a delicate and symmetrical form, to devolve upon the poor females. The features of the Shetlanders are rather small, and have nothing of the harshness that so peculiarly distinguishes many of the Anglo-Saxon provincials in the north of England, or in some of the lowland districts of Scotland. The constitutional temperament of the Scandinavians is generally conceived to be sanguine, and since its characteristics are supposed to consist in a florid complexion, a smooth skin, and hair brown, white, or slightly auburn, the natives of Shetland give satisfactory tokens of their national descent. The elder Linnæus's description of the Northern Europeans well applies to them: " Gothi corpore proceriore, capillis albidis rectis, oculorum iridibus cinereo-cærulescentibus." But Principal Gordon detected a peculiarity among the Scandinavian natives of Orkney, who are of the same race as those of Shetland, that is too curious to pass unnoticed, since it must have wholly escaped the penetrating glance of the great Swedish naturalist. This antiquary discovered that there was not a human eye to be found in Orkney that was not of the colour of sea-green. These are his words : " The inhabitants are generally strong-bodied, and remarkable for the flava cæsaries, and the oculi, cæsii, assigned by Tacitus as distinctive peculiarities of German nations. That sea-green colour of the eye, which I take to be the meaning of the word *cæsii*, is so common in Orkney, that *I never met with any person whose eyes were of a different colour.*"* This is a sweeping assertion, that ought to go far towards removing the scepticism of a French writer, Monsieur Le Grand, who, being as little aware of the modern existence of green eyes, as that they were familar marks of discrimination among the ancients, endeavoured to amend the reading of the "yeux *vers*," or *green* eyes of the early French poets, by converting them, with a slight change of one or two vowels, into "yeux *vairs*," or *grey* eyes. Hanmer also, equally uninformed, proposed, by the substitution of a letter, to change the "*green* eye," of Juliet, which he conceived to be a typographical error, into a "' *keen* eye."†

But Mr Francis Douce, in objecting to such overstrained alterations of Shakespeare's text, has pointed out the ancient familiarity of the expression, by directing the attention to the " oculi *herbei*," alluded to by Plautus‡, to "the great eyes with a *green* circle," which

---

* Journey to the Orkney Islands, by Principal Gordon of the Scots College of Paris, *Transactions of the Scottish Antiquaries*, vol. i., p. 256.

† " *Nurse.* ─────────── an eagle, Madam,
Hath not so *green*, so quick, so fair an eye."
     Romeo and Juliet, *Act* iii., *Scene* v.

‡ " Qui hic est homo
Cum collativo ventre, atque oculis herbeis?"
     Curculio of Plautus.

Lord Bacon affirmed to be significant of long life ; and to a Treatise of Villa Real, a Portuguese, who selected " Green eyes " for his theme, in which they were most marvellously lauded. This able commentator of Shakespeare then arrives at the conclusion, That it is certain green eyes were found among the ancients, though there is a scarcity, if not total absence, of such visual organs in modern times ;—adding with a sneer, " For this let naturalists account, *if they can.*"* Surely Mr Douce could not have been acquainted with Principal Gordon's surprising discovery in Orkney, that a British province was entirely peopled with *green-eyed natives !* It is true, that the residents of these islands may be willing to confess to any description of eyes rather than the " oculi cæsii " of Tacitus ; and it will be no wonder, if, by these individuals, a suspicion may arise of some defect in the learned traveller's own vision, whereby the blue, black or hazel eyes of the inhabitants have been transmuted into the outré tint of sea-green.† If such an affection there really be, it must have frequently attacked the scholars of " olden times," being perpetuated at the present day among a few modern antiquaries. Its symptoms must have been analogous to those which a celebrated natural philosopher recently detected in his own sight ; the tint of pink being found to impress the retina like the sensation of sky-blue, and the colour of red sealing wax like that of a green field. If any disease, then, can be well made out, capable of imparting to a scientific mind the illusion of a green-eyed race of Scandinavians dwelling in the Ultima Thule of the British Isles, it well deserves a place in Nosological Systems, under the name of the Paropsis Archæologica. Certes, there must be some distemper, the bane of learned clerks,

"——————— which o'er the realms of sense,
Oft spreads that murky, antiquarian cloud,
Which blots our truth, eclipses evidence,
And taste and judgment veils in sable cloud."
CHATTERTON'S " *Epistelle t Doctoure Mylles.*"

The dress of the Shetland peasants differs little from that of the inhabitants of the sea-coast of Scotland. To men whose chief occupation is fishing, the common sailor's jacket is a favourite attire. The red cap, which is a distinctive badge of the master of a family, merits particular attention. It is made of worsted, somewhat resembling in form a common double night-cap, but much larger, and gradually tapering to a point, whilst it hangs down the back, after the fashion of the head dress of a German hussar. It is also dyed with numerous colours. Frequently the men wear on their feet *rivlins*, which are a sort of sandals, made of untanned seal-skin, being worn with the hair-side outwards and laced on the foot with strings or thongs of leather. Their lightness is particularly adapted for tramping with velocity over the soft heaths or scattholds of the country. The dress of the women merits little attention, since it does not differ materially from the fashion of the

---

* Douce's Illustrations of Shakespeare, vol. ii., p. 193.

† In a marginal postil, appended to Principal Gordon's Journey to Orkney, now before me, are the following observations, written by a gentleman, a native of these isles. " Black, blue, and hazel eyes, are to be met with in Orkney as elsewhere ; the eyes of the natives are, *in truth, any colour but green.*"

Scotch peasantry. The woollens which are worn are generally imported from Lancashire or Yorkshire, while some few are the manufacture of the country.

We have now lingered sufficiently long among the cottages in the vicinity of Quendal; for, as the Bard of Morven would intimate to us.—Night comes rolling down, and wreaths of mist begin to robe the white cliffs of Fitfiel.—The annunciation of a fine Shetland evening is always expressed by numerous boats covering the surface of the bay, the crews of which are engaged in angling for the small fry of the coal-fish, or Gadus carbonarius. These swarm in myriads within the numerous creeks and sounds of the Shetland Archipelago. They first appear in May, scarcely more than an inch long, and in comparatively small quantities, but gradually encrease as the summer season advances, when about August they become very abundant, measuring from 6 to 8 inches in length. During this time the fry are distinguished by the name of Sillocks.* About the month of May ensuing, they are found to have grown from 8 to 15 inches, acquiring during this period of their growth the name of Piltocks.† Afterwards they thrive very fast, attaining the ordinary size of the cod-fish; a profitable fishery then takes place of them in deep tideways, under the name of *Sethes*.

Although the fry of the coal-fish frequent all parts of bays, yet the fishermen have informed me, that their favourite resort is among the constant floods and eddies which occur near sunken rocks and bars, that are alternately covered and laid bare by the waves. The fishery for Sillocks or Piltocks is, therefore, occasionally fatal to the more adventurous boats, which, in quest of them, angle in such perilous situations. But, besides frequenting tideways, and currents of all kinds, these small fry appear to covet the security of thick plantations of sea-ware, within the shelter of which they are protected from the keen look-out of their natural enemies of the feathered race.

There is, probably, no sight more impressive to the stranger who first visits the shores of Shetland, than to observe, on a serene day, when the waters are perfectly transparent and undisturbed, the multitudes of busy shoals, wholly consisting of the fry of the coal-fish that Nature's full and unsparing hand has directed to every harbour and inlet.‡

As the evening advances, innumerable boats are launched, crowding the surface of the

---

* Known at Edinburgh, (says Mr Neill,) under the name of *Podleys*, and at Scarborough of *Pars*.

† Synonimous with the *pollock*, of the Hebrides; the *glassock* of Sunderland; the *cuddie* of the Moray Firth; the *grey podley* of Edinburgh; and the *billet* of Scarborough. See Nell's Tour, p. 209. The Piltock of Shetland is the *kuth* of Orkney which the following year is distinguished in the latter place by the name of *harbines*, or two year-old kuths, but they are large and coarse, and not much sought after. Acquiring their greatest bulk, they are called *Sethes*. Low's *Fauna Orcadensis*, p. 194. Mr Neill remarks, that the full grown fish is also in different places termed a *Sey*, a *grey ling*, a *grey lord*, &c. Mr Noel de la Moriniere, Inspector-General of the French Fisheries, observes, that the name Sey or Sethe is frequently given by Scandinavian fishermen to the full grown Gadus virens.

‡ Gawin Douglas, the beautiful early Poet of Scotland, has described a scene somewhere similar.

  " For to behold it was a gloire* to see
  The stabled windis, and the calmed sea,
  The soft season, the firmament serene,
  The *lount* illumin'd air, and *firth amene*‡,
  The silver-scalded fishes on the grit,
  Oerthwart clear streams *sprinkilland*‖ for the heat;
  With finnis shinand brown as cinnabar,
  And chizzel taillis stirrand here and there."

* Glory.   † Calm.   ‡ Pleasant plain.   ‖ Darting with a tremulous motion.

bays, and filled with hardy natives of all ages. The fisherman is seated in his light skiff, with an angling rod in his hand, and a supply of boiled limpets near him, intended for bait. A few of these are carefully stored in his mouth, for immediate use. The baited line is thrown into the water, and a fish is almost instantaneously brought up. The finny captive is then secured; and while one hand is devoted to wielding the rod, another is used for carrying the hook to the mouth, where a fresh bait is ready for it, in the application of which the fingers are assisted by the lips. The same manual and labial routine goes on with remarkable adroitness and celerity, until a sufficient number of sillocks are secured for the fisherman's repast. But, in any season of the year the limpet bait may be superseded by the more alluring temptation of an artificial fly. The rod and line are then handled with a dexterity not unworthy the freshwater talents of a Walton or a Cotton.* Frequently, also, instead of launching his light yawl on the ruffled surface of the bay, a small basket is strung across the shoulders, and securely on shore,

" Some rock the fisher climbs, whose hanging brow
Threatens the waves that lash its base below.
A slender twig his trembling hand extends,
The waving horse-hair from the top descends :
Its fraud immerst with equal joys elate,
The shoals pursue, and snatch the lurking fate."†

So easily are captures made of these small fry, that whilst active manhood is left at liberty to follow the more laborious occupations of the deep water fishery, or to navigate the Greenland Seas, it is to the sinewless arm of youth, or to the relaxed fibres of old age, that the light task is resigned of wielding the sillock-rod.

The lavish abundance in which the fry of the coal-fish visit the inlets of Shetland, afford sufficient matter for contemplation to the reflecting mind. Among islands, the severe climate of which is too often fatal to the labours of husbandry,—where the reduced rate of labour, resulting from the debased political state of the country, precludes the purchase of meal at a cost much above the usual price in commercial districts,—under such circumstances, what is there, that can possibly render a few insulated rocks capable of supporting a population of more than 20,000 souls? The reply is not difficult. That kind Providence,

" ———————————— who pours his bounties forth
With such a full and unwithdrawing hand,
Thronging the seas with spawn innumerable,"

---

* It may be of some interest to " brothers of the angle," as Isaac Walton calls his companions, to learn that the Shetland fly, to which Sillocks rise, is rarely intended to represent any particular species observed in Nature. The Shetlander assures us confidently, that two wings are necessary for the insect,—the fish distinguishing nothing more. The inference is, that there is an intellectual gradation among the finny tribe, and that the fry of the coal-fish are not so clear-sighted as the more wary and knowing inhabitants of pellucid trout-streams. For the construction of the bait, the white feather of the common gull, or of the goose, is sometimes used. But the fibres of the tail or back fin of the dogfish, which, when cleaned, shines like silver, is preferred to any other kind of material, being considered by the fishermen as particularly enticing. The fly is attached to a white hair line, and when this cannot be procured, to a brass wire.

† Translation of Oppian's Halieuticks, by Jones, &c., p. 138. Oxford, 1722.

has not neglected the obscure shores of Hialtlandia. Amidst the occasional visitations of famine, the severity of which overwhelms in despair the commercial population of the South, prompting to every act of civil insubordination, the Shetlander has only to launch his skiff on the waters which glide past his own dwelling, and he finds that a bounteous supply of food awaits him at his very door. A late visitor of this country, whose anxious inquiries into the condition of the lower classes of its inhabitants, were creditable to his humanity, has related, that in a period of scarcity, when many of the natives had not the means of purchasing oatmeal for five months, the fry of the coal-fish formed the breakfast,—the dinner,—and the supper of the Shetland peasant.* Brand, the honest Scottish Missionary, recorded about a century ago, a similar fact, upon which he has commented in an inimitable strain of simple and unaffected piety. "In the late years of great scarcity," he remarked, "the poorer people lived upon this fish almost as their only food, they not enjoying a crumb of bread for many weeks. So our Good God, on the shutting up of one door, opened another, in his holy and wise providence, for the relief of the poor."

NOTES TO ITER I.

NOTE I. Page 1.

IN my statement of the latitude and longitude of Shetland, I have been in some degree guided by the remarks of Mr Arrowsmith, in his Memoir relative to the construction of the Map of Shetland, by the longitude of Bressay Island which is given in Captain Ross's voyage to Baffin's Bay, and by the latitude and longitude of Balta Sound, which were accurately determined when observations were made in Shetland on the Seconds Pendulum. But it is probable that a proper chart of the country, sanctioned by Government, will be soon published, when the errors which have been frequently made in determining its situation will be rectified.

NOTE II. Page 4.
FAIR-ISLE.

This is the only isle of Shetland, which, from its little communication with the rest of

---

* " In the course of the last year, when scarcity prevailed in Shetland to a most distressful degree, till partly relieved by the bounty of Government, these Piltocks, or coalfish, formed the principal food of the poorer inhabitants. Even in September 1804, when, in some of the meanest cottages, I inquired what they had generally for breakfast? They answered, 'Piltocks.' What for dinner? 'Piltocks and cabbage.' What for supper? 'Piltocks.' Some of them declared they had not tasted bread for five months." Neill's " *Tour through Orkney and Shetland*," p. 92.

the group, and from its remoteness, I had no opportunity of visiting. In order, therefore, to complete my account of Shetland, I must be indebted for information regarding Fair-Isle to the testimony of other visitors.

Fair-Isle, which is about twenty-five miles S.SW. of Dunrossness, has been stated to be about two miles in length, and about three quarters in breadth. A very intelligent naturalist, Dr Fleming, who visited this island in the year 1808, found that it consisted chiefly of sandstone. He remarked that "in a mineral precipice of this rock, upwards of 300 feet in height to the northward of Naversgill, and directly exposed to the westward ocean, is a vein of copper. It intersects the strata in a perpendicular direction, and its line of bearing is nearly from north to south. Both sides of the vein seem to be composed of greenstone. Between these layers of greenstone, and in the middle of the vein, there is a stratum of soft decomposed rock, containing much clay, and fragments of compact heavy-spar. The principal ore is the copper-glance, or vitreous copper-ore. There is also a small quantity of copper-green, and malachite disseminated through the copper-glance. The vein of ore appeared to be only about six inches in breadth." Dr Fleming again observes, that since copper-glance is known to afford from 60 to 80 *per cent.* of metal, it is an object of considerable importance to ascertain the true size and extent of this vein.*

The following account of Fair-Isle, is an abstract from a MS. Journal, in my possession, of a Mr James Robertson, (I believe of Edinburgh,) who, about the year 1770, visited this place. " Fair-Isle rises in three high lands, known by the following names: The Coasthill to the north west, Sheeperaig to the south-east, and Setterness to the north-east. The whole island is naturally fenced with perpendicular rocks, except on the north-east end, where there are two bays, where boats can conveniently land; the one on the north side, being a tolerable harbour for vessels not exceeding 60 tons. It is, however, to be observed, that two or three only can lie here with safety. The anchoring ground is in the inside of a small rock called the *Stack*, which lies nearly in the middle of the entry. Ships always go in and out by the west side of that rock; and if it chance to blow hard from the north, which leads straight into the harbour, it will be proper to make fast a rope to a stake, and ride under its lee. The number of inhabitants is about 170. The men are employed in catching fish, which they salt and sell to their landlord. The women knit stockings and gloves, or spin lint and woollen yarn. The natives speak the English language with the Norse accent. Their food is mostly milk, fish, wild-fowl and wild-fowl eggs, which they take from among the precipices, by climbing, or going down the rocks by the assistance of a rope."

In the next place, Mr Sherriff, who, in his survey of Shetland in the year 1808, visited Fair-Isle in company with Dr Fleming, remarks, that the arable land is situated on the south-east side, and is of moderate fertility. There is a good deal of meadow, tolerably productive of herbage. The high grounds are in general grassy, and yield tolerable pasture for the sheep and little horses. The latter are kept solely for carrying home peat, which is dug in a vale towards the north end of the island. The inhabitants depend much upon fishing, and catch annually about 30,000 cod and coal fish, with a few ling and tusk.†

Brand, in 1701, found about ten or twelve families in the island, but he observed, that the small-pox had swept away two-thirds of the inhabitants.‡

In Sir Robert Sibbald's time, the inhabitants were noted for their baldness, induced no doubt by Tinea capitis. It was a common expression when speaking of these islanders, to say, That there was not a hair between them and heaven.§

In 1700, Fair-Isle was united to the parish of Dunrossness, the minister of which remained with them annually for six weeks. There was also a little church, with a person appointed every Sabbath-day to read the Scriptures; and it was said to be regularly and orderly attended. " And it is worth the marking," adds Sir Robert Sibbald, " that fornica-

---

* Dr Fleming's Report in Sherriff's Agricultural Survey of Shetland, p. 128.

† Sherriff's Agricultural Survey of Shetland, p. 7.

‡ Brand's Brief Description of Orkney and Zetland; Edinburgh, 1701.

§ Sir Robert Sibbald's Description of Zetland, fol. p. 25.

tion, and other such escapes, (frequent in other places), are very rare here." But, more lately, the Islands of Foula, Fair-Isle, and Skerries, were united in a separate ministry under one clergyman. From the remoteness of these places from each other, this was found an inconvenient arrangement. Fair-Isle was therefore again attached to Dunrossness. Divine service is now performed by a schoolmaster, and the island is visited by the minister annually for a week only.

It may be lastly observed, that Fair-Isle is celebrated for the immense number of the feathered tribe, which abound on its rocks. Mr Bullock of London visited this island a few years ago, and added some rare specimens of birds to his museum. In Brand's time, A.D. 1700, Fair-Isle was noted for hawks, affirmed to be the best in Britain. These feathered marauders were said to have visited Orkney and Shetland for their prey, carrying away from the former place moor-fowls, and flying with them over forty or fifty miles of sea, to bring them to their nests.

NOTE III. Page 8.

TRADITIONARY NARRATIVE OF THE DUKE DE MEDINA'S SHIPWRECK, COMMANDER OF THE SPANISH ARMADA, A.D. 1588.

The Duke de Medina, who figures away so admirably in the Shetland tradition, is described after the following manner by Strada, the Jesuit: "Igitur Alphonsum Peresium Gusmanum, Medinæ Sidoniæ Ducem, militiæ quidem haud ita peritum sed clarum genere divitiisque per Hispaniæ regna præpollentem, pro Sanctacrucio rex substituit, classe non aspernante, ferreo Duci aureum suffectum: quod et primarii milites ampliorem sui usum à novo inexpertoque imperatore sibi promitterent : et reliqui pecuniosum Ducem tanquam obsidem acciperent stipendii non defuturi."

It is proper also to state, that on examining Strada's account of the disaster of the Spanish Armada, I had, at first view, conceived that the narrative of the Jesuit was fatal to the authenticity of the Shetland tradition ; since he mentions, that after the tempest of the Scottish Seas, the Duke was driven to St Andero in Spain. These are the historian's words: " Medinæ Sidoniæ Dux ad Sanctandreanum veteris Castellæ portum appulsus cum paucis navibus, iisque sauciis mutilatisque et velut in magno naufragio collectis male cohærentibus tabulis, ut erat animo æger pariter et corpore, domum permissu regis, curationis causa concessit."* An attentive examination, however, of this passage may shew, that nothing more might have been meant, than that St Andero was a mere rendezvous, for the purpose of collecting together the dispersed remains of the Armada. To this port, therefore, the Duke, on being landed at Dunkirk, might have immediately speeded, where the purpose for which he chose this station would have justified Strada's general narrative. Besides, it was not the historian's object to inquire into personal adventures, but into general historical events. On this account, we are not entitled to expect, that the Duke's particular hardships at Fair-Isle would appear in a summary view of the Wars of the Netherlands. The tradition of Shetland, besides being so current at the present day as to have afforded me much of the matter which I have related, was collected by Sir Robert Sibbald a century ago, from the written communication of Mr Umphrey, a descendant of the worthy Shetlander who landed the Duke de Medina at Dunkirk. Brand, in 1701, received the tradition "from an old gentlewoman," as it was communicated to her when a child, by the country people who saw the Duke.

In page 5 some explanation may be perhaps required, for attributing to Queen Elizabeth an expression usually ascribed to king James of Scotland. Oldmixon, for instance, remarks. "That the Scots nation were very sensible that the danger which threatened England concerned them very nearly ; and that, as King James said himself, if the Spanish

---

* Famiani Stradæ Romani, e Soc, Jes. de Bello Belgico ; Dec. Sec. Ed 1648, p. 559.

enterprise succeeded, he could only hope for the fate Polyphemes menaced Ulysses with, to be the last devoured." Strado, however, in his usual eloquent style, gives a different account of the matter. "Non cessabat illa [Elizabetha] literis, legationibusque placare juvenem regem [Jacobum], et communione periculi in partes attrahere, subinde admonens, caveret sibi a consiliis Hispanorum, quibus decretum esset, post devictam Angliam, continenti opera Scotiam subjugare, nec majus ab Hispano beneficium Scoto expectandum, quam quod Ulyssi promississe dicitur Polyphemus, nempe ut cæteris devoratis, ultimus ipse deglutiretur." But if James was reluctant in embarking in the Protestant cause, it was evident that such lukewarm sentiments prevailed nowhere in Scotland but in Holyrood-House. "The rumour of the great Spanish Armada," says an old author, "being blazed abroad, frequent were the prayers of the godly in Scotland, powerful and piercing were the sermons of preachers," &c. The Spaniards who were cast away upon the Scottish coasts, are also said, in the spirit of the times, to "have begged from door to door, proclaiming aloud the glory of God's justice and power."

NOTE IV. p. 13.

ROMAN ANTIQUITIES FOUND AT DUNROSSNESS.

Mr Ross, (late of Lerwick,) was at considerable pains to collect all the remains of antiquity which fell in his way, that were found in Shetland. In his possession I have seen, among other coins, a copper medal, bearing the inscription of Ser. Galba Imp. Cæs. Aug.; another of Vespasian, and a silver coin of Trajan. Mr Pennant, in his Arctic Zoology, has stated, on the authority of the late Reverend George Low, that a medal of Vespasian had been formerly found at Dunrossness. I possess a note to the same effect in Mr Low's handwriting. "In Dunrossness parish was some time ago found a copper medal of Vespasian, the reverse Judæa Victa. It was turned up in plowing the ground."

In the Plate of Antiquities given in the Appendix, marked Fig. 2, a copper medal found in Shetland, bears on one side the name of L. Ælius Cæsar, and on the reverse "Pannoniæ Curia A E L;" in which Ælius is figured as receiving from a native of Pannonia a cornucopiæ and a household-god. Below are the letters S. C. (senatus consulto.) Ælius was the Roman whom Adrian in his old age adopted as his successor, being better known by the name which he bore prior to his elevation, -that of L. Aurelius Verus. He was created Prætor, and sent to govern the province of Pannonia, in which employment he acquitted himself with a reputation. He was sprung from a noble family, was well versed in most branches of learning, particularly in poetry, and is described as preserving a dignified manner amidst habits of extreme dissipation. His constitution was weak and infirm, and he did not live to attain the high dignity which was intended him as Adrian's successor. See Univ. His., vol. xv., p. 174 to 176.

NOTE V. p. 19.

REMARKS ON THE DARK PERIOD OF THE HISTORY OF SHETLAND.

I have stated that it is impossible to investigate the earliest annals of Shetland to the exclusion of those of Orkney. In giving a concise view of what is recorded on the subject, I have avoided much of the apocryphal matter which has been collected on the occasion by Torfæus. Any antiquary who may possess a relish for the occupation of sifting truth from falsehood, will find abundant materials for his purpose in Buchanan's Account of King Belus of Orkney, in the information of Bede and Boethius that Claudius carried to Rome King Gaius of Orkney for the purpose of gracing his triumph, or in Geoffry of Monmouth's assertion that King Gunfasius of the Orkneys paid a tribute to King Arthur. The same antiquary may also, like the learned Whittaker in his History of Giant Tarquin of

Manchester, plunge at once into the regions of pure romance, where, in "La Morte d'Arthur," printed by Caxton, he will find "how Lot, Kynge of Lowthean and of Orkney wedded the sister of Kyng Arthur;—how Pellinore smote hym a grete stroke thorow the helme and hede unto the browes, and then all the hooste of Orkney fled for the deth of Kynge Lot, and there were slayn many moders sones."

On the subject of the dark period of the history of Shetland and Orkney, I have only to add, that the account of Claudius having, A.D. 43, added Orkney to his government, rests on the authority of Eutropius (lib. 7.) The statement is not corroborated by the testimony of other Roman authors, although it implies the common belief, that about the Christian Era Orkney was inhabited. The narrative of Eutropius is indeed directly opposed to the assertion of Tacitus, who affirms that the Orcades were unknown to the Romans until the visit of Agricola.— See Tacitus, in Vit. Agric. c. 10.

ADDITION TO ITER I.

Sillocks.— I neglected to state in page 27 that the livers of the sillocks are converted to an important use; being collected in a tub, they are boiled for oil, while the overplus is sold. "Thus,". says a female writer of Thule (Miss Campbell) with much eloquence, "the two articles most required in a climate like that of Shetland, have been abundantly provided by the eternal and ever-wise Governor of the Universe, these are fire and light. The natives have, for their labour, as much fuel as they can consume. Whatever wants may be in a Zetland hut, there is seldom or never a good fire wanting. The fish which they catch, almost at their doors, supply them with the means of light. The cold and darkness of their long winters are thus mercifully robbed of their terror; and in the mud-walled cottage of the Zetlander, the providence of God is as conspicuous, and as surely felt, as in those favoured lands which flow with milk and honey, and where the sun shines in all its glory."

Ster II.

SOUTH-EAST DISTRICT OF SHETLAND.

> "And all the Chamber filled was with flyes,
> Which buzzed all about, and made such sound
> That they encombered all men's eares and eyes;
> Like many swarmes of bees assembled round,
> After their hives with honny do abound.
> All those were [Geognostic] fantasies,
> Devices, dreames, opinions unsound."
>
> * * * * * * * * *
>
> Whom Alma having shewed to her guestes,
> Thence brought them to the Second Rowme, whose wals
> Were painted faire with memorable gestes
> Of famous wisards, and with picturals
> Of magistrates, of courts, of tribunals,
> Of common wealthes, of states, of policy,
> Of lawes, of judgmentes, and of decretals."
>
> SPENSER'S *Fairy Queene*, Book ii., Canto 9.

UPON first landing on the shores of Shetland, we were induced to consider, as objects of no little interest, the habits of the people with whom we were to mingle, as well as the memorials which serve to elucidate the early history of the country. It was indeed requisite that there should be some relief of this kind from the monotonous labours of the hammer. For it would be the most irksome of avocations to be condemned for a length of time to toil unremittingly among primitive rocks,—to pore incessantly over mineralogical specimens,—or rather, like Shakespeare's dull solemn foresters, to seek for "sermons in stones."*

---

* " And this our life, exempt from public haunt,
   Finds tongues in trees, books in the running brooks,
   Sermons in Stones."
                    Duke, in " *As you like it*."

In the examination of the south-east district of Shetland, the objects inviting particular attention, are the Burgh of Mousa, which forms no insignificant monument of the military arts of the Northmen by whom the pile was reared ; the Castle of Scalloway, built by Earl Patrick Stewart, which recalls to mind the period when Hialtland first became a Scottish province ; and the modern town of Lerwick, sufficiently indicative of the commercial spirit that has been imbibed from the kingdom to which Shetland was last annexed. These objects, which, in the route we are taking, arrest the notice of the traveller in a sort of historical succession, suggest, at the same time, an inquiry into the causes that have led to the present political state of the country. But this history would be imperfectly understood, without an accurate conception of the state of landed property during the period when Shetland was subject to Norway, and of the changes which Scandinavian tenures underwent, from the introduction into the country of Scottish feudalism. This preliminary information, therefore, I now propose to give.

HISTORY OF THE UDALLERS OF SHETLAND.

Norwegian poets relate, that in the 9th century, Harold Harfagre, or the Fair-haired, hearing of the transcendant beauties of the Princess Gida, credited the rumour to its full extent, and, without ever seeing the damsel, commissioned a Lord to make her an offer of his hand. "The name of Harold is not sufficiently renowned," said the ambitious fair one, "never will Gida esteem the noble suitor worthy of her love, until he has reduced all Norway under his power." The hero was not disheartened by these severe conditions, but vowed to neglect his fine golden locks until the subjugation was accomplished.*

Harold was successful. Most of the petty princes of Norway yielded to him absolute submission : others, less patient of the yoke, sought with their retainers a voluntary exile in Iceland, Feroe, or the islands contiguous to the north of Scotland. Among the remote and steril tracts of Orkney and of Shetland, valiant Norwegians, whose deeds of arms had been so lately sung in their own country, were only solaced by the opportunities of revenge which the earliest breezes of the spring afforded to their piratical barks. Thus did numerous summers attest the devastation and slaughter with which the coasts of Harold were visited.

The monarch was at length roused from his contemptuous disregard of these daring hordes, and, having collected a fleet, immediately put to sea. Shetland, Orkney, and the Hebrides, which had ever afforded shelter for the objects of piracy, fell before him. The liberation of the seas being thus accomplished, Harold offered the provinces of Caithness, Orkney, and Shetland, as one earldom, to Ronald, Count of Merca. But this nobleman being more attached to a Norwegian residence, resigned the donation in favour of his

---

* Torfæus, *Rerum Orcad. Hist.*, c. 6. Mallet's *North. Antiq.* (Translation by Percy), vol. i.

brother Sigurd, who was accordingly elected the first Earl of Orkney.*

During a period of three centuries from the time of Sigurd, the events immediately connected with Shetland deserve little regard, with the exception of the state of landed property, and the admirable system of civil polity by which a small community of colonists was firmly linked together.

In order that the islands and coasts which Harold had subdued, might no longer be a refuge for his foes, it was necessary that they should be peopled by individuals firm in their allegiance to the Crown of Norway; and in a partition of the vanquished territories among the first colonists, the magnitude of shares would be regulated by military or civil rank.† But in measuring out allotments in proportional shares, it would be necessary to resort to some familiar standard of valuation. The Norwegians in the time of Harold, appear to have scarcely known any other than what was suggested by the coarse woollen attire of the country, named *Wadmel*. Eight pieces of this description of cloth, each measuring six ells, constituted a mark.‡ The extent, therefore, of each Shetland site of land bearing the appellation of Mark, was originally determined by this rude standard of comparison; its exact limits being described by loose stones or shells, under the name of Merk-stones or Meithes,—many of which still remain undisturbed on the brown heaths of the country. The Shetland mark of land presents every variety of magnitude, indicating, at the same time, that allotments of territory were rendered uniform in value, by a much greater extent of surface being given to the delineation of a mark of indifferent land than to soil of a good quality. It was some time after the Norwegian colonization of Shetland, that it became necessary to reduce each measurement of ground into still smaller allotments. But although the division was into eight parts, its correspondence to the similar one of a mark of wadmel, was not immediately derived from this measurement. A newer standard of comparison had succeeded to the wadmel, formed of a certain weight of some inferior metal. The division, therefore, of a *Mark-Weight* of this substance into eight Ures§ or ounces, appears to have suggested a name for the same number of portions into which a mark of land began to be resolved.‖

---

* Johnson's *Antiq. Celto-Scandica.* Torfæus, *Rerum Orcad. Hist.*, c. 6.

† It is certain, from Norwegian Historians, that the largest division of property in the Earldom of Orkney, was originally possessed by the Earls themselves.

‡ "In Iceland and Norway all crimes were rated at a certain number of marks. The mark was divided into eight parts, each of which was equivalent to six ells of such stuff as made their ordinary cloaths. Consequently, a mark was in value equal to forty-eight ells of this cloth. Now, a mark consisted of somewhat more than an ounce of fine silver. A cow commonly cost two marks and a half. See *Arngrim.* Jon Crymog, lib. i., p. 86." Mallet's *Northern Antiq.* (Translation by Percy), vol. i., p. 276.
It may be observed, that in Shetland, *Wadmel* continued to be paid in lieu of coin for scat, feu-duties and rent, down to a very late period. In the seventeenth century, however, the name of a mark of wadmel became entirely obsolete, owing to the custom introduced of converting it into money. It was then rated as equivalent to a Zealand Zullen, or to two shillings English. The eighth part of a mark of this coarse cloth then acquired the name of a *shilling of Wadmel*. But notwithstanding this innovation, the eighth part or *shilling* ever continued to retain its ancient extent of six ells. See Gifford's *Description of Zetland*, p. 64. - Published in the Biblioth. Topogr. Brit.

§ An Ure is said to signify a denomination of money, either coined or reckoned by weight. In Iceland,—the Scandinavian colonization of which took place nearly at the same time as Shetland,—the term *Auri*, from which *Ure* is said to be derived, is the eighth part of a *pound* or mark. For the original authorities respecting the word *Ure*, See Jamieson's *Etymological Dictionary.*

‖ "An ure is the eighth part of a merk. The dimensions of the merk vary, not only in the different parishes, but in different towns of the same parish." *Statist. Account of Scotland*, vol. xxi., p. 278.—The division of a mark of land into *Ures*, appears to have been first introduced into the Earldom in the year 1263. Hacon, King of Norway, in an expedition against the Scots, had

Such is the simple detail of events, over which an air of mystery has ever unnecessarily hung, relative to the distribution of territory among the early Norwegian possessors of Shetland; all the leading circumstances attending the partition amounting to no more than this brief statement:—that the standard of valuation to which each divided allotment or mark of land bore reference, was a simple mark of wadmel, consisting of forty-eight ells; that in limiting the area of equivalent allotments of ground, and in adjusting to this simple standard each various quality of soil, every mark of land throughout Shetland would manifest corresponding differences of extent; also, that in the course of time, each mark of land, whatever might have been its area, was supposed to be divisible into equal portions, named *ures*, the term being arbitrarily derived from the eighth part of some inferior metal.

Before the reign of Harold, Scandinavian lands had been held unfettered by any tax or impost. The hardy Northman, after discovering that a soil could be so improved by labour as to afford to the cultivator a subsistence less precarious than that which depends upon the resources of fishing or hunting, would inclose a piece of ground around the cabin he had erected, to which he would affix some unlimited notions of property. Harold is supposed to have been the first monarch of Norway who oppressed his subjects by levying a tax or *skat* upon land.* But in whatever mode the tax might have been exacted in Norway, it appears, that, in the colony of Shetland, the inclosures designed for cultivation were ever considered as property that was sacred to the free use of the possessor; these were never violated by the unwelcome intrusion of a collector of *seat*. Each mark of land bounded by *mark-stones* or *meithes*, naturally contained very little soil fit for tillage. It was, therefore, from pastures, and from the produce of the flocks which grazed upon them, that the seat, or contribution for the exigencies of the state of Norway, was originally levied.† The patch of ground which the possessor had inclosed, being rendered exempt from every imposition to which grazing-lands were liable, it is possible that the uncontrolled enjoyment of the soil destined for culture, first suggested to the early colonists of Shetland such a term as odhal or udal, expressive in the northern language of *free property or possession*; ‡ whilst

---

o. asion to quarter his men on the inhabitants of Orkney. That they might be billeted with a regularity worthy of modern times, he divided the islands int) *Eurelands or Ounzelands*, each of which was the eighth part of a mark. Torfæus thus describes the fact: " Ipse rex (Hacon) in superi oribus ædibus accubuit, insulasque in *uncias* describi curavit *(Eyrisland habetur, continet autem quotlibet merca terra octo eyrer sue uncias,) satrapis et nobilitati*, eorumque turmis, per singulos unciarios agros sustendandis." Torfæus, *Rerum Orcad. Hist.*, p. 169.

* " When King Harold had suppressed all the petty kings, his power extended itself likewise to the Odels-bonden, (free landholders,) and they were obliged to pay him a tax, which was without doubt the origin of the Odels-skat or tax, which is still imposed upon them, though King Hagen Adalsteen afterwards promised that it should be taken off." Pontopp. *Nat. Hist. of Norway*, vol. ii., p. 190.

† *" The Scat was originally the tax or rent paid for pasturing-ground.* This scat was the only land-rent payable to the Crown out of Zetland at first; but in process of time, *some of the arable-land which was at first the property of the improver*, came also to the Crown by forfeitures and donations."—Gifford's *Description of Zetland*, p. 54.

To be in perfect correspondence with the foregoing information, the mark of land ought to have originally included both arable and pasture ground. The following is the reply to a *Query submitted by Mr Shirreff to R. Hunter, Esq. of Lunna*—" When merks of lands are spoken of, is it the land within the Hill-dikes only that is meant to be identified, or is the Scattald or hill-grazings included?" *Answer*: " In the legitimate sense, in sales and in *charters*, it is the *whole arable and pasture-land*, sea-weeds, minerals, &c. unless particular exceptions be made."—Shirreff's *Agric. Survey*, p. 32., *Appendix*.

‡ This is the etymology proposed by Scheffer and sanctioned by Pontoppidan. Blackstone, the English Judge, also conceives it to be the best which has been given. " Schefferus autumat ab Adel et Odel, oriundum esse, quod proprietatem omnimodam, scilicet ab odh *proprietas*, et all *totum* omne denotavit;"—(Pontopp. *Norway*, vol. ii., p. 290.) *Lastly*, With regard to the term, *odhal* or *udal*, it has been imagined, that, by a transposition of these syllables, the term *allodh* would convey the true etymology of *allodium* or absolute property. See Blackstone's *Comment.*, Ed. 1803, vol. ii., p. 44.

UDALLERS.

to pasture-land which was held by the payment of a tax or scat, the distinctive appellation was awarded of Scattald.*

Thus the Shetland mark of land originally included pasture or scattald, as well as inclosed cultivated ground free from scat, and hence named udal. Accordingly, when a mark of land was transferred by sale or bequest from one individual to another, or was even let to a tenant, the proportion of scattald remaining after the patch of free arable ground had been separated from it, was always clearly expressed.†

It is difficult to form an accurate judgment respecting the amount of the scat which was paid by Shetland to the Crown of Norway. When arable ground was inclosed, and subtracted from scattald, becoming by this means udal, or free from the impost of scat, various assessments, for the purpose of equalizing the tax, would be required; and the population of the country encreasing, land would become more in demand, and consequently more valuable. In reference, therefore, to a fixed standard of value, marks of land would be multiplied. At the time when Shetland was separated from the Kingdom of Norway, there are reasons for supposing that the number of marks might be about 13,000 or 14,000, being the same that is recognised at the present day‡, these having been rated for their proportion of the scat due to the King, according to the extent of pasture-ground or scattald which they respectively contained.§

In the days of Harold, the scat was paid in wadmel.‖ In a later period an equivalent of butter or oil was accepted.¶ There is also reason for supposing, that, instead of scattald having been considered as liable to an impost of one or more ells of wadmel, the assessment was made in some rude description of coin, bearing the name of Pennings or Pennies.** The relative value of the penny acknowledged in this

---

* This distinction is evidently implied by Mr Gifford of Busta, in his excellent Memoir of Shetland, drawn up eighty years ago, which displays a degree of research that would do credit to the topography of any province. He expressly says, that it was the *arable-ground* (which he had elsewhere shewn to be not liable to the levy of a scat,) that bore the name of *Udal*. The following are his words: "*The arable ground being all at first the property of the immediate possessors thereof*, went to their successors by a verbal title called *Udell* Succession." (Gifford's *Zetland*, p. 37.) From this and other passages in Mr Gifford's work, it is apparent that the word *udal* was merely meant in Shetland to distinguish *free arable land* from *pasture-land*, which last was liable to a scat-duty, and was hence named *scattald*. Thus were the terms *scattald* and *udal-lands* originally opposed to each other, however confounded these distinctions might have been in later times, owing to the innovations of a feudal nature that had been introduced into the country, when it became annexed to the Crown of Scotland.

† This will be fully illustrated when I have to treat of the law of Udal Succession.

‡ Since the time that Shetland was annexed to the Crown of Scotland, several causes have conspired to prevent the introduction of any innovation in the measurement of the lands of the country; and the ancient land-marks, as they have existed from time immemorial, are still recognised in all transfers of property. As far as I can collect from the description of the different parishes of Shetland given in Mr Gifford's Description of Shetland, the number of marks are supposed by him to be 12,611. Mr Hunter of Lunna has recently supposed them to be about 14,000. —*App. to Shirreff's Survey of Shetland*, p. 32.

§ The amount of the tax paid to the Crown of Scotland, before the oppressive government of Earl Robert Stewart, is supposed to have been the same that had previously been exacted by the King of Denmark and Norway. Mr Gifford says, that before the accession of this Earl, "the Crown rent of Zetland was farmed at 500 marks a-year." *Gifford's Zetland*, p. 63. But no information of the Crown's revenues is conveyed from this circumstance. Tacks of Orkney and Shetland were ever enjoyed by court-favourites, who paid for them an annual consideration, much beneath the real amount of the profit which they derived from these islands.

‖ Money was then unknown. In Pinkerton's History of Medals, (vol. ii. p. 35.) may be found the following quotation from Crantz, regarding the state of Scandinavian commerce prior to the 11th century. "Illa vero tempestate nulla erat in terra moneta; sed rebus res commutantes, vetustissimo more mercabantur."

¶ Gifford's Zetland, p. 62.

** Four penny, six penny land, &c., originally denoted the proportion of scattald contained within the mark. In elucidation

country, when compared with silver, appears in the course of time to have varied materially. But whatever encrease of value the coin might have sustained, either by an addition to the weight, or from causes not purely artificial, four of these pennies were ever demanded as the equivalent of an ell of wadmel, the cloth never having been exacted according to the ratio of its quality, but always in a fixed measurable quantity.* The inevitable consequence was, that, in course of time, the equivalent of an ell of wadmel for every fourpence charged on a mark of land, was transmitted to the government of Denmark in materials of the very coarsest description.† It may be also observed, that the amount of the scat exacted from each mark was within the limits of four and twelve pennings. Hence the designation of four penny, six penny, eight penny land, &c., recognised in Shetland at the present day, no mark having been rated under four pence, or more than twelve pence.

During the period in which Shetland was subject to the crown of Norway, the Grand Foude, or Governor, strictly forbade all commercial intercourse with other nations. The poverty resulting no less from this prohibition than from the disproportionate amount of the tax to which land was subject, ever induced a considerable emigration from these islands.‡

Thus oppressed, it is no wonder that Shetland and Orkney should have always yielded an unwilling submission to the Crown of Norway. Pecuniary mulcts were at various times imposed upon the inhabitants for their disobedience; but these, as they increased the poverty of the country, only served to multiply the causes of irritation.

It will now be proper to take a concise view of the relations in which the different ranks of men belonging to the Scandinavian colony stood to each other.

Shetland being by nature constituted a province distinct from the other divisions of territory belonging to the Earldom of Orkney, had a separate governor appointed by the King of Denmark, as judge of all civil affairs, the country at the same time acquiring the

---

* Of the origin of this and other terms of the like nature, Dr Jamieson has brought forward two quotations from Ihre, which at least shew the familiarity of the term among the northern nations. These are, however, more applicable to the division of the lands of Orkney than to those of Shetland, since the latter country, in the retention of many primeval customs, long after they were abolished in ancient Scandinavia, and even in Orkney, has never yet acknowledged such an innovation as a regular land measurement. Old meithes or mark-stones are still by the Shetlanders religiously preserved; and the mark of land is at the present moment as indefinite as ever it was in the days of Harold Harfagre.

* The ancient *Penning* of the northern nations was less than an *oere*, and, according to one author, an *oere* was less than a farthing; whilst another writer maintains, that a farthing was called *half-oere*. The value, therefore, of the penning, must have been small indeed. (See *Jamieson's Etym. Dict.*, word merk). But in the course of time, so much had the value of the penny increased, that a groat, or four pennies (the fixed price of an ell of wadmel) was, in the old rentals that were examined by Mr Gifford, rated at the sixth part of a Zealand *cullen*, or two shillings Sterling. *(Gifford's Zetland,* p. 61.) It has been before observed, that, in the early annals of Norway, forty-eight ells of wadmel were equal to an ounce of silver. (See Note, p. 178.) But in the old rentals of Mr Gifford it appears, that this commodity had so much increased in value, that the same quantity of silver was considered as an equivalent for no more than twelve ells; so that the Shetlanders, who had been in early times assessed for their scattalds in a definite number of pennies, the equivalent for which was arbitrarily demanded in an unvarying number of ells of wadmel, were by this and other similar oppressions, rendered miserably poor.

† Tradition has not been wholly silent with regard to the fabric of the wadmel. "The Shetlanders were wont," says Dr Sibbald, "to make very coarse cloth, (called wadmiln), the threeds whereof, were as thick as fishers lines, and this they paid to the Danes as a part of their superiour duties; but now they spin it small enough."—*Sibbald's Shetland,* p. 21.

‡ "The poor Udellers were universally oppressed by the Governor or Fowd, and kept under, being forbidden all sorts of commerce with foreigners, as the subjects of that king are to this day in Fairo and Iceland; so there was no such thing as money amongst them; and what they had of the country product, more than paid the Crown rent, they were obliged to bring to the Governor, who gave them for it such necessaries as they could not be without, and at what prices he had a mind, wherewith they were obliged to rest content, having no way to be redressed. Kept under this slavery, they were miserably poor, careless, and indolent, and most of their young men, when grown up, finding the poor living their native country was like to afford them, went abroad and served in foreign countries for their bread, and seldom or never returned; so that these islands were but thinly inhabited." Gifford's *Zetland,* p. 37.

name of a *Fowdrie*.* The Fowdrie of Shetland was divided into five, and subsequently into a still greater number, of districts, to each of which was allotted an inferior foude or magistrate. The foude of a district had only the power of deciding in small matters, his office being intended for the preservation of good neighbourhood: he was assisted in the execution of his duty by ten or twelve active officers under the name of *Rancilmen*, and by a *law-rightman*, who was entrusted with the regulation of weights and measures. Cases of importance were, at stated periods, tried by the Grand Foude, and at an annual court, at which all udallers were obliged to attend, new legislative measures were enacted; appeals were heard against the decisions of the subordinate foudes; and causes involving the life or death of an accused individual, were determined by the voice of the people.

The colonists of Shetland never acknowledged any legal civil authority but that with which the Grand Foude or Lawman was arrayed, who was the King of Norway's representative. To the Earl of Orkney was granted the power of a military commander, but that it was never to be exerted in wresting from the udaller the free possession of his national laws, rights and privileges.† When the native force of the country was required for the protection of its own coasts, or when, for the purpose of embarking in some piratical excursion to the coasts of Scotland, the Earl unfurled the black banner of the raven, crowds of eager warriors repaired to the signal. That the Scandinavian chief had frequently the power of controlling the legislative decisions of the community, is undeniable; but this influence was ever considered as illegal. From his greater wealth, he was daily enabled to spread out a plenteous table, by which means a numerous band of retainers became attached to his household, who knew no other stipend than the liberty of carousing at the banquets of the great hall.‡ Rendered thus powerful, he was frequently tempted, from unworthy motives of ambition, self-interest, or resentment, to commit unjust aggressions on the civil liberty of the community.

Christianity was introduced by King Olaus of Norway into the earldom of Orkney in the year 1014, when the colonists became liable to new burdens. In addition to the seat of wadmel obtained from the produce of the flocks which grazed upon the pastures, tithes of wool were required for the Pope.§ The freedom of the soil, which the Shetlander had inclosed for culture, became, for the first time, invaded by the united authority of the bishop and the priest of the parish. These dignitaries divided between them in equal shares the tenth part of the corn that was inclosed within the udal fence. For the purpose of partition, the lands of the parish were assessed with the utmost exactness, and the dominion over the

---

* It is so named in all old charters, as, for instance, in the grant of the Earldom of Orkney, A.D. 1381, to Lord Robert Stewart: "Totas et integras terras de Orkney et Shetland——ac cum officio vice-comitatus de lie *Fowdrie* de Shetland," &c. *Memorial against Sir Lawrence Dundas, signed Hay Campbell.*

† That a responsibility of this nature was attached to the relation in which the Earl stood to the Udallers, is evident from the whole of the History of Torfæus; and when Lord Sinclair of Scotland received the Earldom of Orkney from the Crown of Denmark, it formed a leading article in his investiture.

‡ Mallet's North. Antiq., vol. i., p. 303.

§ The Pope's tenths in Shetland, were, in the year 1328, very considerable, and said to amount to "22 cwt. of wool less than 16 pounds, according to the standard of Hialtland, being 36 span Hialtland weight of wool." The growth of Shetland wool, as well as of the Pope's power, seem to have diminished about the same period.—For the original authority regarding the Pope's tythes, see the *Biblioth. Topogr. Brittann.* Dr Edmondston has transcribed the document in his History of Zetland.

tenth part of the produce of the husbandman's labour was reduced, by a demarcation of soil, to equal shares. In order also to effect with a still greater nicety, a fair allotment of these temporalities, and to obviate the possibility that the partition which fell to one member of the hierarchy, might not be more lucrative than that which was enjoyed by the other, it was resolved that an annual interchange should take place in the respective shares of the tithe-lands, and that the same ground which belonged in one year to the priest, should be transferred in the following year to the bishop; hence the term umboth, that was given to the corn-tithes, intended to express, in the northern language, such an alternate possession.*
Three districts of Shetland, namely, Tingwall, Whitness, and Weesdale, were formed into an Archdeaconry, the tithes being the exclusive emoluments of the ecclesiastic to whose care it was committed. But besides these compulsory contributions, superstition dictated one burden on the lands that was gratuitous.† A venerable female was introduced into Shetland, recommended by the Bishop as a personage of extraordinary sanctity, that if she slept but one night in a parish, the inhabitants would ever afterwards be blessed with plentiful harvests and fisheries. But the orisons of the matron could scarcely be expected without some pecuniary acknowledgement. Accordingly, the simple natives were easily induced to allow the holy dame, as an annuity for life, a penny for each mark of land.

Notwithstanding all the encroachments of the Church on the free tenure of udal lands, they were prevented from growing into excess, owing to the jealousy with which they were regarded by the Crown of Denmark and Norway. A writer, evidently well versed in Scandinavian literature, has recently observed, that the hierarchy never became so deeply engrafted in the northern commonwealth as in the other countries of Christendom.‡ A proof of the mistrust with which the Bishop of Orkney was viewed by the Danish monarch, is to be found among the conditions under which Lord Sinclair of Scotland received his investiture in the earldom. There was a special stipulation, that he should enter into no engagements to the king's prejudice with the Bishop of Orkney, nor should he be a party in any contract with the Church, that was not ratified by the royal consent.§

During the period when Shetland was a Norwegian province, there was no incident of udal tenures more remarkable than the law ascribed to King Olaus, known by the name of Udal Succession, to which the lands of the country were subject. By this law, the arable ground, which, having been separated by inclosure from the scattald, was the free property of the cultivator, went to all the children of the proprietor, male or female, in equal shares. In order to obviate any evasion of this rule of inheritance, no one could dispose of an estate without the public consent of his heirs. Even the property of the Earls of Orkney was often partitioned out in nearly equal shares among descendants. The annals of the country present a copious detail of conflicting interests arising from this cause, together with the civil discords which they occasioned. It appears that the kingdom

---

* See Gifford's Discription of Zetland, p. 64. "*Umboth* is a Danish word, signifying to change about."

† This burthen was originally but a temporary one; feudal injustice subsequently rendered it permanent.

‡ See Edin. Review, Article on the Ancient Laws of Scandinavia, No. lxvii.

§ Torfæus, Rerum Orcad. Hist., p. 175.

of Harold Harfagre was divided in the 9th century among male successors, in nearly equal proportions.

Before that part of our narrative be closed which appertains to the early state of udal tenures in Shetland, the inquiry, Whether or not the landed property of this country was ever fettered with any kind of feudal restrictions, cannot be devoid of interest. It is well known, that the feudal system of Europe arose from a migratory people, who, in the course of their continued invasions, could not retain land, and therefore returned it to the use of the vanquished, annexing to the tenure the service of arms. But when the military tribes of Europe chose to settle in the country which they had subdued, the chiefs parcelled out the lands among their favourites or retainers, under the obligation of a warrior's oath of fealty. These original possessors dealt out in like manner their lands in lesser divisions, requiring from sub-feudatories the same allegiance which they themselves had been pledged to give to the liege-lord. Lands were thus made accessory to military subordination. But in Scandinavia and its colonies, tenures of this nature were unknown. On the soil of the Northman, "Feudality," as a writer has elegantly remarked, "never expanded beyond the germ."* When soldiers were required to be raised, a popular convocation was held, and the levy was made by fixing the number of men which each village or town could conveniently furnish.† Accordingly, when one of the Earls of Orkney, by impressing soldiers and forcibly carrying them off, had assumed an illegal authority, a meeting of the Udallers was held, and a remonstrance, though ineffectual at the time, was pronounced against the unjust proceeding.‡ Abundant proofs may, indeed, be adduced, that the Earls of Orkney never possessed the uncontrolled power of a feudal lord over the personal services of the community. When Harold Harfagre was indignant at Einar Earl of Orkney and his adherents for the slaughter of his son, he imposed upon the country a fine of sixty marks of gold. The Chief furnished the sum from his own coffers, and in security for that part of the amount which was the proportion due from the Udallers, received in pledge all the lands of the country. But history sanctions not the supposition, that the Earl was enabled to convert the alienated property into feudal tenures; for in a later period, when Earl Sigurd, a descendant of Einar, was desirous to levy troops, in order to ward off a Scottish invasion, he was compelled, before the natives would take up arms in his defence, to offer a free restoration of the impignorated lands.§ This historical event sufficiently proves, that the soil for which the udaller fought was discharged of all personal obligations incidental to feudal tenures. In short, the Earl stood in no other relation to the people, than that of a military chief, who was responsible at the same time to the king, that his influence should be exerted in such a manner as was calculated to preserve to the country its accustomed rights and privileges.

At length it has been shewn, that the lands enjoyed by the udaller originally owed nothing but a contribution to the commonwealth, exigible from the produce of the flocks

---

* Edin. Review, No. lxvii., p. 177.

† Mallet's North. Antiq., vol. i., p. 234.

‡ Torfæus, Rerum Orcad. Hist., p. 47.

§ Torfæus, Rerum Orcad. Hist., c. 7. & 10. Johnson's Antiq. Celto-Scandicæ, p. 11.

that grazed on the wild and uninclosed pastures of the country; that the soil destined for culture, was for a long time sacred to the free use of the encloser,—the udal fence being first broken by the bold hands of the tither, delegated with irresistible power from the Pope, the Bishop, or the Vicar. The causes may now be investigated which led to the annexation of the earldom of Orkney to the Crown of Scotland, and eventually to such a change in the state of udal property, that it became in the course of time almost completely feudalised.

In the fourteenth century,* there was a failure of the male line of the Earls of Orkney, when Henry Sinclair of Scotland, who, from an alliance by marriage, had the best right to the earldom, received an investiture of it from the King of Denmark, on conditions that left undisturbed the ancient laws of the Scandinavian colony, and preserved entire the allegiance due to the mother country.† The earldom of Orkney for a century afterwards continued in the hands of the Sinclairs, when certain events took place, by which it devolved as an appendage to the Scottish Crown.

The Crown of Denmark and Norway had endeavoured to enforce with threats the annual payment of 100 marks, which Scotland had agreed to give for the cession of the Western Isles. The penalties accruing from the non-fulfilment of the contract, had at the same time amounted to a sum little less than ten millions Sterling. A long controversy ensued, the result of which was, that the claim might be conveniently cancelled, by a marriage between the Scottish monarch and the Princess of Denmark. The alliance took place when Orkney and Shetland were pledged to James III. for 58,000 florins, as part of the maiden's dower: a leading condition of the treaty being, that the natives of the Islands should retain their ancient laws and customs.

The right of redemption has not since been resigned by the Crown of Denmark. The historians of Scotland maintain, that the King of Denmark waved his claim to Orkney and Shetland, in joy for the birth of a grandson, the deed of gift being subsequently confirmed by the monarch's successor. The Danes, however, shew that the right of redemption was never surrendered, being formally urged at several distinct periods, the last of which was no longer ago than the year 1667;‡ but it is often an unsatisfactory labour to reconcile the diplomatic contracts and secret understandings of high-contracting parties.

A few years after the impignoration of Orkney and Shetland, Lord Sinclair bartered to James III. his whole right and title to the earldom, in exchange for the castle and lands of Ravenscraig in Scotland; when the first proceeding of the king was, by a formal statute, to annex these islands to the Crown.

We now enter upon the Scottish period of the history of udal tenures. From the year 1470 to 1530, the estate and revenues of the earldom of Orkney, that had devolved by exchange to the Crown, were let out to lease: the civil government was committed to lieutenants and viceroys; and to the Archbishop of St Andrew's was assigned the jurisdiction of the church. The estates were now possessed by the King of Scotland, the hierarchy, and the udallers, when, for the first time, feudal tenures became known to the islands.

---

* A.D. 1379.
† Torfæus, Rerum Orcad. Hist., p. 176.
‡ See Sir Thomas Craig, on the one hand, who advocates the Scottish right; and, on the other hand, Torfæus.

UDALLERS.

The feudal system of Scotland was not introduced into the Earldom of Orkney, until it had made a considerable progress towards a civil establishment. Feudatories had formed attachments to particular sites of ground;—lands were not recalled at the mere caprice of the superior; they were granted for a term of years,—they were even extended to the life of the possessor,—or they were retained by hereditary succession in particular families. When the King of Scotland, in consequence of his marriage with the Princess of Denmark, had acquired the dominion over Shetland and Orkney, becoming also by dint of a subsequent treaty with Earl Sinclair, the sole disposer of the estate and revenues of the earldom, his first care was to annex the property he had acquired to the Crown, not to be given away except to a lawful male descendant of the royal stock. The next object of the Crown was to derive from the property a pecuniary revenue, and to obtain a rent in money or kind, upon terms as little revolting as possible to the prejudices of a people unacquainted with any possessions that entailed upon the inheritors military or servile obligations. In the earliest tenures, therefore, of the crown-lands that were granted to the natives of Shetland, the asperities of feudality were so softened down as to be scarcely perceptible. Leases of the king's property were granted in small divisions for a term of three years ; and when the tenant entered into the possession of the soil for which he had stipulated, a sum for entry of 24s Scots, equal to 2s of English money, was required for each mark of land ; the payment being rendered in butter and wadmel. This duty to the king was named a *Grassum*, being a term of Danish or Anglo-Saxon derivation, importing *a compensation**. In addition to this fee for entry, an annual tribute or rent was paid, known by the name of *Land-mail* †; but in each year where the soil was not under tillage, the acknowledgment of land-mail was altogether remitted. In order, also, to insure to the tenants of the Crown a perfect freedom of settlement, triennial leases were renewed for an indefinite period, without any variation in the amount of the grassum ; or, on the terms of a feu, the possessor enjoyed the lands which he held from the King free from grassum, whilst the conditions of his tenure were rendered the subject of bequest to his most distant posterity. In this attempt to a-similate the tenures of the crown-lands to the unshackled nature of allodial possessions, an unsparing sacrifice was made of all the slavish fetters of a strict seigniory; yet a shadowy form of feudality still remained, which was not overlooked by the keen glance of the suspicious udaller. He still perceived that there was the retention of a feudal principle, which regarded rent in money or kind as nothing more than the substitute for personal service ; and consequently, that crown-lands, on the death of a tenant, naturally reverted into the hands of a superior. For in no other light than as the acknowlegement for possession due to a feudal grant, could he explain in connection with the annual compensation of land-mail, the new investiture required before the son could inherit the soil of his fathers. From this

---

* See Dr Jamieson's Etymological Dictionary. The word Gersome (whence Grassum) is supposed to be from the Danish *Gorsum*, and A.S. *Gaersuma.* The Norwegian word *Gersemar*, simply denotes *treasures*.

In the course of time, the tenants did not become very exact in these triennial payments. Accordingly, the grassum became converted into an annual duty, a third of which, or 8d Sterling, was exacted each year. Under this form it appears in the Shetland rentals of the present day.—See *Gifford's Zetland*, p. 64.

† A.S. *male* ; Isl. *mala*, tributum, vectigal.—See *Jamieson's Etym. Dict.*

period, therefore, the udallers began to distinguish themselves by the name of Rothmen or Roythmen, the import of which term has been most emphatically explained by one of their descendants : "The heritage of the udalman," boasts this Orcadian, "is so entirely his own, that neither homage, nor rent, nor service, is due for it. And the reason is, he owns no seigneural superior, but holds *de Deo et sole*,—of God and heaven only. For this reason, the udalmen were likewise called Rothmen or Roythmen ; that is, self-holders, or men holding in their own right, by way of contradistinction to feudatories, who hold derivatively, or by a dependance on others. And hence their *udals*, at this day, are not transmitted like other lands, but with the *Roth* always, or *Royth*, and the *Roet*, *Aynim* and *Saymin* ; that is, with the very or sole right and dominion, the very or compleat propriety and demesne of the subject."*

We now find, that in the earliest period, when the Norwegian colonies of Orkney and Shetland were pledged to the Scottish Government, three descriptions of tenants occupied the lands of the latter country. Of the first were the udallers, naming themselves Rothmen, whose enclosures destined for culture were free from civil imposts, no authoritative intruder having yet entered them, save the haughty churchman. For their pastures or scathold, they paid to the Scottish Government a scat or tribute. The second description of landed possessors, consisted of triennial tenants, who, for their inheritance, paid scat, church-dues, annual land-mails, and, along with these, a contribution on entry. Of the third were the feuars, in whose favour the grassum was remitted.

A number of wealthy Scottish natives were now induced to settle among the udallers, from whom they found no difficulty in purchasing lands. For, although udal possession was secured to families, by sales being rendered illegal that did not obtain the consent of heirs, and although the power of redeeming paternal lands was allowed to descendants even to the second and third generation, yet, from political causes, the poverty of the inhabitants was often irretrievable, so as to preclude for ever the chance of udal redemption. The first endeavour of these strangers was to set aside the old law of descent, ascribed to St Olaus, by which an estate was divided among all the children of the possessor, male or female, in equal shares, the house of the parent excepted, which was added to the share of the youngest. Since it was indispensable, by virtue of the national treaty subsisting between Denmark and Scotland, that the laws of the country should be purely Scandinavian, the Scottish settlers were enabled, whenever they chose, to supersede the old law of udal succession, in favour of another, derived from Norway, and probably of a more recent date. The newer rule of inheritance was less revolting to Scottish feudality, since it afforded the means of perpetuating family wealth and power, by concentrating them in one individual. It assigned the principal mansion and estate of the parent to an elder son ; whilst to the youngest children equivalents from other estates were given. As for the portion of the poor neglected daughter, it was peremptorily ordained, that she should have her lot in the most remote and uncontiguous lands. If equivalents for the younger children could not be thus furnished, lesser shares were awarded either from soil, from moveables, or from some yearly

---

* General Grievances, &c., of Orkney and Shetland (by Mr James Fea), p. 105.

income, secured on the estates of the chief heir. Such was the later precept of succession that was introduced among the udallers: it was enforced by the Scottish settler; but among the Scandinavian natives never became general.*

In the year 1530, King James V. was induced to make an hereditary grant of the estate of the Crown in Orkney and Shetland to his natural brother James, Earl of Moray. When the islanders saw that a feudal superior was intended to be interposed between them and the sovereign, they were alarmed that the ancient laws of the country were about to suffer a corresponding change. Headed by Sir James Sinclair, the Governor of Orkney, they arose in arms, to resist the arbitrary innovation. The Earl of Caithness, and his kinsman Lord Sinclair, were sent out against them: the udallers met their opponents on the confines of Stennis, and, in a sanguinary engagement, defeated them with great slaughter. The Earl of Caithness, and 500 of his followers, were slain; the rest were taken prisoners. When the King heard of the result of the contest, so far from taking vengeance on the udallers, he appeared, in his subsequent conduct, to be sensible of the justice of their cause, and that they had only resisted the intended dominion of a mesne lord, and the undue attempt to transfer them from the hands of the Sovereign of Scotland, to whose immediate protection they had been committed by their former king. Accordingly, the promoters of the insurrection were pardoned; the Governor of Orkney was not only restored to the royal favour, but he also received various gifts and honours; and at length a complete reconciliation took place between the King and the udallers.†

It appears that the Sovereigns of Scotland, as well as the Bishops, granted various feus of their lands; and since the tenants of the King were, by the Scottish law, subject to taxation, they had opportunities, which it is probable they did not at first embrace, of being represented in Parliament. Kirkwall in Orkney was also erected into a Royal Burgh.‡

We now arrive at the period when a new and great change was beginning to take place in the state of the landed property of Orkney and Shetland. In the year 1565, Queen Mary made an hereditary grant of the Crown's patrimony in these islands, and of the superiority over the free tenants, to her natural brother Lord Robert Stewart, the Abbot of Holyrood, in consideration of an annual payment of £2006 : 13 : 4 Scots. The Reformed Religion had then been introduced into the islands, and a Scottish act of Parliament had passed, declaring that the third of all Popish benefices should be set apart for the support of parochial ministers, who had been always ill remunerated for their duties. Lord Robert, therefore, was entrusted with the controul over the churches of the bishopric.§ But it does

---

* The authorities regarding the old laws of inheritance, will be given on another occasion.

† The cause of this insurrection is narrated by some writers in very mysterious terms. I am indebted for the present explanation of the fray, to the very learned Memorial against Sir Laurence Dundas, in 1776, signed Hay Campbell, (afterwards Lord President of the Court of Session.)

‡ When Orkney and Shetland were under the immediate government of the King, the estates and revenues of the Crown were farmed out for the following sums, viz., From A.D. 1478 to 1502, for £486 13s 4d Scots; from A.D. 1502 to A.D. 1540, for £433 6s 8d; and in 1541, the duties of the King's rental were let for £2000 Scots, with the rights of Admiralty in addition.—See *Shirreff's Agric. Survey of Orkney*, App. p. 29.

§ The words of the grant are; "Omnes et singulas terras de Orkney et Zetland,———— cum tota superioritate libere tenentium, advocatione, donatione ecclesiarum, ac cum officio vicecomitatus de Orkney, et vicecomitatus de lie Foudrie de Zetland tenen., reddendo inde annuatim summam 3010 mercarum."—See *Memorial for Dundas*, A.D., 1776, p. 7.

not appear that this division of ecclesiastical power met with the cordial approbation of the Bishop of Orkney.

We may now consider the exact relation in which the Scottish Government stood to Denmark at this period, with regard to the possession of these islands. It must be kept in view, that, by virtue of the national treaty betwixt these two kingdoms, the ancient laws of Norway, by which udal lands were then held, were to remain undisturbed.* But when King James III. by a subsequent treaty with Lord Sinclair, had acquired the landed property of this nobleman, he assumed the prerogative of creating, on the new estates of the Crown, a number of immediate vassals, who should hold their lands according to the usage of Scotland. On this occasion, the law of udal succession was waved in favour of the Scottish conditions of primogeniture† ; and since Kirkwall was erected into a Royal Burgh, by which means an opportunity was afforded of sending representatives to the Scottish Parliament, an indirect declaration was intended to be made, that the Crown-vassals of Orkney and Shetland were in every respect to be considered as holding their lands agreeably to the tenor of Scottish laws. These proceedings were in evident contradiction to the general terms of the national treaty with Denmark, by which no new conditions of landed tenure could be introduced into the Norwegian colony, that were in opposition to its ancient statutes. But the Danish Government having been precluded by its poverty from doing more than declaring the right of redeeming the islands as the pledge of a royal marriage-dower,‡ it was perfectly useless to insist upon the subordinate points of a treaty, the essential article of which could not be enforced. For, on the supposition that the redemption by Denmark had been successfully urged, Scotland must either have abandoned her right of considering the Crown-tenants of Orkney and Shetland as maintained in their possessions exclusively by Scottish laws, or the country would have reverted into the hands of Denmark, with the strange anomaly presented, of a population composed in part of Scottish and of Danish subjects. But it is sufficiently evident, that a resignation of the sovereignty of these islands was very remote from the contemplation of the power into whose hands they had fallen. The sentiments of Scotland on this point became gradually unfolded ; and when, in the year 1567, Queen Mary, with her usual caprice, chose to revoke the grant which she had made to her natural brother of the Crown-estates of Orkney and Shetland, in order to erect them into a Scottish dukedom for the use of the Earl of Bothwell, it was impossible any longer to doubt, that the ultimate intentions of the Scottish Government were unfavourable to Denmark's just claim of redemption.

The attainture of the Earl of Bothwell having occurred soon after the grant, Lord Robert appears to have been immediately afterwards reinstated in the enjoyment of the

---

* " De nuptiis facile cum Dano transactum omni jure, quod in omnes circa Scotiam insulas, majores ejus sibi arrogarant, dotis nomine remisso ; tantum ut privatis agrorum possessoribus caveretur, ut agros, quos ibi haherent uti ante possederant, ita tenerent.'—Buchanan, Hist., &c. See also Torfæus, Rerum Orcad. His., p. 195, 196.

† Anno 1566, King Henry and Queen Mary grant an estate in the Orkneys to Gilbert Balfour of Westra, and his heirs-male, "Sic quod omni tempore affuturo, unicus hæres masculus successor post alium quamdiu vixerit, possideat et gaudeat hasce terras, secundum consuetudinem Scotiæ, non obstantibus legibus patriæ Orcaden. eandem gavisionem seu possessionem recusantibus."— See Fea's Grievances, &c., of Orkney and Shetland, p. 5, where two other illustrations of similar grants appear of the date of 1587 and 1591.

‡ See Torfæus, Rerum Orcad. Hist., c. 3.

Crown-lands of the revoked dukedom. His first object was to obviate the necessity of participating with anyone in the dominion over the islands of which he was about to take possession; for this purpose he effected an exchange of his Abbey of Holyrood for the temporal estates of the bishopric of Orkney. The Church of Scotland was then under a Presbyterian form of Government. Lord Robert, therefore, left to a Superintendant the spiritual concerns with which he was entrusted, being himself content with the immense temporal influence which the estates of the Crown and of the bishopric gave him, when subsisting under one undivided feu.

The free tenants of the Crown were now intended to be under the sway of a mesne lord, from whom they were to receive investitures. The superiority over them was distinctly expressed in the royal grant; but that such a design was illegal, there can be no doubt: for it is properly argued, "that no act of the Crown could, in law, be effectual to raise up an immediate superiority, which had no existence prior to the grant; that the issues and profits of the *dominium directum* might indeed be assigned, but that the right itself must remain with the Crown, as incapable of alienation, it not being in the power of any superior to place an intermediate person over the vassal without his consent."* Lord Robert, however, found no difficulty in assuming the superiority over the free tenants, which was awarded by the Crown; and, by issuing out at the same time new investitures of the crown lands, he materially increased his revenue. But the chief design of this tyrant was, to wrest, by oppression and forfeitures, the udal lands from the hands of their possessors; to retain the poor natives who might be forced out of their tenements as vassals on his estates, and to entail upon them the feudal miseries of villein service. This he was enabled to accomplish, by establishing a military government throughout the islands, which was intended to impede all avenues to judicial redress. The complaint, drawn up by a Lowland inditer, which eventually reached the ear of the Scottish Government, was, that the udallers were "heavily troublit, *hereit* [robbed] and oppressit be companies of *suddartis* [soldiers], and others, broken men [vagabonds], now remaining in the countries, dependars upon Lord Robert Stewart. They are so halden under thraldom and tyranny, that they can have na passage, neither be sea nor land, to repair to thir partis, to complain heirupon, and sute redress and remeid be the course of justice, nor yet to do others their lefull errandis and business. The ferris and all other common passages are stoppit be the suddartis [soldiers] and others, bearand charge of Lord Robert, quhairthrow the countries and inhabitants thairof is able to be all utterly wrakit and hereit for ever."†

After having established a military force of this kind, Lord Robert, by the good aid of his "suddartis and others, broken men," found it to be a labour of little difficulty to rule in all matters, civil and ecclesiastic. To remove every source of information that might benefit the ends of strict justice, he stormed the charter-chest of the good town of Kirkwall, and did "away put, cancel, burn, and destroy, all the said town's papers and evidents." He received his rents in produce: and the weight named a *mark*, very conveniently multiplied

---

* Memorial against Sir Laurence Dundas, A.D. 1776, p. 17.
† Petition to the Privy Council of Scotland, dated January 31, 1575, quoted in Fea's Grievances, &c., of the Isles of Orkney and Shetland, p. 35.

under his hands from 8 to 10 ounces; whilst the lispund increased from 12 lb. to 15 lb. He learned that the compliment of an ox and twelve sheep from every parish had a few years before been granted to the Earl of Bothwell, in his visit to Shetland. Surely, then, as he marvelled, there could be no very sound reason why this handsome token of respect should not be continued for the support of himself, his suddartis and broken men. It was therefore easily converted into a perpetual tribute under the name of *ox and sheep silver*. This ruler, aided by his "broken men," was perfectly convinced of the salutary effects to be derived from the Reformed religion, and therefore introduced, with few preliminary arguments on the occasion, what he called *the Presbyterian form.* But, that the natives might not altogether forget their old Catholic attachments, he revived an ancient annuity, that had been paid to a holy matron for the benefit of her prayers, and inserting it into his rental converted it into a perpetual oblation to her manes. Yet the most illegal of all these oppressions was to increase the amount of the scat or tax which was levied from pasture lands or scatholds. This measure was in open defiance of the promise of Norway, with which the islanders had been lulled, that when their country was pledged to Scotland, there should be no alteration of the terms under which their lands had been enjoyed.

It is now time to inquire into the more immediate object which Lord Robert appears to have had in view, by the extraordinary pains which he took in desolating the country placed under his rule. By the latest law of udal succession derived from Norway, lands could not be alienated from their possessors, without the consent of the udal-born, or nearest of kin, who had long afterwards the power of redeeming an inheritance at the price for which it had been plighted; neither could lands be sold, but on proof successfully advanced in the Foude's court of extreme poverty. It had been, therefore, the flagitious policy of Lord Robert to create such an universal distress throughout the islands, that, by overwhelming the udallers in one common state of ruin, the poor landed possessor might be qualified, by the urgency of famine, to dispose of his inheritance; whilst his nearest kindred, equally involved in misery, might be prevented from purchasing its redemption. This rapacious scheme was eminently successful; the open violence which was committed on the property of the inhabitants,—the inordinate advance which took place of scat-duties, together with the audacious means to which Lord Robert resorted, of foisting creatures of his own into the Lawting, as judicial officers, caused an extensive tract of territory to fall within his grasp.

These flagrant abuses became at length so notorious, as to attract the attention of the Scottish Government. An investigation took place, the result of which was, that Lord Robert was confined in the Palace of Linlithgow. After remaining a prisoner for six months, he was released, upon condition of giving a large pledge, to ensure his engagement that he would plead at any time to the crime for which he was charged. On the excuse that the accusation against him contained proofs of rebellious designs, the estates of Shetland and Orkney reverted to the Crown.

Lord Robert was withheld from the power of tyrannizing over the natives of Orkney and Shetland for three years, and the rents were paid into the Exchequer. But his interest at the Scottish palace, where his follies or vices were always forgiven, procured for him, in the year 1581, a reinstatement in his former possessions; the feu being subject to the same annual payment to the Crown which had been specified in the previous grant. It had not escaped the attention of this court-favourite, that in his late dominion over the islands, one charge that had been successfully preferred against him was, for corrupting the judicial members of the Lawting, in his design against the lands of Nicol Randall, an udaller whom he had ousted out of the Island of Gersa. That he might be enabled, therefore, to controul the decrees of justice with less chance of detection, he had the address to procure for himself the heritable appointment of Justiciar,* by which he was not only entitled to convoke and adjourn the Lawtings, to administer justice in his own person, and to punish malefactors, but he might select any individuals to fill the various offices of the court, who could be prevailed upon to minister, by corrupt decrees, to the new plots which he was still hatching against the property of the injured udallers.

Along with the office of Justiciar, King James VI. conferred upon Lord Robert the hereditary titles of Earl of Orkney and Lord of Zetland. But it does not appear, that the new Earl, in the resumption of the Crown estates, was equally indulged with the temporalities of the bishopric. The cause of this exclusion from them has not been explained. A Scottish act of Parliament had passed, directing the division of church-lands, for the purpose of securing on a third part of them the revenues which, by evasions and false rentals, had been too often withheld from the Parochial clergy. But in a country like Orkney and Zetland, where a regular land-measurement was unknown, and where the lands of the church were intermixed in the most confused manner with those of the Crown, the purport of the act could not well be carried into effect. It is probable, therefore, that the titular of the church-lands of Orkney and Shetland had readily fallen into the common practice of the day, by concealing the amount of his church rental, in order to evade the full demand of a third which was due to the clergy of parishes. If Earl Robert, from some such cause as this, was at first only entrusted with the appointment of ministers, and the donation of benefices, it was not long before he resumed his dominion over all or most of the temporalities of the bishopric. It was then that he began a new career of injustice, and that his command over the levy of the tithes was rendered subservient to a fresh scheme of operations which he meditated, with the purpose of wresting the right of soil from the ancient udaller. The tither was instructed to exact the dues of the church to the last tenth, and in a mode sufficiently harassing to induce the poor udaller, for the sake of a temporary subsistence offered him by his designing and merciless lord, to appear at the Foude's court, and, with no fictitious tale of woe, to confirm, by such a plea, the validity of his oppressor's purchase.† It is even questionable if the laws of udal succession were not occasionally superseded altogether, by Earl Robert's interpretation of the royal grant, wherein all lands, without limitation, were unjustifiably included within the dominion of the earldom of Orkney and lordship of Zetland. The Earl might consider himself, from this general clause, as gifted with the authority of a feudal superior; as entitled to receive resignations of udal lands,

---

* See Charter of James VI., dated October 28, 1581.

† It is affirmed, that when landholders fell under the censure of the Church, part of their property, by way of penance, was added to the lands of the bishopric.

with the superiority over which, from the very nature of udal tenures, he never could have been invested.

Reiterated complaints against Earl Robert's new acts of tyranny once more reached the Royal ear, upon which he was, for the third time, recalled from the exercise of a dominion that he had so greatly abused.

King James VI., however, did not altogether lose his attachment to his natural uncle, since he granted the earldom in joint shares to the Lord Chancellor of Scotland and to the Lord Justice-Clerk,* on some secret understanding, that the whole would be given up whenever required, in order to be again transferred, on some more favourable opportunity, to its last Lord. Accordingly, the old oppressor was soon afterwards reinstated in his former possessions, and he lost no time in renewing his attempts to wrest the right of soil from the poor udaller. But learning from experience the futility of open violence, he was now prepared to use more covert means, and to illegally support, by a new prerogative, the purchase of udal lands, in opposition to the consent of heirs.

The designs of Earl Robert to gain the possession of the lands of the udallers, had been always impeded by the obligation imposed upon him to obtain a title for his acquisitions in what was called a *Shynd-bill*. Respecting the nature of this document, it may be proper to offer a brief explanation. The udal lands of Orkney and Shetland were originally considered as belonging to the community of Scandinavian colonists, among whom they were partitioned in various proportions. It was therefore to the support of the commonwealth alone, of which the King of Norway was supposed to be the head, that the seat or contribution exigible from pasture-land was paid as a tribute; and it was by the common laws which governed the community, that individual possession was secured. The right of soil was confirmed by the decree of those to whom the power of enforcing the laws of the community was entrusted. Whenever, therefore, an udaller was desirous to make his will, or whenever he died intestate, the Foude convened a regular court of judicature, for the purpose of partitioning the property among heirs, agreeably to the rules of udal succession. A court was also held, when, with the consent of heirs, any purchase of land was intended to be confirmed. Upon all these occasions, the parties applying for judgment produced satisfactory evidence of the legality of their claims. The decree of the court was then recorded, and the authority for entering on the possession of lands conveyed in a shynd-bill: the term *Shynd*, being said to signify in the Norwegian language a *court*, and the familiar word *bill*, implying a document. This record of the court's decree, when signed and sealed by the foude, constituted the only legal title by which udal lands could be bequeathed to heirs, or could be disposed of by sale.† Such being the nature of the Shynd-bill, it is probable that the formalities by which it was obtained, would not be agreeable to Earl Robert's views, since his contracts for land were not such as were calculated to bear the test of a strict scrutiny. But numerous complaints having found their way to the throne of James, against

---

* "The new rental amounted to 1535 meils of *cost*, 3201 meils of bear, 2281 meils of flesh, 72 barrels 12 lispunds of butter, 24 barrels 6 lispunds of oil, and £100 of money-rent, besides a separate rental for Shetland, which the Exchequer compounded at £400 Scots." *Shirreff's Orkney*, p. 32.

† See Gifford's Zetland, p. 54.

the attempts that had been made to change the laws of the country, and these remonstrances having been followed in the latest grants that had been made of the Crown-estates, by provisional clauses in which the functions of the Justiciar of the Islands were rendered comformable to the proper pandects of the Lawting,* the Earl did not yet venture to oppose, in the most open manner, the statutes of the Foude's Court. He rather sought to evade the necessity of having recourse to a shynd-bill, as a title to his acquisitions of territory, by inducing the Government to sanction his pretentions, that the lands of the udallers had been held of the king as of a superior; that the ancient seat or land-tax which was paid for them, was a real feudal acknowledgment;† and, consequently, that udal possessions formed, along with the estates of the Crown, constituent portions of the earldom. Scotland, with little consideration, favoured Earl Robert's insidious designs, and, by specially including udal lands in the new grant, sanctioned, in direct opposition to the treaty with Norway, an infringement of the laws under which the lands of Orkney and Shetland had from time immemorial been held. The Earl of Orkney's charter was dated in the year 1589; and this may be reckoned the most fatal blow that was struck against the ancient rights of the udaller.‡ The little despot now conceived himself fully released from the unwelcome obligation of having recourse to a shynd-bill as a legal title to possession; he had now the sanction of a Royal grant for considering his ill-acquired estates as being resigned or returned into the hands of a superior, thus proceeding on the false assumption that the lands of Orkney and Shetland had been originally dealt out by his predecessors in the earldom to a number of vassals, on terms that involved in them the feudal incidents of sasine, relief, escheat, scutage or homage. Earl Robert had now the power of superseding the shynd-bill as a confirmation of his own acquisitions; but it was not his interest that it should be rendered inert with regard to the contracts of other powerful or wealthy settlers in the country, who in similiar designs on the possessions of the natives, might engage with him, on equal terms, in a course of sordid competition. In order, therefore, to obviate any interference of this kind, the law whereby no purchase could be rendered valid that was not made with the consent of heirs, was retained in full force; and it rendered difficult of confirmation any acquisitions of landed property that did not receive the sanction of the

---

* In the year 1567, the Scottish Parliament discussed it as a question, if Orkney and Shetland were to be subject to their own laws. Among their minutes are these words: "Quhidder Orknay and Zetland sal be subject to the common lawe of this realme, or gif that sale bruike their awne lawis.- Findis that aught to be subject to thair awne lawis." But in after times, the Government was more decisive on this point, as Mr Fea has well shewn: "In the grant made to the Lord Chancellor of Scotland and his colleague, anno 1587, besides their right of convoking and adjourning the Lawting, they have power likewise of appointing Fouds under them, and of administering justice, and punishing malefactors. Also in the grant made to Earl Robert of Orkney, anno 1589, "Cum potestate (says the King) justitiarii et foudriæ deputatos creandi —— justitiam partibus conquerentibus ministrandi, et punitionem super legum transgressoribus et malefactoribus, secundum leges et consuetudinem patriæ Orcaden. et Zetlandiæ, exequendi et puniendi." And in the *Reddendo*, "Ac etiam administrando justitiam in dictis officiis, tenentibus et inhabitantibus dictarum terrarum, et allis quorum interest vel intererit secundum leges patriæ Orcaden. et Zetlandiæ, prout dictus comes, et sui prædicti, Deo omnipotenti et nobis desuper respondere voluerint." See Fea's *Grievances of Orkney*, &c., p. 4. & 5.

† In a legal process which took place several years ago respecting the superiority of Orkney and Shetland, it was an important object to determine whether the Scat was ever paid as a feudal acknowledgment, consequently the primary signification of the word became an object of inquiry. Dr Jamieson has since produced satisfactory authorities for shewing that the term, in its oldest form, whether Saxon or Scandinavian, simply denoted *money*.

‡ The charter of 1589 runs thus: "Totam et integram terram prædict. comitateum Orcaden. et dominium Zetlandiæ, terras firmas, insulas, *lie Holms*, &c., integras terras *lie Udal lands* nuncupat, &c., quæ nobis successoribus nostris pertinent, seu quovis modo, in iisdem pertinere dignoscuntur, reddendo summam 3110 merks."

new self-elected superior of udal lands. If a purchaser of udal property could not confirm his possession by the means of a shynd-bill, which title depended on the consent of the nearest kindred of the inheritor, he could, by ministering to the Earl's avarice, obtain a charter of the lands, whereby they became converted into proper feudal holdings.

As another consequence of these false pretensions to the superiority over udal lands which Earl Robert arrogated to himself, naturally followed the attempt to convert the Lawting into a tribunal of his own, whereby the faithfulness with which his newly created vassals, the udallers, had done their duty, was to be determined by the jurisdiction of a lord's court. Hence the power with which he immediately arrayed himself, of confiscating lands for criminal offences.

Fresh complaints against Earl Robert's tyranny still reaching the throne, it was thought necessary to make his son a participator with him in the earldom. This experiment did not succeed; the joint grant was recalled, and the Earl was again singly invested with the possession of the Crown-estates of Orkney and Shetland, the management of which was, however, subject to the immediate controul of the Scottish Government. But this unwearied persecutor of the udallers soon afterwards dying, the fruits of his iniquity only became fully ripened in the misrule of his successor. Such a scene of universal turmoil and dismay then ensued, as is perhaps unparalleled in the history of any other British province.

Earl Robert Stewart was succeeded in his estates and title by his son Patrick,*

" A fellow by the hand of Nature mark'd,
Quoted and sign'd, to do a deed of shame."†

When Earl Patrick was invested with the earldom, his own patrimony had been much wasted by riotous expences, and these he sought to redeem by fraud and violence. His first object was to supersede the ancient laws of the country, which Scotland had engaged to preserve inviolate, and to hold a court of his own, the statutes of which could be easily polluted by the influence which a feudal lord naturally possessed. The ancient law-book of Shetland, beheld by the Scandinavian colonist with awe and reverence, soon disappeared. The tyrant's newer code of punishment embraced confiscation of lands and property. The loss of soil awaited the crime of quitting the isles without the consent of the superior, or, in any other courts except his, of suing for legal justice. But the forfeiture of both lands and goods was attached to the unpardonable misdemeanour of concealing the amount of personal property, in order to evade or mitigate an impending pecuniary mulct. The feelings of humanity which, at the peril of life, might attempt the salvation of a vessel distressed by tempest, were considered in no other light than as an endeavour to frustrate the chance of lucre from the incident of a wreck on the

---

* I find some difficulty in learning the exact year when Earl Patrick commenced his authority in the Islands. It is probably about the year 1595. A charter in his favour was dated in the year 1600, by which the former grants were revoked, and a new one made, giving him the titles of his father, and the office of Sheriff, Justiciar, &c.; his functions to be exercised according to the laws and consuetude of the country. The feu is subject to an annual payment of 3110 merks. The Earl does not appear to have possessed the lands of the bishopric until A.D. 1600.

† Shakespeare's *King John*.

coast. The act was, therefore, visited, not only with a personal punishment, but with a fine that was of an unlimited amount. The Earl did not even like his father scorn the low, fraudulent act of clandestinely altering the standard weights and measures, in order to increase the revenues of the earldom that were paid in kind. The mark of ten ounces received an addition of a fifth; and the lispund was advanced from fifteen to eighteen pounds. Another act of the Earl was to increase the rents in Shetland, in order to defray the expenses of the new castle which he was erecting at Scalloway. For this purpose the whole country was assessed in money, provisions, and personal labour.

During this dominion of terror, wealthy Scandinavians are reported to have hastily sold to Scottish inhabitants their estates and interests in the country, seeking a refuge in the more kindly bosom of the parent region, from which their ancestors had originally emigrated; whilst the recent occupants, who had acquired a settlement by purchasing udal lands from the natives, were fain to secure even a precarious assurance of protection, by administering to the revenue of the Earl, in the conversion of their estates into regular feudal investitures. As free tenants they now paid to the Lord compositions on entry and annual land-mails. But the poor cottager, who could make feeble resistance against the views of the superior, easily fell a victim to his deep laid designs. Summoned to a court, the arbiters of which were the mere creatures of his will, vain was the plea against the secret plots prepared to ensnare him, or against charges hitherto unregistered as criminal in the revered pages of the lost law-book of Hialtland.* The remonstrance availed not: nothing could arrest the doom of confiscation, that exiled the udaller for ever from the ancient soil of his fathers, that rendered his family outcasts among the barren tracts of the country, or annexed them to the discontented list of menials belonging to the demesnes of the castle. Equity was a stranger in the land. The "udaller looked for judgment, but behold oppression; for righteousness, but behold a cry."

At length, the lamentations of Orkney and Shetland deeply pierced the ears of a Government, which had been ever too indifferent to the concerns of this remote extremity of the kingdom. Earl Patrick was summoned by open proclamation, "to compear upon the 2d of March 1608, to answer to the complaints of the distressit people of Orkney." The charges were fully proved; the Earl had been authorised with the Royal power and commission, and, under colour of his Majesty's authority, had committed many great enormities and insolences "upon his Majesty's poor people." Certain acts had the character assigned to them of rebellion; on which account the estates of the Earl became liable to forfeiture. The Secret Council then directed that the aggressor should be committed in sure ward, until the royal pleasure regarding him should be signified. They also professed the humane intention of making such new enactments in favour of the suffering islanders, as were calculated to prevent a repetition of similar abuses. In the mean time, the government of Shetland and Orkney was entrusted to the humane Bishop of the

---

* The Reverend Peter Barclay communicates the following curious information, which he derived from an inspection of some ancient records in Shetland: "Patrick, Earl of Orkney, in a disposition of the lands of Sand to Jerom Umphray, narrates, that he had evicted seven merks of that land from Powl Nicolson in Cullswick, for stealing a swine; and that he had evicted six merks from ———————— in Cullswick, for stealing bolts from his Lordship's trood; probably some piece of wreck which had been drawn into Cullswick."—See *Statist. Account of Scotland*, vol. vii., p. 584.

Province, by whose active means the charges against the Earl had been matured and successfully preferred.

The Scottish Government did not immediately declare the estates of Earl Patrick forfeited, for reasons apparently creditable to its liberality. An ancient treason-law of Scotland was then in full force, the rigours of which had been originally directed to this important object: it was intended, that, in addition to the allegiance which sub-vassals owed for their lands to a mesne lord, the tenant should be always reminded that there was a permanent obligation of the same nature, that was due to the liege Sovereign. In order, therefore, to enfeeble that unlimited attachment of sub-vassals to a mesne-lord, by which, at the mere will of a subject, they had been often induced to assemble in arms against the King, it was enacted, that upon the discovery of a treasonable conspiracy, all the lands of sub-vassals, the tenures of which had not been previously ratified by the Crown, should, along with the sequestrated estates of the mesne-lord, be involved in one common forfeiture. And to obviate any evasion of the penalty, condemned estates devolved to the Crown, free from every incumbrance; no fictitious claim could be advanced, since the prayer of the creditor was ever condemned unheard.* It was probably in anticipation of some illegal act which Earl Patrick might commit, whilst pursuing the same oppressive course for which his father was called to account, that Sir John Arnot, to whom the tyrant had pledged his basely-acquired udal lands,† was not satisfied with a charter or disposition from the Earl of Orkney, but also procured from the Crown a confirmation of his right, so as to enable him to hold of the King *in capite*.‡ But however construable into treason might have been the illegal proceedings of the Earl, it appears that from this imputation his immediate tenants were perfectly exempt. An ample opportunity was, therefore, allowed them of becoming the Crown's vassals, by which means their tenures would be preserved from the forfeiture of the superior. Of this indulgence some availed themselves before the confiscation was pronounced; others had not their subaltern infeftments confirmed until long afterwards.§ But it was doubtful if this was the only reason for not enforcing the treason law of Scotland. It must be remembered, that in the royal grant to Earl Patrick and his father of the superiority over the free tenants of the crown-lands, a feudal principle had been violated, which denies the right of any superior, whether the King or a subject, to interpose a person between himself and his immediate vassal. On this account, any subaltern infeftments which might have been granted by Earl Patrick to Crown-tenants, were null and void; and they who might have been compelled to accept them, still remained the immediate vassals of the King, whom the treason law of Scotland could

---

* It is remarked of later times, that "this law was considered a great grievance, and therefore it was remedied after the Revolution by act 1690, cap. 33, by which the right and interest of creditors, vassals, and heirs of entail of forfeiting persons, were saved." *Memorial against Dundas*, 1776, p. 20.

† Gifford's Zetland, p. 41.

‡ In implement of a contract entered into by Arnot and the Earl of Orkney, dated A.D. 1601, there is a charter granted by the latter, dated 1603, in which certain lands are held from his Lordship, his heirs and successors, *of his Majesty*, his royal heirs and successors, in feu-farm, for payment to his Majesty of the feu-duties and others contained in the Earl's infeftment. This charter was confirmed under the Great Seal, March 5, 1605. See *Mem. against Dundas*, dated 1776, p. 18.

§ Memorial against Dundas, dated 1776, p. 19 & 20.

UDALLERS.

not in justice affect.* But the discussion of this question was very prudently avoided : the Government did nothing more than declare, that those lands for which no charters from the Crown could be produced, were liable to forfeiture, but that under all circumstances, the King, in his clemency, was unwilling to enforce the execution of the law.†

Three years had now elapsed, when the islanders, who were little acquainted with the deliberation and delay incidental to state affairs, began to manifest, by their impatient clamour, a strong suspicion of the sincerity of the promises with which they had been soothed. It now became necessary that these doubts should be removed: the Bishop was directed to exhort the people " to give no ear to the idle reports which they had heard of alterations and changes to the former condition of misrule, trouble and oppression ;" and soon afterwards the King and Council issued a proclamation, that the lands and earldom of Orkney and Shetland were annexed to the Crown, to remain perpetually and inseparably therewith in time coming."‡

After the act of Parliament had passed in the year 1612, by which Orkney and Shetland were annexed to the Crown of Scotland, and erected into a stewartry, the Government released from mortage Sir John Arnot's security upon the udal lands, that had been so wrongfully acquired by Earl Patrick. The next step was to provide some remedy for the frays and even bloodshed that had resulted from the lands of the bishopric being intermixed with these of the Crown, in every island, parish, and even township. Bishop Law, therefore, the new episcopal dignitary of the islands, received from the King's Commissioners certain crown-lands in Orkney, the extent of which was well defined, in lieu of the scattered possessions from which the church had previously derived emolument. In consequence of this exchange, the Bishop of Orkney no longer possessed any control over the ecclesiastical revenues of Shetland, his share of them devolving to the Crown ; at the same time he succeeded to the King in the right of presenting qualified ministers to all the vicarages.

---

* " It is plain, that such grant of intermediate superiority over the Crown's vassals was of an illegal nature, and could not have effect ; and therefore, supposing the fact to be, that these grantees did take upon them to exercise the rights of superiority, and that the Crown vassals were prevailed on to accept their charters from them, which must have happened through undue influence and concussion, yet the inference will by no means follow, that the persons accepting of such charters, and their heirs and successors in all time coming, are to be considered merely in the state of subvassals. The intermediate authority thus created, was null and void from the beginning, and could not be rendered better by the act and deed of the interposed superior in granting a charter, or of the vassal in accepting of it, this not being the proper feudal form by which a superiority and a subvassalage could be constituted ; for, as the pretended superior was not himself seised in the lands, he could not have a vassal in them."—— .." No act of the Crown could in law be effectual to raise up an intermediate superiority, which had no existence prior to the grant. The only mode in which this can possibly be done, is by the Crown vassal's resigning his lands in the hands of his Majesty, or his Barons of Exchequer, for new infeftment in favour of a third party, and afterwards accepting a subaltern right from such party. It is manifest, that a grant by the Crown in favour of a third party can carry nothing. The full property of the land is in the Crown's vassal, *minus* that right of superiority which is in the Crown *jure coronæ* ; and as that right must necessarily remain with the Crown, so, it is plain, that any conveyance granted by the Crown to a third party, is a mere shadow, and can carry nothing real. The Crown may indeed assign the issues and profits of the *dominium directum*, but the right itself must remain with the Crown, as incapable of alienation, it not being in the power of any superior to place an intermediate person over the vassal, without his consent."—See *Memorial against Dundas*, dated 1776, p. 18 & 16.

† " A charter of confirmation under the Great Seal, dated March 13, 1616, proceeds on the narrative of Edward Stewart and his brother being heritable vassals and tenants to Earl Patrick and his predecessors, in all and haill the eighteen penny land of Sellibuster ; that they were now in his Majesty's hands by the forfeiture of Earl Patrick ; and that his Majesty was not desirous to hurt Edward Stewart's right and title to said lands, but willing to grant a more ample security. The charter contains a *novodamus* in favour of Edward Stewart, ' to be holden of his Majesty and royal successors, in feu and heritage for ever, paying therefor the scat and other duties therein mentioned."—*Memorial against Dundas*, (dated 1776, p. 20.)

‡ Extract from Registers of Parliament 1612, quoted in the Memorial against Dundas, dated 1776, p. 4.

One of the last objects of the Government was to erect a court of stewartry, and to confine the civil judicial power of the church within the circuit of its own proper estate. The Bishop, in the jurisdiction of Commissaries, had the privilege of appointing clerks and other members of court. The form of judicature thus organized, bore still less resemblance to the uncomplicated tribunal of the Foude. Causes were now tried in some hall of the castles of Kirkwall and Scalloway; whilst the open space of the Scandinavian Lawting was devoted to legislative convocations. Here a little Parliament of udallers again began to meet, in order to replace with a fresh code of pandects the ancient law-book which Earl Patrick had destroyed.

When, by the Earl's forfeiture, all the udal lands which had been wrested from their ancient possessors, by the fraud or open violence of the petty tyrants that had been unduly interposed between the Sovereign and the udallers, came into the possession of the Crown, it would have been an act of clemency worthy the exalted rank of the monarch who then held sway over the united realms of England and Scotland, to have instituted a commission, for the purpose of restoring the lands which had been the fruits of evaded laws, and of open rapine. But vainly did humanity intercede in the behalf of the poor udallers;—vainly did justice urge the propriety of restitution.

The King had now made a grant of the islands to Sir James Stewart, in the quality of a farmer-general. Earl Patrick's rental was recorded in the Court of Exchequer, and directions had been given, that it was to be the rule of every future exaction of the revenues of the Crown's estate. Of this cartulary, which is still extant, a late writer has remarked, " that it exhibits, in a strong point of view, the enormous quantity of gross and manufactured produce paid by the country, and affords a sufficient proof of the oppressive means that had been employed to increase the rental."* The money paid was little more than £200 Scots, the rest being delivered in the several species of bear, malt, meal, flesh, oil, or butter. And when the demands could not be answered in kind, the udallers and Crown vassals were subject to the payment of a price depending on the mere will of a rapacious exacter. This perpetuation of Earl Patrick's rental, has, in combination with parochial tithes, entailed upon the landed proprietors of Orkney and Shetland a burden, the oppressive nature of which the resources of the islands have not, for the last two centuries, been able to counteract."†

It may be now remarked, that, in consequence of the resolution of the British government not to sacrifice the smallest abatement of the amount of the scat-duty which had been paid to Earl Patrick, a decisive change took place in the nature of udal possessions The

---

* Shirreff's Agricultural Survey of Orkney, p. 32.

† Mr Shirreff remarks, in reference to that part of Earl Patrick's rental, which concerns the earldom and bishopric of Orkney, that "the scat-duties were more considerable than was generally imagined, consisting altogether of £117 14s 7d Scots of silver, 647 lispunds of butter, 53 lispunds of oil, 954 meils of malt, 1903 meils, or nearly 54 chalders of bear, 922 meils of flesh, 134 meils of cost, and 60 of oatmeal: but there is reason to believe, from some instances in the rental, that the scat itself had in some cases been lately augmented." The entire rents of the earldom and bishopric amounted to £322 Scots of money, 132 barrels and 634 lispunds of butter, 3806 meils of cost, 4251 meils of bear, 3504 meils of flesh, 6 barrels and 127 lispounds of oil, 215 meil sof oatmeal multure, besides poultry and oysters to a large amount.—*Shirreff's Agric. Survey*, p. 32, 33. It is also remarked in a Memorial for the Earl of Morton, dated 1758, that " when the total quantity of these respective articles [of the rental] are converted at the present current prices, [of A. D 1758], the produce of the whole, including the rent of Zetland as it is now let, will extend to £41,500 Scots."

same amount of scat that was paid for a mark of land, was doomed to perpetuation, whatever diminished proportion of arable ground the scathold or pasture-land by new inclosures might contain. The udal fence that was now reared, no longer rendered the soil which it inclosed free from the burden of a tax, and sacred to the unfettered use of the cultivator.* At the same time, the Crown retained the privilege first usurped by Earl Robert Stuart, to confirm the purchaser of udal lands in his possessions, independently of the laws of udal succession; so that, by the operation of a charter from the Crown, the force of a shynd-bill, which sanctioned no contract that was not made with the consent of the udal-born, was easily evaded.

When all these arrangements, so particularly connected with the future political condition of Orkney and Shetland, had been concluded, the King commissioned Sir James Stewart to take a formal possession of the islands. Earl Patrick was then a prisoner in Dumbarton Castle, and hearing of these intentions, he persuaded Robert Stuart, his natural son, to undertake the wild and desperate scheme of raising a party in Orkney, for the purpose of wresting the islands from the power of the Crown. The attempt, as might be expected, completely failed. The brave youth, who to the utmost of his means fulfilled his father's commands, was overpowered, carried a prisoner to Scotland, and underwent a capital punishment. Afterwards, the Earl himself was brought to trial, and being convicted of high treason, paid the last forfeit of his crimes on a public scaffold at Edinburgh.

But the sufferings of Orkney and Shetland did not cease with Earl Patrick. The tyrannical privilege first assumed by the Earls of Orkney of condemning lands, was perpetuated by the tacksmen of the crown revenues. The forfeiture of udal property was the penalty for non-payment of the King's duties. It is even affirmed that the lands thus forfeited were not always applied to the use of the Crown, but constituted part of the private emolument of the fortunate individual who had obtained a tack of the crown-revenues in these islands.† The oppressions which Sir James Stewart, the new farmer, committed, was the occasion in ten years afterwards of his recall. The crown-estates were then successively let out to a number of court-favourites, who felt little compunction in flagrantly abusing their trust. For this reason, there was a frequent revocation of their grants.‡ By means of escheats,—of the exorbitant amount of scat-duties, land-mails, tithes, and the clandestine increase of the standard weights and measures, the resources of the country were drained to the last extremity. The udallers of Orkney and Shetland were now reduced by their overwhelming authority, to the most dispirited state of humiliation. Their udal rights were fled,—the last relic of them, the Shynd-bill, which anciently pro-

---

* It may be proper to remark, with regard to Orkney, that before the time of Earl Patrick, the land which, by being inclosed for culture, became free from scat, was named *Quoy land*. This is a Gothic word, the primary idea of which is, according to Dr Jamieson, simply *an inclosure*. *Quoy*, at the present day, denotes in Orkney a piece of ground taken in from a common. When a patch of quoy-land became reconverted into pasture-ground, by which means it was rendered again liable to a payment of scat, it was named a *Tumail*. Of the etymology of this word I profess myself ignorant.—See *Peterkin's Rentals of Orkney*, No. 2, p. 2.

† See Grievances of Orkney, &c., p. 110.

‡ The Lord Chancellor Hay had the islands for the rent of 40,000 merks Scots, with the heritable office of Steward. This grant was in the course of three years surrendered to the Crown. Various other farmers had subsequent grants, whose names it is of no consequence to record.

tected from the wealthy hand of power the inheritance of their fathers, could now be evaded by a royal charter and infeftment. They now saw no other alternative than to renounce at once their ancient independence of feudal obligations, and, in reminding the monarch of Scotland that they were properly under the influence of Danish laws, to wave this claim, -to style themselves the immediate dependents of the King,—to supplicate a feudal protection, and to implore that the proud arm of oppression which was interposed between the royal superiority and their newly acknowledged state of vassalage, might be for ever removed.* But the Shetlanders conceived that their grievances required a distinct petition; and, as it is recorded by the genealogist of the Sutherland Family, "they complained heavily upon oppressions and disorders committed in that island, far remote from justice, and from the laws of the kingdom." It is then added, that Sir Robert Gordon was selected "to goe thither to redresse and to suppresse these insolencies." In the mean time, the King himself apprised his council in Edinburgh, of the general object of Sir Robert's voyage: He was "to proceed in all things that may tend to the public good, and the *increase of our revenues.*" Sir Robert accordingly set out from London on his mission, but being commanded to previously receive instructions on the subject from the King's council at Edinburgh, he lingered there for two months, these ministers "not having then the leisure to peruse and consider these informations which his Majesty sent unto them concerning Zetland." And now the winter had commenced, and "then went Sir Robert Gordon into Sutherlande to visite his friends;" upon which the King's council excused themselves to his Majesty, that, "in regard to the late season of the year, the difficultie of the passage, and the present estate of that countrey, which is visited with great penurie and want, they had continued his voyage thither until a more opportune time." They had, "in the mean time, established Justices of the Peace in these parts, and had given order for such things as the state of the country did require." It is not remarked whether the poor Shetlanders were satisfied with the wisdom of the council on this occasion, or whether they were altogether convinced that a supply of Peace-officers was the most suitable remedy that could be devised for the relief of the penury of this province. But it is safer to put a favourable construction on the measures of these statesmen, since it is added, that when their letter was received by his Majesty, "the King rested very well satisfied."†

The supplications from the natives of Orkney and Shetland had, however, this effect, that a general act was passed in the ensuing Parliament, annexing the King's property anew to the Crown, by which measure the islanders were, for a few years, saved from the rapacious farmers of the royal revenues. But this respite lasted for a short time only: exacters of the same description again made their appearance, and oppression was again the lot of the udallers.

It may be now remarked, that since the forfeiture of Earl Patrick, new settlers from

---

* The Petition sent to the King in A. D. 1633 contained the following remarkable clause: "*Item,* It is claimed by the Udallers of Orkney and Shetland, who have for these many ages, conform to the Danish law, possessed their lands for payment of skat and teind, that no man be interponed between his Majestie and them, to molest them; but that they remain his Majestie's immediate vassals, for payment of sk at and other duties, conform to their rentals, aye and while his Majestie conform their rights to the laws of this kingdom."

† Genealogy of the Earls of Sutherland, p. 468 to p. 471.

Britain had been gradually introducing themselves into the country, by whom the state of udal tenures was in the progress of undergoing as great a change as had ever been effected under the last Earls of Orkney. It has been shewn that Robert and Patrick Stuart had, by claiming a dominion of a feudal nature over udal lands, removed from themselves the obligation of obtaining a title for their acquisitions in any other way than by accepting them as resignations to a superior; and that the shynd-bill or written decree of the Foude's court, by which no purchase could be confirmed that was not made with the consent of the udal-born, had been preserved as an obstacle to the designs of new settlers in the country, who might be as desirous as the Earls themselves of taking advantage of the impoverished state of the udallers, by obtaining lands from them at a reduced rate. It was the object, therefore, of the Stuarts, to obviate any interference of this nature from the similiar inclination of others, by protecting, with the most anxious solicitude, the force of the shynd-bill, as the necessary authority for confirming every contract of land, but that in which they themselves were parties.* At the same time, the Earls had reserved in their own persons the feudal privilege of confirming any purchaser of udal lands by a feu-charter, which they rendered, by their influence, of a validity equal to the decree of the Foude's court. Such an unwarrantable pretension, therefore, hostile as it was to the ancient statutes of the country, the Crown, upon the forfeiture of Earl Patrick, perpetuated.† The king confirmed all the infeftments of the Earl that had been granted upon udal-lands, and retained the prerogative of issuing out new charters, and of feudalising, if required, all the udal lands in the country. From this cause it was very easy for wealthy purchasers to evade the rigid terms which the Shynd-bill prescribed. The obstacle, therefore, which, in the time of the Earls of Orkney, prevented numerous inhabitants of Scotland from crowding into the country, was at length removed.

By these new settlers, the native islanders are said to have suffered many undue encroachments on their possessions, to which the mixed state of the landed property of the country was calculated to give every facility. In the disputes respecting territory, the udaller was too frequently unable to contend against the influence of wealth and the unjust exercise of civil authority.‡

Notwithstanding the act of Parliament, by which Orkney and Shetland were to be inseparable from the Crown, excuses were still found to annul the decree, and to doom the

---

* In the Law-ting of Shetland, on the 2nd of August 1604, a record under the Earl of Orkney, was made as follows: "Taking consideration of the great confusion, usit within the county of Zetland, anent the buying and selling of land thereinto, continually remembered be the complaints and supplications of the commons of the country, to the great hurt of the commonweal thereof; therefore, it is statute and ordained, that no person or persons frae this forth, either buy or sell ony sort of lands with others, without the samen being first offered to the nearest of the seller's kin, according to the use and constitution of the country."
—*Grievances, &c., of Orkney*, p. 8.

† "From 1612 downwards, there are many charters from the Crown to different proprietors in Orkney, as well as infeftments upon precepts issuing from the Chancery."—*Memorial against Dundas*, A. D. 1775, p. 4.

‡ There in an ancient statute in Orkney, dated A. D. 1632, "anent gripping lands." -"It is statute and ordained, that no man grip his neighbour's lands, under the pain of £10 Scots." No act of this kind appears in the old country laws of Shetland, although Mr Shirreff and Dr Kemp have spoken of the habit as not having been unknown to this country. The latter gentleman has been called to a severe account for the assertion; but, as I have no particular inclination myself to enter into a controversy with my Shetland friends, on the ancient custom of *gripping lands*, (which, by the bye, has not been wholly unknown among much more southerly tracts of Britain,) I shall preserve a cautious silence on the occasion.

islanders to a new change of masters. In the year 1641, the rents of the Bishoprick of Orkney had, upon the establishment of a Presbytery in the islands, been granted to the City of Edinburgh; and two years afterwards, King Charles the First, on the fictitious plea of a loan affirmed to have been made to him by the Earl of Morton, procured from Parliament the confirmation of a grant to this favourite of the lands of the earldom of Orkney and lordship of Zetland, subject to redemption by the payment of £30,000 Sterling.

The Earl of Morton had now power, during the mortgage of the islands, to enter and receive the heritable vassals and tenants of the land, and he had command over all the casualties of the superiority. But it is not evident, from the general tenor of the grant, that the Crown regarded the udallers as holding their lands by feudal tenures; udal lands were specially included in the earldom of Orkney and lordship of Zetland, on account of the scat and other duties which they paid.

Soon after this contract the Earl of Morton died, and his son, on coming into possession of the Islands, immediately endeavoured to sweep away every relic of udal tenures. He acted upon the principle that the Shynd-bill was an illegal infringement of the universal right of superiority which he claimed over the lands of the Province. This was a proceeding that even outstepped all that Earl Patrick had achieved in similar designs to subvert the laws of the country; for although the last Earls of Orkney had always acted as if they had an undubitable right of superiority over Udal-lands, yet the Crown had never retained these pretensions to any greater extent than by admitting the principle, that the validity of a Crown-charter was equal to that of a Shynd bill, and that it was optional to which of these two titles the purchaser or heir of Udal-lands might resort. But Robert, Earl of Morton, now held out the unjustifiable language, that the ancient laws of the country, which Scotland had never verbally rescinded, imparted to udal possessions an imperfect tenure. The words that he used in his charters, when he converted udal lands into heritable feu-farms, were, "That he understood the party had right and possession of the udal land, of [which] he noways was willing to prejudge him, but rather to grant to him and his heirs a more perfect right and security." He then, by a feu-charter, confirmed the udaller in his possessions, taking special care that for this indulgence there should be an augmentation of rental.* Owing to language such as this, which was promulgated as the tenor of the grant from the British Parliament, the Shynd-bill of the Foude's Court began to be regarded with contempt by the wealthy settler, although it was still held in reverence by the ancient udaller, who was naturally tenacious of the laws by which his ancestors had for centuries held their lands undisturbed.

The Earl of Morton, in order to raise a sum of money for the support of the unfortunate Charles, now subjected Orkney to a subaltern and *real* mortage; and at this time a scene of great confusion, from which, indeed, no part of Great Britain was free, began to take place in the Islands. Orkney and Shetland were seized upon by Cromwell, who sent over Deputies into the province. These new rulers committed many irregularities, particularly in the clandestine alteration of the weights; but it is doubtful if they exceeded

---

* An extract from the Charter of the Feu farm, granted to Jerome Fotheringhame, dated September 5, 1640, is the chief authority from which this information is derived. It is to be found in the Memorial against Dundas, A.D. 1776, p. 22.

in oppression their predecessors in the Government. At this period, when the Earl of Morton was no longer enabled to grant feu-charters, when it was doubtful to whom the rights of superiority were due, when the superiority over udal lands was, as a question, still undecided, and when the original udal title of a Shynd-bill was, by the new settlers, regarded not only with distrust, but with dislike, the udaller granted to the wealthy purchaser, under the form of a Scottish disposition and sasine, a charter for his lands, by which they were held immediately from the disponer himself. "Whether," said a well informed historian of Shetland about a century ago, with much simplicity, "the purchases of these incomers were not always such as could admit of a judicial confirmation, or if they wanted to introduce the Scots laws and customs, or partly both, I know not ; – but they began to lay aside the Shynd-bill, and to use dispositions and sasines. And thereupon followed that long train of conveyances, filled with all the clauses and quirks that the lawyer and noter could invent, for lengthening the writing, and making it so intricate, that the true sense and meaning thereof might only be known to themselves. So that it came to pass, in a short process of time, that, instead of the honest, easy, and simple Shynd-bill, Zetland was stocked with rights and conveyances upon the lands, sufficient to find the lawyers and noters as much business as any place of its value in Scotland. Whereby the ancient simple udallers were turned out of their old inheritances, and obliged to improve that ground for others that they had foolishly neglected to do for themselves."*

Upon the accession of Charles II. to the British Throne, in the year 1662, this monarch's first act with regard to these islands, was to restore Episcopacy, and to command that the rents of the church-lands should be paid to the Bishops. He was next inclined to restore the family of Morton to their possession of the Crown estates of Orkney and Shetland, subject to the same terms of redemption as had been specified in the former contract. This grant having been annulled by the general act of revocation that had been passed in the same year, a new mortgage was obtained in the name of George, Viscount Grandison, as trustee for the family of Morton, who were then in embarrassed circumstances. The charter empowered the grant of heritable feus of any part of the Earldom, to be held of the trustees until the extinction of the mortgage, and afterwards of the Crown. Lord Grandison, therefore, appointed Alexander Douglas of Spynie, as factor to receive the Crown-rents of the Islands, and to grant feu-charters. The mission of this individual proved an important era in the history of Orkney and Shetland.

Douglas of Spynie was instructed to dispute the validity of all the tenures in the Islands, which could not produce for them confirmations from the Crown. Most of the lands of the country were then in possession of the new settlers, who, in their avidity to purchase up the little patrimonial possessions of the impoverished udallers, had superseded the ancient security of a shynd-bill for a private deed of transfer, under the form of a Scottish disposition and sasine. This mode of conveyance was, in the first place, objectionable, on the principle that an udal inheritance was specially protected by the laws of the particular community among which udal lands had been originally partitioned ; and, that,

---

* Gifford's *Zetland*, p. 57.

therefore, no title but a judicial decree of the Foude's court could properly transmit an udal right. The second objection to which a private deed of transfer was liable, bore reference to the fact, that prior to the protectorate of Cromwell, no Scottish forms of title for udal lands had ever been given but by the Earls of Orkney or by the King. When, therefore, the title of the Shynd-bill had, by the united influence of the new settlers in the country and the Earl of Morton, gradually fallen into disuse or contempt, the erroneous notion became more easily inculcated, that the King was the proper superior of udal lands, and that, therefore, no property purchased from an udaller could be legally held by a deed from the disponer, unless a prior one had been obtained from the granter's superior. But, as it has been before observed, although the Crown, in violation of the treaty with Norway by which the laws of Orkney and Shetland were to remain undisturbed, had consented to perpetuate the privileges first usurped by Earls Roberts and Patrick Stewart, of feudalizing udal lands, the absolute obligation of the udallers to hold *in capite* from the Crown, had never yet received a direct Royal sanction. The Scottish Government had not acted as if the King *was* the real superior of udal lands, but as if he *might* become the superior of them, whenever an inheritor was desirous to hold his lands by a charter, rather than by virtue of a decree from the Foude's court. But it is doubtful if any distinction of this kind was made by the poor udaller, who could see nothing more than that new landed tenures and new terms of possession, unknown to the lost statutes of the Law-ting, were intended to be introduced into the country, which it was in vain to resist. The udaller was easily intimidated with the hints which were promulgated, that he held his lands on a doubtful right, but that, in consideration of an augmentation of the sums he paid to the King for seat and wattle, he might receive a charter of confirmation, by which he would become, when the King had paid off the mortgage on Orkney and Shetland, an eventual Crown-vassal. This security the udaller gladly purchased, finding in it the soothing words of promise which had been employed thirteen years before, but with less success, on the same purpose of feudalization, that Alexander Douglas of Spynie was no way willing to prejudge him for his udal lands, but to grant unto him, his heirs and assignees, a more perfect right and security of the same. As for the new settlers, whose purchases, as Mr Gifford has remarked, were not always such as would admit of a judicial confirmation, — they readily assented to the principle that the King was the superior of udal lands, and gladly embraced the opportunity of securing the possessions which they had obtained, in opposition to the strict terms of udal succession, by obtaining for them charters of confirmation from the Crown.

From this period, also, may be dated the complete subversion of the ancient laws of the country. The jurisdiction of the Islands had been given to the Earl of Morton's trustee, and the udallers now abandoned for ever the open space of the Law-ting, where, beneath no other canopy than the sky, their fathers had met to legislate for at least six centuries.* They were now required, as new vassals of the Crown, to give their suit and presence to the courts which were held within some covered hall at Kirkwall and Scalloway.

---

* "The practice of making laws in the Law-ting, subsisted till the year 1670." -*Grievances of Orkney, &c.*, p. 4.

The causes have at length been explained, to which the great success that attended Douglas of Spynie's mission to Orkney and Shetland may be attributable. When the Shynd-bill, the ancient security of udal property, had grown into disuse, the feudalization of nearly all the lands of the country became an easy process. There were very few landed inheritors, with the exception of those who had formerly obtained charters of confirmation from the Crown, that did not now hold from the Earl of Morton's trustee. " By granting of these charters from the Crown," remarks Mr Gifford, "Spynie raised a considerable sum of money of the heritors and feuars of Orkney and Zetland, as appeared by a particular account thereof for Zetland, amounting to the sum of £15,000 Scots, which was very heavy upon many of them. But the composition-money paid for the charters, and the great feu-duties payable yearly out of the lands, did, in a short time thereafter, sink many of the heritors so far in debt, that they were obliged to sell the lands for payment thereof. They were utterly incapable of being at the charge of the public securities and frequent confirmations required by law."*

Douglas of Spynie was also commissioned to make long tacks of the Crown lands ; but, as he did not approve of the old country practice of enclosures paying no land-mails when not laboured, he required an annual rent for them whatever might be their condition. At the same time, he disposed in feu, of most of the King's moieties of the umboth or corn tithes.

Orkney and Shetland now began to present a new aspect. Numerous allotments of territory, which had been the result of inheritances equally divided among the nearest kindred of possessors, were laid together so as to form an ample estate. In every part of the islands new settlers were to be found, who began to assume within their small demesnes, all the proud functions of the baronial lord. Each little manor afforded an epitome of the state of the Feudal System, when aided in its civil establishment by the necessity imposed upon feudatories, of resigning to a limited number of their dependents the care of cultivating the soil. The little landlord of Orkney or Shetland demanded, along with his rent, the acknowledgement of a grassum or entry, and many of the menial services that were rendered to baronial lands, such as annual presents, casting the lord's peats, or labouring for him a certain number of days.

It is remarkable, that when the last act of feudalising the udal lands of Orkney and Shetland took place, Denmark appeared to be more seriously bent than ever upon entering into an explicit understanding with Britain regarding her right of redeeming these islands, as the ancient pledge of a royal marriage-dower. But in what state could this ancient Scandinavian settlement have been then restored ? The laws which Britain had engaged to protect, were totally subverted ;— udal lands were transmuted into regular feudal tenures, and were oppressed with the heavy duties, which had first found a place in the wicked rental of the Earls of Orkney, but were perpetuated by the Government to whose care the udaller's rights had been entrusted ;—the ancient Scandinavian inheritor was ejected from his little patrimony, and was become a menial vassal to some wealthier settler,—some

---

* Gifford's *Zetland*, p. 43 & 58.

stranger in the land;—this suffering colony of Norway had been goaded to the quick,—its wounds were yet open. The British Government, therefore, seems to have acted with much less violence to its feelings, in again evading a definite explanation regarding Denmark's claim of redemption, than in restoring the colony in this lacerated state to its mother country. Denmark, not without marks of chagrin, has never since the treaty of Breda persisted in the claim, chiefly from the dread of being implicated on its account in an expensive war ; she has been content with transmitting to posterity, through the medium of her national historian Torfæus, the discussions that have at various times taken place with the British Government on the subject of the impignorated colony, together with the poignant disappointment she has felt at their unsatisfactory termination.* " In tanta igitur historiarum luce," concludes Torfæus, "etiamsi per tot obstacula rerum, cum versati simus, nihil orbem latere potest, quod regum Daniæ, Norvegiæque jus in prædictas insulas ex naturæ gentiumque corroboret pandectis, quibus Anglorum toties injecta, mora penitus adversatur. Nec veritas usquam gloriosius tuetur locum, quam in re tam lucida et contestata, omnium oculis et judiciis expositâ. Causam ideo coram amplissimo orbis terrarum tribunali ulterius disceptare supersedemus, et confisi æquitati remedia a tempore speramus."†

Soon after the conference with Denmark, the English Government was induced to inquire very particularly into the circumstances which led to the dissolution of Orkney and Shetland from the immediate protection of the Crown. The mode in which these islands were mortgaged by Charles I. to the Earl of Morton, became an object of strict investigation, the result of which was, that the transaction was formally declared to be obtained by importunity and obreption, in the face of many acts of perpetual annexation, and without any previous dissolution of Parliament. A reduction of the grant immediately ensued; but although the sum alleged to have been advanced to Charles I. for which the islands were mortgaged, was suspected to be a fictitious loan, the Morton family were satisfied for their claim, as if they had been real creditors of the Crown. These arrangements being completed, a new annexation of Orkney and Shetland took place, accompanied with the profession, that the islands were to remain inseparably with the Crown in all time coming.

With the change of landed tenures introduced into Orkney and Shetland by the Morton family, and with the subsequent annexation of these islands to the Crown in the year 1669, the history of the udallers properly terminates. Some few of this ancient description of landholders still remained unfeudalised ; and their descendants may now have the satisfaction of thinking, that, in their respective families, the hereditary transmission of udal rights has been for centuries successfully opposed to all the feudal obligations of charters, of precepts of infeftment, of casualties of superiority, of compositions for the entry of heirs and singular successors, or of renewals of investiture. The ancient udaller may at the present

---

* Rerum Orcad. Hist., liber iii. " De indefessis potentissimorum Regum Daniæ, Norvegiæque studiis jus suum in Orcades, adjectutemque Hetlandiam pacifice retinendi." At the end of the 2d Book of Torfæus, the assertions of Buchanan and Boethius, that the claim of redemption was surrendered, are ably commented upon.

† Torfæus, Rerum Orcad. Hist., p. 228.

day contemplate his little patrimony with pride, although, alas! his native land,

> ———"bound in with the triumphant sea,
> Whose rocky shore beats back the envious surge
> Of watery Neptune, is now bound in with shame
> With inky spots and rotten parchment bonds."*

This narrative is not closed without the impression, that it is difficult to conceive, how a train of events such as has been recorded, could have ever taken place in a province placed under the protection of the popular government of Britain. But the British Legislature itself, in the manifesto that was published in the year 1669 on the occasion of the fresh annexation of these islands to the Crown, has given so complete a summary of the causes of the misrule, that it may, with the greatest propriety, form the conclusion to the present narrative. The act of annexation recites, "That the islands of Orkney and Shetland were so considerable a part of his Majesty's ancient kingdom, that, for divers ages, they had been the occasion of much trouble and expence of blood and money: That, being of great and large extent of bounds, and so remote from the ordinary seat of justice and judicatures, the inhabitants could not repair to the said judicatures without great trouble and expence, to complain when they were oppressed and grieved: That it is not only fit for his Majesty's interest, but will be for the great advantage of his Majesty's subjects dwelling there, that, without interposing any other lord or superior between his Majesty and them, they should have an immediate dependence upon his Majesty and his officers, being their greatest security against all foreign attempts, and oppressions at home.

"That notwithstanding divers former Acts of annexation, yet, importunity prevailing with his Majesty and his royal father, their goodness and inclination to gratify their subjects, they had been induced to give away and part with so great a jewel of their crown, and to dispone and grant rights of the earldom of Orkney and lordship of Shetland, to the great prejudice of his Majesty, his crown and subjects, and contrary to law."

APPENDIX TO THE HISTORY OF THE UDALLERS.

A slight sketch of the political state of Orkney and Shetland from 1669 to the present period, may be properly appended to this history.

After the act of annexation, the revenues of these islands were let out to different farmers, upon leases not exceeding five years. These tacksmen are said to have been not less scrupulous than their predecessors in the office of contributing to the distresses of the islanders.

In 1697, the Presbyterian form of church-government was introduced into Orkney and Shetland. All lands belonging to the Church then returned to the Crown; but since they

---

* Shakespeare's Richard II.

were not annexed to it, they could be disposed of by the Sovereign at pleasure. Three years afterwards, in consequence of a commission being dispatched to these islands by the General Assembly in Scotland, nearly the whole of the ministers conformed to Presbyterianism. The Bishop's rents in Orkney were retained by the Crown, but the stipends to ministers were paid out of the church funds, though in a less proportion.

In A.D. 1707, Queen Anne, notwithstanding the former solemn annexations of Orkney and Shetland to the Crown, yielded to the importunity of James, Earl of Morton, who had been one of the Commissioners for the treaty of Union, and made a new grant of the islands in his favour, but still in the form of a mortgage, redeemable on the payment of £30,000 Sterling, and subject to an annual feu-duty of £500 Sterling. The Earl had "full power," as the charter specified, "to enter and receive the heritable vassals who now actually hold of her Majesty and Crown, and their heirs, and to grant charters and infeftments." He also obtained a lease of the unappropriated part of the lands of the Church, as well as of those teinds which had devolved to the Crown, by virtue of the exchange, a century before, of certain lands of the King for others of the bishopric. The Earl of Morton was at the same time elected heritable Steward and Justiciar of Orkney and Shetland: he was authorised to appoint deputies for the administration of justice, according to the practice of Scotland; and it appears that he retained a few of the subordinate forms of the ancient legislature of the country. He was made Vice-Admiral of Orkney and Shetland, with all the powers of judicature in the maritime affairs of the country, and with a donation of the rights of admiralty. Lastly, the Earl had conferred upon him the right of patronage to the kirks of Shetland and Orkney, which privilege was taken from the Presbytery, and reckoned a great grievance. A Commissary was retained, who was a judge in consistorial affairs. The revenue accruing from every source of emolument enumerated was about £3000 Sterling *per annum*.

In the year 1742, the Earl of Morton, on the fictitious plea that the emoluments of his concerns in Orkney and Shetland, were not sufficient to pay the interest of the mortgaged sum, had influence enough with Parliament to obtain a discharge of the reversion; an act was therefore passed, making the whole of the estates of which he was in possession, heritable and irredeemable. Five years afterwards, this Nobleman was deprived of the jurisdiction of the Islands, for which he received in compensation the sum of £7200 Sterling. The country now enjoyed nearly the same state of laws as other districts of Scotland. About this period the Earl of Morton became involved in suits at law, chiefly on account of the fraudulent increase of weights and measures that had gradually taken place, by the Earl of Orkney, the farmers of the Crown revenues, and his own ancestors; and although he gained his suit, his property became so troublesome to him, that, in the year 1776, he sold it for the sum of £60,000 to Sir Lawrence Dundas.

The new successor of the Earl of Morton in the estates and superiority of Orkney and Shetland that had formerly belonged to the Crown, appears to have entered on his acquisitions with little historical knowledge of the peculiarities of landed tenure which the Islands had enjoyed whilst annexed to Norway, and of the various changes which they had undergone, during their progress of feudalization. Sir Lawrence Dundas immediately conceived that his powers of superiority were too limited ; and in order to extend them involved himself in an expensive suit at law, in which he completely failed. Since the result of this action did not make the least difference in the relative situation of the various description of landed inheritors in the Islands to the King or to Sir Lawrence Dundas, any particular detail of the proceedings is unnecessary, being a subject less of historical than of legal interest.*

Such are the principal events that have occurred in Orkney and Shetland since the year 1669,—the period when nearly all the lands were feudalised and annexed to the Crown. The Province then became in every respect subject to British laws. It was rendered liable to a land-tax, which was in vain disputed, on the plea that the scatt already paid was a proper equivalent, and that no other could in justice be demanded. Orkney has always paid two-thirds of the cess, the remaining one-third having been rendered by Shetland ; but the latter country having no valued rent, by which the right of individuals to vote can be ascertained, is denied any share in the election of a Member of Parliament. Lord Dundas is the Lord Lieutenant of Orkney and Shetland: and, with regard to the internal legislation of the latter country, it may be briefly remarked, that the offices of Justice of Peace have been lately revived ; that the Sheriff-substitute holds a regular Court, and that there are separate Admiralty and Commissary jurisdictions.

These islands have never been able to recover from the oppressions exercised by Earls Robert and Patrick Stewart, and the farmers and feuars of the Crown revenues, by whom they were succeeded. Of the lands of Orkney, it has been recently said, that " they are now of much less productive value than they were several centuries ago, and were it not for the comparative recent discovery of the kelp manufacture, many of the proprietors would be unable to pay for the total produce of the land, the feu and teind-duties which were paid by their ancestors several centuries ago."† Of Shetland it has been also affirmed, that, " were it not for the profits arising from the fisheries, a great part of the lands would long ago have fallen into the hands of the superior, whose interest in them, under the existing circumstances, is in many instances far beyond that of those who are considered the actual proprietors."‡

But a brighter prospect is perhaps at this very moment opening to the country. The superiority of the Islands is vested in a truly honourable family, and if numerous litigations have occurred between the heritors and the superior, they have been in no less degree attributable to the distracted state of the country during the tyranny of the ancient feuars and farmers of the Crown revenues, than to the ignorance which has since prevailed among all parties of the real state of the tenures of the country, and of the extent of their respective rights. The supply of this deficiency has been the labour of the year 1820. A collection has been made of numerous interesting documents, lately discovered in the charter-room of

---

* I shall give a brief statement of them in the Notes to the present Iter.—See Note 6.

† Memorial against Dundas, A.D. 1820, by R. Jameson, Esq., Advocate, p. 38.

‡ Shirreff's Agricultural Survey of Shetland, p. 18.

Edinburgh, and their publication has been conducted with an ability and zeal that must entitle the industrious editor of them to the lasting gratitude of his countrymen.*

Nothing remains to be added, but that Orkney and Shetland have a long account of arrears against the British Government. The admission into the King's Exchequer of Earl Patrick Stuart's enormous and unjust rental, and the repeated breaches of Parliamentary faith committed in disannexing the islands from the immediate protection of the Crown, are charges of such a serious nature against a free state, that, in justice to the perpetuated sufferings of the natives, ample reparation, even at the present day, is a duty. It is to be hoped, therefore, that an acquaintance with the natural advantages which these islands possess in regard to their fisheries, the manufacture of kelp, or other sources of emolument, may suggest some mode in which a liberal and enlightened Legislature may be enabled to atone for past injuries, and, perhaps, to add materially to the resources of the nation at large.†

The history of Udal Tenures being investigated, the intervals of a Shetland traveller's geological pursuits cannot be better employed than in examining the state of a country which differs little from what it was about a century and a-half ago. Shetland is in the precise state that is calculated to afford much matter for delectation to the taste of some learned member of the Antiquarian Society, well clergyonned in the rolles of old Tyme's Historie.

The land of the country is still as unmeasured as ever it was in the days of Harold Harfagre. Collectors still come round for the annual duties of scat, wattle, ox-penny, hawk-hens, grassum, and land-mails. The tenant labours for his lord a certain number of days. Corn-teinds as well as vicarage-teinds, are severally paid in kind from the produce of cows, sheep, and fishing boats. The single stilted plough is yet in use,—the tusker, the quern and the cassie,—all genuine Scandinavian implements of husbandry,—the description of which can in nowise, without an offence to true Archaiological taste, be mixed up with proposals for introducing at the same time some new-fangled cart, plough, harrow, roller, box and stone wheel-barrow, even though recommended by the Shetland New Agricultural Society.

The course which I intended to take had a reference to the geology of the country. There was consequently a necessity for proceeding in such a direction as would be best adapted for determining the boundaries and mutual relations of the rocks under examina-

---

* There is at the same time no doubt but that the hopes held out by Mr Peterkin (the gentleman alluded to), will be fulfilled; that by the publication of these documents, " the rights of all parties can be adjusted without litigation or expense; that various obstacles to improvement which have checked its progress in Orkney, may be removed; and the basis be established of a more prosperous state of society, in a region which has hitherto enjoyed but little of the beneficence of the British Government, but has been impoverished for centuries past, by a system of leasing the crown-lands and revenues to middle-men of all descriptions."— *Preface to Mr Peterkin's Collection of the Rentals of Orkney,* printed in the year 1820.

† For a particular explanation of the various authorities to which I am indebted for my information in drawing up these memoirs of the udal system, see Note 6.

tion. The result of the investigation forms the subject of a distinct Geological Treatise; but the miscellaneous incidents attending the research constitute the proper details of an Iter.

HOLMS OF QUENDAL BAY.

When the geognost has got in readiness his ponderous hammers,—the well-tried steel of which

"———————the strong-bas'd promontory
Hath oft made shake,"

he cannot, perhaps, more conveniently commence his examination of Shetland, than by first visiting a small insulated rock in Quendal Bay, named Little-Holm; for which purpose he must seat himself in a light Norway yawl, launched on the swelling surge of Dunrossness, whilst he is propelled by the toiling oars of four or six active Shetland boatmen.

On approaching Little Holm, the attention is directed to a mural heap of stones, that, with few interruptions, encircles the island, and presents the appearance of a rude fortification. Upon landing, the mutilated remains may be observed of what antiquaries name Kist-vaens, or stone coffins. Each of these is formed by four flat stones, sunk edgeways into the earth, the upper margins of which do not rise many inches above the common level of the ground. The cavity of the most perfect coffin is about 4½ feet long by about 27 inches broad; of the depth no idea could be formed, from the quantity of earth and rubbish which it contained. With regard to the origin of these stone chests, it is useless to offer any conjectures, as their contents have been removed, and as the use of receptacles of this kind for bones or urns was never restricted to any particular race among the ancient European tribes. It is however remarkable, that antiquaries should have considered that all their speculations on the antiquities of Orkney and Shetland could only refer to a pure Scandinavian or to a Celtic people. It seems to have been lost sight of, that Orkney, and probably Shetland also, was frequented by Saxon pirates, who sustained a defeat by Theodosius. This is so important a fact connected with the earliest annals of the country, that it will be occasionally an object of inquiry, if a proper Saxon race, or even if a mixed people composed of Saxons and Scandinavians, did not inhabit the land prior to the occupation of it by the Norwegians, who had made it their abode after the usurpation of their country by Harold Harfagre. It was now evident, that the stones which encompassed the isle as a sort of defence, were derived from the dilapidation of sepulchral tumuli that covered the stone coffins. Probably this wall might have been hastily thrown up by the shipwrecked party belonging to the Duke de Medina's flag-ship; for, in a different part of the country, where another galleon belonging to the Spanish Armada was cast away, an islet was fortified in nearly a similar manner.

Little Holm is composed of epidotic sienite, and secondary rocks of a conglomerate and arenaceous structure; an interesting exposure here takes place of the junction of the two formations. In Cross Holm, a contiguous islet, nothing but sienite occurs.

FITFIEL HEAD.

In landing at the head of Quendal Bay, the sienite made its appearance close to the house of Mr Ogilvie, being no longer modified by the presence of epidote. In a north-westerly direction, therefore, being that in which the rock is said to have been occasionally exposed by the spade of the labourer, it was proper to proceed, until the granitic mass should become fully exposed on the western coast.—As the fine corn lands of Quendal, and the barren sand-hills to the east of them retreat from view, we become acquainted with the different inhabitants of the Shetland scatholds or commons. The diminutive fleecy tenants of the hills resemble in their form, their nimbleness and fleetness, the Argali or wild sheep of Siberia.* The scene is again varied by the occasional appearance of a little barrel-bellied broad-backed equuleus, of a brown or black colour, which Buchanan, the Scottish historian, has described as "asino haud major;" that is, not larger than a donkey. When the shelty is in his winter or spring garb, it is difficult to suppose that his progenitors were the same animals which travellers have described as prancing over the arid tracts of Arabia: the long shaggy hair with which he is clothed, has more the appearance of a polar dress, or of some arctic livery, specially dispensed to the quadruped retainers of the Genius of Hialtland. Another ranger of the hills is of a revolting kind; he is a little ugly brindled monster, the very epitome of the wild boar, yet not larger than the English terrier:

"His bristled back a trench impal'd appears,
And stands erected like a field of spears."

This lordling of the Shetland scatholds and arable lands ranges undisturbed over his free demesnes, and, in quest of the roots of plants or earthworms, hollows out deep furrows and trenches in the best pastures,—destroys in his progress all the nests which he can find of plovers, curlieus or chalders,—bivouacs in some potato field, which he rarely quits until he has excavated a ditch large enough to bury within it a dozen of fellow-commoners of his own size and weight.† Nor is the reign of this petty tyrant altogether bloodless. When a young lamb is just dropped, it is then that he foams, and, as Blackmore has pompously sung, "flourishes the iv'ry war;" never quitting his ground until the grass is tinged with the red slaughter of his victim.

Continuing in the same north-westerly course, the ocean at length appeared full in view, and near it the fresh-water lake of Lunabister, frequented by numerous web-footed birds. The Cliff Hills, which stretched out far to the north, presented the form of a long, bleak mountain-ridge, muffled up in wet, exhaled mists, and sloping on each side towards the wild superb waste of the Atlantic. For several miles the coast seemed broken into creeks,

---

* To this race they have been compared by Mr Shirreff in his Agriculture of Shetland.
† See Low's Fauna Orcad. for a description of the Sus Scrofa of this latitude.

islets, and sea holms, and, in their pent-up channels, amidst the white foam of tilting waves, the poet might describe the sea-nymphs as keeping up a perpetual coil. In journeying along the west of the lake, the direction of this course was terminated by a little inlet of the sea named Spigga, where the sienite of Dunrossness became fully exposed, where it was in junction with the clay-slate of the Cliff Hills, and with interstrata of hornblend-slate and quartz. After walking due south from Spigga for a distance of two miles along high banks of sienite, this rock had the appearance of reposing upon strata of gneiss and mica-slate. At this place commences the promontory of Fitfiel. The clay-slate of which this headland is composed, has so pearly a lustre, that when the rays of the sun shine fully upon it, a whitish appearance is produced, which seems to have suggested to the early Scandinavian settlers the name of Fitfiel, or the White Mountain. At some little distance from the place where the clay-slate begins, is to be seen a large vein of iron-mica, running from east to west, about 12 feet broad, which was discovered several years ago by a company of miners who worked in the vicinity. This ore is supposed to contain about 70 or 80 *per cent.* of iron, and by the miners of the continent would probably be considered of some consequence. Iron-mica is described in mineralogical works as melting better than common iron-glance, but as requiring a greater addition of lime-stone ; as affording an iron which is sometimes cold-short, but which is well fitted for cast-ware.* Dr Fleming several years ago very properly recommended this vein to the attention of practical mineralogists.

From this point of rock, as we cast our eyes to the north, an extensive view of the country is exhibited ; yet nothing is to be observed but the most frequent constituents of Shetland scenery,—islets, holms, creeks, precipices, and a long line of ragged coast. Bearing off the most distant extremity of the Mainland is the island of Foula, supposed to have been the Ultima Thule which Agricola saw from Orkney. An inland survey of the country shews nothing but a trackless brown desert of hill and dale, which the Forest Nymphs have for centuries forsaken. Towards Fitfiel I found the ascent to gradually increase ; a few signs of cultivation appeared, and some cottages were interspersed among the hills. Still pursuing a course along precipitous banks,

> ———————— " where the murmuring surge
> That on th' unnumber'd idle pebbles chafes,
> Cannot be heard so high ;"

a short walk led to the summit of Fitfiel Head, and to a view of the southerly ocean,—Fair Isle appearing like a speck in the vast expanse. On the easterly brow of this hill may be seen the estuary of Quendal, studded with sea holms ; at the head of the bay are fertile corn lands, a neat white farm-house, and various groups of cottages, around each of which rude dikes of stone or turf irregularly wind, and to the east of these a cheerless contrast of barren sand-hills. More remote is a straitened tongue of land, clothed with a green sward, jutting out far into the sea, and swelling out at its extremity into a bold promontory :—this is the Head of Sumburgh. The prospect in this direction is closed by the ocean, which,

---

* Jameson's Mineralogy, 2d edit., vol. iii., p. 242.

invading the low sandy beach that forms the easterly declivity of the sand-hills, channels out the shore into numerous meandring creeks. In unison with this highly varied, although woodless scenery, are the hoarse screams of the sea-fowl that build among the crags of Fitful. Occasionally the noble, generous falcon whom Isaac Walton's sportsman, in disdain of the Imperial Eagle, has dubbed "Jove's servant in ordinary," deigns to visit this proud eminence.

GARTHSNESS.

In descending the heights of Fitful towards Quendal Bay, I crossed the small ridge of Garthsness, composed of mica-slate and gneiss. Close to the sea there was a piece of ground approaching to a semicircular form, and naturally protected on the west by high banks, on the south by the ocean, and strengthened in other places by artificial embankments of earth. This fortification was probably the hasty workmanship of the marauding parties of Highlanders, who are said to have visited Shetland for a long series of years, and to have secured for themselves within temporary strongholds their booty of corn and cattle, until a sufficient freight of plunder was collected, with which they might sail away to the Western Isles.

At the extremity of Garthsness there is a bed of iron-pyrites, running north and south, of the width of $8\frac{1}{2}$ feet.* This mineral is not worked as an ore of iron, but is in Germany principally valued for the sulphur which may be obtained from it by sublimation, and for the green vitriol or sulphate of iron which it affords by exposure to the air, either with or without previous roasting.† About thirty years ago, Shetland was visited by a mining company from London, who, by the suggestion of an unskillful, trading projector, undertook to work this bed of iron-pyrites, in the expectation that it necessarily contained a deposit of copper. An agreement was entered into with the owner of the estate, for the purpose of introducing a party of Cornish miners into the country, who immediately fell to work upon the mineral, and sunk shafts in various directions of the hill. In the mean time, the wise promoter of the scheme undertook, during the progress of the work, the labour of essaying. The iron-pyrites of Garthsness suffered (as the ancient chemists would say) all the vexations and the martyrizations of metals in the work : solution, ablution, sublimation, cohobation, calcination, ceration, and fixation. But the martyrization was in vain : it is doubtful if a single grain of copper was ever extracted from the ore. At length, a Shetland wight, ambitious for a quiz against the Dousterswivel of the party, slily dropt among the contents of the crucible a copper penny. The effect which was produced exceeded his most ardent hopes of mischief. The crucible was taken from the furnace ; its contents were examined, and joy sparkled on every mining countenance. "I know not," said the deluded visionary, who, from his suggestion of the mining scheme, was allowed to have a

---

* The account of the Garthsness vein is given in p. 143, of this Work ; [the Geological portion].
† Jameson's Mineralogy, 2d edit., vol. iii., p. 309.

proportion of its profits, "Whether I or Bedford's Duke, with all his immense estates, ought most to be envied." This vein of Garthsness

> ——————————— "is the rich Peru,
> And there within, Sir, are the golden mines,
> Great Solomon's Ophir! he was sailing to't
> Three years; but we have reached it in ten months.
> This is the day, wherein to all my friends
> I will pronounce the happy word, Be rich."

But the unfortunate company at whose expense this delectable comedy was got up, were left, notwithstanding the fine promising indications of the laboratory, to wait so long for a cargo of metal from the Shetland Ophir, that their patience was at length exhausted. An emissary from their fraternity was dispatched to Garthsness, sufficiently well qualified to judge of the probable success of the undertaking. He saw the vein, and all the labours of the experimentalist were dissipated *in fumo*.

> " Why, now you smoky prosecutor of Nature!
> Now, do you see, that something's to be done,
> Besides your beech-coal and your cor'sive waters,
> Your crosslets, crucibles, and cucurbites?
> You must have stuff brought home to you to work on."
> *(Probably alluding to the copper penny-piece dropt into the crucible.)*
> " And yet, you think I am at no expence,
> In searching out these veins, then following them,
> Then trying them out. 'Fore God, my intelligence
> Costs me more money than my share comes to
> In these rare works."*

SUMBURGH.

Before quitting the parish of Dunrossness, I paid a visit to the Ness and Links of Sumburgh. After passing along the head of the Bay of Quendal, the rocks appeared to consist either of agglutinated fragments of quartz, granite and felspar, or of a very loose and arenaceous variety of sandstone. Upon crossing the hills east of Quendal Bay, a sandstone succeeded, which much resembled the most common species of primitive quartz rock. I now directed my course to an open inlet of the sea, smaller than that of Quendal, named West Voe. Here, it may be proper to explain a few provincial terms expressive of the different circumstances under which the sea invades the land. The name of Voe, from the Scandinavian *vogr*, is given to a narrow inlet of the sea of moderate extent; but to an estuary of considerable width, the common English term of Bay is applied. An inlet of diminutive size is called a Gio or Geo, from the Scandinavian *gea*. Some idea, though certainly an incomplete one, may be formed of the comparative magnitude of a Voe and a Gio, by supposing that the former, if deep enough, is capable from its width, of affording a

---

* Johnson's Alchymist.

harbour for ships, but that the latter is, from its narrowness, only proper for boats. There is still another small inlet of the sea distinguished by the Shetlanders as being more open than the Gio: it is named a Bite, the word having been probably derived from the popular phrases of English or Scotch sailors, among whom I have occasionally heard it used. The Bite of the Shetland shores is nothing more than the latinised expression of *indentation* of coast, the low metaphor of both terms *(morsu frangere)* in nowise differing from each other. A keen etymologist, indeed, might be at little loss to justify the use of the term Bite, in its application to invasions of the sea on a coast, by citations of the highest classical authority: as, for instance, by a passage from Horace,

"Non rura, quæ Liris quietâ,
Mordet aquâ taciturnus omnis."
HORAT. I. 31.

Francis, in translating these lines, was unwilling to give the closest translation of the term *mordet*, but it is questionable if he has got rid of all the vulgarity of the expression, by the following clumsy version:

" Nor the rich fields that Liris leaves,
And *eats away* with silent waves."

The sand-hills which appear as we approach West Voe from Quendal, are agreeably contrasted with the grassy Links of Sumburgh to the east, and the green headland of Sumburgh. On the confines that mark the devastation of the blowing sand, are to be seen the ruins of buildings, the foundations of which have wholly or in part yielded to the removal of the light arenaceous particles upon which they were improvidently built. An old, plain family mansion, seated in the middle of the green sward of Sumburgh, and erected by the Scottish family of Bruce, remains entire; but at no great distance to the south, being close to the seat of the sand-flood, may be seen the shell of two or three rooms of an ancient house, built in a very plain manner, without any manifestation of a castellated style of architecture. The walls appear of a remarkable thickness, though sunk in several places by the dislodgment of the sand from beneath the foundations. This dwelling was erected by Lord Robert Stuart, the last and 27th Abbot of Holyrood, who was afterwards Earl of Orkney. He was for thirty years the indefatigable persecutor of the ancient udallers of Orkney and Shetland, in his endeavours to subvert their laws, and to wrest from them their landed possessions.

Robert Stuart was the natural son of James V. by Euphemia, daughter of Lord Elphinston. He was generally addressed in the court of Queen Mary by the title of Lord Robert, and very early in life was appointed Abbot of Holyrood*. When the Popish dignitaries of Scotland were compelled, for the sake of securing their benefices, to join the cause of the Reformers, the pliant abbot readily fell in with the prevailing religious sentiments of the times, and probably yielded in zeal to none of those elect,

---

* Chalmers's Caledonia, vol. ii. p. 753. " As the last corruption of a corrupt age," remarks this writer, " the King's bastards were introduced into the greatest bishoprics, and the richest abbeys."

SUMBURGH.

> "Who prove their doctrine orthodox,
> By apostolic blows and knocks."

When the abbot had turned Protestant, he obtained in marriage the hand of Lady Jane Kennedy of the house of Cassilis; and, in a short period, the Queen settled a handsome annuity upon him, out of her thirds of the revenue of Holyrood, in support of his three legitimate children, as well as of two that were base born; for, it may be briefly hinted that the abbot had not in his catholic days imposed upon himself the strictest rules of chastity which might have been expected from his religious order. In the year 1569, Lord Robert exchanged his abbey for the temporal estates of the bishopric of Orkney and Shetland, receiving at the same time a feu of the lands of the crown: it was then that he took possession of his estates in a mode sufficiently indicative of the arbitrary rule which he meant to exercise over the islands. It was the custom of the 16th century, for the nobility and gentry to attach to their retinue a considerable number of men, sometimes to the amount of 200, who were not kept constantly in the house, like other menial servants, but were dispersed over different parts of the lord's demesnes, giving their occasional presence for the purpose of ostentation. Lord Robert brought with him a great number of dependants of this description into Orkney and Shetland, who, from the arms which they constantly wore, agreeably to the fashion of the times, were occasionally named Suddartis or Soldiers, but they were also styled in these islands *broken men*,—an epithet that stands in need of some explanation. Retinues of serving men were engaged, with this intention, that besides giving their attendance for the sake of pomp, their weapons should be ready to decide the quarrels of their masters, or for the perpetration of any excesses or disorders in a country that might be required. It was, therefore, by no means necessary that retainers should be chosen from that class of society who were addicted to the most regular or honest occupations of life:—for, indeed, to no rank of people but of the lowest description, could the conditions of entering the train of a great man be agreeable; such dependents were required to serve for little or no pay, to receive only the perquisite of arms and an uniform livery, and to be content with the chance of quartering themselves upon the country at large, without being made responsible for any dissolute habits to which they might be prone. It was on this account that the name of a *livery* or *lithry*, answering to a retinue of serving men, long became in Scotland the bye-word that was used to signify a despicable crowd.* Lord Robert Stuart's train of dependents that were introduced into Orkney and Shetland, appear to have been composed of individuals of the precise stamp described; they acquired the appellation of *broken men*, a term of opprobrium that finds no synonym but in the more modern word *vagabonds*. It is probable that the moral qualifications of Lord Robert's retinue were not very dissimilar to what might have been found in England about the same period among the kindred description of worthies whose habits

---

* This is the meaning assigned to *Lithry* by Dr Jamieson, though he does not express the same opinion of the origin of the word as I have ventured to give. "In came sic a rangel n' gentles," says an old Scottish writer quoted by the learned etymologist, "and a *tithry o' hanyiel slyps* at their tail, that in a weaven the house wis gaen like Lawren fair." *Hanyiel*, says Dr Jamieson, denotes something in a *dangling* and *dependent state*, and *slyps*, (from Tuet. *slepp*), a train or retinue. *Lithry* or livery, is, therefore, suitably associated with this expression. There is an excellent description in Mr Douce's Illustrations of Shakespeare, of the antient English Serving-men in livery, whose characters are well enough expressed by the Scottish idea of a *Lithry*.

are so well related by early authors; and that there was not one of these *broken men* that could not "rob a ripper of his fish,—cut off a convoy of butter,—or drive a regiment of geese afore him, and not a hiss heard, nor a wing of the troops disordered."* Lord Robert employed an armed retinue of this description, who were dispersed over the islands, to guard all the common ferries, for the purpose of preventing complaints against his exactions reaching the Government of Scotland: in the mean time, he committed what depredations he pleased,—making illegal exactions of rent, and (in the phraseology of the time) *gripping lands* from the udallers; until, at length, a petition reached the royal ear, stating, "That the inhabitants were so *oppressit be companies of suddartis and others broken men, dependers upon Lord Robert Steuart, that they were all utterly wrakit and hereit for ever.*" Lord Robert was then recalled from the islands, but was soon after reinstated in his possessions, with the title of an Earl; "when," says a worthy prelate, "he found out ane uther way to doe his turne. He became Bischope *in omnibus*, and set his rentall of teynds upon these Vdellands, above the availe [value], yea triple above the availe." At the same time, all mortifications and penances for crimes, under the cognizance of the Church, consisted in loss of land; and thus, as Bishop Grahame has added, " the Earl's lands grew daily, as adulteries and incests increased in the country:"† - for these oppressions he had frequently his grant taken from him, but had always interest enough at Court to get it returned.—His Lordship built a palace at Birsay in Orkney, which was remarkable for nothing so much as the whimsical mottoes which adorned its walls. One was "Sic fuit, est, et erit," which the pious men of the time construed as blasphemous; but this is perhaps a mistake; the Earl might have meant nothing more in the expression than an allusion to the unchangeable nature of his moral habits:— *Sic fuit, est, et erit;* that is, A man such as he always was, such is he now, and such he ever will be. Another of the Birsay mottoes is said to have highly displeased the Monarch of Scotland. " When we entered the palace gate," said Brand, the Missionary, about the year 1700, " we saw above it that inscription so much talk'd of, and reputed treasonable by King James VI.:—'*Robertus Stuartus*, filius Jacobi Quinti *Rex* Scotorum, hoc ædificium instruxit:' which inscription could not but offend the lawful heir of the Crown; for it cannot well be thought, that the Earl and all about him, were such blunderers in the Latin tongue, as to put down *Rex* instead of *Regis*, if there had been no design in it."‡ The simple Missionary seems to have erred in his conjecture. A grammatical knowledge of Latin was by no means the indispensable acquirement of a courtier of the 16th century, even though he should have been created the merry Abbot of Holyrood. The Earl died at an advanced age, and though he was not sainted by the udallers of Orkney and Shetland, yet he was at least respected by his own posterity; for when, in thirty years afterwards, an irreverend churl had erected his pew in the Cathedral of Kirkwall, immediately over Robert Stuart's revered remains, he was formally and publicly admonished by the Lord Bishop of Orkney, "not to incur the indignation of such noblemen as the Earl of Carrick, and others

---

* See the qualifications of the *broken men* of England in Beaumont and Fletcher's Beggar's Bush, Act v, Scene 1st.
† Peterkin's Ancient Rentals of Orkney, No. iii. p. 21.
‡ Brand's Description of Orkney, p. 31.

of the worthy name of Stuart ; for it would come to his Majestie's ears how such persone did sit there and trample upon his Hienes' graund-uncle's bellie."*—Such were the eventful features in the annals of Robert Stuart, once Abbot of Holyrood, afterwards a Protestant reformer, but whose latest amusements of life were concentrated in the act of monopolizing all the lands of Orkney and Shetland, whether they belonged to the Crown, the Church, or the unfortunate Udallers.

After loitering a few moments near the ancient mansion of Earl Robert, his virtues not inspiring any extraordinary sensation for the walls associated with his memory, I ascended the adjoining promontory of Sumburgh,—a headland of considerable extent, the easterly side of which having yielded considerably to the ocean, is formed into a steep precipice. It is proposed upon this tongue of land to erect, without delay, a stately pharos, the accomplishment of which is assigned to Mr Stevenson, whose execution of the Bell-Rock Lighthouse is a monument of skill so honourable to the architecture of Scotland.† It is to be hoped that other beacons, equally required on the north and west of the coast, may render these islands no longer the terror of the northern mariner, who, fearing to be benighted near their destructive cliffs, chuses to brave the elements of the open sea, rather than make the still more perilous attempt to steer for the security which the numerous harbours of Shetland are well calculated to afford. But the time is probably not very remote, when it may be said of this country as of other parts of Britain,

"——————————— Lo ! ports expand
Free as the winds and waves their sheltering arms,
Lo ! streaming comfort o'er the troubled deep,
On every pointed coast the light-house towers."
THOMSON.

From Sumburgh Head we have a view of what is named the *Roust*,—this being a term of Scandinavian origin, used to signify a strong tumultuous current, occasioned by the meeting of rapid tides.‡ The sea being calm, there was the appearance of a turbulent stream of tide, about two or three miles broad, in the midst of smooth water, extending a short distance from Sumburgh, and then gradually dwindling away, so as to terminate in a long slender dark line, bearing towards Fair Isle. The explanation of this appearance is, perhaps, to be given in connection with that wave of tide propagated from the great diurnal undulation of the Atlantic, which, in the progress of completing its circuit round Britain, is described by naturalists as passing to the west of Orkney,—from thence to the north of the British Isles, and then taking a southerly direction, so as to form a ridge that extends between Buchan and the Naze of Norway.§ The tides of Shetland appear to be induced by lesser currents, generated during the progress of the wave along the westerly,

---

* Peterkin's Collections, Append. p. 53.
† Sumburgh Head Light-house has been completed since I visited Shetland. A short description of it will be found in Note 7 to the present Iter.
‡ Isl. *roest, raust*, æstuaria, vortices maris, Verel, Ind. Supposed by one author to be synonimous with the A. S. *ræs*, stridor, impetus fluvii.—See Jamieson's Etym. Dict. word *roust*.
§ See Playfair's Outlines of Natural Philosophy, vol. ii. p. 338., and Young's Lectures on Natural Philosophy, vol. i.

northerly, and easterly parts of the country, and these set in nearly an hour sooner on the west than on the east coast of these islands. At the beginning of the flood, the tide in the Roust is directed to the eastward, until it passes the promontory of Sumburgh; it then meets with a south tide, that has been flowing on the east side of the country; when a divergement takes place to the south-east, and lastly to the south. At high-water there is a short cessation of the tide called the Still ; the ebb now begins, first setting north-west and then north, until the recommencement of the flood. The various directions of the tides of Shetland are no doubt owing in a considerable degree to modifications which take place from the number and form of the various headlands and inlets of the coast ; but since they are propagated at successive intervals of time, it is evident that at the northerly and southerly extremities of the Shetland Archipelago, they would be naturally opposed to each other. A gentleman informed me that he has been for five days becalmed in a sloop between Fitful Head and Sumburgh Head, which are only distant from each other about three miles, without being able to pass either point ; one current carrying the vessel into the eastern, and the other into the western ocean : the sloop was often transported by the tide very near the shore, yet another tide always carried her off again.* But although there is an opposition of currents from Sumburgh to Fair Isle, and no doubt from thence to Orkney, the Roust is that part of the stream lying at a small distance from the promontory, the force of which is probably encreased by its proximity to the coast, and by the shallowness of the water. Here there is always a heavy sea, but in a storm the waves are said to rise mountains high. Drayton has given a good description of the occurrence of similar phenomena at the Race of Portland, not however unmixed with a tolerable proportion of poetic bathos :

> " Some coming from the east, some from the setting sun,
> The liquid mountains still together mainly run,
> Wave woundeth wave again, and billow billow gores,
> And topsy-turvy so fly tumbling to the shores."

In the Roust of Sumburgh there is a considerable fishery for the Gadus carbonarius, or coal-fish, the fry of which, named Sillocks, have been already described as entering the bays in myriads. The Gadus carbonarius is known in Shetland by the name of Seethe, although in Feroe and Norway this appellation is given to the full grown Gadus virens. Naturalists have described the coal-fish as being of a very dark or black colour,—hence its name ; but this term is ill applied to those specimens of the fish that I saw in Shetland, which were rather of a lightish brown. The white lateral line with which the fish is marked, has been properly considered as a very distinctive character. The coal-fish, or Shetland seethe, is of a large size, and is said sometimes to attain the length of three feet. It is correctly represented as of an elegant shape, with a small head, sharpened snout, and a lower jaw exceeding the upper in length. I have tasted the fish in a fresh state, but it was dry and coarse. It is, however, cured for sale, and is then sent to a Scotch market,

---

* I am indebted for my information on the direction of the tides at Sumburgh to the kindness of William Henderson, Esq. of Bardister, in Shetland.

where it sells much cheaper than cod or ling. Coal-fish are general frequenters of tideways, but the Roust of Sumburgh offers for them attractions of no common kind ; there they are found in great numbers, being sometimes seen sporting near the surface of the water, whilst, in quest of them, the dauntless Shetlander launches his light skiff among the white waves of contending tides, and, by means of handlines baited with haddock or shell fish, rarely returns without a plenteous freight.

When on the heights of Sumburgh, I omitted to walk round the whole of the head-lands, and, therefore, missed the opportunity of seeing a fortification that appears to have attracted the particular attention of Mr Low, the author of the Fauna Orcadensis. He has described it as a neck of land protected by a ditch and strong wall, at the entrance of which is the foundation of a large structure, that he supposes may have served as a guard-room ; he has also stated, that along the wall, and at some little distance from it, are to be found the marks of numerous small buildings. This defence was supposed to be constructed for the purpose of containing cattle and provisions : not improbably it was the work of the western Highlanders, who, in their predatory excursions to Shetland, are said to have rendered the vicinity of Quendal Bay the great repository of the plunder that they were enabled to levy. In fortifications like those of Sumburgh and Fitfiel Head a considerable booty of cattle, corn, or other provisions, might have been preserved and allowed to accumulate, until a freight had been collected : sufficient to repay the Highlanders for the trouble of their summer's trip.

After descending the promontory, I again passed over the Links of Sumburgh, which have long been commemorated in the traditions of the country, from being the site of an engagement that took place between the Shetlanders and some Western Highlanders. This feud was of a very ancient date. In the 9th century, the Western Isles, which had been originally occupied by a Celtic race, were subdued by Harold Harfagre, and formed into a Norwegian province. But by the arrival of a number of Gaelic colonists from Ireland, the Scandinavian natives were gradually ousted out of the territory which they had acquired, being obliged to occupy the most westerly confines of the coast. In the middle of the 13th century, Scotland was invaded by Haco, King of Norway, on which occasion detachments of these Norwegians were left in the Hebrides, for the purpose of keeping the Western Highlanders in awe. The party that was sent to the Isle of Lewis becoming troublesome, a plan was laid for cutting them off. The lord of the island summoned his attendants, and ordered the Croishtarich* to be constructed, the ritual fire to be lighted, and a goat to be brought forth and slain. The extremities of a wooden cross were then kindled in the flame, and, whilst the blood of the victim followed the knife, they were extinguished in the purple stream. The chief now delivered this emblem of fire and sword to a swift messenger, with the laconic mandate, " Marbhadh ghach shen a bhuana," (let each kill his guest). The nimble footman entrusted with the fire-cross, flew with it to the inhabitant of the next hamlet ;—the receiver heard it announced as the cross of shame, disregarded by none but the

---

* The word *Croishtarich* is said to be derived from Crois, a *cross*, and tarn, a *multitude*, expressive of a *popular signal* ; but this is a very unsatisfactory explanation of the term.—I need not remark how sublimely the great Scottish bard of modern days has explained the use of the croishtarich in his poem of the Lady of the Lake.

infamous; he bowed to the chief's command,—flew to dispatch his guest, and having imbrued himself in Norwegian blood, bore the signal to the next habitation, where a similiar scene of assassination was repeated,—and thus as fast as the message went round from house to house, each Northman was in succession cut off. Haco, King of Norway, was at that time defeated by the Scots at the battle of Largs in Ayrshire, and dying soon afterwards, the treachery of the Lewis men remained unrevenged; his successor contenting himself with the surrender of the Western Isles to the Scots for a pecuniary consideration, but with the stipulation that the ancient Scandinavian inhabitants should be protected in their return to the mother-country with all their effects. Long after this period, the name of the Norwegian became hateful to the Gael; and notwithstanding the Scandinavian colony of Orkney and Shetland was under the protection of Scotland, the natives of Lewis gratified their animosity by annually visiting this province for the sake of plunder. Upon landing in Shetland, they are said to have constructed some sort of inclosures on the steep banks of the coast, for the purpose of holding cattle and other plunder, preparatory for embarkation. Two fortresses well adapted for this purpose, appear on the south shores of Dunrossness; but at the Ness of Skeld, in the parish of Sandsting, there is the vestige of an inclosure to be seen, which is distinctly ascribed to these marauders. The Lewismen are affirmed to have had many battles with the Shetlanders, the last of which was with one of the Sinclairs of Brow, who is said to have marshalled the men of Dunrossness in goodly array on the plains of Sumburgh, and to have resolutely opposed the landing of the Highlanders. A severe engagement ensued, of which no particulars are handed down, except that it had so sanguine a character, as perhaps to have rivalled the best got-up skirmish of the times:

> "Then limbs like boughs were lopp'd, from shoulders arms to fly;
> They fight as none could scape, yet scape as none could die.
> The ruffling northern lads and the stout [Lew'smen] try'd it;
> Then head-pieces hold out, or brains must sore abide it."
>
> DRAYTON.

Not a Lewisman is said to have returned, who might report the fate of his companions. The Highlanders were rudely buried on the Links of Sumburgh, and tumuli of sand raised on their remains. Several of these, about half a century ago, were removed during the devastations of the blowing sand, when heaps of bones were discovered thrown indiscriminately together*.

Quitting the Links of Sumburgh, I again entered upon the sandy tracts of Dunrossness, where vast accumulations of sand, referable, perhaps, to some violent action of the sea, occassionally make their appearance, indicating, that from this cause the form of the coast may have undergone material successive changes. This suspicion is confirmed by the circumstance, that in the year 1778 Mr Low dug up, at some little distance from the water,

---

* Two of these tumuli were opened in the year 1778, by Mr Low of Orkney. In one of them, among the bones, which were laid without any order, he counted nine skulls. In concluding this account of the fray in Dunrossness, I may remark, that the traditional narration of the assassination of the Nurwegians in the Isle of Lewis, may be found in the 1st volume of the Transactions of the Scottish Antiquaries. This account I have connected with the Shetland tradition of the predatory visits of the Lewismen; for the particulars of which I am indebted to Mr Henderson of Bardister.

a number of cockle and limpet shells, which appeared to be arranged in the form of a regular stratum. Along with these were oysters, many of which were no less than nine or ten inches in diameter; and in some of them the pearls remained. This naturalist has supposed that these remains were fossil, as no shell-fish of this sort were to be found alive within twenty miles of the place. But since no forms were discovered among them that could not be referred to the present inhabitants of the sea, this opinion has little weight. Mr Brand, however, the zealous missionary to Shetland, had a century ago a much more wonderful story to tell about the shell-fish buried in the vicinity of Sumburgh; as that a gentleman in the parish of Dunrossness told one of the ministers of this country, who told the credulous traveller, that a plough in this parish did cast up fresh cockles, though the place where the plough was going was three quarters of a mile from the sea; which cockles the gentleman saw made ready and eaten. Brand then adds, "that if only shells were found, such as oysters and the like, the marvel would not be great, seeing such are found upon the tops of high mountains, at a greater distance from the sea, which, in all probability, have lain since the universal deluge; but that any shell-fish should be found at a distance from sea, and fit for use, is somewhat wonderful and astonishing." It is so indeed! and it is unfortunate that no more of these antediluvian cockles should remain in an edible state. A dish of them would make a delightful geognostic treat, and would prove that the worlds of modern cosmogonists are not unreal mockeries.

SUMBURGH TO SANDWICK.

Having now lingered a sufficient time at Sumburgh, being warned to depart by the declining sun, I retraced my steps over the toiling sands of Brow, and reached the house of my kind entertainer at the close of the evening. The morrow was a halcyon day; scarcely a ripple was seen on the surface of Quendal Bay. The sandy plain of Brow strongly reflecting the sun's rays, communicated an uneasy sensation to the vision, which was agreeably alleviated when the eyes turned from the sight of this glittering waste, to repose upon the contiguous green blades of rising corn that were repaying the toil and ingenuity which had rescued a portion of glebe from the devastation of the sand-flood. As the cool of the evening approached, I was induced to take a final leave of the hospitable shores of Dunrossness. Pursuing, then, a route along the eastern side of the parish, over secondary rocks of sandstone, the dreariness of the road in proceeding northward could not well be exceeded. After passing Lamigard Voe, there is nothing for several miles to vary the uniform and dull scenery of the journey. To the right is the wide ocean that separates Shetland from the shores of Norway, bounded by low, ragged cliffs, over which a wild surf continually breaks. On the west is the brown ridge of the Cliff Hills,—beneath which are trackless moors, diversified by no object except the stony land-marks that once separated the little patrimonial possessions of the ancient udaller,—except the ruins of huts, indicative of the desertion of these wild tracts, when, by the poverty of the harassed natives, their inheritances were ceded to some wealthier settler in the islands. At length some cottages appeared, contiguous to an open harbour, resorted to about fifty years ago by the Dutch busses, whilst waiting for St John's day, the commencement of the herring-fishery. At the head of the bay was Channerwick, which I reached about dusk. Several huts were scattered about on its shores ; and as it was on the Sabbath, not a native was absent from the hamlet. The women were attired in the ordinary garb of the country, which consisted of dark woollen stuffs ; but the men were dressed like sailors on a holiday, wearing along with their trowsers neat blue short jackets. The country altogether resembled the good piratical days of King Regner Lodbrog of Denmark, when his subjects were more numerous on sea than on land, when they wore nothing but the habits of sailors, and were ready to embark on the first opportunity. I had intended to have reached a small house at some distance, where an accommodation, though humble, could be procured ; but the mists of the night were fast approaching, and I gladly availed myself of the shelter generously offered me for the night by the schoolmaster of Sandwick.—We were now within a mile or two of the Burgh of Mousa,—the most perfect specimen extant in Scotland of an ancient Scandinavian fortress, the interest of which may perhaps be heightened by a knowledge of the description of warlike weapons that are often found in the immediate vicinity of structures of this kind. This preliminary information is the more necessary, since it is to the form and nature of such instruments, that the construction of the Burgh as a defence must necessarily refer.

ANCIENT WEAPONS OF WAR DISCOVERED IN SHETLAND.

The ancient weapons of war discovered in Shetland are of stone. That such were used by the Teutonic tribes of Europe in the 8th century, and probably very long before, is evident from the fragment of a prose-romance written about that period, in the Saxon dialect of the Teutonic. This manuscript, which is preserved in Cassel, was first printed in Eccardi, Comment. de Rubus Franciæ Orientalis, and it has been reprinted with a Latin and English translation, in an interesting work lately published in Edinburgh, entitled, "Illustrations of Northern Antiquities."* From this very curious document, two or three disjoined passages may be given, by which we may see the reference that is made to the Teutonic Burgh, and to the arms contemporary with this early kind of fortress :—

"I heard it related that Hiltibrant and Hatubrant with one mind agreed to go on a warlike expedition. The relatives [sons of the same father] made ready their horses, prepared their war-shirts, [shirts of mail], girded on their swords [which were fastened] at the hilt with chains.
——————— "well give now, [turn thou this to good,] wielding God, quoth Hiltibrant, whose word is done. I wandered summers and winters sixty out of [my] land ; there they detached me among shooting people [archers] ; never in any burgh [city, castle] fastened they my legs : [but] now my nearest relation will hew my neck with his bill [battle-axe] or I entangle his legs, [tie him as a captive].
——————— "said Hiltibrant,—Good fellow-citizens, be judges who it be that

---
* By Henry Weber and R. Jamieson, Esquires.

this day must quit the field of battle, or who will have both these brunies [hauberks] in his possession.
"Then they first let ashen [spears] fly with rapid force, that they stuck in the shields. Then they thrust together resounding stone-axes; they wrathfully heaved white shields."
—*Illustrations of Northern Antiquities*, p. 218, 230.

These extracts from a composition of so remote a date as the 8th century, may be considered as illustrative of the general mode of warfare adopted at that time by the Saxon and Scandinavian tribes of Europe, among whom a greater similiarity of language and manners then prevailed than was to be found at a later period. We learn from the same authority that the offensive arms of the Teutones were at that early period, (1st), The battle-axe; (2dly), Ashen or spears; (3dly), Bows and arrows; (4thly), Swords fastened at the hilts with chains. The defensive arms were, (1st), Shirts of mail, or war-shirts; (2dly), Brunies or hauberks; (3dly), Shields. We lastly find, that special mention is made of the early Teutonic fortress or Burgh.

1st, *Offensive Arms.*

The first of the offensive arms of the Teutones of the 8th century, was the Battle-Axe. It appears that these axes were constructed of stone. The heroes of the Teutonic romance are said to have "thrust together resounding stone-axes;" these weapons being expressed in the original by the term Stainbort, from stein, a *stone*, and barte or barde, an *axe*. In Shetland, numbers of stone-axes have been discovered, which were wrought from a remarkalby compact green porphyry, probably derived from Scandinavia.* In form, the Shetland Steinbarte† or stone-axe admits of two varieties; it is either (a.) Single; or (b.) Double-edged.

(a.) *Single-edged Steinbarte.*—This variety of blade has one cutting-edge, generally of a semilunar outline, and tapering from opposite points to a blunted extremity or heel. In some specimens both sides are convex; in others, one side only, the other being flattened. All the edges except the broad sharpened margin are bluntly rounded off. The single-edged stone-axes of Shetland vary much in their dimensions, being from four to eight or ten inches in length; their breadth proportionally differing. When the Shetland Steinbarte was used in war, its blunt tapering extremity may be supposed to have been introduced within the perforation made into some wooden or bone haft, and afterwards secured by overlapping cords, formed of thongs of leather, or of the entrails of some animal; twine of hemp not being then in use.‡ Another kind of steinbarte has been said to occur in Shetland, the sharp edge of which describes the segment of a circle, whilst the chord of the outline is thickened like the back of a knife. Probably its blunt edge was fixed within the groove of

---

* The stone contains, along with quartz, a considerable portion of felspar in its composition, and probably some little magnesian earth; it much resembles a rock that I have seen associated with serpentine, as well as a substance that is used in the construction of some of the stone hatchets of the South Sea islands.

† I shall venture to give the name of *Steinbarte* to these remains of antiquity.

‡ A representation of the single-edged Steinbarte, mounted after the manner I have supposed it was, may be seen in Fig. 3 of the Plate of Antiquities in the Appendix. The length of the blade is 6 inches; greatest breadth 2½, and greatest thickness 1 inch.

a wooden or bone handle, so as to form a single-edged cutting instrument.*

(b.) *Double-edged Steinbarte.*—The blade of this instrument is a stone completely flattened on each of its sides, and not more than the tenth of an inch thick; it is of an oblong shape, having one blunted margin perfectly straight, and when the stone is held in such a position that the dull edge is the uppermost, we have the form of a blade presented, in which the two narrow edges are irregularly rounded off at their angles, so that one edge is much broader than the other. Every part of the margin but that which constitutes the summit of the outline, is sharpened; by which means there is a great addition made to the extent of the cutting-edge. The blade is 5½ inches long, and from 3 to 4 broad. Mallet, in his History of Denmark, describes a battle-axe of two edges, as used by the ancient Scandinavians, and he adds, that when it was fixed to a long pole, it constituted a halbert. In reference to this observation, I have supposed a long staff, with the extremity so penetrated at one or two inches from the summit, as to form a long groove 4 inches in length, through which the stone blade, with the blunt side kept uppermost, may be drawn half way, and then secured to its station by means of cross ligatures. The whole would then present the form of a two-edged battle-axe. Antiquaries have remarked, that this weapon was probably in use from the earliest period, but since it was in the course of time wielded by the Trabants, or those who stood upon guard in the castles of their Kings, it was named a Halbert, from the Teutonic *Halle*, a court, and *Barde*, an axe.† In the true spirit, therefore, of archaiological reasoning, it may be pronounced, that the blade of this variety of the Shetland steinbarte, and the hypothetical handle to which it is fastened, constitute the aboriginal rude form of the northern halbert.‡

The blades of steinbartes are very abundantly found in Shetland. Not unfrequently several of them are discovered buried together, thus indicating a little armoury, from which a number of weapons might be distributed on an emergency, by the hand of some chief, to a small band of natives met together on the alarm of common danger. Assemblages of these weapons have been found in the parishes of Walls, of Delting, and in the Island of Unst.§ In Northmavine, says Mr Low of Orkney, seven were discovered under ground, disposed in a circular arrangement, with the points of each directed towards the centre of the ring;—it is a pity that the number of these weapons was not nine, corresponding to the nine wounds of a lance in the form of a circle, which the deified Scandinavian hero Odin gave himself, when, by an act of suicide, he shewed an example of death to his surrounding followers. At any rate, the circular arrangement of the weapons remains, indicative of a mystical allusion, and that is quite sufficient to provoke an antiquarian inference.

Regarding the people by whom these stone axes were used, the natives of Shetland

---

* The blade is represented in the Plate of Antiquities given in the Appendix, Fig. 4, from an original drawing by Mr Low, the author of the Fauna Orcadensis. This gentleman supposes it to be a knife.
† Mallet's Northern Antiq., vol. i., p. 239.
‡ The relic of antiquity which is supposed to be a two-edged steinbarte, was found in the parish of Walls in Shetland, and kindly presented to me by Mr Robinson of Vailey. See Plate of Antiq. Appen. Fig. 5. I possess a drawing, by Mr Low, of a similar instrument.
§ Mr Low of Orkney says, that a deposit of twenty-four in one place was found. The late Mr Archibald, a respectable minister of Unst, has stated, in a communication to Mr Low, that eight of these weapons were discovered together in this island. That more considerable assemblages have been found in other places, I have the assurance of some gentlemen in Shetland.

have not the least tradition, and this circumstance is a proof of their great antiquity. They are supposed to have dropped from the clouds, endowed with the power of protecting the houses in which they are preserved from the effects of thunder; hence they are commonly named Thunder-bolts.

The second description of weapons cited in the Fragment of Eccard's Teutonic Romance of the eighth century, was Ashen or Spears. The extremities of these, which are formed of stone, have been found in Shetland, although rarely. They are about four inches long, containing a groove for the adaptation of a wooden shaft.*

The third kind of weapons used in the eighth century, consisted of bows and arrows. The flint heads of arrows are frequently found in Orkney, indicating that the plains of this country were frequently sites on which battles with the Scotch were fought. But I am not prepared to say if such relics ought to be enumerated among the vestiges of the ancient armoury of Shetland. These arrow-heads are described as having a point of a lozenge-shape, one end more obtuse and shorter than the other, indicating that it was inserted in the wood of the shaft, and that the union was completed by the security of a ligature. Mr Pennant has properly remarked, on the origin of such rude weapons as these, that they must be referred to the earliest inhabitants, at a period in which they were on a level with the natives of the newly discovered South Sea Islands.

The fourth weapon of attack of the eighth century was the sword, no specimen of which has probably yet been found in Shetland.† The northern sword or *swerd* was short, and frequently crooked like a scymitar, hanging to a little belt, which passed over the right shoulder. Sometimes a very long sword was used, which went by the name of Spad or Spada.

Such is the enumeration of the most ancient offensive weapons of the Northmen: slings and clubs stuck round with sharp instruments were also used.

2d, *Defensive Arms.*

In the second place, respecting the defensive arms mentioned in the Teutonic Romance, little may be said; none of them having been yet discovered in Shetland. There is the war-shirt or shirt of mail, and the brunie or hauberk, which, as Monsieur Mallet has remarked, were only for such as were able to procure them. Casques or helmets made of leather, were worn by private soldiers, but those of the officers were frequently of iron or of gilded brass. The shield was of an oval form, usually constructed of wood, bark, or leather‡ ; but that which was worn by warriors of distinction, was frequently of iron or brass variously ornamented: it was also made long, and was used for a protection against arrows,

---

* For the representation of a stone spear-head that was found in the island of Foula by the late Mr Low, see Plate of Antiq in Appen. Fig. 6.

† An ancient weapon was found in the parish of Northmavine, which I have not seen, but it was pronounced to be a Roman Pugio.

‡ A beautiful engraving of the ancient Scandinavian shield, is given in a curious work entitled the Musæum Wormianum, p. 370.

darts, and stones; it is said to have even served the use of a tent, so as to afford a kind of shelter for the night, and when many of such bucklers were locked together in the form of a circle, they constituted a rampart.

It may be, lastly, observed, that there is an allusion in the Teutonic Romance to the defensive Burgh, of which a noble specimen, probably built antecedent to the eighth century, is next to be considered.*

BURGH OF MOUSA.

I passed along the shore of the open bay of Sandwick, which has been the grave of many seamen, who, by mistaking it for Bressay Harbour, have suffered all the horrors of shipwreck upon its exposed shores. In crossing a headland to the east of the Inlet, a small low island, named Mousa, separated from the Mainland by a narrow strait, first rises to view: this spot is little diversified with hill and dale; it contains one good house with out-buildings and cottages. But the most conspicuous object that lines its shores is the Burgh of Mousa, a circular building, which, if it did but taper towards its summit, would present no unapt similitude of a modern glass-house. This ancient fortress stands close to the water's edge; by crossing, therefore, in a boat, a narrow channel, little more than half a mile in breadth, we are landed immediately under its walls.

The Burgh of Mousa occupies a circular site of ground, somewhat more than fifty feet in diameter, being constructed of middle sized schistose stones of a tolerable uniform magnitude, well laid together, without the intervention of any cement. This very simple round edifice attains the elevation of 42 feet; it swells out, or bulges from its foundation, and draws smaller as it approaches the top, when it is again cast out from its lesser diameter; which singularity of construction is intended to obviate the possibility of scaling the walls. The door that leads to the open area contained within the structure, is a small narrow passage, so low that an entrance is only to be accomplished by crawling upon the hands and knees; and in creeping through it, the wall appears of the great thickness of 15 feet, naturally leading to the suspicion of a vacuity within. On arriving at the open circular area included within this mural shell, I found the diameter of the space to be about 21 feet. On that part of the wall within the court, which is nearly opposite to the entrance, the attention is excited by a number of small apertures resembling the holes of a pigeon house. There are three or four vertical rows of them, having each an unequal proportion of openings, varying from eight to eighteen in number. It was now evident that the mural shell of the structure was hollow, and that it contained chambers, to which these holes imparted a feeble supply of light and air. Beneath the whole, at a distance from the ground, there is a door that leads to a winding flight of stone steps, of the width of 3 feet, which communicates with all these apartments; I then discovered that the shell of the Burgh was composed of two concentric walls, each of about 4½ to 5 feet in breadth, and

---

* For additional remarks on the Ancient Weapons of Shetland, see Note 8.

that a space of nearly a similar dimension was devoted to the construction of the inner apartments. In ascending these steps, which wound gradually to the top of the wall, I observed that they communicated at regular intervals with many chambers or galleries, one above another, that went round the building. These were severally of such a height, that it was possible to walk within them nearly upright. The roof of the lowest chamber was the floor of the second, and after this manner seven tiers were raised. On reaching the highest step of the flight of stairs, there appeared no reason for supposing that any roof had ever protected the summit of the building, so that the Burgh of Mousa must have been originally nothing more than a circular mural shell, open to the top. The height of the inside wall was 35 feet, being 7 feet less than that of the outside ; this difference was partly owing to the accumulation of stones and earth, which had filled the inner court.

The mode was now evident in which this Burgh had been intended to give security to the persons and property of the ancient inhabitants of Shetland against the sudden landing of predatory adventurers. The tiers of apartments contained within the thick walls would afford a shelter to women and children from the missile weapons of assaulters, besides being repositaries for grain and other kinds of property, as well as for the stores whereby a long siege might be sustained. The low narrow door within the court, which admits of no entrance but in a creeping posture, might be easily secured at a short notice by large blocks of stone. It has been remarked of the rude forts similar to these which occur on the shores of Scandinavia, that they were seldom taken by an enemy, unless by surprise, or after a long blockade : that frequently terraces and artificial banks were raised near that side of the wall, which was the lowest, and that the besieged were then annoyed with arrows, stones, boiling-water, or melted pitch, being thrown into the fort ;— offensive weapons which they did not neglect to return.* The history of the Burgh of Mousa confirms the correctness of this observation ; its high walls bulging out from their foundation, defied any attempt to scale them ; for, when they were encompassed by one of the Earls of Orkney, he had no hopes of inducing the fortress to surrender, but by cutting off all supplies of food, and then waiting the event of a long siege. Altogether the building was well adapted for resisting the attacks of the ancient piratical hordes of these seas, who, from the short summers of Northern latitudes, and from the incapability of their vessels to sustain a winter's navigation, durst not allow themselves to be detained on the coast by any tedious operations of assault.

Before quitting the Burgh of Mousa, I endeavoured to explore some of the chambers belonging to it, but owing to the ruined state of the floors, the attempt was too hazardous. A lively historian has remarked, that in Scandinavia, such recesses were often devoted in days of yore to the security of young damsels of distinction, who were never safe while so many bold warriors were rambling up and down in quest of adventures. It is also surmised, that galleries like these which ran winding around the walls, were, from the direction which they took, not unfrequently distinguished by the name of Serpents or Dragons ; and hence the many allegorical romaunts that were coined concerning princesses of great beauty being guarded by such monsters. It is unlucky, however, for the historical interest

---

* Mallet's Northern Antiquities, vol. i., p. 244.

of the Dragon-fortress of Mousa, that within the dismal serpentine windings of its apartments, was confined a damsel past her prime of life, and as well entitled to be "shrined for her brittleness," as any of the frail ladies worthie of antiquity.* In the fourteenth century, when, by the rights of udal succession, there were joint Earls of Orkney, Dame Margareta, the widowed-mother of one of them, listened to the lawless importunity of the gay Brunnius. Harold, her son, became impatient of the family disgrace, and banished from the islands his mother's paramour, as well as the illegitimate offspring that were the fruits of the connection. But, in the course of a short time, Dame Margareta's beauties attracted the notice of a more honourable suitor, who was no other than Harold's partner in the Earldom of Orkney and Shetland. Erlend profferred love to the Dame, which she returned, but as her son, from some cause, was averse to the nuptials, the parties entered into a tender engagement without his consent, and afterwards fled from his fury with all speed into Mousa. Then must Harold needs follow them, his hostile barks sailing in pursuit, as fast as if all the winds of heaven had driven them; and then, anon, fled the Dame Margareta and Erlend into the fort, within the dark recesses of which they nestled like two pigeons in a dove-cot. The Burgh was beset with troops, but so impregnable was its construction, that the assaulter found he had no chance of reducing it, but by cutting off all supplies of food, and by this means waiting the result of a tedious siege. And now turn we to the gentle pair in the fortress, that we may speak of what pain they must there endure, what cold, what hunger, and what thirst. In such a dog-hole,—"a conjurer's circle gives content above it; a hawk's mew is a princely palace to it."—But Harold had powerful foes in other places wherewith to contend, and, on this account, he gave heed to the advice of his friends, that Erlend should be retained as a friend and not as an enemy, and that he ought not to despise the new family alliance. A reconciliation took place, and, then, with great joy, returned the parties to their several pursuits, well satisfied with each other. Such is the story chronicled by Torfæus, concerning the siege of Moseyaburgum and the loves of Dame Margareta and Erlend, her last leman.†

On quitting the Burgh of Mousa, I felt no little regret at seeing the ruinous state to which some parts of it were reduced. The form of the low, narrow porch, which was nearly entire when Mr Low saw it about fifty years ago, was much impaired. Mr Stevenson, the engineer to the Northern Light-houses, in visiting Mousa, had laudably interceded with the proprietor for the preservation of the structure. But it can scarcely be expected, that an individual, who may feel little interest in such buildings, should launch out into any expence, with the view of gratifying occasional visitors to the islands. It is from some public fund that repairs of this kind ought to be defrayed; and certainly the integrity of the Burgh of Mousa deserves to be in Scotland of national interest, since a more perfect specimen of the earliest description of Teutonic fortresses does not perhaps exist in Europe.

---

* Mallet's Northern Antiquities, vol. i., p. 243. The story of King Regner Lodbrog's Slaughter of a Snake, has been supposed to imply that "he had surmounted the winding and misshapen wall of the fortress, in which a lovely virgin was confined." Sir Walter Scott properly considers this explanation as forced. See his Notes on Sir Tristrem, p. 295.

† See Torfæus's Rerum Orcad. Hist., p. 131.—For a Representation of the Burgh of Mousa, see Plate III., Fig. 2, and Plate of Antiquities in the Appendix.

I am inclined to date the erection of these holds to an early period, long previous to the arrival of Harold Harfagre. Eccard, indeed, in a specimen of a Teutonic romance of the 8th century, has shewn that they were common at that time; but from their simplicity of contrivance, it is not impossible but that their date might have been some centuries before, and that some of them in Shetland might have been thrown up by the Saxons, who peopled the Orcades and were defeated by Theodosius. The name which the Scots gave to these buildings of Pictish, is scarcely entitled to the smallest degree of notice. The appellation of Pictish Burghs, or, indeed, the notion that a race under the name of Picts, inhabited Orkney or Shetland at a remote period, is not attributable to Scandinavian Historians, who were best acquainted with the history of these islands, but to Scottish writers. The Scots appear, for several centuries, to have given the name of Pictish to every building, respecting the origin of which the tradition was lost: hence, a famous Roman Wall in Scotland was named Pictish. But as another burgh appeared on the opposite shores, though rising a few yards only above the surface of the ground, I deferred extending my speculations on the circumstances connected with the origin of these structures until I had made additional observations.

BURROLAND.

On sailing across a narrow channel to the Mainland, I arrived at Burroland, or the Land of the Burgh. This is a defence that seems to have been originally of greater extent than that of Mousa. The inside diameter of this circular fort is about 48 feet, and it is formed of concentric walls, each from 10 to 12 feet in width, between which are many chambers. The fort is situated on a point of rock near the sea, the land-side of which was originally defended by a stone rampart. Fifty years ago, Mr Low of Orkney detected, in a situation between the burgh and the extreme point of the rock, numbers of foundations of small houses, generally 14 feet long, and 6 or 8 wide, with a foot or two of the wall still standing. He supposed them to have been co-eval with the burgh itself, and to have formed a sort of huts, to which the inhabitants might fly upon any occasion of common danger, in order to be safe under the shelter of the burgh. It is, however, doubtful if this view be strictly correct. There is a greater probability that buildings not temporary but intended for constant occupation were erected near the burgh, and that originally there was no small number of inhabitants collected in any place, that were not provided with a fastness of this kind. The name of Burgh or Beorg at first implied nothing more than what is explained from the Saxon dialect;—*i.e.* a place of defence.* But from the circumstance that a beorg or fortress was an usual appendage to towns, is transmitted to us the name of Burgh, which, in more modern Saxon, stands for the town itself.†

---

* Bairgs, a Northern word, and the A. S. Beorg, burg, are explained mons, acervus, munimentum. Thus, the name of Burg would be given to the site of any rock naturally defended, or to any circular mound or embankment of earth and stones, or to any regular built structure like the Shetland Burgh.

† It has been properly remarked, that Burgh, as a modern Saxon term, signifies either a castle or market town.—*See* Whittaker's *Hist. of Manchester.*

The design of the burgh at length became evident. The imagination may easily figure to itself, on the site of Burroland or the vicinity of Mousa, the first rudiments of a fortified city. Instead of the stately collonades, the palaces, or the lofty fanes of some modern city, environed with regular bastions, curtains, ditches and out-works, we may fancy a few low huts, constructed from rude boulder stones, and protected by roofs of turf, dispersed in the vicinity of a small circular mural shell that forms the defence of this aboriginal garrison town. As the beacon of the hill streams with fire, and an alarm is given that an enemy is off the coast, the inhabitants fly to secure within the fort the property of their dwellings, and to prepare for a vigorous defence, whilst the interior of the walls affords an asylum for helpless women and children.

SANDLODGE.

A short walk of about a mile leads to Sandlodge, the seat of John Bruce, Esq. of Sumburgh. This is a well built white modern mansion, situated close to the shore, adjoining to which is a pavement strewed over with the produce of some veins that were wrought a few years ago. Hæmatites and bog iron-ore have made the road as black as Erebus, and caused it to resemble the vicinity of a smelting furnace. The mineralogist will find some amusement in examining the ores which lie in heaps near the old shafts; these have been by Mr Bruce judiciously preserved :—they present satisfactory indications of the contents of the vein, and may afford a criterion of the hopes to be entertained from any future prosecution of the mining operations of Sandlodge.*

It is now upwards of twenty years since a party of Welsh miners wrought these veins, but without advantage; some time afterwards, in the year 1802, another company undertook the working of them, who spent nine or ten thousand pounds in the undertaking, but were still unsuccessful. Brown hæmatite was a plentiful production of the vein, but copperpyrites constituted the object of search: at the surface it was found much mixed with hæmatite, but towards the bottom of the mine disseminated in sparry iron-stone. The scarcity of the ore, when found imbedded in this matrix, and the difficulty of working it, were stated to be the principal reasons for the abandonment of the undertaking. The copper-ore, after being washed and dressed, was sent to England, where the best sold for £70 per ton, and in the course of two years, 470 tons of copper-ore were exported from this mine to Swansea. Dr Fleming has remarked, that the captain of the mining party did not seem acquainted either with the composition or value of the sparry ironstone or hæmatite; that the persons who were appointed to conduct the work were ignorant of the art of working mines, and of the nature and value of the ores they met with; and that the mine appeared to deserve the attention of an enterprizing company, under the direction of an active and intelligent manager. The same gentleman has recommended, that the ore,

---

* The carbonates of copper obtained from the vein were uncommonly fine; they were in the form of capillary fibres, radiating from a centre. I was presented with a specimen of this ore by Mr Bruce, to whose polite attention to me when visiting this place I am much indebted.

instead of being exported, should be smelted near the mine.*

CONINGSBURGH.

From Sandlodge, I proceeded along the banks of an open inlet of the sea, commanded by the Cliff Hills, and, after passing by the ruins of an old kirk, came into the parish of Coningsburgh. The name given to this district was probably antecedent to the conquest of Shetland by Harold Harfagre, having had an allusion to some Saxon or Scandinavian leader, bearing the Teutonic title of Cyning, and to some burgh, as of Burroland or Mousa, calculated to afford, from its contiguity, a ready protection on the approach of an enemy. In course of time, as the term Burgh expressed a settlement or residence, the fortress being an essential part of it, the appellation of *Conigsburgh* would imply the residence of the chief.

After tracing the banks of the small voe of Aith, and losing sight of the mansion of Sandlodge, a dreary prospect ensued,—misty hills on the left, and, in perspective heaths without a shrub, relieved occasionally by groups of cottages, and surrounded with winding stone-dykes, that were intended to protect from the invasions of cattle, a few patches of lean and hungry earth, somewhat greener than the desart waste which appeared on every side. Nor is the hardy race of people named Coningsburghers, that inhabited this district, said to be less wild than the rugged soil from which they derived their support.† In their form we see few of the peculiarities of the Norwegian cast: they are less nimble and active than their neighbours, but they have a more muscular and robust form: they have a harsher set of features, resembling in this respect the Anglo-Saxons of the north of England, or of Lothian: they have also a dialect peculiar to themselves, that is more rough and guttural. A keen antiquary might amuse himself with the speculation, that this people are descended from the tribe of Saxons that invested the Orcadian seas so early as the fourth century in the days of Theodosius; that they are derived from the original race of warriors, to whom the erection of the burghs were in some part attributable, and that their district, in the name which it bears of Coningsburgh, may find a similar appellation in a town of the north of England contiguous to a Saxon burgh or fortress. But the Coningsburgher was, about half a century ago, distinguished by another peculiarity;—whatever social virtues he might evince to the inhabitants of his own district, he was to the natives of other parts of Shetland surly and inhospitable. The traveller who, in the close of evening, might be compelled to supplicate for a night's lodging, met with a chilling reception, and was awakened at the first dawn of day by a harsh-sounding warning to depart, expressed in the ancient Shetland language in a sort of formula:—This was, *Myrkin i litra ; lurein i liunga ; timin i guestin i geungna.* It is dark in the chimney, but it is light along the heath; it is now time for the stranger to be gone. "It thus became a

---

* I consider the information respecting these mines, during the period in which they were worked, as of such importance, that I am induced to give the report of them in Note 9 of the present Iter.

† "The people of this small spot," said Mr Low in the year 1778, "are a stout hardy race, by all accounts the wildest in Shetland."

custom," said Mr Low of Orkney, who has recorded this expression, "when any one wanted to dismiss a stranger from his house if he staid too long, to recite in Norse the Coningsburgher's phrase." The natives of this district are still proverbially quarrelsome with the inhabitants of other places; for, as I was informed at Lerwick, there is not a fracas that occurs in the town, in which a Coningsburgher is not prejudged to be a party. If the archæologist, therefore, can persuade himself that there is sufficient of the blunt, honest, quarrelsome disposition in this people to identify them with the early Saxons, he has only to go a step farther, and to make the feud between the Saxon Coningsburghers and the Norwegian inhabitants of Shetland, of as early a date as the arrival in the country of Harold Harfagre. "Art thou willing to sell thy coat," said Styrkar Stallarius, a Norwegian in the 11th century, "to an Anglo-Saxon churl?" "Not to thee," said the other, "for thou art perhaps a Norwegian." "And if I were a Norwegian," asked Styrkar, "what wouldst thou do to me?" "I would be disposed to kill thee," replied the boor.* It is, after all, not a little curious, that the Coningsburghers should have been traditionally regarded as a distinct race of people, since they are said to have formerly had many peculiarities among them, by which they were distinguished from the rest of their countrymen. Far be it, however, from me to speak of the hospitality of this people at the present day, but with the greatest respect. On arriving at Fladibister, where a quantity of limestone is burnt for the use of the Town of Lerwick, an offer of accommodation for the evening met me in the way; and from the honest, blunt natives of the place I received a true Saxon *Waes hael*.

FLADIBISTER TO SCALLOWAY.

From Fladibister to Quarf, the road leads for several miles over high banks much indented by the sea; these are formed of conglomerate rocks and sandstone, from beneath which occasionally appeared the outgoings of primitive strata. The prospect was now, if possible, more dreary than ever. The range of the Cliff Hills still continued to the left, and below were rocks with a mere uneven surface, which shewed themselves in naked patches that rose from damp moors and swamps. Such are the too frequent constitutents of Shetland scenery,—materials of description well adapted to the stanzas of some Northern Pastoral, where they may be conveniently mixed up with the sighs of a Shetland Damon:

> "O'er desert plains and rushy meers
> And wither'd heaths I rove;
> Where tree, nor spire, nor cot appears,
> I pass to meet my love."

After a dreary walk of a few miles, I arrived at Quarf, at which place, avoiding the road to Lerwick, I followed the course of a deep valley, that divided the ridge of the Cliff

---

* See this anecdote from Sturleson, in a paper by Dr Jamieson, in the Transactions of the Society of Antiquaries in Scotland, vol. ii., p. 279.

Hills in a transverse direction, so as to extend from sea to sea. This defile is a little more than a mile across, and it is rendered convenient for the transportation of goods by land, from one side of the coast to the other. Arriving at Western Quarf, there is a view of Cliff Sound, which is a channel of very uniform length that washes the base of the steep westerly side of the Cliff Hills, and is confined on the other side by the nearly parallel coasts of House and Trondra Islands. It runs parallel to the course of the strata in as straight a line as a canal; and if the banks on each side were but clothed with wood, nothing could well exceed the beauty of the scene. Taking, therefore, a boat, and sailing along the sound, there being few objects to enliven the view in this leafless desert, I passed the Island of Trondra, and approached the stately turreted walls of Scalloway Castle.

SCALLOWAY.

The first view of this town in sailing to it from the south, is exceedingly picturesque. We come in sight of a fine semicircular harbour, around the sweeping shores of which numerous cottages, of a better description than common, are grouped. A handsome modern white house, and extensive garden walls, enliven the head of the bay. Towering above the whole is the castellated mansion of Scalloway, built in the year 1600. It is a square formal structure, now reduced to a mere shell, composed of freestone brought from Orkney, and of the fashion of many houses of a similar date in Scotland; it is three storeys high, the windows being of a very ample size; on the summit of each angle of the building is a small handsome round turret. Entering the mansion by an insignificant door-way, over which are the remains of a Latin inscription, we pass by an excellent kitchen and vaulted cellars, whilst a broad flight of steps leads above to a spacious hall; the other chambers, however, are not large.

Patrick, Earl of Orkney, was the founder of this building. He succeeded to his father, Earl Robert, in the enjoyment of the estates of Orkney and Shetland about the year 1595, but he only came into the possession of the Church-lands in the year 1600. Spottiswoode gives this account of his character: "This Nobleman having undone his estate by riot and prodigality did seek by unlawful shifts, to repair the same, making acts in his court, and exacting penalties for the breach thereof, as, if any man was tried to have concealed any thing that might inferre a pecuniary mulct, and bring profit to the Earl, his lands and goods were declared confiscated; or, if any person did sue for justice before any other Judge than his deputies, his goods were escheated, or if they went forth of the isle without his license, or his deputie's, upon whatsoever occasion, they should forfeit their moveables: and, which of all his acts was held most inhumane, he had ordained, that if any man was tried to supply or give relief to ships, or any vessels distressed by tempest, the same should be punished in his person, and fined at the Earl his pleasure."*

About the year 1600, Earl Patrick commenced the erection of Scalloway castle; and it

---

* Spottiswoode's History of the Church of Scotland.

is scarcely possible to conceive of a more flagrant exercise of oppression than that which occurred during the execution of this structure. A tax was laid upon each parish in the country, obliging the Shetlanders to find as many men as were requisite for the building, as well as provisions for the workmen. The penalty for not fulfilling this requisition was forfeiture of property. The building was soon perfected; its turreted walls rising from the naked shores of Hialtland with all the feudal haughtiness of a regular baronial mansion,— appearing to mock the humble habitations of the ancient udallers. It was then that Mr Pitcairn, the minister of the parish of Northmavine in Shetland, said to be a pious and godly man, came to pay his respects to the lord of the new mansion. After the usual greetings, the Earl desired the minister to compose for him a verse, which might be put upon the frontispiece of his house. This was an occasion of which the minister availed himself, to lay before the founder of the new castle of Scalloway the sinful enormity of that overbearing oppression which had enforced its structure. The Earl's wrath was kindled, and in his rage he threatened the devout pastor with imprisonment: but afterwards coming to some composure of spirit, Mr Pitcairn said to him, "Well, if you will have a verse, I shall give you one from express words of Holy Scripture,—you will find that 'the wise man built his house upon a rock: and the rain descended, and the floods came, and the winds blew, and beat upon that house, and it fell not. But the foolish man built his house upon the sand; and the rain descended, and the floods came, and the winds blew, and beat upon that house, and it fell, and great was the fall of it.' What think you, then, of this inscription: *That house which is built upon a rock shall stand,—but built upon the sand it will fall!*" Strange to add, Earl Patrick heard with appearant composure the pious man's insinuation of the sort of foundation upon which his habitation was erected; but pretending not to receive the motto in its moral sense, he applied it to his building in such literal terms as might express his disregard of the prophetic words of Scripture;—for, with that happy effrontery which habituated guilt with ease assumes, he honoured the inscription with his approval, as denoting the reason why he had abandoned the house which he had possessed upon the sandy shores of Sumburgh: "My father's house was built upon the sand; its foundations are already giving way, and it will fall; but Scalloway castle is constructed upon a rock, and will stand." Mr Pitcairn was now required to convert the inscription, which in the spirit of zealous reproof he had proposed, into a suitable Latin distich, and this was immediately labelled on the lintel-stone of the gate:

PATRICIUS STEUARDUS, Orcadiæ et Zetlandiæ

COMES, I. V. R. S.

Cujus fundamen saxum est, Dom. illa manebit,

Labilis e contra, si sit arena perit.

A.D. 1600.

Many of these letters can be traced over the door of Scalloway castle at the present day.*

Although the imprisonment of Earl Patrick, and the forfeiture of his estate, seem to have followed a representation to the King of his abuses, yet the disgraceful termination of his career is suspected to have resulted from the plots laid to ensnare him by the Earl of Caithness. An ancestor of this Nobleman had, in the year 1529, invaded Orkney, with the illegal design of interposing himself between the King and the udallers, as the superior of the lands of the country, in which attempt he was secretly countenanced by the Crown; but being defeated and slain, an implacable enmity to Orkney, and to all who might sway that province, was perpetuated among the Sinclairs for several generations. On this account, the Earl of Caithness lost no opportunity to offer Earl Patrick every indignity which, among those who profess the principles of chivalry, could not pass unresented, but at the penalty of dishonour. Some of the Earl of Orkney's servants, whilst navigating the Pentland Firth, had been obliged to land in Caithness, on account of contrary winds and stormy weather. The Earl of Caithness, with insincere professions of hospitality, invited them all within his walls;—he treated them with the best cheer in his house;—encouraged their carousals until they had drunk themselves into a state of intoxication; he then ordered that one side of their beards, and one side of their heads should be shaved, and as soon as they shewed signs of returning sobriety, he forced them to again commit themselves to the storm which was unsubsided. "This was a cryme," said the genealogist of the Sutherland Family, "the lyk whereof I never heard or read of before; onely one example I doe remember: the servants of David, King of Israel, were so intreated by Hannum, King of the Children of Ammon. The Earle of Catteynes thus farr exceeded Hannum, that the Earle, not satisfied with what himself had done, he forced the Earle of Orknay his servants to take the sea in such a tempest, and exposed them to the extremitie of the rageing waves; whereas Hannum suffered King David his servants to depart home quietlie after he had abused them." These poor men are said to have escaped the storms of the Pentland Firth, which, in the best of weathers, is rarely calm, with great difficulty. When the Earl of Orkney came to hear of this indignity committed against the servants of his house, he complained of it to the King;—the King referred the transaction to his council; the council shewed an undisguised reluctance to the discussion of an affair which they might think required among men of honour the private satisfaction of the sword; and thus, when the two Earls came to Edinburgh, ready to inform against each other, mutual friends intervened, so that the result of the mediation is said to have been, that the recriminators "agreed all their private quarrels, lest they should reveal too much of either's doings."

About this time the distresses of the udallers became so insupportable, that, notwithstanding the strict guard which was placed over all ferries, so as to prevent any complaints of tyranny and oppression reaching the royal ear, a few Shetlanders made their escape, attired in the usual skincoat garbs of the country, and in this dress found their way to the

---

* This inscription is copied from Mr Gifford's Zetland. The story of Earl Patrick's interview with Mr Pitcairn will be found in Brand's Zetland. With the reason assigned by Earl Patrick for placing Mr Pitcairn's motto on his walls, Brand was not acquainted.

Court of James, and submitted to him, with true native eloquence, the oppressed condition of their country. Their complaints met with attention; and soon afterwards a representation from the whole of the inhabitants of Orkney and Shetland was forwarded, through the Bishop of those islands, to the Monarch. King James directed a formal investigation, the result of which was, that the Earl was committed to the Castle of Edinburgh, where he lay for two years, and afterwards to Dumbarton, where he was imprisoned for three years longer. It was then that he heard of his castles in Orkney and Shetland being surrendered to the Sheriff, and that he was ready to commit any act of desperation for their recovery. In this mood, it appears that he resigned himself to the counsels of a treacherous servant attending upon his person, of the name of Hacro, who, there is reason to suspect, was bribed by the Earl of Caithness to lay a snare for his master, by which he might be induced to commit some act of treason that would lead him to the scaffold; for so deadly at that period was the enmity of the Sinclairs to the Earls of Orkney, that it was only to be satisfied by their blood. Earl Patrick, at the persuasion of his servant, directed his secretary to write a letter to his natural son Robert, urging him to raise a party in his behalf, for the purpose of regaining his castles. The youth, from an excess of filial duty, complied with the request, and, accompanied with the insidious Hacro, contrived to secure in his interest a few dissolute fellows, by whose means he surprised the Castle of Birsay, and placed in it a garrison of thirty persons. The surrender of Kirkwall followed. When news of this transaction came to Edinburgh, the Earl of Caithness, who was then in that City, laboured much to obtain the command of the party proposed to quell it: assigning, among other reasons for volunteering the service, "that he might thereby be equal with such injuries as the Earl had done unto him before, and to revenge old quarrels upon the inhabitants of Orkney, for killing his great-grandfather." This Nobleman was entrusted with a few soldiers and some pieces of ordnance; and setting sail from Leith, in company with the Bishop of Orkney, he landed at Kirkwall, where he was soon afterwards joined by a much larger force of his own men from Caithness. Robert Stuart was now deserted by all his followers with the exception of fifteen men, and his attendant Hacro, the same faithless wretch, who, after having instigated the Earl of Orkney to treason, was now urging the son to surrender at discretion. But the gallant youth resisted this importunity, and was determined to outbrave the large force of the Earl of Caithness drawn out against him in battle array. First, the steeple and church of Kirkwall were besieged, which Robert Stuart had fortified: these he abandoned, in order to concentrate the whole of his small force within the castle. This fortress was now manfully assaulted; many hundred shot were levelled at it in vain; but so well directed was the fire of the Orkney Leonidas, that numbers of the Earl of Caithness's men are reported to have fallen; one soldier was shot in the act of drinking a health in mockery of the besieged. But, unfortunately for Robert Stuart, Hacro, the Judas of the party, was secretly encouraging his comrades, by the hopes of reward and pardon from the Earl of Caithness, to betray their master into the power of his foes. The youth heard of the meditated treason; and, sooner than be delivered bound by the hands of the wretch Hacro, he made a voluntary surrender of his person to the enemy. He was then conveyed to Edinburgh, in order to be confronted with his father, who was suspected to be accessory to the plot. Afterwards both Earl Patrick and his son were brought to trial, and on the evidence of Hacro and the Earl's secretary, they were condemned to suffer death. Robert Stuart was then conducted to the Market-cross of Edinburgh, and there executed. The similar punishment which was intended for the father, was deferred a little time longer, on the recommendation of the clergy, who had reported him as taking the sentence with great impatience, and as refusing all their proffered exhortations. At the expiration, therefore, of a month, when it was supposed that his mind would be better resigned to death, he was brought to the scaffold, guarded by the Magistrates of Edinburgh, and, in the sight of a numerous concourse of people, beheaded.*

Such was the fate of Earl Patrick Stuart, and with him terminated the sway of the Scottish Earls of Orkney and Lords of Zetland. The misrule of this spurious brood from the royal stock of the Stuarts, remains traditionally current at the present day, and it is mentioned with no other sentiment than that of horror. What Orkney and Shetland were during the tyranny of the Stuarts, cannot be better depicted than in the great poet's description of a similar lot, which had once befallen the country from which these oppressors, armed with illegal authority, had issued.

> "—————————————— Alas, poor country;
> Almost afraid to know itself! It cannot
> Be call'd our mother, but our grave : where nothing
> But who knows nothing is seen once to smile;
> Where sighs, and groans, and shrieks that rent the air,
> Are made not mark'd ; where violent sorrow seems
> A modern ecstacy : the dead man's knell
> Is there scarce ask'd, for whom ; and good men's lives
> Expire before the flowers in their caps,
> Dying, or ere they sicken."†

Since the death of Earl Patrick, no regular inhabitant has ever dwelt within the walls of Scalloway Castle. The house was allowed to fall gradually into decay; and thus the prophetical denunciation over the gate, indicative of the fate of that building which could not boast the solid basis of justice, was strictly fulfilled. For no longer a period than five or six years did these chambers resound with the licentious merriment of this worst of oppressors ; and now no revelry is heard within the castle but that which proceeds from the discordant screams of the foul birds of rapine, that build their nests upon its mouldering walls.

The night coming on, I looked out for the small public house of the village, which having entered, I found my way up stairs with difficulty, through a passage darkened with fumes outbreathing from the kitchen. Here was a modest quadrangle,—a bed in the corner of it,—a chearful peat fire,—and a delightful view of the bay from the window :—the

---

* Robert Stuart was executed on the 1st January 1615, and Earl Patrick Stuart was brought to the scaffold on the 6th of February following. The narrative concerning this last Earl of Orkney is chiefly derived from the Genealogy of the Earls of Sutherland, p. 299 to 301, and from Spottiswoode's History of the Church of Scotland, p. 520 and 521.

† Macbeth, Act 4, Scene 3.

bill of fare consisted of sillocks newly caught, of a hamrasher, tea and eggs; whilst the attention of the family to their guests could not be exceeded. Such is the cheer which the weary traveller may expect from the comfortable hostel of Scalloway:

> "———————————————— It is none
> Of those wild, scatter'd heaps call'd Inns, where scarce
> The host is heard, tho' he wind his horn t' his people.
> Here is a competent pile, wherein the man,
> Wife, servants, all do live within the whistle."*

Before leaving this vicinity, I was favoured by Mr Scott, the laird of the place, from whom I received many civilities, with a sight that was in this country a rarity; opening the door of a high garden-wall, a plantation of trees burst upon my view.—I had not seen a twig before in Shetland. But so cutting are the winds of this climate, that no plant belonging to the Hyperborean Grove of Scalloway could rise higher than the shelter of the garden wall: one tree, eighty years old, and five feet in circumference, was a sycamore: another, of healthy growth, was fourteen years old; there was also an elm well protected, that was 20 feet high: but planes afforded the best promise.

TINGWALL.

North from Scalloway, I entered the Valley of Tingwall, flanked on the east by the Cliff Hills, and by a less steep parallel ridge on the west. The first object that encounters the traveller's notice is a tall unhewn monumental stone, regarding which there are several uncertain traditions. It is said to have been erected in commemoration of a Danish General who was slain in this place, whilst endeavouring to reduce the Norwegian colonists of Shetland to some sort of obedience; others have connected this stone of memorial with the story of a son of one of the Earls of Orkney, who having incurred his father's displeasure, had fled to a strong-hold in the holm of a contiguous loch named Strom. The Earl sent four or five men to Shetland, charging them to bring back the fugitive to Orkney, dead or alive; the party met with him in the Vale of Tingwall, fought with him, slew him, cut off his head, and laid it before the feet of his father, who, upon recovering from his wrath, was so little gratified with the implicit obedience which had been paid to his unnatural command, that he ordered the perpetrators of the foul deed to instant execution, and afterwards erected a stone upon the spot where the slaughter had been committed.†

In the Vale of Tingwall there is a bed of limestone of considerable width, which has communicated to the soil above it a remarkable degree of richness; and in this parish an improved state of agriculture has been introduced, chiefly through the exertions of the intelligent minister of the parish. I now approached the bank of a pellucid loch, which

---

* Beaumont and Fletchers' Love's Pilgrimage.
† Brand's Zetland, p. 122.

watered the valley, and soon arrived at the northerly extremity of it, where was the church of Tingwall, a plain modern building. Close to it were the remains of an old kirk, which was once ornamented with a steeple; but little more than the foundation stones now remain. In the church-yard I observed several ancient monuments covered with lichens and moss. One inscription was very legible; it was to the memory of a Foude of Tingwall, who lived at the period when the udallers were most oppressed; but the stone records nothing more than that he was "An honest Man;" and this is saying a great deal for a Shetland judge, who lived in a period unparalleled for misrule and oppression.* The court where the Chief Magistrate of Shetland issued out his decrees, was in a small holm at the head of the adjoining loch, from which there was a communication to the shore by means of large stepping-stones. But this site of the ancient law-ting of Shetland will be contemplated with more interest, when associated with a knowledge of the Jurisdiction of the country, before this open law-court was removed to some covered hall at Scalloway.

ANCIENT STATE OF THE JURISDICTION OF SHETLAND, DURING THE SUBSISTENCE OF THE LAW-COURT OF THINGVALLA OR TINGWALL.

When, in the 9th century, colonists from Norway peopled Iceland, their first object was to erect at the place where they landed a temple to the God Thor, which served alike for religious and juridical purposes; but at a later period, when Christianity had forbidden the reverence that had been paid to the deified heroes of the Edda, legislative convocations were held at a place called Thingvalla, on the shores of a salt-water lake. It is not a little remarkable, that the same sequence of events took place at Shetland. Harold landed at a bay now named Haroldswick, situated at the Island of Unst; and on the adjoining promontory appears a Scandinavian temple which the early colonists erected, that has from time immemorial been named the House or Seat of Justice; but at a later period, the Provincial Assembly of Shetland held their meeting in a valley on the small holm adjoining the shore of a fresh water lake, which site, like the Icelandic place of convocation, had the appellation given to it of Thingvalla, now corrupted into the name of Tingwall.

It is a character of the Scandinavians who, in the 9th century, colonized Iceland, Feroe, and the islands to the north and west of Scotland, that they had no sooner taken possession of a country, than they immediately proceeded to elect Magistrates, and to give their government a regular form; the whole appearing, as Monsieur Mallet has emphatically remarked, to settle as without any effort. After Harold Harfager had visited Shetland, and subdued the pirates that had infested the shores of Scandinavia, colonizing the country at the same time with subjects attached to his own cause, he extended his sway over the three provinces of Orkney, Caithness and the Hæbudæ. There is reason to suppose, that to each of these four provinces a separate juridical establishment was allotted, and that the whole of these conquered tracts were, like Iceland divided into four quarters or Fiordungar.†

---

* The inscription runs :—"*Here lies an honest man*, Thomas Boyne, sometime Foude of Tingwall."
† Von Troil's Letters on Iceland, p. 71.

Shetland was named for many centuries a *Foudrie*, this being a word that was probably the corruption of some term like that which the Scandinavians of Iceland used to denote one of their four prefectures. It was also not unusual among the Scandinavians to divide a Prefecture into five Bailywicks.* Accordingly, the same number of districts for the controul of an inferior foude or bailiff was formed in Shetland; and whilst the court of Tingwall was devoted to the general jurisdiction of the Great Foude or Lagman, five other tings in different parts of the country were intended for the decision of district causes. But in the course of time, when Shetland became subject to Scotland, a Magistrate was appointed to each parish; so that, instead of five districts of jurisdiction, there were in later years ten.

The municipal laws that were directed to the good order of each district, were framed at a general convocation of the householders of the country, that was held in the law-ting; and this practice of legislating in the law-tings of Orkney and Shetland subsisted so late as the year 1670. Besides this general assembly, each small district of inhabitants formed itself into a legislative community, and as no other kind of punishment was inflicted for minor offences except fines, it was probably from this source, aided by taxation, that distress was removed, when arising from causes that were inevitable. Thus, in Scandinavia, when any man's house was burnt down, or when a stock of cattle was lost by contagion, the bailiff taxed each citizen according to his substance; and, in order to prevent any abuse of such resources of indemnification, no man was entitled to a vote in the municipal assemblies of the country, who had failed in honour upon any occasion, or was too poor.† In the commencement of the 17th century, all the ancient law-books of Shetland were destroyed, and a newer municipal code, under the name of the Country Acts of Shetland, was passed at the general Legislative Meetings of the Law-ting, which was intended for the preservation of good and orderly neighbourhood (as it was called), in each district; by these laws, punishments were inflicted on the dissolute, lands were preserved from trespasses, the equity of commercial dealings was protected, and means were provided for searching out or securing offenders, whose crimes it was necessary to submit to the proper tribunals of the country.

When the householders of a district were assembled, they were empowered to select ten or twelve respectable individuals out of their number, to serve the offices of Rancelmen. The mode of election, which probably differs little from that which existed before the time of Earl Patrick, is to be collected from the ancient Country Acts of Shetland. The clerk of the court read a list of such honest men in the parish as were proper for the office, and these individuals were severally asked if they were willing to serve in it. If any of them, without assigning a sufficient reason, refused the appointment, he was liable to the penalty of £10 Scots. The office of the Rancelman was of a very miscellaneous kind. In the *first* place, he was intended to be the guardian of the domestic morals of the district, being (as the act specifies,) entrusted with the power of inspecting the manners of others;—he was to inquire into the lives and conversations of families, to prevent all quarrels and

---

* Mallet's Northern Antiquities, vol. i., p. 174.

† Mallet's Northern Antiquities, vol. i., p. 175.

scolding, and to levy penalties for cursing and swearing; in every case he was to be an exhorter, and if the parties offending did not obey his recommendation, they were to become liable to judicial interference of a more serious kind. *Secondly*, The Rancelman was to be the guardian of the religion of the district; he was to narrowly inquire who sat at home from the kirk on the sabbath day, and from diets of catechising, and to levy fines accordingly. *Thirdly*, He was to be the guardian of the commercial dealings of the parish; he was to see that all tradesmen made sufficient work, and did not impose upon their customers. *Fourthly*, He was made inspector of the agriculture of the parish; he was to oversee the building of dikes, to punish for trespasses on land, to try the merits of sheep dogs, &c. *Fifthly*, He was to be a steward for landlords; he was to report to them when tenants abused their lands and demolished their houses. *Sixthly*, He was to punish idle vagabond persons, and to take charge of the poor. *Seventhly*, He was to inform against all persons using any manner of witchcraft, charms, or any abominable or devilish superstitions, that they might be brought to condign punishment; and, *lastly*, He was to be the general thieftaker; he had the power of entering any house within the district, in quest of stolen goods; which last office was named Rancelling.

Along with the appointment of rancelmen, a Lawrightman was selected in each district for the regulation of weights and measures. "He was an honest man," said Mr Gifford. "whose business it was to weigh and measure the rent-butter and oil, and to determine its proper quality, and if found insufficient, to return it as not receivable: he was sworn to do justice, and to keep just weights and measures."*

In ancient Scandinavia, and originally, perhaps, in its colonies, it was customary at popular assemblies to appoint a bailiff for each district, who was to be a person distinguished for prudence, and possessed of a certain income in land, for fear his poverty should expose him to contempt or corruption. Judicial officers of this kind were chosen in Shetland, but when the country was annexed to Scotland, the appointment of them was given to some superior of the lands, or farmer of the Crown revenues. In early times, each bailiff of Shetland was known by the name of Foude; this appellation being given to any law officer who presided at a court.† The foude of a division, or bailiff convoked, in later times, two courts in the course of the year, at which all the respectable householders of a district were required to be present.‡ Here the laws or Country Acts, which directed the foude's decrees, were first read over; the foude or bailiff then proceeded to try such causes as were brought before him; but, as Mr Gifford has remarked, "he was only a judge in small matters, such as keeping good neighbourhood, and could decern in no cause above £10 value."

It is difficult to collect the practice of the tribunals of Shetland at an earlier period than the close of the 16th, or commencement of the 17th century. It is evident, that the extensive yet dangerous authority with which the rancelmen were arrayed, had no other

---

* For the ancient directions to the Rancelmen, see Note 12.

† Dr Jamieson has observed, in his Etym. Dict. that he has seen no satisfactory conjecture on the origin of the word Foude, which is the same as the Su. G. *fogde*, *præfectus*, and Germ. *vogd*.

‡ The periods at which they were held in later times were at Martinmas and Michaelmas.—Gifford's Zetland, p. 47.

object than to prevent many causes from coming in a regular shape before the court of the District-Foude or bailiff, and the law-ting of the Great Foude, that could be settled in a more private way. Each rancelman was considered as a domestic arbiter in all the disputes of his district; but when charges came before him in which he could not interfere, he reported them to the District-Foude, who, if they came within his jurisdiction, submitted them before a court of householders; and in passing judgment, he was assisted by the opinion of the whole assembled rancelmen and the lawright-man.

Over the decrees of the subordinate foude or bailiff was placed the controul of the Great Foude or Lagman, to whose superintendence was entrusted the whole of the jurisdiction of the foudrie of Shetland. It is remarked by Mallet of the Lagman of Scandinavia, that he had a power of reversing all the sentences pronounced by inferior judges throughout the island, of annulling their ordinances, and even of punishing them, if the complaints brought against them were well-founded.* It is curious that a similar controul was vested, about the commencement of the 18th century, with the Steward-depute of the country, in whom the functions of the lagman were, up to this period, continued. Mr Gifford has distinctly stated, that "the bailiff was obliged to keep a court-book, wherein all causes brought before his court were recorded; which book must be produced to the Steward-depute, [the successor of the Great Foude,] when called for at his circuit-courts. If the book was regularly kept, and nothing amiss in it, then it was approven, otherwise the bailiff was enjoined to amend what was amiss, or to lose his commission."†

The Lagman or Great Foude of Shetland anciently administered justice in conformity to the precepts of some law-book derived from Scandinavia. When Shetland was first colonized by the Norwegians, it would be governed by the laws which were in force in the mother country; and it was customary in Scandinavia to collect these under the form of a book, when it acquired the name of The Book of the Law. It is perfectly certain, from the testimony of Torfæus, that such a book existed in Orkney and Shetland at a very early date, and there is an allusion to it in many legal documents that are preserved of the decrees of the lagman. An able investigator into the antiquities of these islands, has shewn, that when, in the year 1575, Lord Robert Stuart was indicted by an udaller for ousting him out of his inheritance, having by a packed jury seized upon it for himself, Mr John Sharpe, the solicitor to the defendant, who had endeavoured to skreen this act of injustice under the peculiarity of the laws of the country, was ordered by the Regent and Council assembled, " to bring and produce the Book of the said Law, together with the process and sentence pronounced be the said assize before them." And in an entry in the records of the Privy Council of Scotland, dated August 23, 1602, against Adam Sinclair of Brow, who was concerned in the slaughter of Matthew Sinclair of Ness, the assize is said to have taken " long and mature deliberation, be the inspection of the chapturis of the Law-buik, and practicks of the country in such case."‡ It thus appears that there was not a decree recorded with-

---

* Mallet's Northern Antiq., vol. i., p. 179.
† Gifford's Zetland, p. 46 and 47.
‡ These cases have been collected by the author of the Grievances of Orkney, &c., from the records of the Privy Council of Scotland, and from Lord Haddington's Collections of the Minutes of Parliament.

out reference to some chapter in the Scandinavian Law-book.

Of the particular code of laws which were in use in Shetland, we learn little more than from tradition. The oldest Norwegian Collection is attributable to Haco, the fosterson of Athelstan, the English King, who appears, in the year 940, to have been the first legislator who promulgated a regular code, and new-modelled the laws. This code was afterwards amended by Olafus, King of Norway, who in the year 1014, introduced into Orkney and Shetland the Christian religion, and with it, probably, his new and milder decrees; for, so late as the 18th century, the Shetlanders were accustomed to boast that their laws had been received from St Olla, of whom they were said to have reported strange things in their songs they had of him, called vissacks.* But there is no doubt, that several of the later alterations of St Olla's code were admitted into the law-tings of Orkney and Shetland. Some enactments respecting sheep are ascribed to Hagen, Duke of Norway, and son to King Magnus; and Torfæus remarks, that although Norwegian laws originally prevailed in these islands, they were afterwards intermixed with Danish statutes. During the tyrannical sway of Patrick, Earl of Orkney, the law-book of Orkney and Shetland disappeared for ever; and other edicts were in subsequent times derived from Scotland.

The Prefect or Lagman of Shetland, in presiding at the great Legislative Assemblies which were held in the country, and at those courts where the result of the trial involved the life or death of the party accused, was assisted by counsellors, who had the name of *Raadmen* given to them, from the Scandinavian word *raett*, signifying right; their business being to see that justice was done according to law. Accordingly, it was by the united sanction of the Raadmen and Great Foude that all decrees of the court were confirmed, with the exception of cases involving the life and death of the accused. The criminal might then make a popular appeal to the general convocation of Udallers, who were assembled to take part in the decision. In the functions of the Raadmen there was a great resemblance to those of a Jury; indeed they appear to have been allied to the compurgators of Scandinavia, who, as Sir Walter Scott has observed, "were at first a kind of witnesses, that, upon their general knowledge of the character of the accused, gave evidence of his being incapable of committing the crime imputed, but gradually obtained the character of Judges, who formed their opinion upon the evidence of others adduced in their presence." An illustration of the functions of the compurgators appears in the same author's abstract of the Eyrbiggia-saga, where "Geirrida is cited to a popular assembly and accused of witchcraft; but twelve witnesses or compurgators having asserted upon their oath the innocence of the accused party, Geirrida was honourably freed from the accusation brought against her."† But it appears that the number of Raadmen in Shetland and Orkney was not restricted to twelve. A criminal was ordered to be brought to trial in a law-ting held July 5, 1604, when there sat with the Lagman twenty-two assistants. In the year 1514, a sale of land was

---

* Sir Robert Sibbald's Zetland, p. 42.

† Illustrations of Northern Antiquities, p. 484. Mons. Mallet is evidently mistaken in the character of the ancient compurgators, when he speaks of *the ridiculous practice* of "obliging the accused to produce a certain number of persons called Compurgators, not that these men had, or were supposed to have any knowledge of the affair in question, but they were simply to swear that they were persuaded the accused spoke true." Sir Walter Scott's view of the Compurgators of Scandinavia, whom I suppose to be identified with the Raadmen of Orkney and Shetland, is much more correct.

confirmed by a lawman and thirteen assistants; not unfrequently, however, the number was that of an English Jury.*

The great Foude or Lagman, in dispensing justice, made an annual circuit round the Mainland of Shetland, for the purpose of presiding at the lesser law-tings of each separate district. In his route, he came attended with a large retinue, composed of Raadmen, and other members of his court. At these tings he heard appeals from the inferior courts of subordinate Foudes or Bailiffs; he revoked unjust decrees, and sat in judgment upon all causes, except those upon which depended the life or death of the accused. The custom of making circuits round parishes once a-year, was continued long after the law-tings were abolished, even to the period when the office of the lagman was given to a steward-depute. Mr Gifford, who wrote in the year 1733, has remarked, that "the steward-depute having no salary, could not afford to be at the charge of travelling through the country with such a retinue as all the members of the court made out, and therefore these circuit-courts were much laid aside."†

After these remarks, we may now visit the Law-ting, and with the aid of a lively imagination, suppose the whole of the udallers of Shetland to be in the act of assembling from different parts of the country, for the purpose of attending the general convocation of Tingwall: being mounted on the hardy race of animals known by the name of Shelties. They first halt at the houses on the east side of the loch, where persons are appointed to tether their horses, and to undertake the charge of them; for the loss and trouble of which the occupiers were declared to be free from the usual impost of scat.‡ An immense crowd is now assembled on the edge of the lake; adjoining to them the holm is situated, not more than thirty yards in diameter, which is separated from the land by a shallow channel, and is reached by the aid of a few stepping-stones. This site is destined for the reception of the Great Feude, his raadmen or counsellors, the recorder, the witnesses, and other members of the court. The people stand on the outside of the ting, and on the side of the loch. The President and his Recorder pass through the crowd, trace their way over the stepping-stones, and seat themselves on the large stones of the holm, followed by the raadmen, the whole turning their faces to the east. "We must turn our faces to the east," was the expression of the ancient Scandinavian Lagman, "and pray unto Christ to grant us good tide and peace, that we may keep our land without travail; and our King, the Lord of our land, with health and grace; may he be our friend and may we be his friend for evermore."§—At such a Legislative Assembly, or little Parliament, municipal laws were made, the last of which were the ancient Country Acts of Shetland; causes were determined according to the Law-book of Norway, the business of the Foude being to expound the statutes, in which he was assisted by his raadmen or counsellors. It was also the office of the Foude to pronounce

---

* See Grievances of Orkney and Zetland, p. 8 to 13, and Appendix.

† Gifford's Zetland, p. 46.

‡ "The udallers coming all on horse-back," says Mr Gifford, "had their horses grazed in the neighbourhood thereof, for which the proprietors of Griesta and Astar (two adjoining rooms or towns) were bound to make up their damage, for which one had the scat of some lands in Wiesdale, and the other the scat of Quarf, and half the scat of Coningsburgh."—Gifford's Zetland.

§ Essay on Ancient Laws of Scandinavia, Edinburgh Review, No. 67, p. 179.

the sentence; and there is reason to suppose that the law-book, the pious work of St Olave, was regarded with a reverence that generally ensured a righteous decree. In the year 1519, remarks the author of the Grievances of Orkney, the High Foude or Lagman, in order to give a sacred and venerable authority to his sentence, confirmed it "be the fayth of the lawbuik," as now-a-days men confirm their testimony by the faith of the holy Gospels.* In cases where the criminal was capitally convicted, it was allowed him to appeal to the voice of the people; and the mode in which this was accomplished, still the lively subject of tradition, bears reference to a period antecedent to the introduction of Christianity. When the Scandinavians colonized Iceland, and erected a place of justice on Helgafels or the Holy Mount where the popular assemblies were held, this place, being dedicated to Thor, was esteemed so sacred, that it was not to be defiled by blood: a neighbouring rock was appointed for the performance of any indispensable act that might be considered of a polluted nature. In like manner, at the Island of Unst in Shetland, where the first legislative convocation was held, the place of execution for any criminal who submitted to the decree of the Foude, was on the summit of a high hill named Hanger-Hugh: and if any accused person, after hearing the sentence of the Lagman, was desirous to appeal to the voice of the People, he was allowed to pass uninjured from without the precincts of the site that was considered hallowed. A sanctuary was then fixed at a certain distance, the escape to which depended upon the will of the people. If the popular voice did not accord with the sentence of the Foude, the accused was allowed to reach it unhurt, and his life was afterwards protected. But if the popular indignation was against him, he was pursued on his way to the sanctuary, and any one, before he reached it, might put him to death. This practice was continued in Shetland subsequently to the introduction of Christianity; and when the Legislative convocation held at Unst was removed to the distant holm of Tingwall, the mode in which a condemned person might make an appeal to the people, was still preserved. Mr Brand, in the year 1700, heard the familiar traditional report which is still current, "that when any person received sentence of death upon the holm, if afterwards he could make his escape through the crowd of people standing on the side of the loch without being apprehended, and touch the steeple of the church of Tingwall, the sentence of death was retrieved, and the condemned obtained an indemnity.†

Such are the particulars which may be collected respecting the ancient Jurisdiction of Shetland. The account is very imperfect, owing to the scanty documents and traditions on the subject which are preserved; but that a favourable view is presented of the civil polity of the ancient Norwegian colonists of this country can be scarcely denied. "When we read of Scandinavia," says an eloquent writer on the ancient laws of this region of Europe, "it seems involved in a perpetual snow-storm. Its inhabitants are pictured in our imagination, as a race of stern and barbarous warriors, intent only upon war and plunder; yet, according to their polity, the members of the community were knitted together by the closest social bonds. Moral duties were enforced by the penalties of the law, which came

---

* Grievances of Orkney, &c., p. 6.
† Brand's Description of Zetland, p. 122.

in aid of the precepts and dictates of friendship, of charity, and of natural affection."*

TINGWALL TO LERWICK.

Having left the fertile vale of Tingwall I began to ascend the Cliff Hills to the east of it, and observed what was a real novelty in the country,—a regular paved road, cut across a thick bed of peat moss, and leading to Lerwick, a distance of four miles. The execution of this work is attributable to two private gentlemen, who, several years ago, were at the expence of opening a communication from Lerwick across the Cliff Hills to their estates. If these spirited individuals had lived in Roman days, they would have been honoured at their death by an apotheosis, as being among the earliest promoters of civilization. But, seeing that the Lares viales of Hialtland, whom the Agricultural Society of the country are invoking, meditate another march as far south as Fladibister, as far west as Wiesdale, and as far north as Yell Sound, it is pleasant to contemplate, in the very distant perspective of two or three centuries, when the resources of Shetland for its fisheries may be better known, the gradual effects which will be produced by the new roads, which are intended to connect different parts of the country :—the little shelties, loaded on each side with panniers or cassies, may give place to heavy draught horses imported from Lothian, and dragging behind them a ponderous car :—along the new line of road, convenient quays may adorn the numerous voes which intersect the islands :—at length may arise populous towns, when new and more expensive communications between them will be projected.

> " Lo ! ray'd from cities o'er the brighten'd land,
> Connecting sea to sea, the solid road.
> Lo ! the proud arch (no vile exactor's stand)
> With easy sweep bestrides the chafing flood."
> THOMSON *on Liberty*.

Such is the dream which may be excited by the solitary paved road of four miles that leads to Lerwick. After passing the head of a long inlet of sea named Dale's Voe, the last eminence which I ascended was cut through mud exhausted mosses, where nothing was to be seen but a few sheep employed in grazing the scanty herbage of the hills. The low lands of Lerwick next appeared in view; the sea to the right, splendent as a mirror, with its winding shores ; in front was the beautiful Sound of Bressay, burdened with large vessels, into which a stately frigate was then majestically gliding, while ranged along its shore were a number of white houses,

> " In the sunshine glittering fair,
> Haunts of business, haunts of care."

---

* Essay on Ancient Laws of Scandinavia, Edinburgh Review, No. 67, p. 199.

These formed the town of Lerwick. The prospect was closed by the Island of Bressay, rising into a fine symmetrical hill of a conoid form, and by the distant cliffs of Noss.

Near to Lerwick is a valley through which the road passes, where there is a small fresh water loch, and on a holm may be observed the foundation of a small circular burgh; contained within the wall of it are several distinct chambers, the dimensions of which, as they have been given by Mr Neill in his Tour, are about 10 or 12 feet in length, and 3 in width. At certain places, on the north and north-west of the building, straight walls have been extended from the exterior of the burgh to the water's edge, by which means an additional defence has been rendered, and small inclosures formed for the temporary protection of cattle. South of the holm, stepping-stones communicate with the shore; and to guard this exposed point, a mural out-work, of a crescentic form, shelters this part of the fortress. In one place I traced the remains of a subterraneous passage which led to the water's edge, whereby a supply of fresh water might be obtained for the use of the little garrison that was engaged in defending the holm.

In drawing close to the town, numerous formal inclosures of a stony and steril ground appeared, which were intended for gardens. There is not, perhaps, a poorer soil to be found in the country than about Lerwick; yet, when a large district of moorland was lately disposed of by auction, the high price which it fetched was remarkable. It had then to be converted into garden ground at a considerable expence, owing to the necessity of levelling the small elevated portions of rock, which, protruding from a swampy soil, were laid bare by rains.

LERWICK.

On approaching Lerwick, the houses appeared to be from two to three storeys in height, roofed with a blue, rough, sandstone slate; the descent into the town was by a narrow passage of tolerably uniform width, until I arrived at the main street, the irregularity of which nothing could well exceed. Lerwick seems to have been first built about the beginning of the 17th century, when Bressay Sound was annually visited by not less than 2000 busses. For the sake, therefore, of an easy traffic with these ships in stockings and fresh provisions, the houses, not less than 200, were erected close to the shore; and there was no passage between them and the sea wider than would admit of two men walking together abreast. But great as the disorder was which resulted from ranging the buildings agreeably to the indentations of the coast, it could not be exceeded by the contiguous range of houses which was subsequently planned, with the intention that a street between them should intervene. In one place a taller house might be observed to advance proudly into the road, taking the precedence of contiguous habitations, while, in another place, a lesser dwelling seemed to claim the privilege of encroachment as if it were a fellow-compeer. After this manner houses may be now seen to retreat from one side of the street, like the salient and re-entering angles of a fortification: in other places, they answer to Gray's description of Kendal; "They seem as if they had been dancing a country dance, and were out: they stand back to back, corner to corner, some up hill, some down." But, after all, the town is so remarkably striking, that, woe betide the Hyperborean architect who would reduce the irregular lines of its street, on which its picturesque appearance depends, to the dull uniformity of right lines and squares. Lerwick is laid with flags, which are seldom pressed by any beasts of burden heavier than the little shelties of the country, that are loaded with cassies of turf from the adjoining scathold. No pavement is required, for there is only one cart to be seen, which belongs to a gentleman in the vicinity. A lively appearance is presented in the town from the number of shops with which it is filled; and from the sailors of all nations who are engaged in making small purchases, whilst their vessels are moored in the harbour.

In the town there is no public structure demanding particular attention. There is one plain building, dedicated to the use of a town-house, a court of justice, and a prison; and there is a small neat kirk for the Established religion of Scotland. A dissenting sect, named The Haldanites, have also a regular meeting-house.

The population has of late years much encreased. In the year 1701 many Dutch vessels frequented Bressay Sound, and the number of families residing in Lerwick was said to have been from two to three hundred. When several nations, owing to continued wars, declined their visits to Shetland, the population so far decreased, that, in the year 1778, Mr Low remarked, that the town only contained 140 families. By the last census taken, the number of individual inhabitants was estimated at 1301.

Lerwick boasts no kind of manufactory except one for straw-plaiting, in which 50 girls are said to be employed: the town is much indebted for its support to the vessels which touch at Bressay Sound in their voyage to the Northern Seas, and on their return home; among these are chiefly Greenlanders. In consequence also of the small barters that are made with foreign vessels, Danish and other coins pass more freely in the country than British money.

Provisions in Lerwick are very moderate, being less than half the price which they bear in the Scottish market. A great boast of the inhabitants of Lerwick is the number of vegetables produced in this variable climate. The esculent roots and artichokes are esteemed of excellent quality, and as great a variety of them is enumerated as Drayton has celebrated on the shores of Norfolk:

> The colewort, colliflower, and cabbage in their season,
> The rouncefall, great beans, and early ripening peason;
> The onion, scallion, leek, which housewives highly rate;
> Their kinsman garlic then, the poor man's mithridate;
> The savoury parsnip next, and carrot, pleasing food;
> The skirret which (some say) in sallads stirs the blood:
> The turnip, tasting well to clowns in winter weather:
> Thus in our verse we put roots, herbs, and fruit together.

Lerwick was never invested with any particular privileges; it was formerly governed by a Bailie, whose office was, to the great inconvenience of the place, allowed to become extinct, but lately it has been erected into a Burgh, for the government of which two annual

Magistrates are chosen with the title of Bailies. The Sheriff-substitute holds his weekly courts, where justice is administered according to the forms of Scotland, whilst the force of a few of the country acts of Shetland is still retained: here also are held Commissary and Admiralty Courts.

The general habits of the higher classes of Society in Lerwick differs little from those of any small town in Scotland: it is indeed usual for them to receive a part of their education at Aberdeen or Edinburgh. All strangers have spoken in the highest terms of the urbanity of the inhabitants. The northern voyager, in particular, is wont to descant with rapture on the hours which he has spent in this hospitable harbour. There is only one inn in the place, but it deserves high praise for civility and attention.

On the south of the town is the citadel, built A.D. 1665, which adds much to the beauty of the place: its erection is said to have cost £28,000 Sterling.* In the Dutch war of that time, Lerwick was garrisoned for three years by 300 men, commanded by Colonel William Sinclair, a Shetland gentleman, and they were supplied with about twenty or thirty cannon. Long afterwards, until the commencement of the 18th century, Lerwick was unprotected, when it was visited by a Dutch frigate, which burnt the fort and several houses in the town. The country was also visited by the French, who, says Mr Gifford, "were a more generous enemy than the Dutch, doing little damage to the country, sometimes demanding fresh provisions, which were readily granted them." In the year 1781, the fort was completely repaired, and named, after the late Queen, Fort Charlotte; and in the late war it received a part of a garrison battalion, being mounted with twelve guns, and containing accommodation for two or three companies. There are now no soldiers required in the town, and the fort is destined to an use that must delight every friend of peace; for, next to the pleasure of seeing the sword beat into a ploughshare, nothing can more harmonise with the scene than the conversion of the citadel into the peaceful manse of the pious minister of the parish.

ISLANDS OF BRESSAY AND NOSS.

With the view of visiting the two Islands of Bressay and Noss, I crossed what is named a *Sound*, the term implying, not only in Shetland, but in the Western Islands of Scotland, a narrow passage of the sea, formed by the contiguity of one or more islands to any uninterrupted line of coast.† Bressay presents an interesting appearance: on the shore are the spacious house and grounds of Gardie, the seat of Thomas Mouat, Esq., laid out in a modern style of elegance, and adjoining to Gardie are the manse and the parish kirk. Crossing the scatholds of the country, diversified with numerous cottages, and occasionally varied by the ruins of a burgh, or a rude monumental stone, I arrived at the Ferry of Noss, adjoining to which may be traced the remains of a circular fort, within the foundation walls of which were distinct cavities, each about twelve feet long, six feet broad, and about five

---

* See a view of the Citadel in Plate III., Fig. 3.
† Johnson supposes a Sound to mean nothing more than a *shallow sea*; but it is doubtful if the term was in any country so restricted in its meaning.

feet deep. From the eminence above the water's edge is a good view of the small island of Noss, which consists of one hill rising gradually towards the easterly ocean, and presenting in its outline the similar conoid form shewn by the hill of Bressay.

Crossing in a boat a small rapid channel, I arrived at a neat farm-house, contiguous to which were the ruins of a small chapel, and directed my course to the south-east extremity of the island. Skirting along the steep banks of sandstone, frequently broken into deep chasms, the famous Holm of Noss at length came in view, bounded by precipitous cliffs, and divided by a narrow channel from the equally steep rocks on which I was then standing. The traveller is now struck with the appearance of a tremendous gulf, over which ropes are passed, from which is slung a sort of wooden trough named a Cradle, large enough for the conveyance across of one man and a sheep. How such a device was first contrived, is naturally one of the first objects of inquiry. The holm, which is little more than 500 feet in length, and 170 in breadth, rises abruptly from the sea in the form of a perpendicular cliff 160 feet in height. The chasm which intervenes between it and the no less precipitous banks of Noss is sixty-five feet across.* The original temptation to reach this holm, was on account of the visit paid to it during the season of incubation by innumerable sea-birds, such as black and white gulls, scarfs, sea-pies, and kittywakes, when the grass became whitened with their eggs. It was therefore about two centuries ago, that an adventurous fowler was induced, by the tempting offer of a cow, to scale the cliff of the holm. This hardy and almost incredible undertaking he accomplished, bearing with him two stakes, with the intent of fixing them into that part of the bank which was nearest to the opposite rock. The object of the undertaking was now fulfilled, and the fowler was entreated to avail himself of the communication across the gulf: this he refused to do, determined to descend the way he had climbed, and in so fool-hardy an attempt he fell and perished. When the islanders first availed themselves of this ill-fated hero's success, a stone was fastened to the double of a light cord, and while one man kept in his hands the extremities of the rope, the other threw the part to which the stone was attached across to the holm. By the assistance of a long pole or fishing-rod, the cord was so elevated as to be easily drawn round the stakes; a thicker rope was then attached to the thin cord, and upon the latter being drawn in, the former was in its turn brought round the post. This operation was repeated until a firm cordage formed the medium of transport from bank to bank. In the next place, an oblong box, named a Cradle, was contrived, through the extremities of which two holes were made that allowed ropes to pass along each of its sides, by which means the machine was properly slung. The first visitor of the holm then seated himself in the cradle, and since there was a slight descent towards it, he easily moved forward, and by means of the lateral cords, regulated the celerity of his conveyance. In returning, however, he was assisted by persons stationed on the opposite bank, who were employed in drawing him up by means of a rope that had been for this purpose attached to the cradle.†

---

* By Dr Scott of Lerwick I have been favoured with these particulars of measurement. He found, by a line dropped to the surface of the sea, when he was half way across the gulf, that the height of the Cradle was 162 feet: at the same time the depth of the channel was 27 feet 8 inches.

† In Plate III, Fig. 1. some idea is intended to be conveyed of the Holm of Noss.

At the present day, the Holm is converted into a pasture for twelve sheep. The cradle is slung twice each summer, in a manner differing little from that which was practised two centuries ago. The box is made large enough for the admission into it of one man and a sheep. When Mr Low of Orkney visited Noss, nearly fifty years ago, it was customary to fasten the double of a thin piece of packthread to a fishing-rod, and to allow a favourable breeze to blow it over the stakes; it then proved the medium by which a thicker cordage could be made to supply its place.

I now passed to the highest part of a rock named the Noup, which is a dreadful perpendicular precipice, 480 feet above the level of the sea. The surge beneath is not contemplated without terror, and to a native rose that attaches itself to the crevices of the rock, a peculiar interest is attached by the Shetlanders, which may have originated from the cause that has been so beautifully explained by Dryden.

> "As from a steep and dreadful precipice,
> The frightened traveller cast down his eyes,
> And sees the ocean at so great a distance,
> It looks as if the skies were sunk beneath him.
> If then some neighbouring shrub, how weak soever,
> Peeps up, his willing eyes stop gladly there,
> And seem to ease themselves and rest upon it."

LERWICK TO CATFIRTH.

In returning from Noss, I passed by the beautiful harbour of Aithsvoe in Bressay island, near to which there is a fine stone quarry, and soon afterwards arrived at the Sound, which I again crossed and entered Lerwick. From this town I proceeded north along the west shore of the harbour, past the new quays which are formed by an enterprising gentleman of Lerwick, for the reception of vessels, and shortly afterwards came to Rovie Head, where the conglomerate rocks and sandstone, which I had traced from Dunrossness, ceased altogether. At this place nothing could well exceed the raggedness of the coast, the rocks being formed of immense boulder-stones, cemented by the intervention of smaller fragments. Farther west there is a very thick bed of limestone, which, from its contiguity to Lerwick, may be useful to the agriculture of the vicinity. I had now passed the north entrance of Bressay Sound, when, in directing my course westward, I came in view of a small tumulated hillock, named a Knoll, which crowned the ridge of clay-slate that formed Kibister's Ness. Near this place once lived an unfortunate wretch, who had the reputation of being a wizard. He was a fisherman; and whenever there was a storm which prevented boats from going out to sea, he was wont, say the Shetlanders, to ascend the Knoll of Kibister, and in a deep cleft of the rock, to let down a line, when, for his own provision, he was able to draw up at any time, codlings or ling. From this circumstance the Knoll of Kibister afterwards went by the name of *Luggie's Know*. This act, says Brand the missionary, "was certainly done by the agency of evil spirits, with whom he was in contact and covenant; but the economy of the kingdom of Darkness is very wonderful, and little known to us." Another story of poor Luggie is best related in Sinclair's Invisible World discovered. When fishing at sea with his companions, he was accustomed, whenever hungry, to cast out his line; and, it is added, "he would, out of Neptune's lowest kitchen, bring cleverly up fish well boiled and roasted." This supernatural power became at length so familiar to Luggie's comrades, that so far from being startled at the idea of partaking with him in his infernal banquet, "they would," says Sinclair, "by a natural courage, make a merry meal thereof, not doubting who was cook." This poor fellow was, in the end, brought to trial, and being condemned for sorcery, was burnt at a stake near Scalloway.

If, from the hill of Kibister, we direct the attention to a point north-east of the harbour of Bressay, some little commotion of the sea may be perceived, which is occasioned by a number of waves that break over a dangerous rock named the Unicorn. This shoal is associated with the history of Earl Bothwell, the wicked tool of a more wicked faction, whose views were unremittingly directed to the dethronement of the unfortunate Mary. Bothwell had secretly lent himself to the murder of Darnley, the confederacy with which he was connected having procured his acquittal;—he had forcibly seized upon the Queen, and by the foulest means had left her no resource, but to make him a surrender of her person at the altar. The object of the faction was now on the point of being accomplished,—a marriage had taken place that must render Mary odious to her subjects. Troops were then easily raised for the alleged purpose of compelling the Queen to separate herself from the influence and counsels of the guilty bridegroom. Mary, accompanied by the Earl, prepared to meet her foes; but seeing the unsteadiness of her men, who were disheartened in her cause, she surrendered to their terms, promising to dismiss Bothwell from her presence, and to govern the kingdom by her Nobles. When the plots of the faction were thus far successful, it had been lost sight of, that, in order to be consistent in the object for which a pretence was made for levying arms against the Crown, Bothwell ought to have been secured; but as he was a mere instrument in their plots, he was easily forgotten, and allowed to escape. This forsaken favourite, who had recently been created Duke of Orkney, then conceived, that, in the country which gave to him his title, he should meet with every protection. Sailing thither from Dunbar, with a few ships and men, he arrived at Kirkwall, where he was coldly received by the inhabitants of that place, the governor refusing him admission into the castle. He then came to Shetland,—a country which, from its remoteness, partook much less than Orkney of the party spirit of Scotland. Here he met with a welcome. Bringing with him a number of retainers, an ox and two sheep out of every parish were allowed for their maintenance.* But indigence still overtaking the outcast husband of Mary, he was induced to arm the vessels that had accompanied him, and venturing into the northern seas, he attacked every trading vessel which came within his reach, seeking to procure by piracy subsistence for himself and his followers. The Government of Scotland hearing of these atrocities, sent out two vessels against him, commanded by William

---

* It has been observed, that this voluntary grant became, during the tyranny of the Stuarts, the precedent for an annual demand to the same amount, on the alleged purpose, that the country was bound to furnish provisions for the workmen who were engaged in building Scalloway Castle. Upon the forfeiture of Earl Patrick's estates, the exaction was recorded in the Exchequer under the name of Ox and Sheep Silver; and it is paid at the present day.

Kirkaldy of Grange, and Murray of Tullibardine, the former of whom was accompanied by Adam Bothwell, Bishop of Orkney, who had solemnized Mary's last fatal marriage. Kirkaldy's ship, named the Unicorn, came up with Earl Bothwell whilst anchored in Bressay Sound. The noble pirate immediately abandoned the harbour, took in a pilot, to whom he promised a great reward if he could effect his escape, set all sail and passed through the north entrance of Bressay Sound; while the vessel in pursuit followed him so close, that the ships were within a gun-shot of each other. On entering the open channel, Kirkaldy ordered all sails to be set: the steersman faultered; he was ignorant of the coast,—he hesitated to obey the command of his Captain. Kirkaldy was peremptory;— and still pursuing Bothwell's vessel, which insidiously directed its course close to the hidden rock, his ship broke upon the bank; and, whilst his men were employed in saving themselves, Bothwell had time allowed him for escape. His purpose he effected by stealing from his ship with the aid of a small boat. He then privately entered another of his vessels, which, from the ignorance that he was on board, became not the object of pursuit. From the accident that befel Kirkaldy's ship, the bank has ever since, from the name which the vessel bore, acquired the title of the Unicorn Rock. The sequel of Bothwell's history is well known: flying towards Norway, he met with a ship richly laden and well armed,—he attacked it, failed in the attempt, when he and all his men were carried prisoners to Copenhagen. On his rank being made known in that city, he was saved from the ignominious death which his associates suffered, being condemned to prison for life. "He languished," says an eminent historian of Scotland, "ten years in this unhappy condition; melancholy and despair deprived him of his senses, and, at last, he ended his days, unpitied by his countrymen, and unassisted by strangers."

Crossing Dales Voe to a dreary point of land named Hawksness, I was ferried over a beautiful harbour, which, like the other inlet, flows into the large bay of Catfirth. The soil on the banks was highly fertilized by substrata of limestone, and a lively scene was presented by the neat farm of Mr Hay. Situated close to the water's edge was a good house with out-buildings; at a little distance were barns, stables and lime-kilns, and around them were inclosures smiling with waving corn. Traversing a brown hill to the west, I arrived at the Head of Wadbister Voe, and in the same direction was led to the extremity of Catfirth. This bay, communicating with the channels of several other inlets, stretches many miles north-west into the country. The scenery around it is soon described, since it is diversified with the least possible variety of objects;—it is bounded with unwooded ridges of muirland, inconsiderable in their height;—there is to be seen a solitary good house at the head of the bay, a few cottages, and occasionally the remains of some lonely burgh,

> "With ragged waulles, yea, all so rent and torne,
> As though it had been never known to men,
> Or carelesse left, as wretched thing forelorn;
> Like beggar bare, as naked as my nail,
> It lies along whose wrecke doth none bewayle."*

---

* Churchyard's Worthiness of Wales.

ESWICK TO LUNNA.

A considerable peninsular promontory to the north of Catfirth, bears the name of Eswick. Travelling along the shore of Vassa Voe, a small inlet, I passed over two freshwater lochs, that watered a valley of limestone, and arrived at a fertile little valley named Brugh, well sheltered from the east by a rising hill. In this vicinity was an ample estate, which once belonged to a Scottish family, that anciently held a distinguished rank in Shetland. The lands of Brugh were given by King James VI. to Hugh Sinclair and his heirs, in the year 1587; and in a clause of the grant, there was a special provision, that they should not descend to the family according to the law of udal succession, but according to the rule of primogeniture adopted in Scotland. The charter was expressed as follows: "Secundum formam et modum successionis infra regnum nostrum Scotiæ observat. sciz. quòd unus hæres immediate post alterum succedet, absque divisione, non obstantibus legibus et consuetudinibus patriæ Zetlandiæ in contrarium observatis."* The Sinclairs maintained in Shetland, during the 17th century, an establishment of no small degree of splendour. This is evinced by an inventory of the plate and household-goods of one of the family named Robert Sinclair, which is still extant.† He had also when he died, 82 horses, 38 mares, 60 oxen, 118 cows, 3060 sheep, 165 barrels of oats, 212 barrels of bear, and 3 chalders of bear. The lords of this estate were, on account of the royal grant, generally honoured by the title of Barons of Brugh; but the family is now become extinct, and their estates, which were sold, passed into several distinct hands.

On arriving at the extremity of the Valley of Brugh, near to the sea, the attention is arrested by a ruined chapel of the Sinclairs; a front and part of a side wall being nearly all that remains of the structure. It was built at the close of the 16th century, in the plainest manner. On each side of the door are engraved in stone the arms of the family, and underneath them occur devout mottos. The words of one of them are, "Remember to die, and after that to live eternally." In the other motto, is a sentiment to the following purport: "In earth nothing continueth, and man is but a shadow."‡ Of the house that the Barons of Brugh once inhabited scarcely the foundations remain. The site which was chosen for their residence was judicious; it was a rich valley, sheltered from the east winds by the rocks of Eswick, and beautified by several small lakes with which it was watered. To the front, however, nothing is to be seen but the ocean, into which protrudes the distant promontory of the Neap of Nesting.

I had now arrived at the parish of Nesting, so named from an ancient ting or open law-court, which was held by the great Foude when he made his circuit round the mainland. A wall of a few miles close to the sea, and along the brow of a long mountain ridge of gneiss, led to the kirk of the parish, which is a new building, situated close to a small mount, on which appear the ruins of a burgh. I then came to a promontory, named the Neap, where, in the days of Patrick, Earl of Orkney, an act of savage revenge took place,

---
* Grievances of Orkney, p. 5.
† It was in the possession of Thomas Mouat, Esq. of Belmont.
‡ See Plate III. fig. 4, 5, & 6.

which has not been exceeded in any country, but where oppressive power has inflicted wounds that, rankling to madness, impart to the human breast the passions of demons. It has been shewn that the rapacity of Earl Patrick, in his designs upon the udal lands of Orkney and Shetland, led to his disgrace, and eventually to an ignominious death. His attempts to wrest from the ancient udaller his little inheritance, or to burden him with obligations unknown to his fathers, is perpetuated in the rental of his estate, which, on his forfeiture, was recorded in the King's Exchequer, with the intention that it should be the rule of every future exaction. A more infamous document than this never, perhaps, existed in any age or in any country. Besides requiring duties from lands to an amount that scarcely left for the cultivator the means of existence, Earl Patrick assumed the power of confiscating lands for criminal offences, and thereby, on false charges of theft, witchcraft, or raising marchstones, an immense tract of territory fell within his grasp. If any one also had met with a violent death, his landed property became forfeited. In one island of South Ronaldsay, we find mention made of the lands of four individuals which were seized, because the proprietors of them had been found "deid in the flood-mark." In the same place, the lands of Oliver Sinclair were "escheit for theft." The patrimony was confiscated of Jonet of Cara, "quha was brunt for witchcraft," and of Stansgair, "pertaining to the Couplands, the ane brother [having been] hangit, the other banishit, for theft." It is affirmed, that the parson of the parish of Orphir, in Orkney, was particularly instrumental in administering to Earl Patrick's avarice, which tradition is indeed countenanced by the rent-roll preserved of that parish, dated in the year 1595, where there is a considerable forfeiture of udal property. Among those whose lands fell in escheat, were four brothers, of the names of Sinclair: their estates appearing on the rental to have been confiscated on the accusation of theft.*

When Earl Patrick's degradation had taken place, the popular vengeance was kindled against every instrument of his oppression, in a mode of which no idea can be formed, but by those who have witnessed some revolutionary movement in a country that has long tasted of oppression's bitterest dregs. It was then that the parson of Orphir took flight, pursued by the four Sinclairs of Orkney, who toiled after him like blood-hounds for their prey. The wretched man fled to Shetland; the avengers hunted him out,—met him on the Noup of Nesting, and slew him on the spot. One of the brothers imitated the tiger in his rage,—he laid open the breast of the slaughtered victim,—tore out his heart, and with a ferocity,—from the bare mention of which the mind shudders,—drank of his heart's blood. May the causes which gave rise to such scenes be few on the face of the earth.†

On the summit of the Noup of Nesting, the manse of the respectable minister of the parish is situated.‡ It was built by one of his predecessors, on a site better adapted for a

---

* "Adhuc in land maill of 1 mk terræ in Ingamyre, fallen in escheat to my Lord for theft, pertaining to the Sinclairs, 9 sett, cost, tantum flesh, 1 pultrie." In another place, there is a mention of lands named Be-north-the-Gait, in Swanbuster, part of which were reported as "pertaining to the Sutherlands, fallen in escheat to my Lord, for witchcraft, and raising of ane marchstane," and the rest were "escheat for theft, pertaining to the Sinclairs."

† The forfeiture of the property of the Sinclairs of Orphir, appears in Mr Peterkin's Collection of the Orkney Rentals. The tradition of the horrid tragedy committed on the Noup of Nesting, may be found in Brand's Tour through Zetland. There is no reason to doubt the statement, since history has recorded scenes equally shocking, that have taken place in countries where all the finer feelings of human nature have been obliterated by long and unprovoked acts of cruel oppression.

‡ Now occupied by the Reverend Mr Inches, to whom I feel much obliged for the hospitality I experienced at his house.

light-house. From this eminence there is a fine view of the Isle of Whalsey, stretching out far to the north-east, and situated between a cluster of islands that approach the shore of the mainland, and a remoter group, named the Outskerries. In proceeding northward, my road led through one of the wildest districts of Shetland, where were hills of the most grotesque form, among which were interspersed innumerable small lochs. Passing for several miles along the barren shores of Vidlin Voe, I came in sight of the House of Lunna, situated on the brow of a hill ;* close to it is a very narrow isthmus of land, which communicates with a large promontory, several miles long, that stretches out into Yell Sound.† Near the Isthmus of Lunna, once stood a religious building, but of what description is very doubtful : a broken font was discovered among the ruins, as well as architectural carvings, executed in a soft magnesian stone, of a steatitic kind, named Kleber. Much fish is cured at Lunna, consisting of ling, cod, and the Gadus Brosme, or torsk, commonly named Tusk. The latter, which somewhat resembles ling, though not so long, is very abundantly caught in the deep-water fishery off the coast.

ISLAND OF WHALSEY AND THE OUTSKERRIES.

Whalsey, to which I sailed, is a large island, consisting of irregular ridges of gneiss, that stretch far to the north-east. The approach to it from the south-west extremity is very fine. Near a small bay is a handsome house, belonging to Robert Bruce, Esq., shewing the style of the middle of the last century, with gardens walled round. A system of farming has been introduced in this island, highly creditable to the proprietor. The fields of corn around the house looked beautiful ; and, if the country could only have been clothed with trees, we might transport ourselves, in imagination, to some district of the Lothians. The island to the north-east is very uninteresting. There is nothing to diversify bleak and uneven ridges of gneiss, except a good parish church and a few scattered cottages. I omitted to see a loch which Mr Low noticed, where was a small holm connected to the shore by means of stepping-stones, originally defended by a wall round its margin, and by a breast-work toward the land. A space of ground was thus enclosed, sufficient to contain many people, with their cattle and effects. The Burgh (as it is called) bears the name of Hogsetter.‡

From Whalsey I set sail for the Outskerries, a very remote and detached groupe of small islands and rocks, fifteen miles distant from the mainland of Shetland. Our light yawl was manned by six excellent seamen ; a square sail was hoisted ; and a breeze

---

* Lunna, which was inhabited by Mr Leisk, when I visited it, is the family residence of Robert Hunter, Esq., a gentleman of considerable intelligence, who has the merit of attempting first to introduce into the country a better description of tenures, free from the obligation of fishing for landlords. The obstacles that he met with in his views arose, however, from an unexpected source,—from the tenants themselves, who being by no means prepared for so sudden a change of condition, much abused the liberality they had experienced. The event evidently shews, that a domestic reform, like a political one, should be a gradual process.

† It has been remarked, (p. 173) that, about a mile or two to the north of the house, are several remarkable detached rocks, named the stones of Stefis, of which the largest is about 23 feet in height, and 96 feet in circumference.

‡ There is a rock of gneiss on the west of the island, which, in one place, considerably affects the compass.

springing up favourable for the passage, the buoyant skiff rapidly cut its way through surging waves; whilst the seamen, with admirable adroitness, raised or lowered the sail, according to the force of the wind with which we were impelled along. Passing several solitary holms on which rude huts appeared for the temporary summer accommodation of the seamen who were engaged in the ling-fishery, I arrived at length near the Outskerries. They seemed fenced round about by cliffs frightfully steep and rugged. One of these was pointed out to me, on which was cast away, in the year 1664, the rich vessel, named the Carmelan of Amsterdam, that was bound to the East Indies, laden with three millions of guilders, and many chests of coined gold. The wreck happened on a dark night, when four men, placed among the shrouds, were endeavouring to discover the land. They were not able to descry the rock before the vessel was close upon it, and before they could warn the rest of the crew, the ship struck. The mast broke close to the deck, falling, at the same time, on one of the cliffs, by which means the four men were saved: but the ship itself sank in deep water, and all the crew on board immediately perished. A considerable quantity of spiritous liquors was driven ashore; and, for twenty days afterwards, the inhabitants of the Skerries were in a state of continued intoxication. When the Earl of Morton heard of the wreck, he repaired to the spot, and was actively employed in rescuing from the water several of the chests of gold. These ought to have come to the King's treasury: and, when Charles II. heard of the Earl's private appropriation, he is said to have been decided in the views which he had before entertained, of recalling the Crown-estates of Orkney and Shetland that had fallen into the hands of the Morton family on the fictitious plea of a mortgage by Charles I.*

After passing the rock on which the Carmelan had split, a narrow opening appeared through ragged rocks, out of which ran a strong current of tide, that caused the billows on the outside, impatient of resistance, to boil and foam with uncommon impetuosity. Through these our reeling yawl was guided with infinite skill, when we entered a small harbour, well sheltered by high ground, and presenting on its surface the unruffled tranquil appearance of a mountain lake.

> ———————————————" It was a still
> And calmy bay, on th' one side sheltered
> With the brode shadow of an hoarie hill;
> On the other side an high rock toured still;
> That, t'wixt them both, a pleasaunt port they made,
> And did like an half theatre fulfill."　　　　SPENCER.

As the Outskerries lie so much to the east of Shetland, they are well adapted for carrying on a deep water fishery for ling. On this account, there are a few slight permanent buildings, erected for the accommodation of agents who superintend the preparation of curing; and, along with these, are several rude huts or lodges, for the temporary abode of the fishermen. An old custom, now legalized, allowing any one to erect temporary

---

* The narrative of the loss of the Carmelan, may be found in Brand's Voyage to Orkney and Zetland.

fishing-huts and booths on grounds that had not been previously enclosed for cultivation, has caused frequent disputes between landholders, and others, who were engaged in the ling fishery, some of which frays had even led to bloodshed. Early in the last century, for instance, a contention in the Outskerries arose between two considerable families in Shetland, regarding this right, which proved so serious, that it is still traditionally handed down under the name of the Skerry Fight. The fishermen belonging to the Gifford Family of Busta, came armed, and obtained possession of a booth that they had erected the preceding year. The Sinclairs, also, headed by the valiant lady of the family, took the field. A siege commenced; there was a discharge of fire-arms from each party with little or no effect, until Magnus Flaws, the champion of the Sinclairs, having tried in vain to break open the door of the booth which was occupied by the Giffords, mounted the roof, and swore most stoutly that he would be in the building though the devil should dispute him admission. On effecting an entrance, he was immediately shot dead by the occupants within; upon which the Sinclairs took flight, and, like dastards, abandoned their lady, who was, by the opposite party, made prisoner. It appears that no legal notice was taken of the fray. The head of the Gifford Family was at that time the steward of the island, being invested with the full power of punishing such breaches of law; but he did not think proper to proceed against his immediate dependants.*

The time when I visited the Skerries, was not the season for pursuing the fishing of ling; I thus missed a busy and interesting scene. There are no objects at the Outskerries worth particular notice; a rich bed of limestone passes through the group, near to which the land is remarkably fertile. There are but very few families, perhaps not more than six or seven, who constantly reside at this remote place.

Having at length accomplished my journey through the south-east part of the country, I prepared to sail for the north-east isles of Fetlar and Unst; but I did not quit the district without impressions of the most grateful kind for the hospitable attention I had received in my journey from Dunrossness to the Outskerries.† If there is any district in the globe where hospitality, in flying from crowded cities and courts, has sought some peaceful refuge, it is among the pathless wilds of the British Thule.

I have at length concluded an Iter, the various incidental objects of which were associated with all the leading events connected with the history of Shetland. It will now, perhaps, be sufficiently evident, how little the annals of this country are to be understood, without an accurate knowledge of the original state of the udal laws, that prevailed in this Scandinavian province. The task, therefore, remains of giving more particular illustrations

---

* This tradition of the country has been related to me by Mr Henderson of Bardister.

† I have to acknowledge, in the most grateful manner, the kind attention I received at Lerwick and its vicinity; at Laxfith at the Manse of Nesting; at Lunna and Whalsey.

of them, as well as of the feudal tenures by which they were succeeded, in corroboration of the historical sketches that have been rendered.

ILLUSTRATIONS OF THE LAWS OF UDAL SUCCESSION.

Definition of the word Odel or Udal, and the distinction between the terms of Odel and Feudal.

The original meaning of the word *udal*, in its appplication to land, was *absolute property ;* that of *feudal*, implied *stipendiary property*.

"The real signification of the word *Odel*," says Bishop Pontoppidan, "implies real property, according to Joh. Gramm, in his dissertation upon the word Herremand, " 'ut Adelbonde redeamus, is non alius quam locuples et copiosus colonus aut fundi possessor. Schefferus autumat ab Adel et Odel oriundum esse, quod proprietatem omnimodam, scilicet ab Odh proprietas, et All totum omne denotavit, atque Adelbonde esse eum qui haberet Odel, hoc est proprium et a majoribus, per hæreditatem acquisitum possidebat fundum. Vide acta Societatis, Reg. Hafn. t. 2., p. 272.'" Sir William Blackstone, in his remarks on this passage of Pontoppidan, adds, "the transposition of these northern syllables, *allodh*, will give us the true etymology of the *allodium*, or absolute property of the feudists ; as, by a similiar combination of the latter syllable with the word *fee*, (which signifies, as we have seen, a conditional reward or stipend), *feeodh* or *feodum*, will denote stipendiary property." See Blackstone's Commentaries, 14th Ed., Vol. II., p. 44.

Other opinions on the Etymology of the word *Udal*, will be found in Dr Jamieson's Scottish Dictionary, where they have been collected with great industry, but none of these I have thought proper to adopt. Some of them are nearly as amusing as that which was given in the year 1642, by Bishop Grahme of Orkney, in reply to a query by the Magistrates of Edinburgh, *to know what the lands haldin* of Udil were : " Ratio nominis, alse far as ever I could trye," answers the worthy prelate, " is, that the kings of Norroway sent one Udillaus, wha divyded the lands of Orknay and Shetland, in pennie lands and used lands, as Ireland is now divyded in aikers ; from yat divisione, to this day, they have possesst yair lands as heritors without wreate." Peterkin's Rentals of Orkney, No. 3, p. 20.

The author of the Grievances of Orkney has observed that the word Udal was by the Germans and Scandinavians called Aoidal, Audal, Othel or Odal ; and by the Orkneymen and Shetlanders, Authal, Uthel or Udal."

Nature of Udal Tenures.

Feudal lands were originally possessed by military chiefs, and they were granted to inferiors on certain conditions of homage, rent or personal service. The incidents of feudal tenures, which were at the first connected with military subordination, have been considered as seven in number, viz., the heriot, relief, escheat, wardship, scutage, marriage-licence and homage.

Udal lands, however, did not render the earliest possessors of them liable to obligations of a military, or even of a civil nature ; for it was in later times that they became liable to a seat or tax. Yet this impost was not devoted to the service of a military chief, but to the support of a popular government, of which the King was supposed to be the head. It also appears, that on the introduction of Christianity, tithes on udal lands were levied by the clergy. But although religious and civil tributes became eventually imposed upon udal possessors, their estates were ever free from those incidents of feudal tenures which originated from military obligations.

No community can exist without regulations for its internal government, and for its independent preservation; contributions would, therefore, be required for the purposes of civil jurisdiction, upon which its validity would depend, or for the exigencies of war. The earliest tax of this nature, that existed in Scandinavia, was a *Nose tax!* "We are told," says the author of an article on the ancient laws of Scandinavia, in the Edinburgh Review, "that Odin set such laws in the land, as before were in use among the Asi; and throughout all Swedland, the people paid unto Odin a Scotpenny for *each nose.*"*

The origin of the scat or land-tax, is ascribed to Harold Harfager, at the time that he had suppressed the petty kings of Norway, and had made himself sovereign of that country. But the duty was never paid as a feudal acknowledgment to a superior, but merely as a contribution for the support of the Government. Scat is an old northern word, that merely denotes money or treasure, and its etymology conveys no information of the latest acceptation of the term. But it has been shewn from the Norwegian versions of the Bible, that a tax or tribute was always expressed by the word Scat. (Grievances of Orkney and Shetland, p. 100 and 101.)

When Harold Harfager subdued Orkney and Shetland, and promoted the colonization of these countries by Norwegians devoted to his interest, it appears that he only exacted a scat from pasture or grazing land, and this was named Scathold; but the land which was inclosed for cultivation became free from scat, and consequently retained the ancient name of Udal. The scat was also rated at a certain number of ells of wadmel; but in a later period, the assessment was made in some rude description of coins that bore the name of pennings or pennies. At this time the lands were divided into marks; a mark of land being of such an extent as would be equal in value to a mark of wadmel, a rate of silver, or a mark of some baser kind of metal. A mark of land would, then, include a certain area of scathold, and of inclosed or cultivated soil, retaining its original name of Udal, because it was free from a tax; an estimate, therefore, of the quantity of scathold included within the mark, was expressed by the number of pennies which were rendered as a tax to the King. The largest extent of Scathold, incidental to a mark of land, was liable to an impost not exceeding twelve pennings; this sum being rendered equivalent to a certain measure of wadmel: for the least extent of scathold, a sum not less than four pennies or one ell of wadmel was required. It was, therefore, within the limits of four and twelve pennies, that an appreciation was intended to be made of the proportional quantity of scathold, which, with udal or arable soil, formed the individual mark. But as the population of the country increased, and as soil became more valuable, a diminished area of the mark of land would be the equivalent of a fixed standard of comparison, and minuter divisions of scathold, by means of mark-stones, would become inconvenient. It was, therefore, within the enlarged compass of districts and parishes, that the proportion of scathold belonging to each mark of land was adjusted. Thus, in time, the term Penny became expressive of the proportion of scathold contained within the mark of land; a six-penny mark of land denoting a division that contained six proportions of scathold; an eight-penny mark a division that contained eight proportions, and so on. This is all the knowledge that a Shetland landholder has at the present day, of the quantity of soil which he possesses. That the mark of land, as some have stated, is not less than half an English acre, and does not exceed two acres, is a mere conjecture; it is as indefinite in its extent as ever it was in the days of Harold Harfager.

The lands in Orkney, however, do not appear to have been always in this unmeasured state. It was, probably, during the stay of King Hacon in Orkney, when he wished to billet his men over the country, that estates were for this purpose divided, in order to regulate the area that was necessary to support a certain number of men. The mode in which this was effected, is explained by a well informed author. "In Domesday-book," he remarks, "the entries of land in order to *Hidage,* are first by counties, then by towns or manors, and lastly by hides, half-hides and virgates of land, according to which the *Hidage*

---

* "The Latin translators," says the reviewer, "have absurdly and unfaithfully converted the nose tax into a capitation tax."

is fixed and limited. So also with us, the entries are first by islands or parishes, then by towns or villages, and lastly by mark-lands, pennies and farthings, according to which the *Skat* is fixed and limited. Therefore, *Skat* with us, is in the nature of *Hidage* in Domesday-book, that is tribute real, *land-tax* or ground-subsidy." (Grievances of Orkney and Shetland, p. 102.)

A mark of land had thus divided into eight ures or ounces;* each ounce-land into eighteen penny-lands, and each penny-land into four farthing-lands. The cultivated soil free from scat, was then named Quoy-land, a term meaning nothing more than an enclosed field. In No. II, p. 3 of Mr Peterkin's Rentals is this explanation :—

"Ane buoy-land or outbrek is ane peece of land newly win without the dykis, and payis no scatt.

"Ane tumall is ane peece land whiche wes quoy-land, but now enclosed within the dykis."

It was also a humane provision, that no mark should pay a tax for its proportion of scathold, unless the inclosed udal land was in a cultivated state. By this means the burden of the tax was much alleviated.

Thus, it appears, that Harold Harfager first invaded the udaller's rights in Orkney and Shetland, by rendering grazing lands liable to a tax, by which it acquired the name of Scathold; but the land which was enclosed for cultivation, was long afterwards sacred for the free use of the possessor, until the udal fence was first broken by the rude hands of Ecclesiastical power. The author of the Grievances of Orkney and Shetland has remarked that "Olaus, King of Sweden, was sirnamed Shot-Konung, *i.e.*, the tributary king, because he sent tribute to the Pope, and made his kingdom subject to the Holy See. Rex Sueciæ Olaus, Skot-Konung, *i.e.*, tributarius Rex cognominatus esse existimatur, quod hortatu Præsulum Sueticorum ad Pontificem Romanum misisset tributum. Loccen. Hist. Succ., lib. ii." Ever since, udal lands have been burdened with tithes.

But although lands became eventually liable, but to civil duties and to tithes, it is almost unnecessary to repeat that there is no reason to suspect that allodial or udal land ever rendered the occupier liable to personal service in the field, or in maritime excursions; but if it did, the obligation would by no means have resulted from the absolute will of a superior lord, as in feudal tenures, but from the popular voice of the cummunity. When the ancient kings of Scandinavia were desirous to raise an army, they convoked a general assembly of the free men of the nation. In this council, the requisition of each province, to furnish a certain number of soldiers or ships, was rendered proportional to its means.†

It may be also observed, that when Orkney and Shetland were united into an Earldom, the chief had no legal power over the inhabitants but when called into the service of war, when he held the rank of military commander. His engagement to the people appears, from many circumstances recorded in the early history of the Orcades, to have been like that which the King himself was bound to maintain; it was "to observe the laws : to defend his country ; to extend its boundaries ; to revenge whatever injuries his predecessors had received from their enemies, and to strike some signal stroke which should render him and his people famous." An obedience to the laws of Orkney and Shetland, appears, in fact, to have been alike obligatory on the ancient Earls of Orkney and on the people.

Origin of Udal Laws and their diversity.

It was at popular assemblies that laws were enacted for the decision of hereditary claims, and for preventing the alienation of lands from those who might be considered as proper heirs ; by this means, rights of succession we protected by the general regulations of the community, to which the udaller belonged. In the ancient laws of udal inheritance,

---
* See Torfæus, Rer. Orcad. Hist., p. 169. The greatest division of land at the present day is named an ounce-land.
† See Mallet's Northern Antiquities, Trans., vol. i., p. 257.

the proper successors to estates on the death of those who enjoyed them, were named the Udal-born.

It is stated in Erskine's Institutes of the law of Scotland, that when Orkney and Zetland were first transferred from the crown of Denmark to that of Scotland, the right of lands was held by natural possession, and might be proved by witnesses, without any title in writing, which had probably been their law formerly, while they were subject to Denmark. This is a mistake. Since the lands of the Scandinavian colony of Orkney and Shetland were considered as under the protection of common laws, no title for estates could be established, without a written decree of the Foude's court, delivered under the name of a Shynd-bill; the word Shynd being said to signify a Court. This bill or deed was signed and sealed by the Foude and a number of witnesses. The practice of confirming the possession of estates by means of Shynd-bills, continued long after these islands were annexed to the Scottish Crown. It was only when feudal oppression sought to destroy the force of the Shynd-bill, and with it the common laws which protected the rights of landed property, that great irregularities took place in the conveyance of estates, and that the poor udaller, alarmed for the security of his little property, knew of no other way in which his little patrimony could be held, except through the means of a charter from some superior, when it would be converted into a regular feudal tenure, or, on the other hand, by that sort of natural possession described by the celebrated Scottish lawyer, which consists in the proof of a right before witnesses, without any title in writing.

It has indeed been a common mode of defining udal lands, to say, that they were a property which was transferred from one hand to another without writing, possession being the only right. But, in reference to the principle, that the rights of udal lands were protected by the laws of the community of individuals among whom they were partitioned, the possession of them was never guaranteed but by a written judicial decree, which was made agreeably to the laws of udal succession, that had been passed at some popular legislative meeting.

The enactment of laws declaratory of those who were the udal-born, or had claims of hereditary succession to the enjoyment of udal-lands, is to be referred to a date long prior to the period when Harold Harfager converted Orkney and Shetland into a Norwegian colony.

That the laws of udal succession are antecedent to the reign of Harold Harfager is admitted by Pontoppidan, and many other Norwegian writers. There is an obscure illusion to the udal laws, in one of the most remarkable ancient poems that has been preserved; it is entitled Rigs-Mal, the song of King Eric.—" Rig (Rich), or Eric the second," says Mr Jamieson of Edinburgh, in his illustrations of Northern Antiquities, "was one of the first of the Goths in Scandia, who assumed the denomination of Kong (King), his predecessor having been stiled Diar or Drottnar; that is, Chiefs or Lords. He was likewise the first who divided his subjects into the three distinct classes of nobles, husbandmen and slaves, distinguishing precisely the rights and privileges of each; and upon this foundation, an allegorical poem was constructed, which was no more than a personification of the different modes of society, and making them the children of King Rig." In this very ancient poem, then, supposed to have been written about the eighth century, is an allusion to some decisive regulations which had taken place relative to the possession of udal lands. King Rig's directions to his son Jarl, *(comes)*, are thus related :

Thann had hann eignatzt	Eum possidere jussit
óðal völlu	avitos agros
óðal völlu	avitos agros
oc alldnar bygdir.	et antiqua rura.*

---

* Illustrations of Northern Antiquities, p. 456.

The oldest law of udal succession that existed in Shetland, and no doubt in Orkney also, is thus described by Mr Gifford. " The most ancient way, how lands and heritage was transmitted to posterity, was by a verbal deed called Udal Succession, founded upon an old Norwegian law called St Olla's Law, by which a man could no way dispose of or burden the lands he had by his father ; neither had he any power to make a will contrary to the said law ; but whatever children he had, male or female, they all succeeded equally to the father in his estate, heritable and moveable, and the youngest son had the father's dwelling-house, because the elder children were commonly *foris familiat* before the father's death, and the youngest son staid with him, and supported him in his old age, and thereby had no opportunity to provide himself in a settlement ; and, therefore, was provided with his father's dwelling-house, which was also an inducement to make him more careful of his old father. By this way of succession, most of the inhabitants were proprietors of the lands they possessed, and very few tenants amongst them ; and this Udell succession continued with many of the small Udellers of Zetland, till the year 1664, that they took heritable tacks of their own Udell lands from Spynie." (Gifford's Zetland, p. 54.)

It is well known that the Scandinavians succeeded to the Celts in the possession of certain of the northern districts of Europe. It is not improbable, therefore, that this law, which is that of Gavelkind, might have been borrowed from the custom of the earlier tribes who were dispossessed of their settlements, particularly as it is certain that many religious customs peculiar to Celtic nations became introduced among the rites of Odin. In the old Welsh laws, every man's inheritance was divided among his children, but the youngest son had the principal house. The Celtic females, however, were precluded from the inheritance, for, sooner than that an estate should devolve to them, it escheated to a superior. There is reason to suspect, that in some partial cases, an exclusion of this kind existed in Orkney ; for although the estates of the Earldom were, in an early period, equally divided among all the sons of the father, so that by this means there were at one time several Earls of Orkney, yet in no instance do we find that a female was made a partaker in such an inheritance. This exclusion may be accounted for, when it is considered that the Earls of Orkney were hereditary military leaders ; they were appointed to the command of all predatory expeditions, and they headed the forces of the country that were united for common defence. Among the Scandinavians and Saxons, it also appears that there was a distinction made between spurious and legitimate children. But by the ancient Welsh laws, and the Irish custom of Tanistry, the inheritance of a deceased landholder was equally divided among his sons, whether bastards or lawfully born. (Whittaker's History of Manchester, vol. i., p. 266, Ware's Antiq. of Ireland, vol. ii., p. 73, and Bingley's North Wales, vol. ii., p. 257.)

Mr Gifford has recorded the manner in which the udalborn of Shetland came into the possession of their rights ; this is so curious that I shall give it at full in his own words : " The first right that is to be found upon lands in Zetland, is that called a Shynd-bill, and that was only used by the most considerable heritors.* Shynd, in the Danish language, signifies a Court, and Bill was a common name to any deed or writing made in court ; so it may be translated in English a judicial right. The way how it was done was this ; a man having a mind to dispone his estate, invited the Fowd and three or four of the best men in the country to his house, where he had an entertainment provided for them. And being all convened, the Fowd kept a court, before which the heritor compeared, and did there judicially made his will, disponing his estate, heritable and moveable, particularly mentioned,

---

* Mr Gifford is here under a mistake. Before the introduction feudality into Shetland, the Shynd-bill was obtained by all heritors, considerable or inconsiderable, as a title for their estates.

and divided to his children, reserving his own liferent of the whole, and a liferent of a part to his wife, if she survived him ; which will the clerk of court wrote, and being done, was publicly read, all being concerned being present, and if approven by the disponer, it was signed by the Fowd, and these three or four gentlemen that sat with him, as assessors, and all their seals were put to it, and being recorded in the court-books, the principal was delivered to the disponer, who kept it till his death, and then all the heirs mentioned in the Shynd-bill, entered to their respective portions contained therein, and were all equally chargeable for the defunct's debts and funeral charges. And if there was no such will made by the udeller in his lifetime, after his death his children, or nearest of kin if he had no children, made application to the Fowd to divide the inheritance amongst them, who appointed a day and place, ordaining all concerned to attend ; and having called a court, he caused the heirs to give up a faithful inventory, upon oath, on the whole subject left by the heritor deceased, which he divided equally amongst them, according to the Udell or St Olla's law, and caused a Shynd-bill to be written thereupon, which was signed, sealed, and delivered to the heirs, and was as good as if made by the udaller while he lived." (Gifford's Zetland, p. 54 and 55.)

At a later period in the annals of Orkney, primogeniture appears to have been favoured to a certain extent. Newer laws of inheritance were introduced in the country, which afforded the means of perpetuating family wealth and power, by concentrating them in an individual. But it does not appear that this later law of Norway was enforced to any extent, until the annexation of Orkney and Shetland to the Scottish Crown. Recent settlers from Scotland then found a Norwegian pandect, in which primogeniture was respected, much less revolting to their notions of feudality, than the law of Gavelkind, which had originally existed in the country. A translation of the rule inheritance, from the law-book of Norway, (Lib. vi. cap. 2. act 63), is given in the scarce work entitled the Grievances of Orkney and Shetland.

—" Does a father leave odals behind him ? Then shall the eldest son succeed to the principal mansion and estate ; the other children receiving an equivalent out of the other land ; everyone his own lot, a brother, a brother's lot, and a sister, a sister's lot, according to the estimation of neutral men.

" Is there no son ? Then descends the chief manor to the grandson by the eldest son; or by the second, or any other son in order, as nearer the inheritance than daughters. Are there no grandsons? Then belongs the chief manor to the eldest daughter, the rest of the sisters getting land in equivalent, as said concerning the children in general.

" Is there not land enough to compensate the chief manor? Then must the co-heirs be satisfied in money or goods. Do these fall short too : The eldest shall yet keep the manor, giving the rest a share only of the income, as by neutral men shall be determined. As for the other manors, these, with the woods, shall belong to the sons ; for daughters shall only have their lot in the most remote and discontiguous lands. But can they not have a lot in these, nor in moveable, nor city-goods neither ? Then shall the brothers who receive the manors, make up their lot by some other equivalent ; otherwise they shall admit them for partners in the manors, for so much as the sisters have right to."

Pontoppidan remarks on this latter law,—" One great evil arises from this odal's right, namely, many an undutiful and wicked son, because he is the eldest, and depends on his odal right, which nothing can affect, behaves extremely ill, not only to a deserving mother-in-law after the death of his father, but also to his own parents. This might certainly be remedied, without infringing the odal's right, when there are younger children of better disposition, and more deserving of the inheritance. By this means, great sins against the law of Nature might be prevented, if the legislature would think fit to set proper restrictions to the odal's right."—*Pontopp. History of Norway*, vol. ii., p. 291.

I shall now subjoin two illustrations of the mode in which property was assigned to heirs, as they appear in the memorials of the Foude's Court. It will be evident, from the tenor of these decrees, that the law of primogeniture was directed to invalidate a prior division of lands, which had taken place according to the more ancient law of St Olave, which was that of Gavelkind. It may be, however, premised, that the principal mansion and estate that formed the share of the oldest son were often named the *head-buil;* in other records, they were called the *chemis place;* the term *chemis* being from Old French, *chesmez,* importing the principal house on an estate which was inhabited by the lord or proprietor.—*See* Jamieson's *Etym. Dict.* word *Chemys.*

- "*August* 19, 1602. Anent the action and cause persuit be Margaret Murray, oy to umquhil Niager Williams' daughter, heretrix of the lands underwritten, and Hierome Umphray her spouse for his entres ; against John Murray of Stendail, and Robert Murray his son, anent the richt and tytil of six mark land uthel, lying in the town of Gruting, disponed be the said umquhil Niager to the said Margaret Murray her oy, in her minority : Compeirit Hierome Umphray, pruifit sufficiently the said umquhil Niager to have conquest and giftit the foresaid six mark land, and disponit the samen to her sa'd oy, and placit her in possession thereof, be casting of peits, and uplifting the debts and duties thereof, in her name. Compeirs the said John Murray and his son, and alledgit that the said six mark land was the *head-buil, (i.e.* the principal manor), and so could not be giftit nor disponit frae the principal air. Quhilk alledgance was found relevant, and therefore assigns them to pruif the samen at the next *laweting,* this heand the first diet of the actioun, and then justice to be ministred in the said matter as law lewis. And in case the samen beis provin to be the *head-buil,* the complainer to have als meikle, als guid other land in another part, according to the use and consuetude of the country."

"*July* 21, 1603. Anent the action and caus persuit be Alexander Cheyn, ane of the sons and airs of unquhil Mr Robert Cheyn of Ury, agains Thomas Cheyn of Walla, his eldest brother, for making an airff and division of all lands and moveables appertaining to the said unquhil Mr Robert, amangs the haill airs, to the effect the said Alexander many be kend to his part thereof. Quhilk being considerit be the assize, in presence of the said Thomas, they ordain him to make an lawful airff and division of all lands and moveables pertaining to his said father, at the airff-house of Norby, be twelve neutral men, to be chosen with advice and consent of the said hails airs,—and to make every one of the said airs, either sister or brother, to be kend to their own parts, according to the laws, use and consuetude of the country."*

The author of the Grievances of Orkney, &c., in his desire to shew that the udal right had its foundation in the Mosaic institutions, observes, that " by the law, the eldest son had right to a double portion of his father's estate, and the other sons had their equal shares ; the daughters, in this case, being incapable of any inheritance, but of legacies only, in money or moveable goods. And thus, for the most part, it is by the law of Norway, which in this matter is much alike, differing more in modification than in substance."

It is difficult to say when the right of primogeniture was introduced for the first time into Orkney and Shetland. Torfæus, in speaking of a period about the beginning of the 12th century, has the following remark :—" Sucinus omnibus allodiis quæ parter, quæ frater Valthiofus possidebat sibi assertis (jure profecto a Norvegico, vel etiam eo, quod septemtrionalibus hisce regnis in usu erat alieno, sed occidenti usitato, primogeniturae privilegio) magnifice deinde vixit," &c.—*Torf. Rerum. Orcad. Hist.* p. 113.

Another Scandinavian law, incidental to udal tenures, was the incapability of an inheri-

---

* Grievances of Orkney and Shetland, p. 9 and 10.

tor to dispose of his patrimony without the consent of the next heirs, or the udal-born. In the law-book of Norway, (lib. v. cap. 3. act 1.), is the following injunction.—"Will a man sell his odalland? Then shall he summon all the odal-born [his kindred] and notify to them, that he is to sell such odal-land, making them the first offer, if they will buy, and have no impediment, such as the want of money, and the like. Also he shall proclaim, or cause to be proclaimed, in the public market, that he is to sell such odal land, and shall again offer it to his own kindred, the odal-born, whether known or unknown; but first to those who stand in the nearest degree of relation to him, whether male or female, that so the thing may come to their knowledge, though they should not be there present."*

Mr Gifford has testified to the introduction of this law into Shetland. He has remarked, that "if any man was to make a purchase from an udeller with consent of his heirs, without which the purchase was not good, the property was conveyed to the purchaser by a Shynd-bill, with this addition, that the disponer did judicially acknowledge that he had received the full value of the land disponed, and desired that his property therein might instantly be transferred to the purchaser and his heirs; and the apparent heirs of the disponer being also present, consented to the sale; and the Shynd-bill being signed and sealed, was delivered by the Fowd to the disponer, who did judicially deliver it to the purchaser, with a benediction."†

Another confirmation of the prevalence of this law, is the mandate of Earl Patrick, quoted in p. 59, ordaining, "that no person or persons frae this forth, either buy or sell ony sort of lands with others, without the samen be first offered to the nearest of the seller's kin, according to the use and constitution of the country."

Besides the incapability of an udaller to dispose of his patrimony without the consent of the udal born, it also appears that the lawting of Orkney and Shetland did not allow him to sell his lands, unless he could substantiate before the court, that it was poverty and wretchedness alone which prompted him to an alienation of the inheritance of his fathers.

This is evident from the copy of a Shynd-bill, which has been preserved by the author of the Grievances of Orkney and Shetland.

Decree of the Lawman of Orkney and Shetland, and his Council, affirming a Sale of Land in these Islands, as made according to Law.‡

"At Kirkwall, on Tuisday in the Lawting, in the moneth of Junii, the zeir of God ane thousand fyve hundreth and fourtein zeiris: A dome dempt be me Nicoll Hall, Lawman of Zetland and Orknay for the tyme, and ane certane of famows, discreit and unsuspect personis, of Rothmen and Rothmenisonis,§ chosin, the grit ayth sworne, and admitit to dissyd in ane matter of heritag: their names followis, that ar to say, Johnne Flet of Harray, Hendrie Cragie, Thomas Craigie, Nicol Craigie, brether-german to Johnne of Cragie, umquhile lawman of Orknay, Peiris Loutfut, Hendrie Fowbuster, Andro Linclet, William Clontheath, Alexander Housgarth, Magnus Comra, Magnus Aitkin, Andro Skarth, and Johnne of Bristo; betwixt Thomes Adameson, in the umbuth of ane nobill and potent man,

---
* Grievances of Orkney and Shetland, p. 7, 8.
† See Gifford's Zetland, p. 56.
‡ "From the protocol of Mr William Peirson, and another notary, in possession of the Lord Sinclair."
§ "The Udalmen were likewise called Rothmen, or Roythmen, that is, self-holders, or men holding in their own right, by way of contradistinction to feudataries, who hold derivatively, or by a dependence on others."

Schir William Sinclair Warsetter knycht, and in the umbuth of Nicoll Fraser, sone and lauful air to David Fraser, on the ane part ; and Alexander Fraser, the said Nicollis fatherbrother, in his awin umbuth, on the tother part :

"Quhafr the said Thomas Adameson, in the name and behalff of the said Schir Williame, producit lauchfull witnesses, of full hying and selling of all and haill the said Nicollis father heritag, that he airit, or mycht air he ony manner of way, lauchfullie sauld frae him and all his airis, to the said Schir Williame and all his airis ; and gart reid the writtingis maid thairon, as it beiris : and proponit, allegit and schew ressonabill caussis, as the law levis, that is to say, that the said Nicoll, divers sindrie tymis, come to the said Alexander, and offerit him the bying of all and haill his rychtis, and his fatheris heritag, befoir ony utheris, and he refussit it all tymis : and thaireftir, he come befoir the best and worthiest in the countrie, and diveis and sindrie tymis, in courttis and heidstenis ; and maid knawin that he was fameist, and perachand of hungar, in falt of fude, and naikit in falt of cleithing ; and tuk witnes, that sen the said Alexander had refusit the bying of his rychtis and heritag, that it was force till him to sell to ony that wald by ; Quhilkis the said Schir William thaireftir bocht, as his chairtor maid thairon mair fully proportis. And the said Alexander shew for his evidentis, that he had gewin the said Nicollis father, his broder, foure markis usuell money of Scotland, in part of payment of his part of heritag.

" All the saidis parteis allegance and evidentis, he ws avisitlie and ryplie considderit, hard, sene and undirstand, havand God befoir é,* hes deliverit, decreitit, and, be the cheptor of the Law-buk red thairon, for final dome gewin, that the said Schir William's bying and selling fra the said Nicoll is lauchfull, and thairfoir he sall bruk, joiss and posses, perpetuallie to him and all his airis, the saidis Nicollis father part of all and sindrie his rychtis, landis, heritag, malingis, steidingis, togidder with the principal chemis place† in Toob,‡ as eldest brother thairto. And the said Alexander bying and selling, fund of nane availe, becaus it is weill knawin, and fund, that he smikit and defraudit his brother foirsaid, and did sielych to the said Nicoll, his brother sone. And the said Schir William to lous ane sister-part of the foirsaid landis and heritag, togidder with the tane halff of the teind pennie, and the feird, as the eldest brother in the foresaid heritag. And the foirnamit four markis usuell money, gewin be the said Alexander to the said David, with all utheris that he may preiff gewin to the said Nicoll, before the said Schir William's bying and selling of the said heritag, sal be allowit in the landmaillis and ogude, sa far as it extendis to. And siclik, all that the said Alexander may prief that his foirsaid brother David Fraser tuk upe of the pament of the tenement in Sowyr, mair nor he gat, sal be allowit in pament of the said landmaillis and ogude, sa far as it extends to ; and all the wanttis be rycht compt and reknyng, the said Alexander sall mak pament to the said Schir William, togidder with the landmaillis of the eldest brotheris part, frae the day and dait of the said Schir William's bying and selling, quhyll the making of this present writ. And the said Schir William and Alexander to be at the arff-hows and chemeis, betwixt this and Allhallow-evin next eftir the dait of this present writ, to mak ane lauchfull shone and ayrfkest, as law levis.

" In witness of the quhilk thing, I the foirsaid Lawman hes hungin my seill to this present dome. And for the mair verificatioun and sikkerness, we the foirnamit domismen hes procurit, with grit instance, the scilis of venerabill and discreit men, that ar to say, Fredrick Newplar notar-publick, and Gilbert Kennedy burges of Kirkwall, for ws, to be hung to the present dome, befoir thir witnessis, Thomas Tullo of Ness, James Murray, Williame Scot and Alexander Borthwick, with utheris divers, day, zeir and place abovewrittin, befoir thir witnessis, Schir Umplair Clerk officiar, Schir Matho Farcar and Schir William Boswale, with otheris divers.

" Hæc copia concordat cum suo originali in omnibus, aliena manu (me aliis præpedito negotiis) fideliter copiat, ac collationat. per me magistrum Willelmum

---

* That is, before their eyes.
† The head-buil, or principal manor. See p. 125.
‡ Now Tob, a village near Saba, upon the mainland of the Orkneys.

Peirson notarium publicum, teste hoc meo cyrographo.
"Ita est.—Willelmus Peirson notarius publicus manu propria.
".Alterius notarii testimonium et subscriptio avulsa sunt."

There was a law in Shetland empowering the possessors of udal lands, with the consent of their heirs, to dispose of their patrimony to any person who would undertake their support for life. Such disposers were then received into the house of their maintainer under the name of his *opgesters;* whence the law by which estates could be alienated from the udal-born for such a purpose, was named the *custom of opgestery*.

In the possession of the late Thomas Mouat, Esq. of Belmont in Shetland, was a curious document, dated A.D. 1602, in which William Mansone accepts as his domestic inmate for life, or *opgester*, Freia Rasmusdochter, and her aged mother; and for their support he receives the amount of foar marks of land. It also appears that Freia Rasmusdochter was married, and had children. Hence the husband's agreement to part with his wife was requisite, as well as the consent of her children, or udal born, to the alienation of their grandmother's estate. It is but too probable that extreme poverty rendered necessary this deed of opgestery. The document I shall take the liberty of subjoining.

"Be it kend to all men, be this presentis, me, Freia Rasmusdochtir, to haif overgiven and transferit, and be ye tenor hierof overgivis and transferis my mither Enggegerth Thomesdochtir, with all and haill hir landis and heritag, viz. twa mark and ane half sax pennies ye mark lyand in Ronan in Sound, and ane mirk and one half in Gardom, all within ye south herischour of Unst, and lordship off Zeittland, to my guid frien Wm. Manssone of Gardie, his airis and assignayis, togidder with all my haill guids and geir, movabill and unmovabill, aperttening to me, or yat heiraftir may be found to aperttein to me; and I the said Freia, and my husband Ingillbrycht Nickellsom, grantis us weill content, satisfeit and thankfullie payd for our guid will and overgcom of our said mother, to ye said Wm. and his airis for now and ever, and yat of opgestrie, be virtue off ane laudabill custome and form of ye cunttrye of opgestrie, and with express consent of my hail bairnis, I am become lawfull opgester to ye said Wm., to be sustenitt in meat and claith all ye dayis of my lyfetyme, ratteficing, confirming, and aproveing ye forsaid gift given to ye said Wm. and his airis, to stand firme and stabill, without recovattioun or backcalling wnatsomever; and for the better seeurittie and veriefficattioun to ye said Wm. and his forsaide, becauss I culd not writt myself. I haif procurit the seallis of famous and discreit men, viz. Magnus Thomassone of Ronins seal, with ye seal of Nickell Acklay of Hiegaland, and Malcolm Mowatt of Wadbester is seall, and wt ye subscriptioun of Jhone Arschair, to be affixit and sett to yis present widd + + +

"At Gardie, in Unst, ye tent day of May 1602, beffor this witnes forsaid, and under subscryveand, wt eithers divers.

"Freia Rasmusdocther, wt consent of my husband Ingillbricht Nickellsone, wt our hands led at the pen, be me Jhone Archair, becaus we could not writt oursel.

"Jhone Archair, witnes to yis premisses."

The last law of udal possession, which is that of redemption, is stated after the following manner by Pontoppidan: "According to the old law, called Odelsbalken, thirty years possession was required to establish the odel's right. The law now requires but twenty years. This right could then never be forfeited to the Crown, unless by treason or felony. No odels-gods or freehold, can be alienated by sale, or any other way whatsoever from him, that can make it appear that he has the best title to it, by being the right heir or odels-mand. If he has it not in his power to redeem it, then he must declare, every tenth year at the sessions, that want of money is the only reason; and if he surmounts that difficulty, or, if he or his heirs, to the second or third generation, be able to redeem it, then he that inhabits it, who is only a possessor *pro tempore*, must turn out directly, and give up the premises to the *odels-mand*. For this reason, they keep a strict account of their pedigree: and formerly, about midsummer, every family used to meet together, and make themselves merry; and if any of their kindred had deceased since their last meeting, they marked his name in the tal-stock provided for that purpose."*

Respecting the law, Bishop Pontoppidan has made the following excellent remarks: "This odels right is preferable to that of the sele-eyers or freeholders in Denmark, not only because it is better secured to their families by the right of redemption, but because they possess it with all the privileges which a nobleman has in Denmark; for the Norwegian's odelsgaard or freehold, is only subject to the Crown. Whether this odels rights be to the advantage or disadvantage of the country, is a question that cannot easily be resolved. However, we may say of this as of most human institutions, which are always imperfect, that it may produce both good and bad consequences. It has this good effect, that it fixes the peasant's affections on his native place, with hopes of keeping his little patrimony in his family, and consequently improves with pleasure those possessions which he looks upon to be strongly secured to him. It likewise induces many a peasant's son, who sees the possession that must one day devolve to him, to keep near at hand, with hopes of enjoying and improving it by his industry. On the contrary, when it must be sold to a stranger, it never fetches its value, because the buyer possesses it with a great uncertainty, and does little to improve the ground that cannot be called his own, according to the words of the Poet:

" Sic vos non vobis nidificatis aves."

The very learned author of the Grievances of Orkney and Shetland, has made the following curious observations on this law of udal redemption: "If we consider the law-book of Norway, under the head of selling and redeeming udal land, it is plain that the udal right has its foundation in the Mosaical institutions. It was allowed by the Law, that if a man had sold his land, and was not able to redeem, his next relation might redeem, and the buyer could not refuse. So likewise by the law-book of Norway, not only may the odal-born, or the next heir of an odal-man, redeem from a stranger; but if he is not able, any of his kinsmen may; and so may another kinsman, if nearer than he who redeems, redeem back from him, till the land returns to the odal-born.— By the Law, no man was allowed to sell his house or his field, till the time of jubilee, except for necessary provision, compelled by poverty. And just so in Norway, or in these islands, which is the same, when one was to sell his land, it was not enough to make the first offer to his kindred; but he could not sell at all, except for the relief of his necessities.—By the Law, a man whose poverty had constrained him to sell his land, might redeem it before the year of jubilee, and so might any of his near relations: But then (say the Hebrew doctors) this was to be honestly done, and not with borrowed money, on purpose to carry the land from the buyer to another. By the law-book of Norway, the odal-born cannot redeem but for himself; and if the buyer mistrusts he must clear himself by oath, that he seeks back the land to his own odal, and to no other.—By the Law a man was to redeem his field according to what was given for it, though the buyer (say the doctors) had sold it to another for twice as much. By the law book of Norway, the odal-man, or odal-born, is to redeem his land for the price which was first paid for it, according to the letter of sale, and this though he redeems from one of his

---

* Pontoppidan, Nat. Hist. of Norway, vol. ii., p. 290.

own kindred, who had already redeemed it for more.—By the Law, houses within walled cities, if not redeemed within a year after the sale, remained with the buyer as his own, and the jubilee would not restore them. By the law-book of Norway, the owners of houses and lands within cities, may freely alien them, without making any offer to their kindred, as the law provides when odal land is sold."

The power of reversing any sales of land that were made contrary to the law-book of Norway, seems to have been vested, before the impignoration of Orkney and Shetland to the Scottish Crown, and even some little time afterwards, in the Law-man of Bergen.

This is evident from a curious document which has been given by the author of the Grievances of Orkney and Shetland.

Decree by the Law-man of Bergen, in Norway, and also by the Law-man of Shetland, and their Council, reversing a Sale of Land in these Islands, as made contrary to Law.

"Allum manum som dette breff see elder hore, sender Sebiorn Gottormson, Gulatings og Berwen lagman, Neils Willemson lagman i Hieltland, Erland Anderson-Frack, Jon Sturkason, Mattis Jenson, Endrith Swenson-Rostungh, Asmond Salmonson, raadmen ther samesteds, Willem Thomason lagrettisman i Hieltland · · · kuniktgorende at mith worse i Sacreffiet i Kros-Kurkie, liggende i Fornefnte stad Berwen, Manedaghen neft for St Lauris dagh, anno Domini 1485. Soghon ogh gordan aa at their heldo handon saman aff enen halffwo Beskedelig man, Jeppe Zeirsen radman, i tratnefnte stad, i fullo umbode hustrue Marion Jons-dotter, eighte kono sinne En aff Andro halfuone, Thomas Engilisk, i fullo umbode Dyoneth Alexanders-dotter, eighte kono sinne · · · saa mange Jorder som Thomas foresagd ulogligh koyt hadde af Anders Scot, aftnefnte hustrue Marions fader broders, som liggeri Hieltlando, eh herefter nefnes, *primo*, i Liungoyo i sunde thio Marker vrenda viii penninga aff marken. *Item*, i Yaale i Hedderokill vii marker, nio peninga aff marken. *Item*, Ulstadt i Jala sex marker, sex peninga aff marken. *Item*, i Hawle i Jala nio marker, sex peninga aff marken, undan tratnefnte Thomas och hans Erffvinga, och under ofuennefnte Jeppe hans hustrue och theris Erffvinga, til ewineligh egn. och als forrad innengords och utthen, til lands och Fiarls i mindelwch eder meira med allo tui, som tilliger eller tilliger hafuer · · ·. Til ytermer vissu hengia, wii ivor insigle for dette breff, med forsagdo Thomas som screffuit, er dagh och aar som forfagher.

Ex originali, penes Dominum Sinclair; sub octo sigillis, quorum sex avulsa sunt, duo supersunt."

Translation.

"To all men who shall see or hear this decree, Sebiorn Guttormson, law-man of Gulating and Bergen, Neils Williamson, law-man in Shetland, Erland Anderson-Frak, John Sturkarson, Mattis Jenson, Endrith Swenson-Rostungh, Asmund Salmonson, council-men of the same place, William Thomason, lagrettman in Shetland, (send greeting). Know, that in a convention held in the quire of the Cross Church of Bergen aforesaid, upon the Monday before St Lawrence Day, A. D. 1485; there being present, on one side, a judicious man,* Jeppe Zeirson, council-man of that place, in right of his lawful wife Marion, John's daughter; and, on the other side, Thomas Engilisk, in right of his lawful wife Dyoneth, Alexander's daughter: We said · · · that the lands in Shetland, herein after mentioned, which Thomas aforesaid had unwarrantably bought from Andrew Scot, the above Marion her father's brother, viz. *primo*, in Linga in Whalsey-sound, ten marks land, VIII pennies the mark less: *Item*, in Yell in Hedderokel, VII mark land, nine pennies the mark less: *Item*, in Ulstadt in Yell, six mark land, six pennies the mark less: *Item*, in Hule in Yell, nine

---

* *Beskedelig* man; in Latin, *providus vir.*

mark land, six pennies the mark less; shall all pass from the said Thomas and his heirs, and return to the above Jeppe his wife, and their heirs, for an everlasting possession; with all the appurtenances likewise, within the hamlets, or without the hamlets, where the lands lie, whether hills or dales, that do belong, or have belonged to them · · ·. In confirmation of which thing, we, and also the said Thomas, do seal this decree, the day and year mentioned above."

There is a passage in this document that requires some explanation. It has been shewn, that when land was separated from scatthold, and enclosed for the purpose of cultivation, it became udal, or the free property of the cultivator. It appears, then, that in the notice which has been taken of the estates of Shetland by the law-courts in Norway, the quantity of udal lands contained within the mark was made the subject of free bequest; but as the proportion of grazing land or scatthold, expressed by the term *pennies*, had not, for the purpose of culture, been surrounded by an udal fence, it was considered as held conditionally from the State, to which it paid a tax or tribute, and for this reason formed the subject of an exceptional cause. Hence the expression *ten mark land, eight pennies* [or eight proportions of scathold] *the mark less*; *seven mark land, nine pennies* [or nine proportions of scathold] *the mark less*, and so on.

In concluding this account of the udal system of Orkney and Shetland, it may be generally noticed, that there is not the slightest proof that feudality ever prevailed in these islands, whilst they constituted a colony of Norway; but the feudal system was immediately introduced on their annexation to Scotland; and it has been shewn, that the feudalization was completed by an unparallel course of injustice exercised in the country, by the illegitimate and tyrannical race of the Stuarts, Earls of Orkney, by needy farmers of the revenues of the Exchequer, and by fictitious mortgagees of the Crown estates.

It has been affirmed, that when Harold imposed a fine upon Orkney for the slaughter of his son, and when Einar received in pledge all the lands of the country, on condition that he would pay the fine from his own private coffer, the natives lost, for a short time, their udal rights, and they were reduced to the state of feudal vassals, who were bound to the Chief by a sort of military tenure. But it ought to be considered, that the soldiers of ancient Scandinavia never received any regular pay for their services in predatory expeditions, but were recompensed by a division of the booty; and if the natives of Orkney and Shetland, who had pledged their lands to the Earl, were allowed to retain them, and if they, in consequence of the impignoration, were more urgently impelled to follow the standard of the Earl when he embarked on some plundering excursion to the Scottish coast, it was with the hopes of obtaining such a share of spoils as might afford them the means of regaining their inheritance. That this hope of redemption was never finally abandoned, is evident from the sequel of the narrative; for when Earl Sigurd, a descendant of Einar, was desirous to take the field against a Scottish Chieftain, the udallers seized that opportunity of insisting that their services on this important occasion should be accepted as a redemption of their impignorated lands. "Singulis deinde civibus agros allodiales," remarked Torfæus, "a tempore Einaris de Cespite, in possessione Comitum sub hypotheca dedentos, restituit, quò militiam hanc sequerentur. Inde convincitur, non ibi magis, quam in Norvegia aut alibi, licuisse principibus cives ad militiam extra patriæ fines pro libitu cogere."—Torf. Rerum Orcad. Hist. p. 27.

It has been also supposed, that when, in A. D. 1379, Earl Sinclair received an investiture of the earldom of Orkney, there entered into his engagement with the Norwegian Monarch some obligation of a feudal nature. This is true enough; for the Earl was obliged to find the King a hundred good men, well armed, as often as required. But if this feudal relation existed between the King and the Earl, it was impossible that it could affect the relation in which the udaller stood to this nobleman. Their possessions were as unburdened as ever from military obligations; consequently the Earl had no other way left him to fulfil his engagement with the Monarch, than by regularly hiring the voluntary services of those who might be induced to serve the King of Norway.

ILLUSTRATIONS OF THE FEUDAL TENURES OF SHETLAND THAT SURVIVED THE EXTINCTION OF UDAL RIGHTS.

It has been remarked, that, in the earliest tenures of the Crown-lands that were granted to the natives of Shetland, the asperities of feudality were so softened down as to be scarcely perceptible. The lands that devolved to the Crown, by virtue of the treaty of James III. in the fifteenth century with Earl Sinclair, were named Property-lands; and the king, in letting them out on triennial leases, subjected them to an annual rent named Land-maills, and to a fine or compensation on entry, named Grassum. But if a tenant wished to convert his lease into an heritable feu, the triennial compensation of grassum was dispensed with, and he merely paid the annual tribute of land-maills. When, also, lands were ley or not laboured, the land-maills were humanely remitted. The earliest feuars of the Crown estates were named The Kindly Tenants of the King.

By no author have the relation of kindly tenants to their monarch been better explained, than by Sir Walter Scott, in his remarks on the Rentallers of Lochmaben. The kindly tenants of the four towns of Lochmaben, who are each entitled to a small piece of ground, are said by this author to have been "the descendants of Robert Bruce's menials, to whom he assigned, in reward of their faithful service, these portions of land, burdened only with the payment of certain quit rents, and gassums, or fines, upon the entry of a new tenant. The right of the rentallers is in essence a right of property; but, in form, only a right of lease: of which they appeal, for the foundation, to the rent-rolls of the lord of the castle and manor. This possession, by rental or by simple entry upon the rent-roll, was anciently a common and peculiarly sacred species of property granted by a chief to his faithful followers; the connection of landlord and tenant being esteemed of a nature too formal to be necessary, when there was honour upon one side, and gratitude upon the other."—(See *Minstrelsy of the Scottish Border*, vol. i., p. 87.) It is evident, that, in Orkney and Shetland, the king created a number of these kindly tenants on the Crown-estates, in order to assimilate their feus as much as possible to the free nature of udal tenures.

When the superiority of the country was granted to mesne-lords, and when the revenues of the King were let out to farmers, Crown-lands paid rent whether they were ley or laboured; and, in the course of time, the terms on which the rentallers of the Crown were allowed to possess their lands, were rendered particularly rigorous. The consequence of the fraudulent encrease of the standard weights of the country, and other oppressions that have been pointed out, which took place during the feudalization of Orkney and Shetland, have entailed such a burden on lands, as to perpetuate the greatest of hardships upon all classes of tenantry.

The mode in which lands have been feud or let out to tenants since the feudalization of Shetland, will now be pointed out. A mark of land was supposed to contain within it a greater or less extent of scathold, in proportion to the number of pennies which entered into its denomination. Thus a twelve penny mark of land contained a greater proportion of scathold than a ten penny mark. Appellations like these, anciently expressed the proportion of scathold which remained after arable or udal ground had been separated from it by inclosure; and although, upon the record of Earl Patrick Stewart's rental in the Exchequer, inclosed arable ground became no longer exempt from the impost of scat, yet the term was still of use to perpetuate the proportion of the annexed scathold. Frequently, in any division of commons, proportions were awarded, according to the number of pennies with which each mark of land had been long designated.

These preliminary observations being made, it may be now remarked, that, when Crown-lands were first let out to lease, they were supposed to consist wholly of scathold; and, therefore, the amount of the rent annually required for each mark, was regulated by its denomination of pennies. Thus, for instance, a mark of twelve penny land, containing twelve proportions of scathold, was charged with a greater rent than ten penny, eight penny, six penny, or four penny land that contained only ten, eight, six, or four proportions of scathold.

When Shetland was first annexed to Scotland, the Crown-rents were paid in wadmel and butter. Originally, a mark of wadmel was divided into eight parts, each of which contained six ells; and when, in the course of time, this coarse cloth was, for payment, converted into money, an eighth part of a mark, or six ells, was made equivalent to a Zealand zullen, which, again, said Mr Gifford, was equal to 24s Scots, or 2s Sterling. Hence six ells, or cuttels, were named a shilling of wadmel; and, in the old rentals, the quantity of cloth that was exigible from each estate, was marked down in shillings and cuttels. The amount of butter required from each lease holder from the Crown, was in lispunds and marks. A lispund was originally of 12 lb. weight; and it was farther divided into 24 marks, each of 8 oz. This weight was fraudulently raised during the tyranny of Earl Robert from 12 to 13 lb. Earl Patrick clandestinely advanced it to 18 lb. In the year 1690, under the oppressive exactors of the Crown-rents, and needy farmers, the lispund had further increased from 18 to 24 lb. weight. In 1710 it was again advanced to 26 lb. Mr Gifford of Busta in 1734, found that it was 28 lb. It is now said to be 32 lb.* By this augmentation it will be seen, that the produce fraudulently exacted from the injured and empoverished husbandman, was more than doubled. On this subject, the author of the Grievances of Orkney and Shetland has stated, that, "As a consequence of this encrease, numberless little heritages, and some fair estates also, are swallowed up, the Crown-rents having so encreased with the weights, that, when the years are not very plentiful, the whole fruits of the ground are not sufficient to satisfy them."

The ancient rental of Shetland, which has remained unaltered from the annexation of this country to Scotland down to the present period, may be now given.

Ancient Rental of Shetland.

Proportions of Scathold contained within the mark expressed by the term Pennies.	Butter paid, as computed according to Lispunds and Marks; the Lispund having been fraudulently increased. A Lispund is also divided into 24 Marks.	Wadmel computed in Money.
12 Penny land.	12 Marks Butter.	16s Scots.
10 Ditto.	14⅔ Ditto.	14s 8d do.
9 Ditto.	12 Ditto.	12s do.
8 Ditto.	10⅔ Ditto.	10s 8d do.
7 Ditto.	9⅓ Ditto.	9s 4d do.
6 Ditto.	8 Ditto.	8s do.
4 Ditto.	6 Ditto.	6s do.

* 24 marks are said to be equal to 32 lb. Scots troy, upwards of 35 lb. avoirdupois.

It may now be farther added, that when the chamberlain set a tack or lease of the property-lands to a tenant, it was for three years; and he caused him to pay the usual fine or compensation of Grassum. This amounted to 24s Scot, or 2s Sterling, for each mark of land; but, in progress of time, it was found more convenient to convert the grassum that was due every three years, into an annual demand of 8s Scots, or 8d Sterling. The annual land-maills, therefore, for a mark of the King's land, was estimated by the general rental of the country that had been given; and, added to this, was the annual sum of 8s Scots for grassum. This is the rental for all the lands in the country at the present day, whether they belong to private landholders, or to the superior of the country. When the number of pennies *per* mark determines the value of land, and when the annual grassum is added to the amount it will be found that

1 mark of 12 penny land pays yearly 16 marks of butter, and £1 4 0 Scots,
— — — 9 ————————————— 12 ————————————— 1 0 0
— — — 6 ————————————— 8 ————————————— 0 16 0 —

In the Appendix to Mr Shirreff's Agricultural Survey, p. 17, it is stated, that each penny *per* mark paid 1⅓ mark of butter, and 1⅓ in money: for instance, six penny land paid 8 marks of butter, and 8s Scots in money, to which was added 8s Scots *per* mark of Grassum.

Thus, although the nominal rents have not been raised since the islands were annexed to the Crown of Scotland, yet, by the gradual fraudulent increase of the lispund from 12 lb. to 32 lb., the produce exacted by the landlord has nearly tripled. Mr Morrison, in his statistical survey of Delting parish, has also remarked, that "till a few years, it was considered a standard regulation, that the butter part of the rent should be charged at 5s Sterling a lispund, or 2½d a mark; but the factor for the superior thought proper to charge the current price for the feu-duty butter, and many of the proprietors followed his example; so that a mark of butter, which weighs 1¼ English, is sometimes 3d, 4d, and 4½d, instead of the old conversion of 2½d a mark. This the tenants considered as a hardship, as few of them can pay their butter rents in kind."

The lands which were originally udal, but which were feudalized at a later period by the Earls of Morton, are enjoyed on tenures that are comparatively light. Some very ancient patrimonies having never been held by a charter from the Crown, are still in a limited decree udal. But the vassals who having inherited the proper estates of the Crown and its donators, have been rendered liable to the charge contained in the ancient rental of Shetland, labour under heavy burdens. All landholders, however, still pay the old scat that was rendered to the Kings of Norway; they pay a duty named *Wattle*, in commemoration of the prayers of a good sainted lady which the Shetlanders, in Popish times, purchased as an intercession for their manifold sins, and which Earl Robert Stuart, a Protestant reformer, contrived to perpetuate, by inserting in his rental: they pay the ox and sheep money that was granted as a compliment to the Earl of Bothwell, when he obtained a refuge in Shetland, after his marriage with the unfortunate Mary. The average of scat, wattle, and ox money, is said to be about 8d Sterling; some lands being charged for them as high as 1s 4d. According to Mr Shirreff, in his account of the agriculture of the country, the landholder pays one-half the cess or land-tax, and rogue-money; a premium for killing eagles, ravens, and hooded-crows; bounty to seamen and other casualties, with a proportion of schoolmasters' salary, which may altogether amount to about 6d Sterling *per* mark of land. The duties to the superior, which were originally exigible in the *ipsa corpora*, have long been commuted for money; the amount being regulated by the rise or fall of butter and oil, according to the prices of the market.

After Shetland had become subject to the Scottish Crown, the falconer of the Royal household came annually to collect hawks for the use of the King; and to feed these birds a hen was demanded from every house; or (as it is called) from every *reek*, under the name of Hawk-hens. Long after the sports of hawking had gone out of fashion, the payment was continued; and it is, at the present day, said to be perquisite assumed by one of the officers of the Exchequer, who has been in the habits of letting out the privilege of collecting them, for an annual compensation in money ; but I have not learnt that the claim has been very recently advanced.

It was shewn, (page 63) that when the udallers had become so distressed by poverty, that they were obliged to dispose of their property to wealthy strangers in the land, numerous allotments of territory were laid together so as to form an ample estate ; and in every part of the islands new settlers were to be found, who began to assume within their limited demesnes all the proud functions of the baronial lord. The little landlord demanded, along with rent, the acknowledgment of a grassum or entry ; and in many menial services, such as annual presents, casting the lord's peats, or labouring for him a certain number of days.

The proprietor of the lands of Shetland has been in the habit of setting them according to the ancient rental of the King; and he has imitated the superior of the Crown estates, in adding the King's ancient requisition of grassum, to the amount of his land-maills; he has also taken for his precedent all the subsequent mode of exactions adopted by the inheritor of the Crown-estates. But, indeed, considering the nature of the lands of Shetland, and their undivided state, this assimilation of tenures, to those that were granted by the superior, was almost unavoidable.

Among the private proprietors of Shetland, but more particularly of Orkney, many ancient feudal customs were continued, long after their extinction in Scotland from whence they were derived. Of these, none is more remarkable, than the perpetuation of those exactions which had their remote origin in a capitation tax, that prior to all feudal institutions, was paid for the support of some Commonwealth. It has been observed, that the most ancient tax of Scandinavia, instituted by Odin, was a *Nose-tax*. When countries, therefore, were, by the invasion of an enemy, feudalized, the chief feudatories, who had allotments of conquered land granted them by some liege lord, subjected their newly acquired vassals whom they found on their estates, to the same impost to which they had been accustomed, by inserting it in their rentals. We find traces of this most ancient of all duties, in the old rent-rolls of many manors in England, as well as Scotland. In the latter country, it was perpetuated under the name of *Canage :* this term being said to be derived from the Gaelic Cean, signifying the head ; and, therefore, supposed to import the capitation duty, which had preceded feudal vassalage. This tribute was generally paid at one period in the year, often at Christmas, in fowls, in cheese, or in oats ; which were hence named cane fowls, cane cheese, or cane oats. I have an account of this exaction being introduced, though late, into Shetland, by a gentleman of that country, which is related with so much of the spirit of the ancient udaller, that I shall give it in his own words : " About the beginning of the last century, the first Sir John Mitchell of Westshore in Shetland, married Margaret Murray, daughter of Francis Murray of Pennyland, who was commissary of Caithness. Sir John, as steward of Shetland, held the supreme judicial power in that country. His lady being accustomed to the oppressive feudal impositions then laid on the poor peasantry of Caithness, introduced some of them on her husband's estate, viz. the payment of a hen for every merk of land possessed by them, under the name of *Poultry Fowls.* In other cases, she imposed the burden of casting and carrying home peats to the manor-house, and of furnishing packages employed in the carriage of them called Cassies or Maizeys. The poultry is still paid, but the other exactions have partly gone into disuse, or have been commuted for money, or the annual labour of a certain number of days." Another mode of collecting the capitation tax, was by requiring from tenants an annual present at Christmas ; and this was spent in providing a treat, in which both the landlord and tenant partook. This feudal custom, which I have reason to believe is little know among antiquaries, is so curious, that although it was only introduced in Orkney and not in Shetland, I shall, perhaps, be excused, for giving some account of it on this occasion, though a little out of place. It was continued so late as the beginning of the last century, by the petty landlords of that country, feuars of the Crown-lands, in imitation of the lordly Barons of the south. In a very small pamphlet, entitled, *The True Causes of the Poverty of Orkney*, published in the year 1760. I find the following account of what are termed Boumacks, or Bummacks, a word which Dr Jamieson supposes to be of Scandinavian origin, derived from the Isl. *Bua* parare, and *mage socius*; that is to make preparations for one's companions. "The ancestors of the generality of the present Lairds of Orkney," says the writer of the pamphlet, "were mean men, feuars of the King's property; by their tenures they became bound to pay the full rent by way of feu-duty; they were wise enough to reckon nothing their own, except what, by their labour and industry, they brought the ground to yield, over and above the rents payable to their superior. They were plain, simple, sober, countrymen, frugal, industrious labourers, unacquainted with tea, coffee, rum, silks and velvets. Their tenants were their friends and companions; every tenant feasted his laird at least once a year, in the Christmas holidays; these feasts are called Boumacks by the country people. A late landlord of a good estate, looking on these boumacks as what the tenant was obliged to give his master, converted the boumacks of every house on his estate to 4 stettins of malt, and charged that in his rental as a fixed and constant rent; for now a-days most of these lairds would be affronted to sit down at a boumack with his tenants."* That a custom similar to the one described, existed in the north of England among the powerful landlords of that country, I have shewn in a paper which I had the honour of reading to the Antiquarian Society of Edinburgh. The return of an annual present from tenants, for the sake of partaking at the feast of Yole or Yule, I have detected in the rent-roll of a knight of Ashton-under-line, near Manchester, who lived in the reign of Henry VI. In the preamble of the rental are the following words: "The service of the said tenants is this; that they shall give their presents at Yole, every present to such a value as it is written and set in the rental, and the Lord shall feed all his said tenants and their wifes, upon Yole day, if them like for to come; but the said tenants and their wifes, though it be for their ease not to come, they shall send neither man nor women in their name, but if she be their son and their daughter dwelling with them; for the Lord is not bounden to feed save only the goodman and goodwife." There is no doubt, but that these annual presents were of the same nature as the Scotch canage, and that they are to be identified in the Orkney boumacks. They were, in fact, perpetuations of a capitation-tax, in use before the introduction into the country of feudality. It may be also observed, that the amount of the presents thus collected, was, in the manor-roll which I have examined, of such a considerable magnitude in proportion to the rent paid, that it would more than repay the expences of the table, leaving to the lord a handsome surplus. Accordingly, it is not improbable, that the name of Landlord was originally attached to the host of an inn, as a satirical allusion to the manorial landlord, who never provided a dinner for his guests, without receiving for it an adequate recompense. I may further remark that in the old halls of manorial residences in Lancashire, may be commonly seen an occasional elevation of the floor, or sometimes a lofty gallery, which was for the purpose of accommodating the Lord of the manor or his family, that they might not be incommodated with the coarse freedoms of the tenants below; also to preserve due decorum, was frequently introduced a diminutive pair of stone-stocks, about eighteen inches in length, with holes for fastening the fingers of the unruly. This instrument was entrusted to the general prefect of manorial festivities, the king of misrule, whose office it was to punish all who exceeded his royal notions of decency.—Thus much in illustration of the canage or cane-fowls of Shetland, and of the kindred acknowledgment of boumacks in Orkney.

The landed proprietor of Shetland has also long been accustomed to exact in addition to cane-fowls, the labour of each tenant for three or six days in the week, for the purposes of casting peats, or other labours of husbandry. We find this requisition in the rent-rolls of the powerful feudatories of more ancient times. In a manor-roll in my possession, every

---

* Some account of these Boumacks or Bummacks, may be found in the 15th vol. of the Statistical Account of Scotland, p. 393, 394. But the best notice of them is in the scarce pamphlet to which I have alluded, for the perusal of which I am indebted to Mr Neill.

tenant at will is thus commanded: "He that plough has, shall plough a day, whether the Lord be liever [more willing] in wheat seeding or in lenten seeding; and every tenant harrow a day with their harrow in seeding time, when they bin charged; and they shall cart every tenant ten cartful of turve from Doneam Moss to Assheton, and shere four days in harvest, and cart a day corn." This service, so profitable to the lord, was in the north of England called *Boon-work;* and hence, an old adage, when a man was compelled to work for nothing, "I am served like a Boon-shearer." No one, perhaps, but an antiquary, will be delighted to hear that *boon-work* is not still extinct in the British isles, and that it is still felt with all the impatience of the ancient boon-shearers of the South. "The three days labour in each year to the landholder," says Dr Edmonstone, with much justice, "is certainly a serious hardship on the tenant, especially as he has to work three days also to the clergyman. Both the heritor and the clergyman now live in a new enlightened state of society; and it becomes their duty to concur in abolishing a practice which keeps alive the recollection of feudal oppression, and stifles the feelings of generous freedom."

Having now taken leave of the ancient udal and present feudal state of Zetland, I shall briefly notice the state of the tithes which constitute one of the greatest burdens on lands that is at present experienced in this country, since they are generally drawn in kind.

The teinds of Shetland are partly of corn; these are paid by some lands in every tenth sheaf, after being cut down; in other lands the teinds are compounded for in butter and oil, and in a few lands only in money. For every thirty sheep three marks of wool and one lamb are exacted. For each cow three marks of butter on an average, and for each calf 1s Scots. Each six-oared boat pays of teind fifteen ling; and each four-oared boat ten ling. In the last place, the minister claims a right to three days work from each family in the parish, for the purpose of casting, raising and bringing home his peats. *See Memorial for the Parishioners of North Mavine, in Mr Shirreff's Agricultural Survey of Shetland,* p. 24—33.

There are no poor rates; the poor are said to be quartered upon the parishes in rotation, living on each family for periods varying from one week to a month.

NOTES TO ITER II.

NOTE VI. HISTORY OF THE UDALLERS, Page 34 to 68.

IN drawing out a narrative of the history of Udal Tenures, although I have made many references to the authorities on which they are given, yet several of them I shall acknowledge under general sources of information. Of the first of these is Mr Gifford's Historical Description of Zetland, given in No. 38 of the Bibliotheca Topographica Britannica. This is an excellent work; 'lit was written in the year 1733, in conformity to the wish of the Earl of Morton, by whom he was appointed' a Steward-depute in the county; but the fear of offending this Nobleman, by allusions to the conduct of his ancestors, led him to be very careful of entering with great particularity into the history of Udal Tenures. It is indeed questionable, if, after all, Earl Morton did not think he had explained too much on the subject; for the book was not printed for more than fifty years after it was written; and the publication is attributable to a late celebrated antiquary of Edinburgh, Mr George Paton, into whose hands the MS. had fallen. It is from some hints thrown out by Mr Gifford in the course of his work, that I attempted to explain, in connection with the laws of udal succession, the series of causes by which the ancient landed tenures of the country became feudalized. The difficulty of the task has been infinitely greater than I was aware of, and it can only be estimated by those who may still recollect the disputes which took place about forty years ago, regarding the rights of the superiority of Orkney and Shetland. That the statement which I have ventured to give of the feudalizing process which took place in the country may not be free from inaccuracies, I am prepared to expect; nor do I need to be reminded, that an individual who may possess a very trifling degree of knowledge of the feudal peculiarities of Scotland is ill qualified for the attempt. But, unfortunately, I had commenced the inquiry with little foreknowledge of the difficulties attending it; otherwise I should have long since shrunk from the task. My last object was to illustrate, from examples, the curious laws of udal succession; and as this is accomplished, I shall soon take my leave of the subject.

Another work that contains much curious information relating to the early state of the laws and udal tenures of Orkney and Shetland, is usually ascribed to a Mr James Mackenzie ; it is named *The General Grievances and Oppressions of Orkney and Shetland*. I am, however, given to understand that it was written by an Orkney gentleman of the name of Fea, on whose abilities it reflects great credit. It was drawn up in consequence of a law suit that was impending relative to the encrease that had taken place in the weights of the country ; and the object having been to prove that the laws of Orkney and Shetland ought not to be conformed to those of Scotland, it became necessary to state what the peculiarities of the subverted statutes were. Of this scarce work only fifty copies were printed ; one of these is in the possession of Mr William Laing, bookseller, of Edinburgh, who kindly favoured me with the perusal of it whilst I was drawing up my narrative of Udal Tenures.

The information which I have received relative to the various feudal grants that have been made of Orkney and Shetland, is chiefly derived from the arduous and learned researches of the legal gentlemen who drew up Memorials of the date of 1776, in an action brought by Sir Laurence Dundas, relative to his assumed right of superiority. An allusion is made to this law-suit in page 67. I shall now state its nature.

Sir Lawrence Dundas asserted, 1*st*, That he was superior of such of the lands belonging to the defenders as had once been held of the Earls of Orkney, or other grantees of the Crown, and of which the vassals were not *actually* seised by infeftment from the Crown in 1707.

2*dly*, That he had a right, as the King's *Commissioner*, by virtue of the charter 1707, to enter even the Crown vassals, by giving them charters and precepts for infeftment ; and that no Crown vassal in Orkney or Zetland had a right to the charters from the Exchequer, or precepts from his Majesty's Chancery.

3*dly*, That, as grantee of the feu and other duties, and causalties of superiority, he was entitled to insist for the compositions due on the entry of heirs and singular successors, and renewals of investitures, even from the Crown vassals, whether they received their entries from him or from the Exchequer.

Lastly, That if any of the udallers should at any time chuse to be feudalized, they could not take their charters and entries from any other than him, and were bound to hold of him for payment of the skat-duties in use to be paid out of these lands, and the usual casualties of superiority.

The termination of this action is given in a MS. addition to Campbell's Political Survey, which is in the possession of the Antiquarian Society of Edinburgh ; this document I have not seen, but it is quoted in the Appendix to Dr Edmondstone's History of Zetland. Sir Lawrence Dundas's pretension is said to have been " successfully resisted on the part of the defendants, in whose favour the Judges determined the suit. Some points of lesser moment were remitted to the Barons of the Exchequer ; but the plaintiff's title to the feu-duties in use to be paid to his predecessor not being disputed, was confirmed ; leaving the principal heritors at liberty to recur, as formerly, directly to the Crown, while the small udallers had an option, if they chose, either to subject themselves to the Sovereign, or to acknowledge Sir Lawrence Dundas."

In page 47 and elsewhere in page 95, &c. it has been shewn, that the agents by whom the Stewarts were enabled to inflict unparalleled atrocities upon the country, were a class of people known by the name of Dependants. These differed from mere vassals in this respect, that they were not only required to take up arms in the quarrels of their master, but to give their presence at all times when required, for the sake of pomp and ostentation, particularly when their lord rode abroad. Mr Francis Douce, in speaking of the English custom of clothing persons in liveries or badges, remarks that " it was not confined to menial servants. Another class of men, called Retainers, who appear to have been of no small importance among our ancestors, were habited in a similar manner. They were a sort of servants, not residing in the house, but attending occasionally for the purpose of ostentation, and retained by the annual donation of a livery, consisting of a hat or hood, a badge, and a suit of clothes. As they were frequently kept for the purpose of maintaining quarrels and committing other excesses, it became necessary to impose heavy penalties on the offenders, both masters and retainers." In process of time they were licensed. The same author quotes an extract from a work of Jervis Markham, dated A.D., 1596, to shew that these retainers were not always men of low condition, but consisted of the sons of noblemen, of "*Esquire's sonnes*, and of *gentlemen younger brothers, that wears their elder brothers' blew coate and badge.*" "Let us congratulate ourselves," adds Mr Douce, "that we no longer endure such insolent aggressions, the result of family pride and ignorance, and which had been too often permitted to degrade the natural liberties and independence of mankind." In treating of Earl Bobert Stewart's atrocities, I have had occasion to state, that the retainers or dependants which he brought with him from Scotland, were distributed over the whole of the country of Orkney and Shetland, having no establishment given them for a constant residence, but that they were allowed to quarter themselves at a free cost on the country ; and that they were hence named *broken men*. This mode, however, of keeping retainers, does not seem to have been general in Scotland ; and in this respect the country was better governed than in England. Retainers had, in many well regulated demesnes, lands given them, with the obligation annexed, that they and their heirs should be loyal and true men, and servants to their lord, and "*ryde, gang, and serve yame, and tak plain part with yame in all and sundrie yare actiones, causes, quarrellis,*" &c. though not to the detriment of the liege Sovereign. When any one, therefore, enlisted himself among the retainers of a superior, for which engagement lands were sometimes granted, he was said to be in *manrent*; which significant term scarcely requires any explanation. Two bonds of Manrent have been shewn me, which are so very curious, as illustrating a prominent trait in the Scottish manners of the 16th century, that I have scarcely any apology to offer for inserting them in this place.

BOND of MANRENT, A—— B—— of that Ilk, to C—— D——, dated 19th October 1555.

BE IT KENT TILL ALL MEN be yir p'nt Lres me A—— B—— of yat ilk Forsamekle as he vertew of an contract and appoinctment maid betwix an Noble man C—— D—— of —— on yat ane part and me on yat uther part toucheing ye infeftment of alienatioune maid and gevin be ye said C—— D—— to me my airis and assignais off all and sundrie ye landis of   and   wt comoun pasture frie ische and intre in ye Comoun of ye Lordschip of   usit and wount and als of ye   myln of ye   wt the mylne landis thirle multure pertening to ye samin and comoun pasture frie ische and intre in ye landis of   usit and wount wt all yair pertinentis lyand in ye   I am oblist by vertew of the said contract to mak sele subscryve and deliver to ye said C—— D—— ane Band of Manrent byndand and oblissand me and my airis to be lele and trew men and servandis to ye said C—— D—— of —— and his airis in ye maist ampill forme yat ye said C—— D—— can devyss oure allegeance to our Soverane Lady allanerlay except as ye said contract at mair length proportis Thairfoir to be bundin and oblist and be ye faith and treuth in my body lelelie and trewlie bindis and oblisses me and my airs in Manrent to ye said C—— D—— of —— and his airis and yat we sall be leill and trew men and servandis to yame and ryde gang and serve yame and tak plain part with yame in all and sundrie yare actiones causes quarellis pleyis contraversys and debaitis lefull and honest quhatsumever movit or to be movit be yame or agains yame be'and agains quhatsumever persone or persones yat leif or de may in ye law or by the law oure Soverane Lady ye Queuis Grace and her auc'te allanerlie except and sall nowther here se nor knaw yare skaith but sall revele ye samin to yame and stop ye samin at the utermaist of oure poweris and further sall leif nathing undone yat men and servandis aucht and suld do to yair maisteris And hereto I bind and oblisses me and my airis faithfullie to ye said C—— D—— and his airis under the pane of forfalting and tinsel of ye foresaidis landis mylne thirle multuris and utheris abovewri^n And gif I or my airis failzies hereintill to ye said C—— D—— and his airis the saidis landis to returne againe to ye said

NOTES TO ITER II.

C———— D————— and his airis and be fre in yair handis In witness hereof to yis my p'nt Band of Manrent subscryvit with my hand my proper sele yrto hingin at Edinburgh the 19th day of October the yeir of God Ane thousand fyve hundreth and fyftie fyve yeirs, before yir witnes And howbeit ony failzie above-written happynis to be made be the said A———— B———— and his airis to the said Laird of   or his airs zit notyesless he nor his airis sall not haif regress to ye foresaids lands be resone of ye said failzie unto ye tyme ye soume of xviij^c & l merks ressavit be ye said Lard of   for ye alienatiounc of ye saids landis be refundit again be the said A———— B———— wt ye annualrent of xxi mks yrely   and   again to yaim. Before ye witnesses &c.

A———— B————

BOND of MANRENT, A———— B———— of   to C———— D————

BE IT KEND TYLL AL MEN by yir p'nts Lres Me A———— B———— of to be bundin and oblist and be ye tenor of yir p'nts fathfully bindis and obless me to ane Honerable man C———— D———— of   to becumin his man for all ye dayis of my lyff and to tak his part at all tymess him to supple wt my kynd servants and frends at or power in all his rycht honest and just pleis and querellis before al oyr p'sones excepand ye Kings Grace & allegeancy to ye Croun And forther newer to her nor to se seaitht...... no pert in body fayme or his gudes bot I sal resist defend and reweil to ye said C———— D———— at my power at al fraud & gyll excludit For ye observying keping and fulfilling p'misses I ye said   bindis and oblisses me be ye faith and treucht in my body in the mast sekarest form and stratest still of obligation In witness of ye quhilk for ye mair securitie I ye said A———— B———— hes affixit to my seil at   ye 2d day of September ye zer of God ane thousand fyff hundrett xxi zers and wt my subscription manuel before yer witnesses, &c.

A———— B————

NOTE VII. SUMBURGH LIGHT-HOUSE, Page 77.

The Shetland Islands, owing to their detached form and central position in the North Sea, present several situations whereon light-houses would be extremely beneficial to shipping; aud the Commissioners of the Northern Light-houses have lately extended their operations to these islands, and have erected a light-house on Sumburgh-Head, the most prominent southern extremity of the Mainland. The light-house here is known to mariners as a stationary light. The buildings were founded in the month of March 1820, and the house was lighted on the 15th day of January 1821. The light is from oil with reflectors, elevated 300 feet above the medium level of the sea, and has been distinctly seen, in a favourable state of the atmosphere, at the distance of no less than eight or nine leagues.

NOTE VIII. STEINEARTES OR STONE-AXES, Page 86.

Dr Chalmers, in his Caledonia, has made the following remarks on the subject of the stone-axes found in Shetland : " The curious fact, that Druid remains and stone monuments exist, and that celts and flint arrow heads have been found in the Orkney Islands, while none of them have discovered in the Shetland Islands, evinces, that the same Celtic people who colonized South and North Britain, also penetrated into the Orkneys, but not into the Shetland Islands; and this fact also shews that those antiquities owe their origin to the Celts, who early colonized the Orkney Isles alone, and not to the Scandinavians, who equally colonized both the Orkney and Shetland Islands." I am sorry that Dr Chalmers had been misinformed on this subject, since stone-axes are much more abundant in

Shetland than in Orkney; but it is still more unfortunate, that the same learned antiquary should have enfeebled the excellent arguments which he had advanced relative to the Pictish question, by dwelling on such fallacious incitements to antiquarian inferences as stone-axe or barrows. Whittaker, in his History of Manchester, has given a plate of a stone-axe which he supposes to have been used by the Celts, but it differs materially from the form of the Teutonic steinbarte. The blade of the Celtic stone-axe exhibits hollow sides; that of the Shetland steinbarte is convex on one or both sides. The blade of the Celtic stone-axe contains an orifice, calculated to admit within it a wooden shaft; but there is no orifice displayed by the blade of the Shetland steinbarte; on the contrary, it is itself passed through the aperture of a wooden or bone handle, for which its tapering extremity is adapted.

NOTE IX. SANDLODGE MINES, Page 91.

I consider the information of those gentlemen who have seen the Sandlodge Mines as so important, that I shall insert the testimony of all the mineralogists who have visited Shetland while they were worked. Professor Jameson, who saw the mines about twenty years ago, thus describes them: "At a little distance from the shore, in the sandstone, which is here still continued, there is a vein of copper pyrites, or sulphuret of copper, which was worked for some time by a party of miners from Wales, with very flattering prospects; but the vein gradually decreased in width, until it was not above an inch broad, when it was thought proper to leave it. On the opposite side of the house there is another large vein of iron-ore, above six feet wide, having a very scorified aspect. This was also worked for some time, but the great expence, and the small proportion of copper obtained, soon made it to to be given up."

"At Sandlodge, in 1803," says Dr Traill, "a copper-mine was wrought, which has, I understand, been since given up, but which, I have been told, it is in contemplation soon again to open. There was then a small but well constructed steam-engine on it. The principal shaft was sunk within a few fathoms of the sea. The miners had penetrated to the depth of about twenty-two fathoms, and were but little incommoded with water. The upper rock was sandstone; and below it, at twenty-two fathoms, lay a petrosiliceous, or perhaps quartzy rock, traversed by many veins of brown quartz. This was the greatest depth to which they had then penetrated; and I believe that the hardness and unpromising nature of this rock was the cause of their so quickly giving up. At that time there were but two Cornish miners, besides a Cornish *Captain of the Mines*, engaged, and these were chiefly occupied in giving directions to the natives employed to work in the mine. The want of men sufficiently skilled in mining, was certainly one cause of their failure. The principal manager was a partner, who had chiefly directed his attention to the corn-trade, as I was informed, and who was totally ignorant of the art of mining. The principal *lode* or vein lies between the sandstone and the petrosiliceous rock, in a direction from NE. to SW. The copper-ore is chiefly green carbonate, and the sulphuret; it is imbedded in an iron-ore, which is sometimes pulverulent, and was called by the Cornish miners *gozzan*. The iron-ore is by much the more abundant. When Mr Jameson visited this place, the copper-mine was not opened; and he only mentions iron-ores as the product of the mine, which many years ago had been wrought by an English iron company, but afterwards abandoned. It was subsequent to Mr Jameson's visit that the copper-ore was much noticed. The iron-ores here found, are, 1. Dark-brown, fibrous, and mamillated hæmatites; 2. Columnar bog iron-ore; 3. Micaceous iron-ore; 4. Iron-ochre of a brown colour; 5. Stalactitic iron-ore, colour, dark-brown; 6. Earthy matter, much charged with iron, seemingly arising from the debris of other ores. The copper-ores are, 1. Friable and amorphous carbonate of copper, colour rich green; 2. Beautiful carbonate of an emerald green, crystallized in capillary fibres of a silky lustre, diverging in radii from a centre. This species is found imbedded in iron-ore; 3. Sulphuret of copper, disseminated through felspar in some places, and, in others, in great masses in iron-ore. The rich carbonates were found near the bottom of the mine. The levels and shafts of the old company seem to have passed within three or four feet of this rich vein, but never to have touched it. I walked through the galleries scooped out in former attempts, for about forty fathoms, but saw only little appearance of copper-ores, while there was iron in abundance all around. The roads near the mine were all paved with fine iron hæmatites, which the Cornish miners who were there did not seem to regard as of any value, or indeed almost to know. Some of them imagined it was a new kind of copper-ore. Some pieces of bog iron-ore I had collected, were called *copper-spume* by one of them; hence, it is evident, we cannot trust much to the mineralogical opinions of the generality of miners. From the saline taste of the waters of the mine, and the crust of copper it left on my knife, I proposed to the workmen to try to procure *copper of cementation* in the usual way. This company had already expended between £9000 and £10,000 on the work, and had shipped one or two cargoes of ore; for, when dressed and washed, it was carried to England to be smelted. I was informed that the best of it sold for £70 per ton. The hills in the vicinity afford both copper and iron-pyrites in considerable quantity. Near Coningsburgh Cliffs, a vein of copper-pyrites was wrought a few years ago, which yielded Mr Jameson 18 *per cent.* of copper; but it so much decreased in width as they descended, that it was finally abandoned. The appearance of the ores was judged, by the Cornish miners, to improve as they descended in the Sandlodge mine; and, at their lowest level, the quantity of fibrous malachite, when I visited the mine, was such as to afford a most beautiful specticle by the light of our candles. They have since, however, I am told, unfortunately met with such obstacles as to induce them to give up the work. Still, it appears to me, that it would be worthy the attention of some Mining Company, who had capital and enterprise to prosecute the undertaking."—App. to Mr Neill's Tour, p. 169, &c.

Dr Fleming, who last visited the mines in the year 1808, states as follows:—" Copper-pyrites was the ore which the miners sought for. Near the bottom of the mine it is disseminated in sparry ironstone, along with iron-pyrites. The difficulty of working the sparry ironstone or veinstone, and the small proportion of copper-ore which it contained, were stated to me as the reasons for abandoning the mine. Among the rubbish thrown out from the vein I observed a few pieces of *grey copper-ore*. *Fibrous malachite* occurs in abundance in the cavities of the other ores, or in the form of a surface coating. Specimens of native copper have also been found.

"Besides these ores of copper, the vein contains a great proportion of iron-ores. Common iron-pyrites is found in company with the copper-pyrites, but does not seem to be very abundant. Brown hæmatite is found towards the surface of the vein in great quantity, and nearly occupies its whole breadth. The sparry ironstone appeared in plenty towards the bottom of the mines, and constituted the veinstone." (Appendix to *Shirreff's Agricultural Survey of Shetland*, p. 130.) The substance of Dr Fleming's opinion on the Productiveness of the Sandlodge mines will be found in p. 90.

NOTE X. ANCIENT JURISDICTION OF SHETLAND, Page 101.

Anent making of Ranselmen, and their Instructions.

IN a Bailie Court lawfully fenced, the whole householders in the parish being present, the Bailie is to cause his Clerk read out a list of such honest men in the parish as are fit to be ranselmen, and then he is to inquire each of them if they are willing to accept of the office of ranselmen, and if any of them refuse, and give no good reason for his refusal to accept, the Bailie may fine him in £10 Scots. And those that accept, the Bailie asks the whole householders present if they have ought to object against any of these men why they may not be made ranselmen. And no objection being made, then the following instructions are to be read to them.

1. You are, at any time of night or day you see needful, to call for assistance, and to enter into any house within the parish and search the same as narrowly as you can, and upon any suspicion of theft, if they refuse you the keys, you are to break open heir doors

or chests, and if you find anything that is stolen, you are to bring the thief and the fang to the Bailie, or secure both, and acquaint the Bailie. If you have any scruple about any thing you find in the house, you are to inquire how they came by it, and if they refuse to tell, take witness upon their refusal, and let the thing be secured until you acquaint the Bailie. You are also to examine the household stores of flesh and meal, and see if they be correspondent to their stocks, and likewise the wool, stockings, yarn, webs, &c. and inquire how they came by all these, and if they cannot give a satisfying account thereof and brough and hamell, you are to inform against them.

2. You are to inquire into the lives and conversations of families, whether there is any discord or any unbecoming carriage betwixt husband and wife, parent and child, master and servant, or any other unchristian or unlawful practice in the family, and you are to rebuke such and exhort them to amend. If they obey, it is well, if not, you are faithfully to represent such to the judicatory competent, and bring the best evidences you can against all such offenders.

3. You are to prevent all quarrels and scolding as far as in your power, by commanding the contending parties to peace, and if they persist, require witnesses against them, and call for assistance to separate them, and give in a faithful report thereof to the Fiscal or Clerk of Court; and in case you are not witness to any scolding or quarrelling that happens, you are to gather the best information thereof you can, and make report of the same as aforesaid.

4. If you hear any person cursing or swearing, you are to demand of them the fine of Twenty Shillings Scots, and if they refuse to pay it, you are to require witnesses against them, and report it to the Court, the one-third of which fine to yourself, and two-thirds to the poor.

5. That you narrowly enquire into your neighbourhood, who sits home from kirk on the Sabbath-day, and from diets of catechising, and if they can give no sufficient reason for their so doing, that you cause them pay the fine, being twenty shillings Scots, to be applied as aforesaid. And that you take particular notice in your neighbourhood anent keeping the Sabbath-day, and if you find any breach thereof that you report the same.

6. You are strictly to observe the country acts anent good neighbourhood; such as none injure others in their grass and corn, and rebuke the offenders, with certification if they continue so to do, you will inform the Court against them; and that they big their dikes sufficiently and timeously under the pain contained in the Acts.

7. That you take notice that tenants do not abuse their lands, nor demolish their houses, through sloth and idleness, and that you reprove such, and if they continue so to do against the land-masters, you are to report them.

8. You are to inquire if there is in your neighburhood any idle vagabond persons, and to acquaint such that they must take themselves either to some honest employ, or you will inform against them, so as they may be punished and ordered to service, and that the poor be taken care of in your respective quarters, and not suffered to stray abroad, nor are you to allow any begger or tigger from any other parish, to pass through your bounds, and if they offer so to do, you will secure them till they be punished, conform to the country Acts.

9. That you try all the dogs in your quarter, and that none be allowed to keep a dog that can take a sheep, unless allowed to keep a sheep-dog by the Bailie, and that none keep scare-sheep otherwise than in the Act; and that the Acts be observed anent punding, hounding, marking, and taking off sheep.

10. You are to inquire in your quarters anent all persons using any manner of witchcraft, charms, or any abominable or devilish superstitions, and faithfully inform against such, as that they may be brought to condign punishment.

11. You are to examine all tradesmen in your bounds, and see that they make sufficient work, and do not impose upon any in their prices, and if you find any such transgressors, inform against them so as they may be punished as law directs.

12. Upon any suspicion of theft, two or three ranselmen may take as many witnesses with them, and go to the neighbour parish and ransel, and if they catch the thief, they are to acquaint the Bailie of that parish thereof, who will order the thief to be secured.

And, in the last place, as you are entrusted with a power of inspecting the lives and manners of others, so let your own good life and conversation be exemplary unto them for good, and take care you are not found guilty of these faults yourselves, that you are called to reprove in others; for if you should, your punishment shall be double to theirs. Now, all these instructions, as far as it is in your power, you promise and swear solemnly in the sight of Almighty God, and as you shall answer to him at the great day, faithfully and honestly to observe and perform. So help you God.

ADDITIONS TO ITER II.

FURTHER ILLUSTRATIONS OF UDAL LAWS.

Since drawing up the History of the Udallers, a document fell into my hands, that would have been noticed in the account of these ancient landholders if it had arrived in time. Early historians have asserted, that the oldest law of Udal succession was "*Gavel-kind*, which," says Sir Robert Sibbald, "is the division of the heritage moveables equally, *sine discrimine sexus vel ætatis* amongst the children of the deceased, only *by the custom of Shetland*, the youngest got the dwelling-house, beside his share." The early Scottish settlers, however, readily availed themselves of an edict that gave them the opportunity of concentrating and perpetuating family wealth and power in one individual; the principal features of it being, that the oldest son should have the *head buil*, or principal manor; that the youngest sons should, if possible, have equal compensations in other lands, or in income, but that the daughter should have her share in the most remote and discontiguous lands.

Although this law seems to have been evidently framed on the principle of gavel-kind, yet it left room for many evasions of it, with the sinister view that the oldest son should not only succeed to the manor of a deceased udaller, but should enjoy the bulk of his landed property. Accordingly, it appears to have been resisted by many of the wealthier landed proprietors, who, in their law-ting, framed an act of their own, by which primogeniture was no farther respected, than that the first choice of such lands as were *equally* divided among all the sons of a deceased udaller, fell to the oldest. If, however, the rights of sons were reduced to an equality, those of the daughters were little respected; since, in a division of property, two sisters' shares were allotted for one brother's part. The law was explained in the year 1610, when an estate was awarded to Edward Sinclair of Marrasetter; but the allegation that it was "inviolablie observit," has been shewn to be incorrect.

"Till all and sundrie quhome it effeiris, to quhais knowlege thir presentis sall cum; we, vndersubscryveand, dois testifie and beir witnes, That in all tymes bygane, past memorie of man, thair hes bene an ancient law, custome and consuetude, within the cuntrey of Zetland, be the quhilk it hes bene inviolablie obseruit, that quhan ony landit man haveand landis within the said cuntrey, depairtit this mortall lyffe, the haill landis and heretage appertening to him in his lyftyme, immediatlie efter his deceis, war equallie and lawtyfullie diuydit amangis his haill bairnis, alsweill sones as dochteris, comptand alwayis twa sisteris pairtis for ane brotharis pairt; and being sua diuydit, the eldest brother had na farder prerogative abone the rest of his brethers, except the first choiss of the pairtis and parcellis of the lands diuydit."

This Law ought to have been noticed in pages 45 and 123.

Iter III.

THE NORTH ISLES OF SHETLAND, THE MIDLAND DISTRICT OF THE MAINLAND, AND THE ISLANDS OF THE BAY OF SCALLOWAY.

"*Piscator*—So Sir, now we have got to the top of the hill out of town, look about you, and tell me how you like the country.

"*Viator.*—Bless me, what Mountains are here! are we not in Wales?

"*Piscator.*—No, but in almost as mountainous a country; and yet, these hills though high, bleak and craggy, breed and feed good mutton above ground, and afford good store of metal within."

Complete Angler, Part ii., Chap. 2.

HAVING prepared to quit the Outskerries, with sentiments of gratitude for the attention which Mr Bruce of Whalsey had paid to my accommodation in this detached and dreary group of islets, I set sail with a moderate breeze for the North Isles of Fetlar, Yell and Unst; the distance to the nearest point of them being about twelve miles. Landing at a low, barren rock north-west from the Outskerris, named the Meikle Skerry, which I found to be composed of gneiss, and leaving to the west, the dismal shore of Yell, which appeared to consist of a number of dark and tenantless ridges of hills, the steep rocks on the south of Fetlar began to appear more distinct; and, in a short time, I came to a north-westerly point of land where the banks were much lower, and where the presiding deity of the place, was

"Clad in a gown of grass so soft and wondrous warm,"

that the traditional account seemed highly probable, which gave to Fetlar the name of the Green Island; its early designation was Fœdar Oi.

ISLAND OF FETLAR.

I landed on the north coast of the Island, at Urie, where was a plain family mansion, built early in the last century, which, with most of the estates of the place, belonged to a Scottish family of the name of Bruce. A fine fertile valley lay to the south, bounded on the west by a high ridge of gneiss, and on the east by the barren serpentine hill of the Vord; to the north were the distant shores of Unst. The island is considered to be from five to six and a half miles in length, and about five in breadth; and in my circuit round it, I first arrived at Odsta, where there was a rock of serpentine which much influenced the compass. Continuing my tour along banks of gneiss, in a southerly direction, I observed a site of ground where were the remains of a remarkable fortification, unlike all others I had seen in the country. It was situated in a very low and level green sward, close to the edge of the ocean, but a considerable part of the defence has been washed away by the sea, in its inroads on the coast. A small quadrangular area, the original dimensions of which cannot be well determined, was inclosed by a wall of uncemented stones and earth, about eight yards in breadth, and about two in height; it was also protected by a double ditch. There was likewise an outer rampart of less magnitude, being about five yards broad and two yards high, which Mr Low of Orkney conjectured, and with reason, was for no other use than to secure for the small garrison, the possession of a well of water that had been sunk in the *fosse*. About ten yards distant from the fortification, was a mound of earth about thirty-seven yards in circumference. If the antiquary does not fear being contradicted in his conjecture, by some unlucky Edie Ochiltree, such as the learned occupant of Monkbarns met with in his newly discovered camp of Agricola, he may fairly set down his fortress as showing more marks of a Roman construction, than of one that is either Saxon or Scandinavian. Shaw, the historian of Staffordshire, has proved from examples, that the Romans always took great care to have a supply of water for the soldiers, and even placed their camps very near a regular road, that, on an emergency, the men might be in immediate readiness to march; but less civilized nations, as the Saxons for instance, with no provident view of this kind, fixed their camps on high hills, with a steep precipice before them; thinking that this kind of security was more to be regarded than water, which they were forced to carry a great way to the considerable inconvenience of the army when large. The Romans also selected a quadrangular spot of ground, and made a single graff; but the Saxons gave themselves no trouble about the form, and, where they apprehended the fortification to be weak, would often make two or three ditches. These judicious remarks of Mr Shaw, apply sufficiently well to the strong hold of Fetlar, which, from its smallness, and very plain construction, could never have been intended for more than a temporary fortress, and might have been constructed by a few of the troops that manned the vessels of Theodosius, when, in the fourth century, they rooted out the Saxon pirates from the Orcadian seas. The site of the camp of Fetlar was not upon a hill such as the Saxon barbarians would have selected, but upon a low site of ground near to the sea, and, as it has been shewn, special care was taken to preserve, adjoining to the station, a well of water which the experienced artificers defended by an outer vallum.*

The southerly direction which I took, led me along very steep cliffs to Lamhoga, a south-westerly point of land which has long been the resort of the Peregrine Falcon. Not far from this place, is a considerable accumulation of decomposed gneiss, which appears under the form of porcelain earth. In turning round the point of Lamhoga, I came in view of the wide open bay of Triesta; at the head of it stood a neat white kirk and manse, built contiguous to a small fresh water loch, which was divided from the sea by a low sandy beach. Behind the manse was some good corn land enlivened by several cottages. The westerly banks of the bay were high and barren; the easterly shore, which was terminated by a promontory named the Snap of Fetlar, was much less steep. Arriving at the Loch of Triesta, I staid to examine its sands, which have long been celebrated for the magnetic iron-ore, in the form of grains, with which they are intermingled. To the south-east of the manse is Houbie, near to which town are the ruins of two burghs. One of them was once a circular fort, formed by two walls, with chambers between them; it was situated on a bank close to the sea, being further protected by segments of three concentric ramparts, and by one cross or flanking wall.† Another burgh was placed on an eminence having no out-works; but contiguous to it were the foundations of numerous small houses now in ruins, that had been built on this site, for the purpose of being under the protection of the burgh.

My examination of the mineralogy of the coast that lined the bay of Triesta having been concluded, I again set out in a north-westerly direction for Urie, having received from Mr Ingram, the worthy minister of the parish, much kind attention on the way. From Urie, where I was hospitably entertained by Mr Nicholson, the principal proprietor of the island, I journeyed the next morning in an easterly direction, and soon reached the summit of the Vord Hill, which was so named from the ancient watch-tower that crowned its summit. The rock is composed of serpentine, and its surface exhibits a yellowish ferruginous coating, which is exceedingly hostile to vegetation. On this hill once stood three circles, each of which was of the diameter of about thirty-six feet, formed by loose stones. These remains, which were probably ancient Tings or Courts of Judicature, are now much injured. Descending the high banks on the east, I came in view of the open bay of Gruting, and after having become an inmate, for one night, at the house of Mr Smith

---

* A plan of this Camp has been given in Mr Pennant's Arctic Zoology, from a drawing by Mr Low, the original of which is now in my possession. To the strict correctness of it I cannot assent, but as the general view which it gives is not very remote from its present appearance, it is recopied in the Plate of Antiquities given in the Appendix, Fig. 1. I may remark, that as no part of my observations, except on the Geology of Shetland, was originally intended to appear before the public, I neglected to take such a plan of the fortress as the object deserved.

It has been said, that not far from this place, on digging in a moss, six brass relics were found, shaped like fetters, and wrapped in a strong hide. Their form has not been described, and it would, therefore, be absurd to offer any conjecture regarding their use.

† See Plate of Antiquities in the Appendix, Fig. 11.

of Smithfield, from whom I received a generous welcome, I arrived at the north-east extremity of the island, where is an old fortress that bears the name of Strandiburgh. My road then led along steep banks of conglomerate rocks to Funzie, a small open bay, on the banks of which a booth has been long erected for the convenience of several boats that prosecute the ling fishery during the summer months, at a distance of forty miles from land.

It is affirmed by tradition, that the fleet under Harold Harfagre, which invaded Shetland, first sailed to Funzie, but that the Norwegian Monarch finding he could not procure anchorage in this insecure harbour, steered for some other part of the country, where, at the island of Unst, he was more successful in effecting a landing for his soldiers.

About the middle of the last century, the Vandela, a Swedish vessel, trading to the East Indies, perished within a short distance of the booth of Funzie; she had on board a sum to the amount of £22,000 Sterling, in various coins and pieces of silver. About £18,000 of this money was fished up by means of diving apparatus.

At a small distance from Funzie, a remarkable instance of the effect of thunder, took place about the middle of the last century. A rock 105 feet long, 10 feet broad, and in some places more than 4 feet thick, was in an instant torn from its bed, and broken into three large and several lesser fragments. One of these, 26 feet long, 10 feet broad, and 4 feet thick, was simply turned over. The second, which was 28 feet long, 17 broad, and 5 feet in thickness, was hurled across a high point of a rock to the distance of 50 yards. Another broken mass, about 40 feet long, was thrown still farther, but in the same direction, quite into the sea. There were also many lesser fragments scattered up and down.*

From Funzie, I proceeded south to the promontory named the Snap of Fetlar, which had terminated, on a former occasion, my examination of the mineralogy of the coast of Triesta Bay. From this point I crossed the country in a direction to Urie. It was impossible, in this route, not to admire the rich loam with which the valleys were enriched, and this fecundity was often singularly contrasted with the bare and yellow surface of the serpentine of the Vord Hill, which was overspread with a ferruginous matter fatal to vegetation. A considerable number of shelties were roaming over the scatholds of the island, the breed of this place being considered as some of the best that Shetland produces.

I was presented, in the Island of Fetlar, with specimens of pumice, which, from their small specific gravity, easily float on the water, and appear to have been driven to the coasts of Shetland from the volcanic rocks of Iceland. It is then a question, from what cause were these substances conveyed to Shetland; were they thrown here by currents of tide, propagated from the great diurnal undulation of the Atlantic? The ridge of one wave must, in its northerly course, have passed between Feroe and Iceland, and, in taking a southerly direction, might have fallen in with another current which passes between Shetland and Feroe, or Shetland and Norway; whether, from such a cause, these specimens of pumice have floated to the shores of Shetland, I shall not pretend to determine. There

---

* For the narrative of this effect of lightning, I am indebted to the MS. of the late Reverend George Low.

are indeed reasons for supposing that the vicinity of this country itself has been the seat of a submarine volcanoe. "In the year 1768," said the late Andrew Bruce, Esq. of Urie, in a communication to Mr Low, "we had the visible signs of a submarine shock, which threw ashore vast quantities of shell-fish of different kinds, and of all sizes, with conger eels and other sorts of fish, but all dead; at the same time, the sea for several miles round was of a dark muddy colour for several days after." The late Mr Gordon, minister of the Island of Fetlar, in allusion to the same event, stated, that, "some years ago, there was a marine eruption, or some such phenomenon, which we could not account for in any other way. There was a vast quantity of sea-fish driven ashore, and many that had never made their appearance on this coast before. Conger eels above seven feet long, but all dead. The water in the bays was so black and muddy for eight days after, that when our fishermen were hawling haddock, or any small fish, they could never discern them until taken out of the water."

It is, again, a curious coincidence, that whilst specimens of pumice, thrown on the shores of Shetland, indicate directions of current from the North Seas, the West Indian products, known by the name of Molucca beans, which float to the coast, should give tokens of extensive and opposite currents, branching from the gulf-streams that are directed from the south-west. Three descriptions of the seeds that are cast on the shores of Shetland and Orkney, are enumerated by authors; the first of them belongs to the *Mimosa scandens* of Linnæus; it is so large that the fishermen of Orkney make snuff-boxes of it; the second is the seed of the *Dolichos urens*, distinguished by the *hilus* or welt with which it is surrounded; and the third is a round hard seed of the size of a musket-bullet, belonging to the *Guilandina Bonduc*.*

ACCOUNT OF DAVID GILBERT TAIT, A LAD BORN DEAF AND BLIND.

Before quitting the Island of Fetlar I accidentally heard of the existence of a lad of the name of David Gilbert Tait, who had been born deaf and blind. The knowledge of his case seems not to have extended beyond the insulated place of his nativity, where he has dragged on an unnoticed existence for twenty-five years. I, therefore, hastened to contemplate so remarkable an object, being accompanied in my visit to him, by Mr Nicolson of Fetlar, and Captain Macdermid, two gentlemen to whose hospitality, in Shetland, I have been much indebted.

We soon reached the miserable hovel, one of the worst in the island, occupied by the family of the Taits, and on entering it, the lamentable object of our visit first arrested our attention. He appeared to be in a squatting position, and was warming himself by a fire which occupied the centre of the hut. He was almost in a state of nudity, and we learned that he had never been accustomed to wear any thing more than the apparel that he then possessed, which was a coarse blanket, slightly tied round him so as to cover his back. In his limbs, he showed much emaciation and feeble muscular powers; being little disposed,

---

* For a more particular description of these seeds, see Neill's Tour to Orkney and Shetland, p. 60 and 213.

perhaps from the mode in which he was brought up, to exposure in the open air. His countenance certainly appeared very idiotic. His forehead, which in the lower part protruded, was in the upper part retreating, whilst the occiput was disproportionably large, yet flattened on its surface. His chin was very prominent, his mouth remarkably wide, and his nose particularly sharp. The pupil of the eyes shewed the pitchy black appearance characteristic of amaurosis, and the iris did not contract or dilate upon the sudden application or withdrawing of a candle.

Upon first hearing of this youth, I naturally expected that his sense of odorous substances would be as acute as that of tangible bodies. But in this expectation I was disappointed; there was no evidence of a very perfect sense of the power of smell when I was present; nor, from the representation of his parents, am I inclined to think that it was ever exhibited. The question rather is,—Was the sense blunted or suspended? From my own observations, and the enquiries which I made, it certainly did not seem to be obliterated.* It is, therefore, not improbable, that the circumstance of the youth's idiotism, ascribed to him by his parents, might have prevented the particular exertion of this organ.

In the course of my interrogation relative to the degree of intellect which this singularly destitute being has exhibited, I learned from his mother, that she had brought ten children into the world, some of whom were living, but that she had a daughter, who soon after her birth became blind, and had always exhibited unequivocal marks of mental imbecility. This female was two years older than her brother David, being of the age of twenty-seven. The torpor of her intellectual faculties was indicated by an indocility of apprehension, and confused articulation, which could not be rendered subservient to the purposes of speech. Thus, the probability of the son's idiotism was strengthened by the hereditary predisposition to it, which appears to have existed in the family. But it must be confessed, at the same time, that such a state of fatuity is difficult to be proved, in an individual possessing so few avenues by which external objects can be conveyed to the mind. The lad's sense of touch, for instance, appeared to be perfect, and we are entitled to suppose, that it necessarily included every abstract notion of perception which a sane intellect would possibly entertain;—that it involved the individuality, number and position of material objects as they co-exist in space, or as they are continuous in point of time. His careful selection of the objects which he chose to handle, indicated correct notions of form, magnitude, and of the comparative hardness of bodies, as they more or less resist his muscular contractions. His preference of particular kinds of food, also evinced the comparative distinction which he was accustomed to make in the varied nature of sapid bodies. Respecting, also, the generation of ideas in the mind, after the causes which have excited sensations are withdrawn, there appeared to be a sufficient state of efficiency in the law of ideal association, although the evidence on this point was confined to a few of the most simple events. Previously to receiving food, the mother of

---

* I paid a second visit to David Tait, for the purpose of satisfying myself upon the state of the organ of smell, by the application of various substances to his nostrils; but, unfortunately for my purpose, the day on which I returned, happened to be the time of his repose, when his parents were naturally very unwilling that he should be disturbed.

David taps his hand with a spoon, which is recognised by the poor object as a signal that she is preparing to satisfy his hunger. In an instant, therefore, his hands are extended to receive the bason in which is contained his pottage. If, then, the senses of touch and taste are perfect, and if the law of association by which perceptions are reproduced in the state of ideas be equally efficient, in what way is the youth's supposed deficiency of intellect to be detected? Metaphysical writers conceive that the reasoning power of man is only elicited when, upon the occasion of two or more objects being brought into the view of the mind, their mutual correspondences are discovered; hence are supposed to arise our notions of relation. At length, then, we may perhaps draw the distinction between idiotism and a sane state of intellect. The perceptions of relation comprehended by the youth, were derived from the contemplation of the fewest possible objects; but no relations could be felt, that must result from the reflection of a numerous train of ideas associated in the mind, particularly if they were of an abstract nature, as those which belong to number and mensuration. The reason, then, of Tait, resembled the feeble discrimination of the lower race of animals, being limited to few objects, and being incapable of much variety or improvement. In this respect, the interest of the present case is much diminished; particularly when placed in comparison with that of James Mitchell, a deaf and blind youth of much discrimination, whose situation has been so ably described by the pen of Professor Stewart.

It was, in the next place, an important enquiry, What were the particular objects which, in affecting a youth of this kind, would appear to be original sources of gratification. It is very manifest, from the delight which infants take in certain colours, sounds, odours and sapid bodies, while certain other objects are disagreeable to them, that there is a predisposition to receive pleasure and pain from particular objects in preference to others. When first observed, David had no sensible object within his grasp. It was then curious to observe the innumerable muscular contractions of his fingers, and the velocity with which each motion was executed, in order to produce a rapid change of their position. The solitary circumstance of varied muscular contraction, exerted in parts of the body best calculated to produce the effect, was, in fact, the origin from which much of the enjoyment of this individual was derived. Metaphysicians may refer all our enjoyments of touch, as of many other senses, to the same source of varied position, but it is only in such a destitute being as Tait, where these are unmixed with motives of action arising from any other organs of sensation, except occasionally those of smell or taste, that speculations on the abstract sources of sensitive pleasure can be confirmed. It was of importance to ascertain, in the next place, what objects, by being opposed to, and by consequently resisting the muscular contractions of his fingers, (which is all we mean, when we speak of objects of touch,) appeared to afford the highest gratification. The answer given by the mother, when an interrogatory to this effect was put to her relating to her son, was in the highest degree satisfactory. It afforded the most direct proof of the law to which our pleasures are subject. That there may be a continuation of agreeable sensations, it is necessary that the causes of them should be continually varied. The most beautiful landscapes, or the most exquisite monuments of art, when long opposed to vision, lose all their captivating power. Applying this principle, therefore, to the case of Tait, and conceiving it highly possible, that the abstract causes of pleasurable sensations in touch, might in this individual be exemplified, I proposed a question to the parent, "What did the lad like best to handle?"—"Every thing that he can alter the shape of," answered the mother. This direct reply comprehended all that might have been anticipated. She at the same time referred to the flexible substances in the cottage, as to wollen and linen clothes, materials of cotton, or to straw. These were the objects the form of which he could change, and they consequently yielded him the greatest sum of enjoyment.

At the same time, when different substances were presented to the lad, he preferred those which had smooth surfaces to those which were uneven or rough: thus the outside of the tea-kettle, coated with sooty matter, was particularly disagreeable to him. The sense of taste, owing to the poverty of his parents, has had little opportunity of being gratified by variety: all that I could learn on this subject was, that, in preference to fish, he chiefly lives on meal pottage, with which he is generally fed by his mother from a spoon.

I have heard a celebrated metaphysician enumerate as original objects of desire, society, knowledge, power, the esteem of men, the happiness of those whom we love, or the affliction of those whom we hate. All or most of these, which I should be disposed to consider on a different theory as original sources of gratification, may, I think, be traced in Tait; though it would necessarily require a long acquaintance with his habits to detect in him those affections which we may be disposed to consider as purely instinctive. That he is susceptible of resentment, as well as of friendly attachment, can be easily shewn. The attachment which he expresses towards his mother, who constantly feeds him, is said to be remarkable. This is denoted by a restlessness, when he cannot, by feeling every object around him, detect her presence; her maternal offices of kindness are also preferred before those of any other individual.

It may be now noticed that David's interval of time, set apart for sleep, is never regular, being very indeterminate in length; it may also so happen, that either the day or the night constitutes his hours of vigilance. This circumstance affords an additional proof how little his habits have been under the controul of proper tuition.

An opportunity having occurred to me, of examining more narrowly the person of Tait, I found that the sternum was much protruded, and that the lumbar and dorsal vertebræ were somewhat curved; but whether this effect could be attributable to some disease, as to rachitis, or whether, on the other hand, it resulted from a mere habitual position of the trunk, which had been bent forwards equally with the sternum, I could not learn. It however appeared, that this state of the body much favoured the attitude in which I first observed him, when he was warming himself by the fire. He was in a posture not unlike that which is described as peculiar to the Moors;—he was not actually seated, but seemed most at his ease, when his extremities were gathered up to the trunk, and his chin was at perfect rest upon his knees. I was, however, not a little surprised to find, that a squatting position was maintained in his gait. The usual erect attitude of man was certainly not habitual to him, and when I directed that it should be induced by coercion, it was maintained with very uneasy feelings, whilst its continuance met with his decided resistance. I also learned from the mother, with equal astonishment, that no attempts had ever been made to teach her son to walk erect. The parents of poor David had, from his birth, regarded him in the hopeless light of a forlorn creature, whose peculiarly bereft lot no tuition could ameliorate. Consequently, if we could be assured that disease had not induced the position of body most easily sustained, it might possibly have afforded a reply to the question, Whether the erect attitude was the natural or acquired position of man?

David's intonations of voice, which I only heard when his painful feelings were intended to be expressed at the erect position in which he was placed, were somewhat remarkable. They were highly melodious, being uttered in almost every key; and if music, as some philosophers state, be the natural language of passion, this idea was perhaps never better illustrated by example, than in the case of this untaught youth.

Pauca de appetitu venereo in hoc adolescente manifesto restant. Hanc enim quæstionem, vir illustrissimus Dugaldus Stewart, de Jacobo Mitchell agens, sic defendit: "Neque inutile foret, neque ab honestissima sapientia alienum, novisse quo modo hic miserandus, jam puber factus, se habuerit quoad ad res venereas." Davidis Tate seminudum corpus hanc propensionem detegendi facultates quidem copiosissimas præstat.

Genitalia ipsa solito ampliora videntur. Mater ejus (nam pater piscatu occupatus domo longe abfuit) mihi ad rogata respondere parum hæsitavit. In memoriam revocandum est, Davidem semper in casulæ aream suo more sedere assuetum esse. Sæpe ideo evenit, ut crura nuda paupercularum familiariter domum invisentium, pueri omnia contrectantis, digitis occurrant. Talibus igitur occasionibus, mater confitetur se sæpius admiratam esse, qua cupidiate manus earundem cruribus adhærerent, quanta maxima celeritate, per summam omnem cutem haud vestimentis contectam, ideoque tactui subjectam, digiti aberrarent. Interea in miseria corpore, notæ veneris desideratæ (scilicet priapismus) in oculos adstantium sese manifestas darent. Hæ autem res arcanum quiddam nec notis legibus subjectum, et naturam appitus venerei insitam, quem nullus imaginationis vel idearum impetus hoc exemplo sed contactus solus accendere potuit, clare comprobare viderentur.

Oporteat quoque hoc loco adjicere, ut in dejectionibus alvi vel vesicæ, nullo pudoris sensu hic miserandus cohibeatur.

These are the leading circumstances in the case of David Gilbert Tait. I was sorry that the time which I could conveniently detach from other avocations was so limited, as to prevent me from devoting that long attention to his habits which was necessary to the completeness of his history. The feelings with which I retired from the cottage, were by no means of an unpainful nature: an observer, though shrinking from an involuntary association of the name of man, with the rank of any earthly creature which may exhibit no emotions beyond those that are produced by mere natural appetite, is still incapable of withholding the confession, that, in an exclusion from all sounds, in a deprivation of sight and intellect, this unfortunate object has an existence in no degree advanced above that of a race of animals occupying the lowest scale of creation.

BELMONT TO WOODWICK, ISLAND OF UNST.

The distance from Fetlar to the island of Unst is about six miles, being across a channel diversified with several sea-holms. Belmont, the handsome seat of Thomas Mouat,

Esq., is situated on the south-west extremity of the island, being built on a site of rising ground at the head of a small inlet of the sea, and commanding a clear view of the ragged and indented coast of Yell ; on the east arises a ridge of serpentine, known by the name of Gallow-hill, which was an occasional place of execution in the country, during the oppressive period when feudality exercised its lawless dominion over the injured udallers ; on the west is a steep headland, defended by two semicircular ramparts of earth, the inner one being five yards, and the outer one ten yards in breadth. A ditch intervenes, much filled up, that is now about five yards broad and two deep ; there is also an outer fosse, of nearly the same dimensions. In the area thus defended, may be traced the remains of a burgh ; but whether this structure is to be considered as cotemporary with the fortification, is highly questionable :—I scarcely dare pronounce with much confidence the camp to be Roman.

The tumultuous channel of Blomel Sound separates the west of Unst from Yell, where there always occurs an opposition of tides, that is to be explained in connection with the great wave of tide which performs its circuit round the shores of Britain. Lesser currents are generated during the progress of the wave, which, running in a direction of north with the flood, and south with the ebb, set in nearly an hour sooner on the western than on the eastern coasts of the country. It will be evident, therefore, that in any channel which communicates with the opposite coasts of the country, as in Blomel Sound, tides propagated at successive intervals of time will be naturally opposed to each other. Sir Robert Sibbald has long since remarked, that the tide in Uyea Sound, on the east of Unst, flows an hour later than that of Blomel Sound on the west, though only two miles distant ; and Mr Gifford has also stated, that when the great current in the middle of the sound sets north, there is an eddy, deriving its course from opposite shores, that sets as fast south, and so shifts about as the great current alters.

About five miles from Belmont is the open bay of Wick, where there is a house and fishing-booth belonging to Mr Scott of Greenwell. On a large headland to the south, foundations of small huts have been traced, which probably were places of refuge for the ancient inhabitants of Shetland on the appearance of an enemy, where they safely lodged their cattle and other property. The *Moul* or promontory is naturally protected by the steepness of its banks, which overhang the sea, and on the land side by rough crags and rocks, the defence of which was assisted by the erection of a strong wall, no part of which now remains. West of the Moul is a rock, where are the remains of an ancient burgh, destroyed by time and wilful dilapidation. It is, I believe, a little south of Wick that Mr Low of Orkney found a burgh named Snaburgh, formed by a double circular wall, which contained large apartments, severally of a shape that was oblong, and widening at each extremity. The situation of the fort was close to a loch, defended partly by the water, and partly by a wet ditch, and rampart composed of loose stones.*

At the head of the inlet of Wick the dreary hill of Vallafiel rears its lofty head, on the opposite side of which, is a long valley, watered by several lochs, that runs parallel with the

---

* The figure of this burgh, which is copied from Mr Low's original Sketch, is given in the Plate of Antiquities, Appendix, Fig. 12.

coast. The hill terminates close to the sea, at a well-sheltered fertile dell near Woodwick, rendered interesting to the mineralogist by the crystals of grenatite which are so abundantly diffused throughout its rocks.

KIRK OF BALIASTA, ISLAND OF UNST.

A walk through the valley near Woodwick leads to a large open lawn at the head of the Loch of Cliff, which seemed very populous and well cultivated. I arrived there on the Sabbath morning: the natives of the Vale were all in motion in their way to the Kirk of Baliasta. The peasant had returned home from the bleak scathold, where he had ensnared the unshod poney that was destined to convey him to the parish kirk. No curry-comb was applied to the animal's mane, which, left to nature's care, "ruffled at speed, and danc'd in every wind." The nag was graced with a modern saddle and bridle, while on his neck was hung a hair-cord, several yards in length, well bundled up; from the extremity of which dangled a wooden short pointed stake. The Shetlander then mounted his tiny courser, his suspended heels scarcely spurning the ground. But among the goodly company journeying to the kirk, females and boys graced the back of the shelty with much more effect than long-legged adults of the male sex, whose toes were often obliged to be suddenly raised, for the purpose of escaping the contact of an accidental boulder that was strewed in the way. A bevy of fair ladies next made their appearance, seated in like manner on the dwarfish steeds of the country, who swept over the plain with admirable fleetness, and "witch'd the world with noble horsemanship." The parishioners at length arrived near the kirk, when each rider in succession, whether of high or low degree, looked out for as green a site of ground as could be selected, and after dismounting, carefully unravelled the tether which had been tied to the neck of the animal. The stake at the end of the cord was then fixed into the ground, and the steed appeared to be as satisfactorily provided for during divine service, as in any less aboriginal district of Britain, where it would be necessary to ride up to an inn, and to commit the care of the horse to some saucy lordling of the stables.

The kirk was remarkably crowded, since there was a sermon to be preached incidental to the administration of the Sacrament; on which occasion I had an opportunity of seeing the convulsion fits to which the religious congregations of Shetland are subject. The introduction of this malady into the country is referred to a date of nearly a century ago, and is attributed to a woman who had been subject to regular paroxysms of epilepsy, one of which occurred during divine service. Among adult females, and children of the male sex, at the tender age of six, fits then became sympathetic. The patient complained, for a considerable time, of a palpitation of the heart; fainting ensued, and a motionless state lasted for more than an hour. But, in the course of time, this malady is said to have undergone a modification such as it exhibits at the present day. The female, whom it had attacked, would suddenly fall down, toss her arms about, writhe her body into various shapes, move her head suddenly from side to side, and, with eyes fixed and staring, send forth the most dismal cries. If the fit had occurred on any occasion of public diversion, she would, as soon as it had ceased, mix with her companions, and continue her amusement as if nothing had happened. Paroxysms of this kind prevailed most during the warm months of summer; and about fifty years ago, there was scarcely a Sabbath in which they did not occur. Strong passions of the mind, induced by religious enthusiasm, were also the exciting causes of these fits; but, like all such false tokens of divine workings, they were easily counter-acted, by producing in patients such opposite states of mind, as arise from a sense of shame: thus they are under the controul of any sensible preacher, who will administer to a mind disease,—who will expose the folly of voluntarily yielding to a sympathy so easily resisted, or of inviting such attacks by affectation. An intelligent and pious minister of Shetland informed me, that being considerably annoyed on his first introduction into the country by these paroxysms, whereby the devotions of the church were much impeded, he obviated their repetition, by assuring his parishioners, that no treatment was more effectual than immersion in cold water, and as his kirk was fortunately contiguous to a fresh-water lake, he gave notice that attendants should be at hand, during divine service, to ensure the proper means of cure. The sequel need scarcely be told. The fear of being carried out of the church, and into the water, acted like a charm; not a single Naiad was made, and the worthy minister has, for many years, had reason to boast of one of the best regulated congregations in Shetland.

When I attended the kirk of Baliasta, a female shriek, the indication of a convulsion-fit, was heard; the minister (Mr Ingram of Fetlar) very properly stopped his discourse, until the disturber was removed; and after advising all those who thought they might be similarly affected to leave the church, he gave out in the mean time a psalm. The congregation was thus preserved from farther interruption; for, on leaving the kirk, I saw several females writhing and tossing about their arms on the green grass, who durst not, for fear of a censure from the pulpit, exhibit themselves after this manner within the sacred walls of the kirk.

HERMANESS TO HAROLDSWICK, ISLAND OF UNST.

After skirting along the east of the Loch of Cliff, which is situated in a beautiful valley of limestone between rocks of gneiss and serpentine, I crossed some low ground at the head of the water, and arrived at Burrafiord, (generally named Burra Firth), which is a wide bay, so open to the ocean as to afford no refuge for ships: it is bounded on the east and west by lofty banks of gneiss, and at the head of the inlet is a low, sandy shore, contiguous to which several cottages appeared, along with a small building intended for the curing of fish. The heavy sea and surf, which had succeeded to a few boisterous days, prevented me from visit- ing two large caverns which communicated with the water; the larger of these is said to be formed by a grand natural arch of considerable height, and wide enough to admit the sail- ing of a boat for a distance of 300 feet. The high banks of Burra Firth, and the stacks contiguous to it, are frequented by numberless flocks of birds, such as gulls and scarfs; and along with these the lyre, or *Procellaria puffinus*,—the Tomnorry, or *Alca arctica*,—and the kittiwake, or *Larus Rissa*. Their nests are annually visited by the nimble and adventurous rockmen, who, for the sake of plunder, land with boats at the foot of the most hideous precipices, which they easily scale, or are let down from the summit of them by means of ropes. The eggs thus obtained are considered as a great dainty; the carcases of the young birds serve for grosser food, and the feathers form an article of commerce.

On the east of the bay is the hill of Saxavord, the occasional resort of the Skua gull, which is estimated at a height of 600 feet. The view from this eminence affords little variety; hills of serpentine, "cold, barn, bleak, and dry," lie extended to the south; and to the north there is an immense prospect of the wide and wealthy sea. On the summit of the ascent are several loose stones, which bespeak the ruins of an ancient watch-tower, the erection of which is fabulously assigned to a giant of the name of Saxe. In the old Shetland dialect, a watch-tower is said to have been expressed by the term *vord*, this being a word that finds a kindred signification in the English expression *ward*. Accordingly, the name of Saxavord indicates Saxe's Vord, or watch-tower. There is also a deep cleft of the rock which is said to have been the residence of this tall warrior, whose name is well calculated to excite the speculative views of some ardent antiquary. For if it be admitted that Shetland was once possessed by the Saxons, who were defeated in the 4th century by Theodosius, the conclusion might be, that tradition, in perpetuating the memory of the giant of Unst, has still preserved in the country the name of Saxe or Saxon. The appellation of Hermaness, by which the adjacent headland on the west of Burrafiord has long been known, is said to have been derived from the residence of a similar gigantic chief of the name of Herman.

East of Saxavord, are the high cliffs of Braewick, composed of mica-slate, which appear remarkably prone to disintegration, and at the north-east angle of Unst, is to be seen a small cottage, which may be considered as the most northerly habitation in the British isles. To the north of Scaw, a small sea holm, there is a considerable opposition of tides, named a *Roust*, which arises from the same cause that I explained in treating of the Roust of Sumburgh-head, on the south of Shetland, (See page 77.) During the circuit of a great wave of tide round the British isles, lesser currents generated from it meet the west and east coast of Shetland, at successive intervals of time; and, by this means, the tides at the north and south extremities of the country are opposed to each other. The tumultuous Roust of Scaw is much frequented by the *Gadus carbonarious*, or Shetland Seethe, for which there is a good fishery.

In continuing my excursion, I arrived at Lambaness, a considerable headland stretching out far to the east, and presenting a favourable situation for the erection of a light-house, that would be an highly useful signal for vessels in sailing from the north. A booth or two is erected in the vicinity for the purpose of conducting from this extreme point the deep water fishery for ling. Near this place, at the distance of a few yards from the brink of a precipice, we look down upon a very deep sloping cavity of a circular form, arising from the disintegration of gneiss, which, at the bottom, communicates by a subterranean channel with the ocean, so as to admit into it the flowing of the tide. This hole is named Saxe's Kettle, being a culinary vessel (and certainly a leaky one) that was used by the Shetland Giant. A short walk in a southerly direction leads to the open Bay of Norwick, which is bounded on its two sides by the steep cliffs of Lambaness, and by brown hills of serpentine-

At the head of the inlet, where a heavy surf continually breaks, is a fishing-booth with several cottages, and well cultivated patches of land : the picturesque effect of the whole being heightened by the shattered remains of an arch belonging to St John's Kirk of Norwick.

After crossing some bleak hills of serpentine, an open bay appears in view, much exposed to the ocean, and affording not the least shelter for shipping. This inlet, named Haroldswick, is celebrated for being the place to which Harold Harfagre sailed after he had touched at Funzie in the Isle of Fetlar, and it was here that he landed, in order to wrest Shetland from the possession of Norwegian pirates, to whose vessels its numerous bays had long afforded a protection. On the brow of a hill are the remains of a sepulchral tumulus of loose stones, which bears the name of Harold's Grave, but as the death of this monarch did not occur in Shetland, it would be idle to offer any conjecture upon the origin of the appellation. The Barrow was opened some years ago, but what description of relics it contained I could not learn.

CRUCIFIELD, ISLAND OF UNST.

South of Haroldswick are bleak and barren hills of serpentine, the most conspicious of which is Crucifield, where there are circular ranges of stones that have, with little reason, been supposed *Druidic*. The Druids believed that the peculiar residence of their deity was among groves of oak, and it was beneath the shade of such trees that Celtic oratories were constructed. But the Scandinavians had no veneration for any trees, with the exception of the ash, their temples being often built on high exposed places, where no forests had ever insinuated their roots. As it is evident, therefore, that the bare surface of the hill of Crucifield never could have supported the growth of trees, we must be prepared to consider these circles of stones as Scandinavian Temples, sacred to the rights of the deities of the Edda. While, in this record of the tenets of the Teutonic tribes who followed Odin into the wilds of Scandinavia, an universal and beneficent Father was acknowledged under the name of Alfader, as well as a personified evil principle under the name of Surtur, various fables are narrated concerning the origin of giants, of dwarfs, and of the proper human race, as well as of a man named Brure, from whom were descended three gods, stiled Odin, Vile and Ve, who ruled between them both heaven and earth : of these Odin was the most powerful. This god in a short time married Frigga, from whom was descended the family of the Ases, or of the gods, whilst Thor, or the first born, was the most renowned for valour. It was promised to the freeborn of Scandinavia, that if they fell by the sword, they were to be admitted to Valhalla, or the hall of Odin, where heroes might have the pleasure of daily cutting each other to pieces in battle ; but, as soon as the hour of repast should approach, they would be restored to life and health, in order that they might eat boar's flesh, and drink beer and mead out of the skulls of their enemies. On the other hand, there was a place, consisting of nine worlds, where Hela, with the direst horrors, inflicted punishments on those who had died of disease or old age.

It is not unlikely that the Scandinavians, in the circular ranges of upright stones that composed their temples and courts of judicature, imitated the religious structures of the Celtic people, whom they had succeeded in the possession of certain European territories; it is also probable, that many Druidic temples which had been abandoned by the Celts in their flight to more secure realms, became occupied by their invaders, who dedicated them to some deity of the Edda. Yet, as lofty columns of stones do not seem to have been absolutely necessary to the construction of Scandinavian temples, we often find that the limits of a holy site of ground were described in the most simple manner, by shallow furrows scooped into the earth, within which loose stones of various sizes were strewed. Accordingly, such a structure distinguishes the juridical remains that appear on the hill of Crucifield.

A remark has been made, (page 99), that when, in the ninth century, colonists from Norway peopled Iceland, their first object was to erect a temple to the god Thor. It is, therefore, singular, that near to the place where Harold Harfagre landed in the Island of Fetlar, and near Haroldswick, to which he subsequently sailed, certain appearances should be presented, indicative of similar honours that were paid to some deity.

The sites of ground now under examination are three in number. The first of these is not far from the Kirk of Baliasta; it is formed by three concentric circles, cut into the stratum of soil that covers the serpentine, into which boulder stones or earth were thrown, until they rose above the level of the ground. The diameter of the outermost circle is 67 feet, of the middle one 54¾ feet, and of the innermost 40 feet. There is a small central tumulus of stones in the middle of the inclosure, 12 feet in diameter, the presence of which is no unfrequent indication of a Scandinavian temple. It was customary on a central stone, or heap of stones, to sacrifice human victims to Thor, which was effected by crushing or breaking the spine. Rites of this kind were also mingled with the duties of legislation; it was at some general convocation for this purpose, after the altars and worshippers of Odin had been sprinkled with the blood of immolated victims, that leaders were elected under a vow to defend their country, to revenge its injuries, and to extend its boundaries; that taxes were levied for the maintenance of religious rites and ceremonies, and that supplies of men and vessels were voted as necessary for the support of predatory excursions, or for defence. In such convocations, therefore, the concentric ranges of circles might be intended to separate individuals of greater or lesser rank, who officiated in the ceremonies of religion or legislation, while the populace stood on the outside.

About a mile to the east of the temple thus described, is a second, yet smaller site of ground, formed, like the first, by three concentric circles, in the centre of which is a tumulus; the diameter of the outermost circle being 55 feet, and of the central heap 10½ feet; and at the distance of about 80 feet from the second temple is a third, consisting of a central tumulus, inclosed by no more than two concentric circles, the diameter of the outermost being 22 feet, and of the innermost 17 feet.* There are reasons for supposing that these sites of ground were intended for popular juridical assemblies; the central space being

---

* For a representation of these concentric circles, See Plate of Antiquities in the Appendix, Fig. 15 and 16.

devoted to the reception of the Foude or Judge, the accused, and the evidences; while the concentric circles divided in an order of precedence, counsellors, men of landed rank, and the lowest orders of society. The place of execution for any criminal condemned by the voice of the people, was without the precincts of the site that was considered hallowed, being on one of the contiguous peaks of the hills named the Heogs; for, probably, like the Holy Mount of Iceland which was dedicated to Thor, the site of the temple was considered so sacred, that it could not be defiled by the blood of a criminal. One of the small peaks, which rises abruptly, like an artificial tumulus, from the high platform of a hill, is named Hanger Heog, and at the foot of it is a heap of stones, which went under the title of the Place of Justice. The top of the peak was reached by a flight of rude steps, where another heap was to be seen, named the Place of Execution. A tradition prevails, that whatever criminal ascended the steps of Hanger Heog never came down alive; and, in confirmation of the account, two bodies, supposed to have been executed criminals, were, about sixty years ago, found buried in disorder near the base of the lower heap of stones. But if any accused person, after hearing the sentence of the Lagman, was desirous to appeal to the voice of the people, he tried to effect his escape in a direction that led to the more westerly circle of stones situated on an adjoining hill, and if he could reach in safety that sacred site of ground, his life was preserved; but if the popular indignation was against him, he was pursued on his way to the sanctuary, and any one before he reached it might put him to death. Such a practice was long continued; but on the conversion of the country to Christianity, the Pagan temple was superseded by the erection of a church, which formed the latest place of refuge. Several crosses, scooped in the earth, shew the places where malefactors have been slain in pursuit; hence the name which has been given to the hill of *Crucifield*. The juridical assembly held at Unst was afterwards removed to the Vale of Tingwall on the Mainland, where the same mode in which a condemned person might make an appeal to the people, was, till a very late period, preserved.

Torfaeus states, that the Pagan supersitions of Shetland were first abolished by the arrival of King Olave Triguesson into the earldom of Orkney, who introduced Christianity among the colonies of Norway at the point of the sword. Landing at South Ronaldsay, he invited Earl Sigurd on board one of his vessels, with which request the unsuspecting chief, accompanied by his young son Hindius, complied. "You are now," said the monarch, "fallen into my power, and I propose to you one of these two conditions; Profess, with all under your dominion, the Christian religion, present yourself at the font for baptism, yield me homage, and while your liberties are enjoyed according to the usage of your ancestors, consider your possession of the country as due to my courtesy: be also my friend for ever, and, by obeying the mandates of God, participate with him for the time to come in his heavenly kingdom. Or, on the other hand, hesitate to comply with my demand, and immediate death awaits you. Unless also your people chuse to profess, upon this very spot, what will be to them their true liberty,—the rites of Christianity,—the whole of the islands shall be destroyed by fire and sword. Refuse me,—and ye may expect, as mere mortals, that at this instant of time, an extreme calamity awaits you, while *hereafter* a much more severe consequence will ensue,—an eternal punishment." "Truly, O King!" replied the Earl of Orkney, with much mildness, "I cannot be induced, either by choice or fear, to prostitute the religion of my fathers, or to deny the established worship of the gods; for I am not conscious of being more clear-sighted than my ancestors, nor do I know in what respect that adoration, which you command, excels our own." The King seeing him thus obstinately bent to idolatry, drew his sword, and seizing upon Hindius, exclaimed, "Now, be assured that I shall keep my word, that I shall spare no one who is opposed to the worship of the Heavenly God, and to the Gospel which I announce. You are a father obstinately bent against your own interest, and unless you, and all under your dominion, shall profess yourselves the servants of the great Deity whom I revere, your son shall perish before your eyes, and one common destruction shall follow." Earl Siguard could not resist this powerful argument: he submitted, along with his son and the whole of his people, to baptism. The King then left ministers of the divine word, with other holy men to give the proselytes farther instructions, and taking with him Hindius as a hostage, he set sail, with pious delight, to communicate his success to his good people of Norway.

BALTA SOUND, ISLAND OF UNST.

After crossing Crucifield, I arrived at Balta Sound, a fine inland harbour, stretching from east to west, the mouth of which is closed in by the small island of Balta.

> "Within a long recess there lies a bay,
> An island shades it from the rolling sea,
> And forms a port secure for ships to ride,
> Broke by the jotting land on either side,
> In double streams the briny waters glide
> Between two rows of rocks."

Two large merchantmen were safely anchored in the Sound; the low bounding shores were arrayed with a few large spread meads, adorned with summer's green, and at various intervals might be seen some good houses, which communicated a cheerful addition to the scene, when contrasted with the brown and barren scalp of the dreary hills of serpentine and euphotide, that rose to the north and south. Balt Island is a rock of inconsiderable height, chiefly inhabited by rabbits of a brownish-grey colour, the natural enemies of whom are ernes, hawks, ravens, and the great horned owl, or *Strix bubo*. The shieldrake, or slygoose, builds in these rabbit burrows; and when the breeding season is past, takes its flight from the country, to spend its winter in some warmer clime. Near the head of Balta Sound is Buness, the residence of Thomas Edmonston, Esq., which place will be long celebrated as having been the site where the French philosopher Biot, in the year 1817, carried on his experiments for the purpose of determining, in this high latitude, the variation in the length of the second's pendulum. He was succeeded in the following year by Captain Kater, who occupied the same station with the same intent. Mr Edmonston rendered every accommodation in his power to facilitate the scientific views of these gentlemen, for which he obtained the warmest thanks of the Royal Society of London, and of the National Institute of Paris. The party who, during M. Biot's visit, prosecuted the trigonometrical survey of Great Britain, were encamped in Balta Island.

The Hill of Crucifield, Hagdale, Buness, and other places in the immediate vicinity of Balta Sound, abound with that valuable substance hitherto chiefly obtained from America, named the Chromate of Iron. I discovered it in different parts of the serpentine rock, in the form of insulated masses of various sizes ; and those portions of the mineral which have been loosened by the disintegration of the rock in which they were contained, seemed to be strewed about the hills, in a direction west from Hagdale, for an extent of several miles.*

Among the serpentine hills, which, in quest of the chromate of iron, I took much labour in exploring, there is a pure stream that has long been celebrated for its supposed sanative virtues. It was of late years usual to walk to its source, and on an adjoining site of ground to throw three stones. This custom is so old, that a considerable pile has been raised by these offerings ; but as the influence of the water god has been long on the wane, the acknowledgment is now much less frequently paid. It was also usual, after the sacrifice to the deity had been made, to drink of the water of the spring, which insured health to the zealous imbiber. Hence the stream acquired the name of Yelaburn or Hielaburn, that is, the Burn of Health.

CASTLE OF MOUNESS, ISLAND OF UNST.

My next excursion was across the Vord Hill, so named from some ancient watchtower which crowned its summit, when I came in view of the long bleak line of the east coast, that is terminated on the north by the Islands of Hunie and Balta. On reaching the Bay of Sandwick, the fine white sand of which strongly reflected the rays of the sun, I ascended a headland that forms the south-east extremity of Unst, and arrived at the ancient castle of Mouness, founded by a Scottish gentleman of the name of Lawrence Bruce. His mother was Euphemia, daughter to Lord Elphingston, the same frail dame who, having born a child to James V., afterwards entered into an honourable alliance with Bruce of Cultmalindie. He who was the fruit of this marriage, thus became the half brother of Robert Stewart, Abbot of Holyrood, and afterwards Earl of Orkney. It unfortunately happened, that Lawrence Bruce, in a private altercation, slew his antagonist. It is then supposed, that, through the intercession of his relation Earl Robert Stewart, who possessed great interest at court, he was allowed to form an undisturbed settlement in Shetland. On reaching this country, where he was accompanied by his cousin William Bruce, he bought up a quantity of land from the distressed udallers of Shetland, and, on the estate which he thus acquired, completed, in the year 1598, the spacious mansion of Mouness. This castle, the principal walls of which still remain entire, stands near the sea, surrounded with a few low hovels. It is three storeys in height, two of its corners being surmounted by round hanging towers, whilst at two other angles, much larger turrets rise from the ground. At

---

* The account of my discovery of Chromate of Iron will be given at the close of the work.

the same time, the castellated stile is intended rather for show than for real defence. On entering a passage of no great width, a kitchen and apartments leading into it, may be found to occupy the lowest storey. Above, is a well shaped dining-room, about thirty-two feet long, and twenty-one broad, with chambers contained within the towers nearly three or four yards in diameter. The upper storey consists of bedrooms. On returning, I noticed, over the outside of the door-way, an undefaced inscription, well engraved on a tablet of freestone :

> " List ze to knaw this building quha began ?
> Lawrence the Bruce he was that worthy man,
> Quha arnestlie his ayris and afspring prayis,
> To help and not to hurt this work always."

Unhappily for the peace of Lawrence Bruce's shade, his supplication was in vain. Owing to the imprudence of his posterity, the estate of Mouness has passed into other hands; the castle then became uninhabited, and the rank weeds of desolation were allowed to fix their roots among its walls, and to wave with every wind. Many beautiful ornaments of masonry have been robbed from the mansion, which now appear stuck up for show among the rude unhewn stones that constitute the fabric of several vile hovels. Yet, after all, there is not so much of the tenement fallen into decay, as would prevent its restitution at a moderate expence; and since the structure does not appear too large for the seat of a country gentleman, it would reflect great credit on the taste of the country, if the disturbed ghost of the anxious founder could, by the restoration of the building, be appeased.

I can find little or no mention made of the family of Bruce in the histories of Shetland. Brand states, that when, in the year 1699, the Laird of Mouness was in a boat with nine or ten persons, a *flann*, or blast off the land, came with such force against the sail, as to overturn the vessel, and to consign to a watery grave the Laird and all his party, with the exception of one servant. From Lawrence Bruce, the founder of Mouness Castle, and his cousin William Bruce, are descended two respectable families in Shetland; from the former the Bruces of Simbister, and from the latter the family of Sumburgh.

UYEA SOUND, ISLAND OF UNST.

A short walk of two miles across the bleak scatholds of the country, brought me to a harbour formed by the low shores of Uyea Island and the coast of Unst. A gleam of sunshine played lightly on the gay white dwellings that were ranged along the circling shore of the sound. Numberless bones belonging to the small whales called *Bottle-noses*, or *Ca'ing Whales*, which had been killed in the harbour, lay bleaching on the strand. The ground to the rear of the hamlet was beset with green patches of corn land, and the humbler habitations of the Shetland peasants. Bleak moorlands closed the prospect, the forbidding summits of which rose with a gradual and dull ascent. But on a small eminence to the east might be seen a rude unhewn obelisk, supposed to have been an ancient land-mark, which directed the vessels of Scandinavia that were steering into the harbour, while some have conceived that it commemorated the site of a battle, where some chief of heroes fell.

Uyea Sound is a great resort for vessels that trade from Leith to Shetland. After touching at Lerwick, where they discharge and take in fresh goods, they sail with the same intent to the north isles of the country.

On landing at the Island of Uyea, which is scarcely a mile in breadth, and about a mile and a half in length, I learnt that a *barrow* had been recently opened, which contained urns of a interesting description. One of these I had indeed seen, when I was on a visit to the hospitable house of Mr Leisk of Lunna. It was a well shaped vessel, that had been apparently constructed of a soft magnesian stone, of the nature of the *Lapis ollaris*. The bottom of the urn had been wrought in a separate state, and was fitted to it by means of a circular groove. When found, it was filled with bones, partly consumed by fire. The barrow was composed of heaps of stones, but by what people it had been raised no idea can be formed; most probably it was of Scandinavian origin. The stones of the sepulchre were completely removed, for the purpose of being applied to the uses of a contiguous building.

In the island of Uyea, the soil is very fertile, and it is likely to be much improved, having become the residence of Mr Leisk, who was then employed in erecting upon it a good house, prior to his removal from Lunna. To the east of Uyea, are two holms, named Weather-holm and Haaf Grunie, the latter of which is a great resort for birds during the period of incubation.

Whilst the rowers rested off the island of Uyea, our boat was visited by one of the large seals of the country *(Phoca barbata)*, named by the natives a *Haaf fish*, because it usually appears at that remote distance from the main coast, which, in the language of the fishermen, is called the *Haaf*. This stray animal was much larger than the common seal, being not less than seven or eight feet in length.* The curiosity which it shewed upon approaching us was remarkable; it played round the edge of the boat for at least half an hour, appearing to inspect the vessel and its occupants with the most marked attention. The boatmen often lamented that the visit which the animal paid to us was upon a Sunday, since the sanctity of the day prevented them from shooting him through the head; and they also attributed to his supernatural sagacity, the choice of a time wherein he could securely make his observations. But how could it be regretted that these fellows were deterred by a religious dread from making an ill return for that unsuspicious confidence which the creature seemed to repose in man? Upon sailing away, the seal was unwilling to quit us, and pursued the boat for a considerable distance. A new dread now arose in the mind of one of the rowers; he was plying his oars on a Sunday, and for this profanation of the Sabbath, the Haaf fish was come to welcome the intended transfer of one of them to the unfathomable depths of the ocean: his object, therefore, was to fly from the influence of the seal's evil eye :—

---

* Mr Low has stated in his MS. Tour, that a seal which was taken in Shetland was not less than twelve feet in length and seven feet in breadth.

> "So forth they rowed, and that ferryman
> With his stiff oares did brush the sea so strong,
> That the hoare waters from his frigot ran,
> And the light bubles daunced all along."

In leaving this foreboder of mischief far behind us, we arrived at Haaf Grunie, where all the remorse of the occasion was stifled by the sight of the numerous eggs of the sea-birds which covered the holm. These were the property of Mr Leisk, and although I had given strict injunctions that not one of them should be taken, I was sorry to find on my return to Uyea, that the sacredness of the Sabbath had not prevented the conscientious boatmen from committing a far greater violation of the day, by charging their pockets to the utmost height with the plunder of the nests.

UYEA SOUND, UNST, TO THE ISLAND OF HASCOSEA.

Along the cultivated land on the south coast of Unst, which extends from Uyea Sound to Belmont, there is little to arrest the attention of the traveller. In the absence, therefore, of any particular object of notice, we may stay to contemplate the inclosures connected with the habitations of the peasantry that bear the name of *Towns* or *Rooms*. It has been pointed out, that Harold Harfagre first levied a tax upon all the land of the country that was intended for pasture: hence the term *scathold*, which was applied to it. But the inclosures destined for cultivation were ever considered as sacred to the unfettered use of the possessor, and not obnoxious to the impost of any seat; they thus acquired the name of Udal or Free Property. When the ancient udaller, therefore, had built a habitation on the land which he had inclosed, he gave to it the name of *Town*. Thus, the word *town*, in this aboriginal country, signified nothing more than udal land which was cultivated and occupied by a proprietor, although there might be upon it but a single cottage. The nature of a Shetland town may afford a curious subject for antiquarian speculation. It is possible, that among many Scandinavian and Saxon nations of Europe, where land was originally allodial, a solitary inclosure, within which was built no more than one habitation, was styled a *Town*; but along with the introduction of feudality small solitary possessors would be more rare, and as the name of *Town* would include not only the mansion occupied by the lord, but the cottage of his dependants, it would thus be in time associated with a large collection of dwellings.* It is, therefore, only in thinly inhabited districts, or in countries unfeudalized until a very recent period, that the original meaning of the word would stand a chance of being retained. Thus, at the present day, if a Shetlander incloses land from the scathold, and surrounds it with a fence, it is still called a Town; and when a stranger is directed to repair to the town before him, he may be surprised to descry that it consists of a single inclosed habitation. A similar use of the term is not wholly unknown in some parts of

---

* I have before had occasion to remark, that, in some countries of Europe, it would, in an early period, be necessary that each town, when it consisted of a number of houses, should be under the protection of a fortress or burgh; and since such a defence became in time an usual appendage to towns, the name of Burgh eventually signified the town itself.

Scotland, but when settlers from this country came into Shetland, a town was also named by them, according to their own phraseology, a *room*; the expression signifying a limited space inclosed from the commons for a place of abode and for culture.

It is a tradition of Shetland, that the most ancient houses which belonged to the wealthier udallers were composed of wood; and that planks were cut out in Norway of such a shape, as that they might form, when joined, proper habitations. These were said to be constantly imported from the mother country in large, twelve-oared boats, named *Scudas*. The best description of houses may be probably found described by Torfæus. There was a spacious cellar for the preservation of casks of ale, a large refectory, with a fire-place in the middle; certain apartments for repose, and often-times a private chapel was attached to the building. But the hovels of the peasants were rude enough, being composed of unhewn stones, with roofs of straw or turf.

Most of the *towns* or *rooms* which had originally belonged the small udallers of the country, fell, in the course of time, into the hands of some rich settler from Scotland, who attempted to connect the various small inclosures that had been made by a single dike. At this day, therefore, nothing can well surpass the irregularity of such circumscriptions, which often wind in every direction in the most zig-zag manner. One dike may include thirty or forty towns, and every farmer is obliged to repair a certain extent of his fence, proportional to the land which he occupies; but so imperfect are these inclosures, which consist of turf or stone, that, by the incursions of sheep, horses, and swine, they are thrown down every year.

Before quitting the island of Unst, I may notice the peculiar mode in which cows are housed. The black cattle of Shetland are of a very diminutive breed; a cow is said to weigh from two to three hundred weight upon an average; an ox from three to four, but not exceeding five hundred weight. These animals have long, small horns, and are of a bridled white, brown, or black colour, rarely displaying an uniform hue. In the summer season they are tethered during the day-time in some adjoining pasture, but at night they are kept within the house. Upon the conclusion of the ling fishery, which is generally in August, the Shetlander repairs to his scathold, and cuts down a large quantity of grass and short heath, which he spreads abroad upon the hills to dry; it is afterwards stored within the enclosure of his small farm, being piled into stacks like hay. When intended for use, the heath is strewed along the floor of the byre, for the purpose of being well mingled with the dung that accumulates from the cows. The wet stratum is then covered over with a layer of *duff mould*, or dry decomposed moss, which substance, in like manner, remains until it is well moistened with the dung that falls, when the whole is again covered with a layer of heath; and after this manner, successive strata of heather and mould, mixed with the ordure of the animal, are allowed to accumulate to a considerable height, until the pile attains such an elevation, that its removal is necessary, in order that the cattle may find sufficient head-room beneath the roof of the byre; but how far the effluvia of putrid matters may conduce to the health of the animals that inhale the tainted atmosphere of such confined places, is a question of unnecessary discussion. When the compost is removed, it is well blended together with a spade, and is then adapted to the land destined for cultivation.

Leaving Belmont, I sailed on the turbulent channel of Blomel Sound, in order to visit the Holm of Linga, contiguous to the shore of Yell, and from thence rowed to the small island of Hascosea, situated between Yell and Fetlar, which is composed in like manner of gneiss. Hascosea is inhabited by a very few families; the land is low, and is in some places tolerably fertile. Some little kelp is burnt in this place, but it may be generally remarked, that the quantity of this substance annually made in Shetland is very inconsiderable, not exceeding 500 tons; for, among the bold shores of these islands, but a small extent of surface is left by the tide, for the collection of sea-weed.*

ISLAND OF YELL.

From Hascosea I was ferried across a narrow channel to Yell, an island six miles in breadth and about twenty miles in length. The rocks are wholly composed of gneiss, and little more is to be seen than parallel mountain ridges, which have a dull and uniform course from south-west to north-east, and slope gradually towards the shore. Landing on the south of Refiord, a voe closed in by the island of Hascosea, my journey south possessed little or no interest. After passing a few good houses at Gossaburgh, Otterswick and Quhon, I arrived at the south-east of Yell, where is the small harbour of Burra Voe, which is well sheltered, and visited by the Leith traders, who land goods from Scotland, and accept in return fish, oil and kelp. An old fashioned house, erected early in the last century, is occupied by Mr Leisk, who keeps on the shore what is named a *Booth;* that is, a small ware-room filled with vendible articles, chiefly imported from Scotland. This is after the manner of the Hamburgh and Bremen merchants, who, in their visits to Shetland, above a century ago, for the sake of trafficking with the natives for fish, opened booths in various parts of the country, for the sale of fishing-lines and nets, coarse cloth and linen, spirits, strong beer, and other articles.

It was in Burra Voe, probably, which is so well situated for trade, that a Bremen merchant dwelt in the days of Buchanan. "In hac" (insula) "habitare ducitur Bremensis, qui omnes merces exoticas, quarum illic usus, abunde omnibus suppeditet, adportet." Near the ruins of a burgh which gives its name to the voe, are the later remains of a building named a *Skeo,* several of which may be indeed seen on the shores of Shetland. A *skeo* is a small square house formed of stones without any mortar, with holes through which the air may have a free passage; for which purpose the building was erected on a small eminence, being at the same time protected from the rain by a roof. It is not long since it was

---

* On taking my leave of Unst, I must acknowledge, in the most grateful manner, the attention I received from several families in this island. There are no inns in the place, except a small one at Uyea Sound, kept by a civil family, of the name of Gardner. But however regardless I might be of this deficiency, and unwilling to intrude myself on the hospitality of the inhabitants, the invitations which I received were so frankly tendered, that I had little or no difficulty in availing myself of the kind welcome that met me on my way. The families to whom I would particularly own my acknowledgments, are those of Mr Edmonston of Buness, Mr Spens of Hammer, Mr Scott of Greenwell, and Mr Nicolson of Haroldswick. I was in like manner indebted to the late Thomas Mouat, Esq. of Belmont, a gentleman of considerable literary attainments, who, from his writings, evidently possessed an intimate acquaintance with the ancient history of this country. I felt much regret in hearing of his death a few months after my visit to Shetland.

customary, before using beef or mutton, not to salt it, but to hang it up in one of these places, until the wind, by which it was penetrated, should, at the necessary degree of temperature, have so completely dried the meat as to preserve it from putrefaction : it was also found, that any cave within which the tide flowed, named a *helyer* or *hiallar*, (the Iceland name at the present day for a skeo), had similar antiputrescent powers. When beef or mutton was thus treated, it was named *vivda ;* but much of the latter description of food appears to have been previously salted, and, says Sir Robert Sibbald, it then acquired the name of *blown meat.* Fish was also hung up unsalted in the skeo, but in this case a slight degree of putrefaction was promoted, that is even at the present day as agreeable to the Shetlanders as the tainted flavour of venison is to an English stomach. "Of the fishes they take," says an early writer on the country, "some they hang in skeos till they be soure, and these they call blowen fishes, which, indeed, are very delicious, and easy to be concocted ;" but when Mr Low travelled through Shetland in the year 1776, he felt much annoyance from the relish which the natives had for tainted fish. "Nothing," says this traveller, "can smell stronger than a number of these skoes placed near one another ; and this, together with the natural fogs of the country, must render it unhealthful and pernicious, particularly for strangers." Many fish, however, which were caught during the period that the Hamburgh merchants trafficked in Shetland, were more carefully dried in these houses, so as not to run into an incipient stage of putrefaction, or they were salted ; they then became an object of barter at the booths of the traders, under the name of *Stock-fish.** About the middle of the last century, the practice of curing beef and mutton in skeos without salt was much given up, and, at the present day, such buildings are not even receptacles for blown-fish, being roofless, and allowed to fall into decay.

A dreary walk to the west, along the south coast of Yell, leads to Hamna Voe, the shore of which is whitened by the numerous bones of the Ca'ing Whale, and from thence past several towns to the south-west point of the island, (named the West Sound of Yell), near to which are the ancient ruins of a small, yet firm built church. The road to the north is along a dreary line of coast, commanding a good view of Yell Sound, with its tumultuous *rousts*, and its various holms and islets ; the prospect being closed on the south by the dark hills of Delting and Northmavine. Sandwick, which I next visited, is the most fertile place in the island, and is well inhabited. To the north is a high headland, forming the south of Whaleford Voe, named the Neaps of Graveland. Lofty banks stretch along the remaining westerly line of coast, where the grotesque forms presented by the immense granitic veins that traverse the strata of gneiss, aided by the solitary appearance of some ancient burgh, serve to beguile the labour of walking through this trackless desert. The north-western extremity of this line of coast is remarkably bold, and at Gloup several naked skerries, the refuge of innumerable sea-birds, appear to have been torn from the neighbouring foreland, while their caves form the great resort of seals. At this place, scories and kittiwakes are caught, by lines being let down perpendicular cliffs, and *jerked* into the young birds. The

---

* The same custom of treating fish occurs at the present day in Iceland. Dr Henderson remarks, that they are hung up and dried in houses called *hiallar*, which are so constructed as to admit the wind through them : the fish are then named *hengi-fish*, or hung-fish, in contradistinction to *flat-fiskar*, or flat fish dried on the rocks.

north and east coasts of North Yell are well inhabited, owing to the lowness of their shores, and their greater breadth of soil that admits of cultivation. At Burra Ness, a point of land near the mouth of a large open inlet named Basta Voe, are the remains of a burgh, that consists of two concentric walls, the outermost of which is about 10 feet thick, and 150 feet in circumference. The inner wall is 4½ feet in breadth, and the space between the outer and inner wall, which has been formed into chambers, is about 2 feet in breadth. About fifty years ago, when Mr Low visited this burgh, the walls were 20 feet in height, but from subsequent dilapidation they are now much lower. The area contained within the fort is about 31 feet in diameter.

Returning to Refirth, I found the prospect relieved by the appearance of some more cultivated land, together with three or four neat white houses. Near the voe is a small church, to the porch of which is affixed an ancient description of pillory named the *juggs*, which much resembles the *carcan* that in former times was well known on the Continent. In Mr Douce's Illustrations of Shakespeare, may be seen the copy of a print from Comenius's Orbis Pictus, representing a woman mounted on a platform, and confined to a pillar by means of an iron collar. The same ring characterises the Shetland punishment, being suspended by a chain to the kirk-porch; and when it was fitted to the neck of a criminal, he was rendered the scorn and gaze of the parish, as they entered the kirk to hear divine service. Such an ignominy is not unknown in Scotland, and was probably introduced into Shetland by settlers from that kingdom. It is enacted in the bye-laws of the country, that all tiggers [beggars] of wool, corn, fish, and others, "be punished with the stocks or *juggs*." The word *juggs* is supposed to be of monkish coinage, being derived from the Latin *jugum*, significant of the Roman infliction of the yoke, which, like this description of pillory, was not attended with corporeal pain, but with moral degradation. The exposure is now considered of such a humiliating kind, that it is not inflicted; and, although the acts which render the Shetland *carcan* a penalty are still extant, yet they become no longer a terror to evil doers, but are rendered easy objects of transgression:

> "We must not make a scarce-crow of the law;
> Setting it up to fear the birds of prey,
> And let it keep one shape, till custom make it
> Their perch, and not their terror."

To the west of Refirth is a dell that leads to another voe of the name of Whalefirth, confined within high banks, open to the Atlantic, and beset at its entrance with dangerous rocks. Refirth and Whalefirth nearly divide the island into two equal parts, which are named North and South Yell.

The interior of the island, which I explored in different directions, will give little interest to the mineralogical traveller, being, for the most part, covered with an impenetrable moss. Brand the missionary tells us that one of the ministers of his time, fell into such a loose piece of ground, that his horse, furniture and all, sank beneath him, and were no more seen, while he himself, with great difficulty, struggled out and was saved. I may add, however, that, during the summer months, the moss is firm enough.*

YELL SOUND.

In Yell Sound there is always a very troubled sea, owing to the currents of tide which are opposed to each other. The flood that sets south between the parish of Northmavine and the Island of Yell, encounters a tide on the east of Shetland, which sets in an hour later, between Lunna Ness on the Mainland, and Burra Voe in Yell. These torrents are again broken in their direction, by the number of islands and sunken rocks that offer resistance to them in their course.

The Islands of Yell Sound, which are in general low, amount to the number of thirteen, or more, Brother Island, Biga, Samphray, and Little Rhoo, which are severally inhabited by a very few families, being the largest. Many of the holms afford a very fine succulent pasture for black cattle, and for sheep destined for the table, such spots being indeed the chief places where they are fattened. So great is the value attached to holms, that an ancient law of the country ordains, that no person trespass upon them, under the penalty of £10 for the first fault, of £20 for the second, and for the third, of being prosecuted as thieves; one-half of the penalty accruing to the judge, and the other to the owner of the holm. Several of the rocks, particularly Linga, are the resort of the Tern, or *Sterna hirundo*, named by the Shetlanders the *Tirrock*. This bird may be often seen in its hovering flight to suddenly dart upon the surface of the water; and, in its successful capture of a sillock, to utter a shrill cry; the *Scouti aulin* or parasitic gull, hears the well known note of success, and instantly repairing to the spot, forces the captor to drop his prey, which he intercepts in its fall. Numbers of the small, low rocks that rise but a few feet from the surface of the water, afford a basking-place for seals, or are frequented by the great black cormorant, or the common scarfs. In the smaller bays that open into the Sound, the eider duck *(Anas mollissima)* may be observed to dive in pursuit of its food. Frequently numerous shoals of sillocks, or young herrings, swarm in every creek. Nor is this channel wholly free from the mightier inhabitants of the deep. Large porpoises roll among the waters; and sometimes appear the *Delphinus orca*, or Chaffer, anciently the dread of boatmen; and the *Squalus maximus*, or basking shark. But an interesting frequenter of the Sound is the large animal lately named in systems of natural history *Delphinus Deductor*, styled by the Shetlanders the Ca'ing Whale; and by the natives of Feroe, the *Grindaquealur*. Adult whales of this kind, which have been often slain on the sands of Hamna Voe, in Yell, seldom exceed 22 feet in length. They are of a shining black colour; though frequently white or grey about the belly. The skin may rival in softness the texture of silk. The head is round, short and thick, having the under jaw shorter than the upper, by three or four inches. The eyes are remarkably small; the teeth, which are of the average length of an inch, and of a sharp, subconoid form, vary with the age of the animal, being, in the

---

* There is a deficiency of puplic accommodation for the traveller at the large island of Yell. I have, however, to acknowledge the hospitality I received from Mr Irvine, Mr Leisk, and a gentleman whose name I do not recollect, in Gossaburgh.

largest size, about 24 in number. There is a blow-hole near its neck, from which it is able to spout water to the height of a few feet. It has a tail that is cleft and vertical, a short, stiff dorsal fin, and two long and narrow pectoral fins. The females have two nipples, although they are much concealed by an adipose substance. These whales often appear in a gregarious concourse to the number of from one to five hundred.*

I had landed at Mr Leisk's of Burra Voe in Yell, when a fishing boat arrived with the intelligence that a drove of Ca'ing Whales had entered Yell Sound. Females and boys, on hearing the news, issued from the cottages in every direction, making the hills reverberate with joyful exclamations of the event. The fishermen armed themselves with a rude sort of harpoon, formed from long iron-pointed spits;—they hurried to the strand, launched their boats, and, at the same time stored the bottom of them with loose stones. Thus was a large fleet of yawls soon collected from various points of the coast, which proceeded towards the entrance of the Sound. Some slight irregular ripples among the waves shewed the place where a shoal of whales were advancing. They might be seen sporting on the surface of the ocean for at least a quarter of an hour, disappearing, and rising again to blow. The main object was to drive them upon the sandy shore of Hamna Voe, and it was evident that the animals, with their enemy in the rear, were taking this direction. Most of the boats were ranged in a semicircular form, being at the distance of about 50 yards from the animals. A few skiffs, however, acted as a force of reserve, keeping at some little distance from the main body, so that they might be in readiness to intercept the whales, should they change their course. The sable herd appeared to follow certain leaders† ; who, it was soon feared, were inclined to take any other route than that which led to the shallows on which they might ground. Immediately the detached crews rowed with all their might, in order to drive back the fugitives, and, by means of loud cries and large stones thrown into the water, at last succeeded in causing them to resume their previous course. In this temporary diversion from the shore, the van of the boats was thrown into confusion ; and it was a highly interesting scene to witness the dexterity with which the Shetlanders handled their oars, and took up a new semicircular position in rear of the whales. Again the fish hesitated to proceed into the inlet, and again a reserve of boats intercepted them in their attempt to escape, while a fresh line of attack was assumed by the main body of the pursuers. It was thus that the whales were at length compelled to enter the harbour of Hamna Voe. Then did the air resound with the shouts that were set up by the boatmen, while stones were flung at the terrified animals, in order to force them upon the sandy shore of a small creek ; but before this object could be effected, the whales turned several times, and were as often driven back. None of them, however, were yet struck with the harpoon ; for if they were to feel themselves wounded in deep water, they would at all hazards betake

---

* I was little aware when in Shetland that the external characters of a whale frequently seen in Feroe and the north of Scotland, were imperfectly known to many naturalists, otherwise I should, by independent observations on its form, have been spared the necessity of comparing my recollections of it with the previous remarks of other writers. I have, however, to subscribe to the general correctness of Captain Scoresby's representation of the shape of the Delphinus Deductor, as given in vol. 1, p. 496 of his work on the Arctic Regions, which was derived from communications on the subject by Mr Neill and Dr Traill, who have the merit of being the first to point out the distinctive characters of this animal.—See also Landy's *Description of Feroe* (transl.) p. 217.

† From this circumstance, Dr Traill, with great propriety, first proposed to give the animal the title of *Delphinus Deductor*.

themselves to the open sea. The leaders of the drove soon began to ground, emitting at the same time a faint murmuring cry, as if for relief; the sand at the bottom of the bay was disturbed, and the water was losing its transparency. The shoal of whales which followed increased, as they struck the shore, the muddiness of the bay;—they madly rolled about, irresolute from the want of leaders, uncertain of their course, and so greatly intimidated by the shouts of the boatmen, and the stones that were thrown into the water, as to be easily prevented from regaining the ocean. Crowds of natives of each sex, and of all ages, were anxiously collected on the banks of the voe, hailing with loud acclamations the approach of these visitants from the northern seas;—and then began the work of death. Two men, armed with sharp iron spits, rushed breast-high into the water, and seizing each a fin of the nearest whale, bore him unresistingly along to the shallowest part of the shore. One of the deadly foes of this meekest of the inhabitants of the sea deliberately lifted up a fin, and beneath it plunged into the body of the animal the harpoon that he grasped, so as to reach the large vessels of the heart. A long state of insensibility followed, succeeded by the most dreadful convulsions; the animal lashed the water with his tail, and deluged the land for a considerable distance: another deathlike pause ensued, throes still fainter and fainter were repeated with shorter intermissions, until at length the victim lay motionless on the strand. The butchers afterwards set off in a different direction, being joined by other persons assuming the same functions. Female whales, appearing, by their hasty and uncertain course, to have been wrested from their progeny, and sucklings no less anxiously in pursuit of those from whose breasts they had received their nutriment, were severally arrested in their pursuit, by the relentless steel of the harpooner. Numerous whales which had received their death-wound soon lined the bay, while others at a greater distance were rolling about among the muddy and crimsoned waves, doubtful whither to flee, and appearing like oxen to wait the turn of their slaughterer. Wanton boys and females, in their anxiety to take a share of the massacre, might be observed to rankle with new tortures the gaping wound that had been made, while, in their blood-thirsty exultation they appeared to surpass those whose more immediate business it was to expedite the direful business. At length the sun set upon a bay that seemed one sheet of blood: not a whale was allowed to escape; and the strand was strewed over with carcases of all sizes, measuring from six to twenty feet, and amounting to not fewer than the number of eighty. Several of the natives then went to their homes in order to obtain a short repose; but as the twilight in this northern latitude was so bright as to give little or no token of the sun's departure, many were unremittingly intent upon securing the profit of their labour, by separating the blubber, which was of the thickness of three or four inches. It was supposed that the best of these whales would yield about a barrel of oil; and it was loosely computed that the whales were on an average worth from two to three pounds Sterling a-piece, the value of the largest being as much as six pounds.*

The division of the profits that accrue from these whales, was, from very ancient times,

---

* In Captain Scoresby's work, the measurement of an adult ca'ing whale appears as follows: Length, 19½ feet; greater circumference 10 feet; pectoral fin (the external portion) 3½ feet long by 18 inches broad; dorsal fin 15 inches high and 2 feet 3 inches broad; ...readth of the tail 5 feet.

regulated by strict laws, which on the introduction of feudality varied from those of Denmark. " As soon," says Mr Gifford, "as the whales are got ashore, the Bailie of the parish is advertised, who comes to the place, and takes care that none of them are embezzled ; and he acquaints the Admiral thereof, who forthwith goes there, and holds a Court, where the Fiscal presents a petition, narrating the number of whales, how and where drove ashore ; and that the Judge thereof may give judgment thereupon, according to law and the country practice. Whereupon the Admiral ordains the whales driven on shore to be divided into three equal parts ; one of the parts to belong to the Admiral, one part to the salvers, and one-third to the proprietor of the ground on which the whales are driven ashore; and he appoints two honest men, who are judicially sworn, to divide them equally. The minister or vicar claims the tithes of the whole, and commonly gets it ; the Bailie also claims the heads for his attendance, and if the Admiral finds he has done his duty, the heads are decerned to him, otherwise not." In consequence, however, of frequent disputes that took place on this tripartite division of the whales, the Earl of Morton, who was invested with the droits of Admiralty, appears to have compounded with the landed proprietors of Shetland, by agreeing to accept a definite sum for his share of the capture ; but his successors have, I believe, relinquished the claim altogether.

Nothing can better display the debased state of the husbandry of Shetland, than the fact that the carcases of the whales are in general allowed to taint the air until they are completely devoured by gulls and crows. Mr Hay and Mr Bruce are, I believe, the first agriculturists in the country, who have sent for them from a considerable distance, in order to apply their carcases to the land as a manure ; but many of those which were caught during my visit to Shetland, were allowed to rot on the shore. At Feroe, the flesh of these animals is cured like beef, which it is said to resemble in taste, and is considered as a great dainty ; and in the year 1740, a time of great scarcity, it was eaten from necessity by the natives of Northmavine.

LUNNA TO AITHSVOE.

After crossing Yell Sound to the Mainland, and experiencing a rough passage, from the waves caused by the Roust, one of which half-filled the boat, I arrived at Lunna, and from thence steered north-west, along the east coast of Delting, where several considerable mountain-ridges of gneiss terminated in bold headlands. In the intervals between them, the sea finds access for some little distance. Swinnin Voe runs a mile and a half into the land ; Colafirth Voe a mile ; and Dale's Voe, the banks of which are highly enriched by strata of limestone, is three miles in extent. On the shore of the latter inlet once stood an open ting or court of justice, that gave its name to the parish of Delting or Daleting. My next sail was round the peninsula of Foreholm, which shelters the entrance of Dale's Voe. To the north of this land are four projecting capes, formed by gneiss and sienite, between which run the North Voe of Swinnister, Firth's Voe, and Taph's Voe ; their course is respectively not more than from half a mile to a mile inland. Taph's Voe is visited by Leith traders, for the purpose of discharging and taking in goods, while, on the shore between this harbour and the most northerly point of Mioness, may be seen the booths of a few small traders employed in the ling fishery, and the cottages, or rather *towns*, as they are called, of several fishermen. But as the coast is viewed from the water at some little distance, the patches of cultivation that vary the surface of the land, seem so comparatively scanty, when compared with the extensive desert which forms the interior of the mainland, that, by enabling the spectator to contrast the general complexion of the country with what ought to be its hue, the gloomy sensations excited by the prospect are not diminished but increased. On approaching the dwellings of a humbler description, the traveller is often surprised with the great number of domestic fowls that are reared, the encouragement given to this race having probably originated in the ancient requisition of an annual number of fowls due to the falconer of the Royal household, for the alleged purpose of supporting the King's hawks that were collected in Shetland. It is supposed that the goshawk, or *Falco palumbarius*, was the object of the falconer's search; but the bird which was held in chief estimation, was the *Falco peregrinus niger*, said to be recognised at a distance by a white band that he wore; he was found in Fair Isle, Foula, Lamhoga, Fitfiel and Sumburgh Heads. No more than one pair would inhabit the same rock, and from the memory of man would continue in the same place. In such request were these birds, that when the earldom of Orkney and lordship of Zetland were disannexed from the Crown, there was a clause in the act of Parliament, stating, "that all hawks should be reserved to his Majesty, with the falconers' salaries, according to ancient custom." During the Scottish government of Shetland, each parish afforded the falconer who was sent over the means of feeding the King's hawks, by an obligation to furnish for this purpose a certain quantity of carrion, dogs, horses or other garbage: but as food of this kind was not always to be procured, the requisition was commuted for a certain number of fowls from each parish, or for a hen from every reek or house. Fowls were said to be thus collected for the food of the hawks; but during the tyranny of Robert and Patrick Stuart, they rather administered to the supply of the Superior's table.* When hawks ceased to contribute to the amusements of the king, who in later times lived in England, the continuation of the levy was considered a great hardship, and the falconer found much difficulty in levying his *hawk-hens*. In revenge, therefore, for the trouble which he experienced, he brought one year into the Mainland some weazels, which he turned loose, in order to destroy the fowls. But the object was not successful; on the contrary they were said to be of some little use of clearing the island of rats. It also appears, that the early inducement for the Shetland peasantry to rear poultry, was not only attributable to the requisition of hawk-hens (due even at the present day,) but to a feudal custom of the south, which was the payment of a certain number of fowls at Yule or Christmas to the new settler, who was aping, in his little demesnes, the exaction of some mightier feudal chief of Scotland.

The most common tenants, however, of the inclosures are the small swine peculiar to

---

* It has not been unaptly remarked to me, that the most insatiable of the hawks that required poultry for their maintenance, were the Stewarts, Earls of Orkney.

the country, which are of a dunnish-white, brown or black colour, with a nose remarkably strong, sharp pointed ears, and back greatly arched, from which long, stiff bristles stand erect. The hog is said to weigh from 60 to 100 lb. Being often very lean, his flesh is as food proportionally coarse; but when fattened, the meat is sufficiently sweet and delicate, and when cured forms excellent hams. The swine are too often suffered to roam abroad, and to root up turnips, potatoes, corn, and other herbage, so that they are scarcely a profit, but an absolute loss to the country. There is an ancient law in Shetland, that "none have more swine than effeiring (proportional) to their land labouring;" and that "none have swine pasturing in their neighbours' lands,—under the pain of £10, besides damages." But this proper regulation is little regarded.

There is generally a piece of green pasturage, never dug up, that surrounds the Shetlander's farm-house, which he names his *town mails*.* On this spot horses are always tethered, when wanted for immediate use, or upon the close of a summer's day, the small black cattle of the country are in like manner secured, previous to their being lodged for the night within the byre. Cows are kept in the house every evening during the year. Their litter is composed of heath and sometimes of *duff mould* or decomposed moss. Their food is in general so little, that during very severe winters, numbers have been known to perish for want. When Dr Kemp travelled through the country a few years ago, so great was the dearth for food, that he witnessed a kind of mash served up for a cow, consisting of a large pail filled with boiled fish-bones, which had been broken down. Such an unnatural mess, however, though by no means uncommon in Iceland, is much less frequently seen in Shetland. The quantity of milk given in the day by the Shetland cow is very inconsiderable, not amounting, in the middle of summer, to more than from three to five English quarts in the day. The operation of churning takes place every second or third day. A little time before the butter is about to part from the serum, the dairy-maid throws red-hot stones into the churn, by which the separation is hastened, and rendered more complete. The attention she pays to the purity of the butter depends upon its destination,—whether it is intended for consumption within the house, or must be rendered in payment of feudal duties, or of teinds; thus the proverbial quality of teind-butter, which is fit for little more than for greasing cart-wheels, is notorious; nor has the impurity ever been counteracted by an act of the country, which declares, that no butter be rendered for payment of land-rent, or for sale, but such as is clean from hairs or bland, and other dirt, and sufficiently salted, under the pain of forty shillings Scots for each offence; and for the first fault, the insufficient butter to be returned, and for the second, to be forfeited for the use of the poor of the parish. Into the buttermilk that remains in the churn hot-water is poured; the caseous part, named *Kirn-milk*, subsides, and is used for food: the mixture of serum and water that is left, forms a common drink named *Bland*, which when allowed to rest, undergoes a slight degree of fermentation, and acquires in the course of a few months a remarkable degree of transparency, and along with it a very acid yet agreeable taste. A similar beverage is familiar at the present day to the Icelanders, among whom it is known by the same

---

* In the ancient Shetland language, the green pasturage attached to a dwelling was named a *Setter* or *Seater*.

appellation that it bears in Shetland. Another product of the dairy, is obtained by adding to a quantity of sour cream some sweet milk ; the mixture then undergoes a sort of fermentation, after which the whey or serous part is poured off, and more new milk is added. The process is thus repeated several times, until the firmer part resembles a sub-acid and highly pleasant taste.

On turning round the point of Mioness, I steered south-west past the mouth of Orka Voe, an inlet two miles in extent, and reached the narrow entrance of Soulam Voe, confined on the west by the peninsula of Glus and by Foula Ness, and on the east by the promontory of Coldback. Soulam Voe soon afterwards sends out a considerable arm into the low land on the east, which acquires the name of Garth's Voe ; and to the south, at a distance of seven or eight miles from the mouth, are two or more smaller inlets, near one of which named Hardwell Voe, is the manse of the minister of Delting. This large channel was evidently at one time nothing more than an inland lake, being connected to the sea by the disintegration of the granitic cliffs that appear at its entrance between Foula Ness and Coldback. The vicinity of Garth's Voe was one of the last retreats of the native Dryads, before they foresook in despair the British Thule. On the low land of this place, the encroachment of the sea, long since exposed the remains of a very ancient forest, consisting of hazel and several large aquatic plants, the stocks of which were from half an inch to eight inches in diameter, that struck their roots into a bed of gravel, while above them was an accumulation of peat-moss about ten feet in thickness. The disclosures that are made throughout the country in digging for peat, shew that certain kinds of small trees, such as hazels, willows or birch, once braved with success the cutting blasts of Shetland, while the introduction of sheep into the country, which would prevent new plants from springing up, or inundations arising from the incursions of the ocean, have probably been the conspiring causes to which their decay is attributable. It was in an early period of the historical annals of the country that the want of food was first felt. The first Norwegian colonists were acquainted with no other kind of fuel than that which they had collected from the forests of their own native mountains, and when Einar, Earl of Orkney, pointed out to them that a fuel was to be obtained from dried peat, he was almost deified for the discovery, having ever afterwards the honorary title prefixed to his name of Torf. The celebrity that Torf-Einar thus secured for himself among the songs of the Northern Scalds, is by no means remarkable : the dark annals of many European nations celebrate the names of individuals, who are considered as benefactors to the human race, from inventions no less simple. Thus, in the Welsh Triads, three Bards are renowned as modellers of the Island of Britain, one of whom made a vessel with a sail and helm for the race of the Cymri ; a second taught the use of stone and lime, and the third the use of a mill with a wheel.

It is in the time of *Voir* or Spring, after the seed has been sown, that the Shetlander generally repairs to his scathold for the purpose of cutting his peat. Thus, there is an ancient law in the country, "that none cut floss before Lammas-day in their own scathold, without due advertising of their neighbours belonging to the same scathold, under the pain of 40s Scots *toties quoties.*" When the natives are assembled to cast their peat, their first object is to pair off the vegetating moss, named the *feal*: this is always called *flaying the moor*. For this purpose an ancient description of spade is used, the shaft of which is long and light, while the iron-plate at the bottom of it is of a different shape, and much narrower than that which distinguishes the common spade of England and Scotland, *(See Plate of Antiq. in the Appendix*, Fig. 25.) There is one man, who, with this implement, makes a ditch seldom wider than two feet, while another is employed in disengaging the feal that has been cut, which he throws on the delver's right hand-side, in the most slovenly manner. When the moor is thus *flayed*, an ancient Scandinavian implement of husbandry is used for casting the peats, named a *tuskar* : its shaft is rather longer than that of a common spade, whilst to the bottom of it is affixed a sharp iron-plate, styled a *feather*, which projects from one place seven inches, and from another a little more than an inch, *(See Plate of Antiq., Fig.* 24). Thus, when the Shetlander, in wielding his tuskar, pushes down the feather into the moor in a perpendicular direction, a corresponding shape and size is given to the peat that is cut ; he then with the greatest activity, lifts up each portion as it is severed, and whilst it rests upon his tuskar, throws it abroad on his left hand-side, or piles it in such a manner, that proper intervals may subsist for the admission of air. The ditch is dug very narrow, and its depth rarely extends beyond the depth of two peats. When this labour is finished, the feals appear in loose slovenly heaps, being but seldom deposited at the bottom of the ditch, with the verdant surface upwards, so that vegetation might be continued. With regard to the length and direction of the excavations, they are governed by no rule, the tenant having the unrestricted liberty of making what devastation he chooses upon his pasture. Often, as Mr Shirreff in his Agricultural Survey has remarked, the cuts are at right angles across a declivity, so as to catch all the surface water that runs down the slope, and to prove traps for drowning sheep ; or not unfrequently the water bursts over the lower sides of the trenches, and converts the ground, for a considerable distance, into an unsightly gulley. In the course of a fortnight or three weeks after the peats have been cast, they are set up on one end that the drying may be completed ; but the close of the process is in the middle of the summer, when the Shetlanders build up their peats in large stacks near the place where they were dug, or, by means of the little shelties of the country, carry them home. For this purpose, a saddle, named a *Klibbar*, is contrived, which consists of two flat pieces of wood that meet on the ridge of the shelty's back, being rounded off in their summit, and connected together, by means of two long attached pieces of wood, which transversely fit into each other, and project upwards ; the boards are then secured below by girths, that pass under the animal's breast and tail, while from the two cross pieces of wood that rise from the top of the saddle, are suspended a couple of *cassies* or baskets made of straw.* When a number of horses are thus accoutered, they are driven to the scatholds ; the cassies which they bear are filled with peat, which, on arriving at its destination, is stored up in piles close to the Shetlander's house, for his yearly stock of fuel.

It appears that the use of the shelty, which is seldom more than from nine to eleven

---

* A klibbar or *klibbari* is in use in the Feroe Islands ; but its form is very different to the Shetland saddle. See Landt's Feroe Islands, (Transl.) p. 278.

hands high, is principally confined to the carrying home of peat; yet, in the transportation of other kinds of light burdens, his back is still surmounted with a wooden saddle. When hay or any light bulky substance is to be carried, *maiseys* are used, which are made of ropes prepared from *floss* or rushes, these being reticulated in meshes of some inches in width. A net of this kind is passed round the horse, so as to secure the hay or other light substance that rests upon the boards of the klibbar. This ancient saddle is also found of use when the shelty is required by the female rider to bear her to the parish kirk; she then throws over his back a native coarse manufacture of the country, woven into the shape of a saddle-cloth, and when, upon this covering the klibbar is fixed, its projecting pieces of wood which the female holds by, form it into a kind of side-saddle. But, amidst the various services which the poor shelty renders to his owner, the revolting task remains of recording the treatment which in spite of them he undergoes. He is left to feed on the hills during the whole of the year; and in the most inclement weather of winter, is never admitted within the warm walls of a stable, being frequently compelled to subsist on the drift ware that is left by the ebb. On my arrival in Shetland early in the spring, I found these animals in such a half-starved state, owing to their scanty supply of winter food, that the growth of the summer herbage was necessary before they had so sufficiently recovered their strength, as to bear a rider over the moors of the country.

At the head of Soulam Voe there is a small isthmus about 100 yards broad, that separates this inlet from the westerly seas, while there is a larger neck of land to the south, though not more than a quarter of a mile across, that leads to another spacious harbour, diversified with islands and holms, which is not only the common centre at which several voes and sounds meet, but the site where the common junction takes place of several mountain masses, consisting of granite, sienite, epidotic sienite, quartz rock, greenstone and gneiss. The traveller now perceives that he is treading upon a regular paved road, several yards in breadth, which, though scarcely a mile in extent, gives to a visitant of Shetland, who for several days may have seen nothing before him but trackless deserts, a delight that is wholly inexpressible. At the termination of the walk is the substantial and respectable old fashioned mansion of Busta, built at different periods, but of a style characteristic of the commencement of the last century, being closed in by spacious garden-walls, the height of which is coequal with the tops of a grove of trees. Near the shore is an excellent landing place for boats, and a dove-cot, of dimensions that might rival in magnitude the buildings of a similar kind, that are to be found in the south. This prospect of comfort and civilization is still more enjoyed, in connection with the rocky tract of country and wild seas that appear on every side; but on entering the garden amidst a grove of mountain ashes, plane trees and elders, the gratification is complete; nothing can give greater cheer to the fatigued vision, when so long satiated with the superfluous waste of bare and tenantless scatholds.

> " It is a chosen plott of fertile land
> Amongst wild waves set, like a little nest
> As if it had by nature's cunning hand
> Bene choicely picked out from all the rest,

And laid forth for ensample of the best :
No dainty flowre or herbe that grows on ground,
Nor arborett with painted blossoms drest,
And smelling sweete, but there it might be found
To bud out faire and throw her sweet smells all around."—SPENSER.

The garden is laid out in a style, in regular parterres, that shews much of the formal taste of the last century. The trees are, however, stunted as soon as they get above the shelter of the wall. Mountain ashes may be found near 20 feet high, and from 2 feet to 2½ feet in circumference, when reckoned within the limits of six feet above the ground. Planes are of a similar height, and from 2½ feet to nearly 3 feet in circumference. There is also an elder, having dimensions little different. The trees that thrive the best are those of which particular mention has been made : the growth of other kinds, with perhaps the exception of the scyamore, having hitherto defied the attempts of the planter; but the result of his success, should seeds be imported from Norway, or raised in the country, might perhaps be very different. In the parish of Delting, near the Burn of Valyor, native mountain-ashes may be found growing in sites secure from the attacks of cattle. It is said that plants from this place have been transplanted into the garden of Busta, where they now flourish.

Busta is the seat of Arthur Gifford, Esq., the worthy representative of an ancient family, who settled in Shetland in the sixteenth century. Some of their land was purchased from Earl Patrick Stewart, since a feu-charter is recorded, dated July 8, 1583, of certain lands on the opposite shore of Wethersta, in which this nobleman reserved for his own use two or three rooms in the mansion-house that belonged to the estate. As Busta was the habitation of a gentleman who published the earliest statistical description of this country worth notice, on account of the acquaintenance that it shews with the laws of this ancient Scandinavian colony, this family-seat ought to be for ever held in esteem by the inhabitants of Shetland. The author of the History of Shetland married the sister of Sir Andrew Mitchell of West Shore near Scalloway. It is recorded of the Gifford family, that, in the year 1748, no fewer than four of the sons belonging to the Laird of Busta, accompanied by a cousin, were lost in a boat whilst crossing a bay. A more melancholy accident than this, it is seldom the fate of the provincial historian to record.

Not far from the house of Busta, is a large stone of granite, that appears as erect as if it had been fixed there by art.* Not improbably it was a large boulder-stone, brought thither by natural causes, and placed in an upright position, as the memorial of some battle or death of a chief. It is supposed by the vulgar to have been thrown there by the Devil from some hill in Northmavine. A similar origin is ascribed to appearances like these in other countries.

"And whereto serves that wond'rous trophy now,
That on the goodly plain near Walton stands;

---

* See Plate iv. Fig. 1.—I cannot take leave of the vicinity of Busta, without expressing my sense of the hospitality I received from the truly respectable resident of this place. I have singular obligations due to Mr Barclay of Olnasfiord.

> That huge dumb heap that cannot tell us how,
> Nor what nor whence it is, nor with whose hands,
> Nor for whose glory it was set to shew?
> How much our pride mocks that of other lands!—
> Then Ignorance, with fabulous discourse,
> Robbing fair art and cunning of their right,
> Tells how these stones were, by the Devil's force,
> From Afric brought to Ireland in a night."—DANIELS.

South of Busta is the Island of Meikle Roe, divided from the Mainland and the Island of Vementry by two narrow sounds, and to the east of it is Linga, a small holm of a perfectly round shape, that is situated at the common entrance into two voes; the first, which is named Gonfiord, runs two miles from north to south, and the second named Olnafiord, is a broad inlet, the channel of which intersects, at right angles, the gloomy ridges of gneiss that run from south-west to north-east, stretching at the same time from five miles to the eastward: at the head of this voe stands an ancient kirk, where are some good monuments of the Gifford family, and adjoining to it is the mansion of Mr Barclay, a very intelligent medical practitioner. Entering a yawl, I was rowed across the mouth of Gonfiord Voe, and reached the headland ot Hoobensetter, where are the remains of several tumuli, probably of Scandinavian origin, from which rude earthen urns have been taken. From this point there is a good view of Aithsvoe, the entrance of which is nearly closed by the island of Papa Little. Several buoyant skiffs were floating on the blue trembling waves of the bay, while the active Shetlander was wielding the light rod, and throwing his line among the throng of sillocks with which the inlet was filled; his successful competitors in the pursuit were the rapacious maws, who, in their hovering flight, darted down frequently on the surface of the waters, though in the abundance of their finny victims, they failed in outnumbering the captives which had been secured by the adroit hand of the busy angler. Small patches of cultivated ground and dwellings lined the circling coast of the voe, indicating the cause that had designated it by the title of *Aith*, which implied the vicinity of a fertile soil. Near the head of this voe is East Burrafiord, an inlet so named from a holm that contains an ancient burgh, of which scarcely the foundations remain. The shore is commanded by the hill of Scallowfield, exceeding a thousand feet in height, which forms the highest point of a ridge that extends from Weesdale to Olnasfiord.

ANCIENT AND PRESENT STATE OF THE SHEEP PASTURES OF SHETLAND.

The country to the south and south-west of Olnasfiord consists of bleak and uninhabited hills, which form part of the scatholds of the Mainland, where there are neither partridges, moorfowl, nor hares to afford amusement for the sportsman; but, in the place of them, he may hear the shrill and plaintive notes of the curlew and plover, or the whistling of the snipe.

The tenants of the scatholds were the wild sheep of the country, celebrated for their small size, and known by naturalists under the name of the *oves cauda brevi*, that at the present day range among the mountains of modern Scandinavia and Russia: in very few places are the Shetland sheep mixed with a Northumberland breed. Their colour is exceedingly various, being grey, black, dunnish brown, white, or they are streaked and speckled in the most curious manner with a combination of various tints and shades. Besides the distinctive character which they possess, from the shortness of their tails, their horns also are very small. In summer, they collect from the pastures that kind of food which the natives still designate by the ancient Scandinavian term of *Lubba*, expressive, in the original sense, of coarseness or roughness. Lubba comprises those common productions of the hills which are found where heath is absent; thus it consists of several kinds of Carices, of *Nardus stricta*, *Eriophoron* or cotton-grass, which is the food of sheep in spring, and of other plants.* *Burra*, which is the provincial name given to the *Juncus squarrosus*, serves the animals during the winter. But besides these productions, the *Erica vulgaris* and *tetralix* are the last resources. The sea also affords provision for the wild inhabitants of the Shetland scatholds, and there almost appears to be a peculiar instinct, which, in the severer months of the year, prompts them, upon the ebbing of the water, to flee to the shore, where they remain feeding on marine plants until the flow of the tide; they then return to the hills. The diseases to which they are subject are as various as in the several districts of Scotland; thus they are afflicted at times with what the Scotch call *braxy*, or an inflammation in the bowels, with the *sturdy*, or water in the head, with blindness, from which they frequently soon recover, and with the rot. About thirty or forty years ago, the scab was unfortunately introduced into the Mainland, and proved very fatal, reducing the number of these animals in some places to a third. The natural enemies of the young lambs are eagles, (named Ernes), ravens, hooded crows, and the black-backed gull. Of these, the ravenous sea-eagle *(Falco ossifragus)*, and the ring-tailed eagle *(Falco fulvus)*, are the most formidable; nor is the *Vultur albicilla*, or white-tailed eagle, unknown as an assailant of the Shetland pastures. In order to encourage the destruction of these birds of prey, there was an ancient law of the country that set a liberal price upon their heads, whenever they were brought to the court of the Foude. The reward was much less in value when paid by the Commissioners of the Land-tax, amounting to 3s 4d Scots for an erne, 3d for a corbie or raven, and 2d for a crow. Other formidable invaders of the flock are the swine, which, to the approbrium of the husbandry of the country, are suffered to roam uncontrolled over the scatholds, and to die their tusks in the blood of young lambs when just dropped.

The sheep are allowed to run wild among the hills, herding and housing being almost wholly unknown in Shetland. There is an old law, that was probably introduced by the Scotch settlers, ordering that every scathold have a sufficient herd, and that builling, punding, and herding, be used in a lawful way, before, or a little after, sun-setting; and that

---

* The provincial term *Lubba* is well explained by Mr Neill in his account of the heathy eminences of Yell. This author remarks, that "Narthecium ossifragum (bastard asphodel), Pinguicula vulgaris (butterwort or sheep-rot), and Pedicularis palustris (marsh lousewort), were indeed too common. Melica cœrulea (purple melic), Nardus stricta (heath matweed), and Festuca vivapera (viviparous sheep's fescue), were the principal grasses; together with Carices recurva, distans, panacea, &c., and some junci or rushes. To a mixture of all these, when heath is absent, the natives give the name of *Lubba*."—*Neill's Tour through Shetland*, p. 74, 75. Mr Shirreff remarks, that the Anthoxanthum odoratum is seldom touched by the sheep.

none scare, hound, or break up their neighbours' punds and buills, under the penalty of ten pounds Scots, besides damages; but the regulation has not, for a long time, been enforced. On the contrary, the sheep are almost to be regarded as in a state of nature, since they range at large over the scatholds during the whole of the year. No food is provided for the poor animals during deep falls of snow, nor is there any friendly shepherd to drive them to some *buill*, or dry place of shelter, where the lives of numbers of them might be preserved. Upon the approach of a storm, a sense of common danger causes them to congregate for self-defence beneath the shelter of some rock on the sea-shore, where they protect themselves from the cold, by the warmth which arises from their bodies in a crowded state; or, if they are covered with snow, hunger impels them to tear portions of wool from each other's backs.

Whenever it is requisite to catch any sheep, they are hunted down with dogs, trained for the purpose, which Wallace, the historian of Orkney, describes as a sport both "strange and delectable." When a flock is in sight, the Shetlander seizes hold of his *had-dog*, (the ancient Scandinavian name for a sheep-dog,) and points out to him a particular sheep. The dog then bounds after his prey: the flock are immediately alarmed, but soon perceiving the particular individual that is the intended victim, they restrain their flight, and allow the pursuit to be uninterruptedly confined to one object of selection. The poor animal is then chaced from hill to hill, until he falls into the power of his pursuer, who is taught to seize him by the foot, the nose, or the ear; or perhaps he perishes by tumbling over some precipice, where he is either dashed to pieces upon the stones, or falls into the sea.

As the sheep of one scathold, island, or parish, constitute a promiscuous flock, which may belong to more than a hundred individuals, it is remarkable that more frequent disputes should not arise respecting the rights of possession. No property of this kind was ever secured without the means of had-dogs; it was therefore a proper regulation that none of these animals should be kept in secret. An ancient act of Shetland declares, "that none keep sheep-dogs but such as are appointed or allowed by the Bailiff, with the advice of the honest men of the parish, whose names are to be recorded in the Court-books; and each of them to be accountable for their actings." It was also ordered, that all dogs should be tried yearly by the Bailiff, the ranselmen, or other honest men belonging to the parish in which they are kept; and if any individuals should be found to possess a had-dog, who had no property in a sheep stock to entitle him to keep such an animal, he should be fined and the dog hanged. The next object of the ancient legislators of the country, was to see that each dog which might be kept to take sheep, was under proper controul, and that he was not what was named a *running dog*, whom the old acts of Orkney characterise as "a dog that runs frae house to house, or through the country, the neighbours' sheep;" such a dog would be not only prompt to seize a sheep for his master, but would have little hesitation in providing mutton for himself. Whenever, therefore, the ranselmen in their annual examination of dogs, found out any of these freebooters, they put in force the act, "That all running dogs be discharged, under the pain of forty shillings, to be paid by the owner of the dog, *toties quoties*, and the dog to be hanged. But since this act was framed, a sort of demoralization has taken place in the character of the canine race of Shetland,—and it

SHEEP PASTURES OF SHETLAND.

would be difficult to say, at the present day, what dog was not a *running dog*. Mr Shirreff, in his agricultural survey of the country, has complained, with great justice, of a rapacious ranger, of this kind, which he observed, who, without any order from his master, would break off at the first unfortunate sheep that he saw, throw him down, give him a good biting, and then return, unchided for his cruelty, to his owner, who seemed to consider the treatment as a matter of course. "The fact is," adds the narrator, "that there is so little profit arising from sheep stock, in the present state of landed property, compared with fishing, that the landowners and tacksmen do not put as much value on a sheep, as in Great Britain on a hare."

When sheep were considered of more value than they are at present, it was of great consequence that no wild or *scar* sheep should be at large in any particular district, which might have the tendency of scattering the flock. Thus there is an ancient act, "that none keep *s ar* sheep except it be in holms of nesses diked in, and properly belonging to themselves, under the pain of ten pounds Scots, and forfeiture of the sheep after six months advertisement." But, at the present day, most of the sheep of the country are so wild, that the old distinction of scar sheep seems to be nearly lost; and as summer herding is almost unknown, these animals are by no means in a progressive state of tameness.

In the last place, as the seizure of sheep took place by means of dogs, it was necessary for the preservation of individual property, that no capture should be private. Every proprietor in claiming his share of a promiscuous flock, had a particular mark of his own, that was formed by various kinds of incisions, which were inflicted on one or both of the animal's ears ; these received such names as a shear, a slit, a hole, a bit out of the right or left ear, before, behind, or from the top. In this way an infinite variety of private marks was devised, but none of these could be lawfully used without the sanction of the bailiff of a district, or civil officer, whose duty it was to insert in a public register a descriptive account of all the tokens which any individual wished to adopt, for the recognition of the particular share which he had in a joint flock of sheep.* It was, therefore, a proper regulation, that the marking of sheep should be a public act, and that no property could be thus claimed, but in the sight of a whole district. The period appointed for marking lambs, was when all the proprietors of a flock were assembled for the purpose of *rucing*, or tearing off with the hand the wool from sheep, after it had naturally begun to loosen ; this was about the middle of May, or near midsummer. Thus there was a law, that no one mark lambs, or rue sheep, where there are different owners in the flock, but in the sight of sufficient witnesses, under the pain of ten pound Scots for the first offence, of double the amount for the second, and for the third fault of being reputed and punished as thieves. The time of marking and rueing is still publicly proclaimed, and on the day fixed, all the men of a district turn out, and drive their common flock, without any preparation of washing, into rude inclosures, named *punds* or *crues*. If the *punding* be delayed too long, the sheep become so wild that they are

---

* Mr Shirreff has given a curious specimen of the register of a sheep-mark, as taken from the parish records of Orkney, where a custom nearly similar to the Shetland practice prevailed : " I John Gillies, baron-bailie of the parish of Orphir, hereby grant warrant to Edward Wishart, in Mill of Claistran, to assume and use the sheep-mark following, as the same is recorded in the register of sheep-marks, on the 4th day of July 1770 years, in the name of John Flett in Skelbister, viz. The crop of the right lug and a bit behind, a rip in the left lug and a bit before, and the tail off."—*Agricultural Survey of Orkney*, p. 132.

hunted down and taken by dogs; but when at last they are secured within the *crues*, the civil officers (who were in former days the bailiff and ranselmen of a district) appear as arbiters of all disputes. Each owner now searches the crue for his property, which the civil officers confirm by their register, and also claims the lambs that are produced from the particular stock that he possesses, in order that his right to them may be secured by a proper ear-mark. At the same time the general *rueing* begins, the proprietor seizes hold of his poor sheep, and, disdaining the use of shears, tears away the wool from the struggling animal's back in the most brutal manner; and if the fleece has not begun to naturally loosen, the operation is attended with most excruciating pain. Such a cruel mode of fleecing, which is of true Scandinavian origin, is at the present day retained in Iceland, as well as in Hialtland.

Thus it is shown, that no claims of individual property among sheep could, by the ancient laws of Shetland, be sanctioned, if made in secret. An act expresses, "That if any person use a sheep-dog, and run therewith after his own sheep unaccompanied; if he mark, rue, or take any home without showing the mark, he shall pay for the first fault four angels, for the second six angels, and for the third be holden and repute as a common thief, and punished accordingly." It also appears that the last penalty was awarded for even a first offence, if committed under cloud of night. If any one also killed a sheep without first showing the mark to a ranselman, " or other honest man," he was liable to a fine of £10 for the first offence, with payment of damages: of £20 for the second offence; and for the third crime, of being reputed and punished as a common thief, and of being prevented in all time coming for keeping a sheep-dog. It is a pity that, in reference to the undivided state of the seatholds, the salutary tendency of these good laws has not been perpetuated. Mr Shirreff has properly remarked, that the Shetlander, who may possess the best sheep-dog, is by repute the greatest sheep-owner in Shetland; and that thieves are greater enemies to the sheepstock than either defect of food or the inclemency of the weather:—he produces as an example, some natives of Yell, who, for many years, had severally contrived to secure for themselves, on an average, two sheep each week. But how can such a state of the Shetland sheep pastures create much surprise? Husbandry has long sickened under oppressions of the most galling nature; the fisheries have become the only sources of profit in the country; and thus has the care of the individual property which may exist in a common sheep-stock, become an object of little moment.

The carcase of the Shetland sheep is very small, being said not to weigh more than thirty pounds. The flesh is peculiarly sweet, and may rival in flavour the best Welsh mutton, that is so esteemed in England. But, owing to the crooked policy of proprietors leaving none but the worst lambs, which are unacceptable for the table, for breeding rams, the race of Shetland sheep has been long supposed to be in a state of degeneracy.* The wool is short, yet very fine. From the amount of the tithes paid in this commodity to the Pope, so early as the 14th century, it has been

---

* Mr Sheriff conceives, that the same strange policy is operating to the disparagement of the Shetland wool. He states, that if a proprietor observe among his lambs any one that is particularly fine wooled, all his alarm is that it should stray away to some other pasture; he does not hesitate, therefore, to stifle in the animal any inducement which he may have, during the tupping season to ramble after the ewes. Thus are the best rams incapacitated from perpetuating a race of fine woolled sheep, whilst the worst serve for breeders.

supposed that the breed of sheep in this country was much greater in ancient times than at the present day. Their wool, which was manufactured into the coarse cloth named Wadmel, afforded the means that this ancient colony of Norway possessed of paying the tribute which was due to the King of Denmark under the title of *Seat*. The tax for each mark of land being exigible in a certain unchangeable measure of wadmel, it was found convenient, in a later period, to lessen the burden of the exaction, by making the threads as thick as fish-lines; but, upon the commutation of wadmel into money, the weavers of Shetland soon obviated the aspersions that were thrown upon their manufactures, and their cloth was woven fine enough. There were originally no walk-mills in the country, and the web was thickened by the hands and feet; at other times it was securely spread along the bottom of a narrow passage among the rocks through which the tide ebbed and flowed, so that the action of the sea, which, in such pent up channels was much encreased, might *walk* or full the cloth. When thus prepared, the fabrick was said by Sir Robert Sibbald to have acquired the name of *Tavacathoe*. Early in the last century, the Earl of Morton ordered a walk-mill to be built, but the manufacture of wadmel was then much on the decline. There is, however, at the present day, a considerable quantity of woollen cloth made for home-consumption.

The chief use to which the Shetland wool is applied at the present day, is for the stockings and gloves that are knit. The fleece of the sheep, which is remarkably soft, has been wrought into stockings so fine, that they have been known to sell as high as 40s *per* pair. I had not the good fortune to see articles of this value, but several pairs were shewn to me, which, from the fineness of the workmanship, might be considered reasonable at half a-guinea or fifteen shillings each. The price of the most common quality, however, is about three or four shillings, whilst they are manufactured so coarse as to be worth no more than fivepence or sixpence. When the Hamburgh traders, who had encouraged the fishery of cod and ling, had ceased to visit Shetland, the manufacture of stockings for the demand of the Dutch busses, which annually anchored in Bressay Sound, was so considerable that the sale of them was a principal resource that enabled the Shetlander to contend, for the sake of a bare subsistence, against the numerous feudal oppressions with which he was overwhelmed; but when the Dutch fishery had dwindled away, the peasantry became so wretchedly poor, that, if their landlords had not succeeded to the Hamburghers in the prosecution of the ling fishery, the country must have been almost rendered a perfect desert. The knitted covering for the head, which the master of a family wears, is an object of the Shetland manufactures; its shape has been described, as resembling a common double nightcap, with this variation, that its extremity, to which is affixed a small tassel, hangs so low down the back, as to resemble, in this respect, the cap of a German hussar. The variegated and fantastical colours which it displays are produced by native dyes, the collection of which was anciently an object of great importance, particularly when the manufacture of wadmel was a leading employment in the country. The *Lichen tartareus* yields a tit or dye, that was formerly an article of commercial notice, named Korkelit; it is scraped from the rocks after a fall of rain, reduced to a powder, steeped for many days in stale household-ley, and kneaded into balls of the weight of a pound and a half, which are dried. When boiled with cloth, it communicates to the fabric a reddish purple colour. The *Lichen saxatilis* (provincially named *Old man*), when treated partly in the same way, yields a yellowish or reddish brown colour. The *Lichen parietinus* (named by the Shetlanders *Scriota*), dyes cloth of an orange colour. I believe that the *Lichen omphaloides* is also occasionally used for the purpose of affording a brownish or blackish purple colour. From a collection of plants, (no names of which I could learn, with the exception of the marigold), a yellow colour is procured. A good black is extracted from the mossy earth of the country, when found much impregnated with bog iron-ore.

Another sort of woollen cloth that was manufactured, was expressed by the term *Kiverins*, or *coverings* for the beds of the peasantry. These were composed of very coarse materials. Sometimes they formed a ground, into which different coloured worsteds were sewed, so as to display various figures of more or less beauty, according to the taste or ingenuity of the operator. Manufactures of this kind were then used for rugs or hearth covers ; when intended for superior coverlids, the figures of them were, with a view to warmth, produced by thicker threads, the thrums of which were left about two inches long. The last use for which kiverins were designed, was for saddle-cloths ; these were placed under a klibbar, when the shelty was mounted by a female rider.

The skins of the Shetland sheep are in requisition, for the purpose of affording the fishermen a sort of surtout, that covers his common dress. The *tormentilla erecta* has been long used in the process of tanning.

Among the ancient laws of Shetland, there are some remarkable regulations respecting the rights of Ranselmen to inspect at any time the stock of wool, skins of sheep, and the cloth or stockings made of wool, which may be in a house. Such functions would appear inquisitorial, if we did not advert to the circumstances that might have rendered them necessary. A flock of sheep belonged to a number of proprietors, and the guardianship of them actually devolved upon the civil officers of a district. In order, therefore, to prevent theft, it was not only necessary that every seizure or slaughter of sheep should be forbidden, without being reported to the Ranselmen, but even that the produce of flocks should not be applied to any use, without the knowledge of such guardians of the general sheep-stock of the community. On this account, it was a proper regulation, that each Ranselman should always have access to the stock of wool or sheep-skins in a house ; in order that he might compare with his register, the amount of sheep that each individual had, before legal witnesses, claimed by proper ear-marks, as his own. Thus it was ordered, "That the Ranselmen should be yearly sworn and examined, or as oft as needful, and give an account to the Sheriff or Bailiff anent their diligence, and that they should see all wool, skins, heads and marks whatsoever ; and that they should see all cloths and stockings made of wool, and compare the same with the stock of the makers ; and that they should take up inventories from weavers, of all work wrought by them ; and that none refuse ranselling, or to give up inventories, or quarrel or offend at ranselling, under pain to be repute and prosecute as thieves." At the same time, a general warrant was given to the Ranselmen, to search, whenever occasion required, any part of a house, and to examine " the wool, stockings, yarn, webs, &c. ; and enquire how the inmates of the dwelling came by all these ; and if they could not give a satisfying account thereof, and brough and hammell, to inform against them."

These are all the remarks which I have to offer on the sheep of this country, and the manufactures to which they give rise. It will be evident, that if lands are still destined to remain in their present uninclosed state, no improvement can ever possibly take place in the state of the Shetland pastures, unless the salutary operation of the ancient acts of the country be in their full force revived.* It is true, that such regulations are, in their inquisitorial nature, little accordant with the present spirit of British liberty; yet they are still well calculated to excite our high admiration for the ample security which they must have once afforded to every scatholder, that his proper interest in a promiscuous sheep-stock should be preserved to him entire.

TROLHOULAND.

A south-westerly walk from Aithsvoe led me for two miles across a brown moor, unenlivened by a single habitation; but this cheerless scene at length receded from the view, and was replaced by the different reaches and windings of a large irregular inlet of the sea, that penetrates the mainland for a distance of six miles. As the eye traced the widening of this estuary in its flow with silent majesty towards the southerly expanse of the ocean, a few spots of verdure and scattered cottages might be detected, above which frowned the dark parallel ridges of gneiss, that form the Western Kaim. Leaving the head of Bigsetter Voe, I ascended a high track of moorland, where the barking of the house-dog, in signal of the traveller's attempt to explore the indistinct tracks before him, might still be heard; a few scanty human habitations presented themselves, closed in by a melancholy waste of hills and lakes. In this wild abode of man, a knoll shrouded in clouds and mists has long been dreaded as a domicile for unclean spirits; hence its name of *Trolhouland*, or the Hill of Demons or *Trows*. Several other hills in Shetland are also celebrated for affording, within their internal recesses, a habitation for evil genii; and it is remarkable, that certain places in Norway have, for many centuries, from a similar superstition, been associated with the name of *Trol*; thus, Olaus Magnus, in speaking of a place rendered awful, by the descent of a rapid and tumultuous river, adds, "Nomen vulgare habet *Trolhetta*, hoc est, *caputium Demonis*, forte propter horrorem, quem sono, stridoreque generat, in paludinosam planitiem cadens." In Iceland a number of craters are known by the name of *Trölla-dyngiar*, which is translated *magic heaps*; and an ancient volcano is called *Trölla-kyrkia*, or the Giants' Church. The word *Trol* thus applied, is of very obscure etymology; possibly it may be an old Teutonic word, the meaning of which is perpetuated in the French *Trôler*, signifying to lead, draw along, seduce or entice; and an epithet of this kind might have been applied in the early age of Christianity, to the fabulous deities of the Edda, who were considered as still capable of exerting a seductive or alluring influence over the souls of mankind.

---

* Some of the Sheep-laws of Shetland bear evidence of a date so early as A.D. 1040. See Note II. at the end of the present Iter.

The Trows of Shetland, who inhabit the interior of rocks, are the same race of beings whom the natives of Feroe describe as *Foddenskemand*, or underground men; in the Icelandic Edda, they appear under the name of *Duergar* or dwarfs, the origin of whom is thus stated: Odin and his brothers killed the giant Ymir, from whose wound ran so much blood, that all the families of the giants were drowned, except one that saved himself on board a bark. These gods then made of the giant's bones, of his flesh and his blood, the earth, the water and the heavens. But in the body of the giant, several worms had, in the course of putrefaction, been engendered, which, by order of the gods, partook of both human shape and reason. These little beings, which were of the most delicate figure, always dwelt in subterraneous caverns, or clefts of rocks. They were remarkable for their riches, their activity, and their malevolence.

It has been supposed, that this mythological account of the Duergar bears a remote allusion to real history, having an ultimate reference to the oppressed Fins, who, before the arrival of invaders under the conduct of Odin, were the prior possessors of Scandinavia. The followers of this hero saw a people, who knew how to manufacture the produce of their mines better than they themselves; and, therefore, from a superstitious regard, transformed them into supernatural beings of an unfavourable character, dwelling in the interior of rocks, and surrounded with immense riches.*

The subterraneous Trows of Shetland, who resemble the malignant Dives of the East, in every thing but their hideousness of form, have, in more recent times had the improper name given to them of *Fairies*, which is of comparatively modern introduction into Europe, being derived from the Persian *Peris*, an imaginary race of intelligences, whose offices of benevolence were opposed to the spiteful interference of evil spirits. Another later term of *Elves*, is equally objectionable, if, as some suppose, it is to be found in the Teutonic *helfen*, translated *jurare*.

Sir Walter Scott, in an elegant and learned dissertation on the fairies of popular belief, prefixed to the tale of 'Tamline, has shewn that the modifications which the rudiments of elfin superstition have undergone, are to be sought for not only in the traditions of the East, but in the wreck and confusion of the gothic mythology, in the tales of chivalry, and in the fables of classical antiquity; yet in such an obscure and detached country as Shetland, few of these causes could have operated in changing the earliest traditions of the country. A few tales of chivalry might have been introduced; but the fables of classical antiquity, and the learned fictions of the poets of the 16th century, have never found growth on the distant soil of Thule.

The Dwarfs of Shetland, then, who dwell among the hills, are to be considered as the same malevolent beings who are to be found in the Scandinavian Edda; and as it is deemed dangerous to offend them by any terms of obloquy, however well merited, they are also named the *guid folk*, words of similar import being used at the present day for the self-same reason in the Feroe Islands, as well as in other places.

It does not appear that the popular belief in the personal appearance, habits, and

---

* Minstrelsy of the Scottish Border, vol. ii., p. 276.

influence of these land Trows has much varied, since, as objects of Pagan worship, they were enumerated by pious Catholics among the list of fallen angels: for the Shetlander still *sains* or blesses himself, as he passes near their haunts, in order to get rid of his fearful visitants. Although, according to the theory of the early Divines of Scotland, the light of the Reformed Religion ought to have long ago expelled from the land these agents of heathenism and popery, yet they are scarcely less seen than formerly, and cannot be considered as in the act of emigrating to climes where they will be more cherished. They are described, at the present day, as a people of small stature, gaily dressed in habiliments of green. Brand, however, says, that in his days they were often seen in Orkney, clad in complete armour. They partake of the nature of men and spirits, yet have material bodies, with the means, however, of making themselves invisible. They have also the power of multiplying their species: thus a female of the Island of Yell, who some years ago died at the advanced age of one hundred years, or more, once met some fairy children, accompanied by a little dog, playing, like other boys and girls, on the top of a hill. At another time, whilst in bed, she had occasion to stretch herself up, when seeing a little boy, with a white nichtcap on his head, sitting at the fire, she asked him who he was. "I am Trippa's son," answered he. Upon hearing which, the good woman *sained* herself, that is, called on God to be about her, and Trippa's son immediately vanished.

Several Shetlanders, among whom are warlocks and witches, have enjoyed a communion with the *guid folk*, and, by a special indulgence, have been transported in the air, whenever occasion served, from one island to another. In their visits to Trolhouland, or any other knoll of a similar description, they have been allowed to enter the interior of the hill at one side, and to come out of it at the other; and, in this subterraneous journey, have been dazzled with the splendour exhibited within the recesses through which they have passed. They report that all the interior walls are adorned with gold and silver, and that the domestic utensils of the place, peculiar to Fiary-land, resemble the strange implements that are sometimes found lying abroad on the hills, which sceptical antiquaries ascribe to an early race of inhabitants who peopled Shetland. Thus there are innumerable stories told of Trows, who, in their rambles, have carelessly left behind them utensils of a shape unknown to human contrivance. Sometimes the dairy-maid observes a fairy woman in the act of clandestinely milking the cows in the byre, upon which she sains herself, when the evil spirit takes so precipitous a flight, as to leave behind her a copper pan, of a form never before seen.

The Trows of the hills have a relish for the same kind of food, that affords a sustenance to the human race, and when, for some festal occasion, they would regale themselves with good beef or mutton, they repair to the Shetlander's scatholds or town-mails, and employ elf-arrows to bring down their victims.

> "There ev'ry herd by sad experience knows
> How wing'd with fate these elf-shot arrows fly,
> When the sick ewe her summer food forgoes,
> Or stretch'd on earth the heart-smit heifers die."

In Scotland, the *guid folk* are not the best of archers, since the triangular flints with which the shafts of their arrows are barbed do not always take effect, and are therefore found strewed on the hills; but the Shetland dwarfs are much more successful, none of their arrows having ever glanced aside, so as to afford a fertile theme of speculation for the northern antiquary, who, if they could have been found in the country, might have assigned their origin to some imaginary Pictish race that had fled from the pursuit of King Kenneth.

When the Trows are so successful as to shoot one of the best fatlings that is to be met with, they delude the eyes of its owner with the substitution of some vile substance possessing the same form as that of the animal which they have taken away, and with the semblance of its sudden death, as if it were produced either by natural or violent means. It is on this account that the bodies of animals which have perished by accident are condemned as unlawful food. A Shetlander at the present day affirms, that he was once taken into a hill by the Trows, when the first object that he saw was one of his own cows brought in for the purpose of furnishing a savoury supply for a banquet. So precarious at the same time was the man's individual preservation, that he considers himself as indebted for it to the gracious protection of a fairy lady, under whose special favour he had been admitted within the cave. On returning to his friends whom he had left on the earth's surface, he learned that at the very moment when, with his own organ of vision, he had observed the cow conveyed into the interior of the hill, other earthly eyes had beheld the animal in the act of falling over the rocks. In this instance, then, the real cow had been abstracted, and an illusory image left in its place, lacerated and dead.

As the Trows are not altogether secure from diseases, they possess among themselves medicines of as invaluable efficacy as those which, in the seventeenth century, immortalized the name of Anne Jefferies of Cornwall, who, with salves derived from fairies, performed many special miraculous cures. There was, for example, a good man in the Island of Unst, who had an earthen-pot containing an unguent of infallible power, which he alleged was obtained by him from the hills, and, like the widow's cruise, it was never exhausted of its contents.

These spirits are much addicted to music and dancing, and, when they make their excursions, it is generally with an imposing effect, being accompanied by most exquisite harmony:

———————————— "Like Fairy elves
Whose midnight revels, by a forest side,
Or fountain, some belated peasant sees,
Or dreams he sees, while over head the moon
Sits arbitress, and nearer to the earth
Wheels her pale course; they, on their mirth and dance
Intent, with jocund music charm his ear."

A Shetlander, while lying in bed, heard one morning before day-light the noise of a large company of Trows passing his door, accompanied by a piper. Having a musical ear, he readily learnt the air that was played, which he would afterwards repeat, calling it by the name of the Fairy-tune. The site where dances of the *guid folk* are held, is, as in other countries, to be detected by the impressions in the form of rings which their tiny feet make on the grass ;* and within such unholy precincts it is hazardous for a Christian to enter:

> "Their nightly dancing ring I always dread,
> Nor let my sheep within that circle tread;
> Where round and round all night, in moonlight fair,
> They dance to some strange music in the air."

The Trows are addicted to the abstraction of the human species, in whose place they leave effigies of living beings named Changelings, the unholy origin of whom is known by their mental imbecility, or by some wasting disease. Although visits of such a purpose are to be particularly dreaded at midnight and at noon, yet to childbed-women who may be designed for wet-nurses to some fairy infant of quality, the latter hour is, as in certain Asiatic countries, by far the most formidable. On this account, it is still a point of duty not to leave, in so fearful an hour, mothers who give suck, but, like pious Saint Basil, to pray that the influence of the demon of noon may be averted.† Children also are taken away to the hills, in order to be play-fellows to the infant offspring of the Trows; on which occasion, all the lamentable effects have been produced that have been so well depicted by an elegant poet of Scotland, in his address to the muse of the Highlands.

> "Then wake (for well thou canst), that wondrous lay,
> How, while around the thoughtless matrons sleep,
> Soft o'er the floor the treacherous fairies creep,
> And bear the smiling infant far away :
> How starts the Nurse, when, for her lovely child,
> She sees at dawn a gaping idiot stare!
> O snatch the innocent from demons wild,
> And save the parents fond from fell despair."‡

When an impression prevails that any childbed-women or infants, pining away with disease, or betraying a mental fatuity, are beings of a "base elfin breed," substituted by the Trows, in the place of those whom they may have taken into the hills, no inducement can persuade a family, labouring under such a persuasion, to afford the objects of commiseration entrusted to their care, the attention which their situation demands. Nor, on such melancholy occasions, are there wanting persons who pretend to the power of entering the caves of the fairies, and of restoring the human beings who may be immured in them, to

---

* The cause of Fairy-rings is ascribed to the growth of certain species of Agaric, which so entirely absorb the nutriment from the soil beneath, that the herbage is for a while destroyed.

† "The Celts," says Dr Percy, "with the same view offered sacrifices. One says pleasantly, the true demon of noon is Hunger, when one has nothing to satisfy it."

‡ Supplemental Stanzas to Collins' Ode on the Superstition of the Highlands. By Wm. Erskine, Esq., Advocate.

their friends. A warlock of the parish of Walls is said to have amassed a considerable sum of money by assuming such an influence over the demons of the hills; his success being denoted by the apparent recovery of childbed-women or children from the disease under which they had laboured.

When the limb of a Shetlander is affected with paralysis, a suspicion often arises that it has been either touched by evil spirits, or that the sound member has been abstracted, and an insensible mass of matter substituted in its place. A tailor now living reports, that he was employed to work in a farm house where there was an idiot, who was supposed to be a being left by the Trows, in the place of some individual that had been taken into the hills. One night when the visitor had just retired to his bed, leaving the changeling asleep by the fire side, he was startled by the sound of music; at the same time, a large company of fairies entered the room, and began to bestir themselves in a festive round. The idiot suddenly jumped up, and in joining their gambols, shewed a familiarity with the movements of the dance, that none but a supernatural inhabitant of the hills could be supposed to possess. The observer grew alarmed and *sained* himself; upon hearing which, all the elves immediately fled in most admired disorder; but one of the party, a female, more disconcerted than the rest at this inhospitable interruption to their sports, touched the tailor's big toe as she left the room, when he lost the power of ever afterwards moving that joint.

Such are the details which I was enabled to collect, relative to the Trows that inhabit the interior of the Shetland hills. In no country are there more habitations remaining of unclean spirits than in Thule. All these had their origin in the mythology of the ancient Scandinavians; and when Christianity was introduced into Shetland, a belief in the existence of gods, giants or dwarfs, still remained, with this qualification only, that they were fallen angels of various ranks belonging to the kingdom of darkness, who, in their degraded state, had been compelled to take up their abode in mountains, springs or seas.* These were tenets conveniently subservient to the office of exorcism, which constituted a lucrative part of the emoluments of the inferior Catholic clergy, with whom Orkney and Shetland were in ancient times overrun. We may, therefore, reasonably expect that the industry of these Papists would resemble that of the holy freres of England, so well described by Geoffery Chaucer:

> "That serchen every land and every streme,
> As thikke as motes in the sonne-beme,
> Blissing halles, chambres, kichenes and boures,
> Citees and burghes, castles high and toures,
> Throps and bernes, shepenes and dairies,
> This maketh that ther ben no faeries."

Demons or Trows were thus kept in order by a kind of spiritual police, which prevented them, owing to the interference of exorcism, spells, or charms, from breaking into human habitations, or trespassing on the lands of the udallers, to the injury of live-stock

---

* A doctrine nearly similar was inculcated by Debes in his description of Feroe, and by Olaus Magnus.

and to the fruits of the earth: and on the suppression of Popery, the Reformer left the popular belief in Trows uncontroverted, contenting himself with the allegation, that the means employed by the Catholic of expelling them were delusive, but that they were to be effectually banished the land by the pure light of the Gospel.* On this view, the reason why these spirits have not yet fled the islands of Shetland remains to be explained; but as an inquiry of this sort is out of my province, I shall prefer leaving it for the discussion of learned divines.

CULLSWICK TO THE VOE OF SANDS.

Cullswick is situated at a distance of five miles from Trolhouland, in a south-westerly direction; the way to it lying across a trackless waste, where, in a peculiar formation of the hills of quartz and granite that characterise this district, a sort of undulating surface of moorland is presented, that is covered over with a deep heath, and is dotted with numerous pools embosomed in irregular hollows. At length the circular burgh of Cullswick appears in sight, fixed on the brink of a menacing cliff of red granite, below which the ocean dashes in relentless fury. Innumerable loose crags, a dusky pool, and a few wretched cottages, are interspersed on the barren surface of an irregular plain, while the darkening shadows of higher rocks cast around an indescribable gloom. The westerly cliffs of Valey Island and Gruting's Voe appear to the west, where few other inhabitants are to be seen

" But yelling meawes, with sea-gulles hoars and baee,
And cormoyraunts, with birds of ravenous race."

The fortalice of Cullswick is constructed of unhewn stones of granite, closely built, without any cement; it exhibits a double concentric wall, inclosing a space 26½ feet in diameter. The thickness of the outer wall is four feet, and of the inner wall three and a half feet, while the interval is two feet wide. So much of the burgh has been destroyed of late years, that it rises but a very few feet from the ground; and its utility, even as a seamark, could not preserve its stones from being applied to the erection of a vile set of hovels. In the memory of man its height was known to be about twenty-three feet from the ground; chambers were formed within the walls, but whether they ran round the building in a spiral direction, so as to resemble the burghs which antiquaries maintain were, from this peculiar construction, metamorphosed by poets into serpents or dragons, I could not learn. Mr Low seemed to think that the roof of the lowest room was the floor of an upper room, and so on; the whole communicating, as in the burgh of Mousa, by steps; but I have heard this assertion doubted. The entrance to the internal area was by a door about two feet

---

* Sir Walter Scott, in speaking of the belief of fairies in Selkirkshire, says, that "the most sceptical among the lower ranks only venture to assert, that their appearances and mischievous exploits have ceased, or, at least, become infrequent, since the light of the Gospel was diffused in its purity."

high, strongly lintelled at the front with a large triangular stone, while other supports of the same nature which rested on both walls, formed the internal structure of the entrance. The passage, when besieged, would of course be blocked up by large stones rolled from within the area. The fortalice was surrounded by a ditch, now filled up, the breadth of which was thirteen feet. An outer rampart secured the whole, 19½ feet broad. *(See Fig. 14 of the Plate of Antiquities.)*

A walk of three or four miles, along a coast thinly inhabited, leads to Skelda Ness, a bold headland, worn in deep recesses, the abode of ravens, sea-gulls, or wild pigeons : one of the larger caves is said to have been in former times the haunt of a Norwegian pirate. Crossing Skelda Voe, an inlet three miles in extent, I reached Reawick, where the ancient family of the Umphrays have a residence ; an ancestor of whom afforded, by his vessel, the means whereby the Duke de Medina, the commander of the Spanish Armada, escaped, after shipwreck, from Dunrossness to Dunkirk. Selie Voe, (said to signify, in the Norse, a Herring Voe), lies to the north-east, which I reached in a boat. This is an inlet, open to the sea, and about a mile in extent ; the banks of which are adorned with a few good houses, and by a neat manse. The sea in the vicinity abounds with haddocks, whitings, piltocks, and sometimes with mackarel. Kirkholm lies off a point of land to the east of the bay ; being an islet celebrated for the refuge that it afforded to the crew of a galleon belonging to the famous Spanish Armada, which sank on a haddock-sand near Reawick Head, now called the Meeth. The Spaniards having effected their escape on the shore, took possession of Kirkholm, sank a well of good fresh water, fortified the banks with a wall, and built for themselves several huts. Sands Voe, which is about half a mile to the east, is a small open bay, near to which are the ruins of a very neat chapel, erected by the Spaniards during the time they were detained in Shetland ; it was originally dedicated by them to St Mary, as a tribute of gratitude to the Virgin for their preservation on the hospitable shore of Thule.* On the west of the inlet, Sir Andrew Mitchell of Westshore, formerly built a large house, three storeys in height, which is now possessed by John Scott, Esq. The shore of the Voe was strewed over with the bodies of a numerous herd of ca'ing whales, that had recently been driven on the sands and slaughtered.

BAY OF SCALLOWAY.

The rocks, holms and islets in the bay of Scalloway are very numerous, and the mineralogical examination of them, which I undertook, was very tedious ; my labour being much impeded by the Shetland boatmen, who, notwithstanding they were engaged at a specific sum, for the purpose of landing me at different points of the islands, were as impatient of the least delay as they were extortionate in their charges. In no part of great

---

* A medal, that was long in the possession of a Shetland family, commemorating the defeat of the Armada, is given in Fig. 26 of the Plate of Antiquities, Appendix. It is now in the hands of Mr Ross of Edinburgh, late collector of the customs in Lerwick. The coin materially differs from one relating to the same event, that is described in a number of the Spectator.

Britain is boat-travelling more extravagant than in Shetland. There are no regular ferries; and although the Magistrates of the county have attempted to fix a rate of fares, and to express their determination, in case of any disputes coming before them, to make it their standard of reference, the regulation is altogether a dead letter. There are few gentlemen who, in the trips that they make, are not rowed by their own tenants, and they take such an opportunity of ingratiating themselves in the favour of their dependents, by paying them above their due; it is, therefore, unfortunate that the sum thus given is the least that is demanded from the stranger. It is also impossible to bind the Shetlander down to any specific agreement:—whatever sum he may contract for as a fare, he endeavours to encrease, and there is a great degree of unpleasantness in entering into a new agreement during the whole of the passage, this being the chief object of the boatman's gratuitous conversation with which the passenger is perpetually annoyed. All this meanness might have been expected from the poor peasant, when in a debased state of vassalage, which would naturally prompt him to treat the higher ranks with mistrust and artfulness; but since the country is by no means what it was half a century ago, it is time that a different line of conduct, indicative of a more improved state, should be adopted. The fishermen whom I had engaged from the parish of Walls were under the influence of an old boatman, whose unaccommodating and surly disposition, was in perfect correspondence with the hideous appearance of his figure; his person had been so long entrusted to Nature's care alone, that his beard hung down to his breast; he was in truth

> "An uncouth, salvage and unciville wight,
> Of griesly hew and foule ill-favour'd sight;
> His face with smoke was tand, and cies were blear'd
> His head and beard with soot were ill bedight,
> His cole-black handes did seeme to have been sear'd
> In Smythes fire-spitting forge, and nayles like clawes appear'd."

The Shetlander is too often in the habit of considering the extortion to which he makes the stranger submit, as of the same nature as the right that he assumes to plunder a wreck; for he enumerates under the blasphemous title of the "*God-sends*," a wreck, a drove of whales, and a boat-fare.

After landing on the Sandistura Rocks, which rise but a few feet above the level of the sea, I visited the cluster of isles composed of epidotic sienite or gneiss, named Hildazoo, Papa Little, Oxna, Longa, and the Cheyneys.* Burra is a island of gneiss, about four miles in length and two in breadth, rendered memorable in Holland for the disaster which befel the Dutch navy in the summer of the year 1652. The vessels were driven by a gale on the west side of the island; a fire-ship was wrecked, and a man-of-war sank to the bottom. The rest of the fleet ventured among the small isles and rode in safety. In Burra, formerly

---

* Mr Low has remarked, that he found on these holms the long-leaved sorrel, the sea gilliflower, the sweet smelling garlick, also the *Lychnis dioica, petalis rubris et albis*.

stood a church, adorned with a spire, but the whole is now rased to the ground. House Island, which lies so near to Burra as to be connected with it by a wooden bridge, was anciently the residence of a Sinclair who joined the force that, in defence of the rights of the Udallers, opposed and slew the Earl of Caithness. He obtained a respite, along with Sinclair and Strom, for nineteen years. Great Havery is a small inhabited isle, partly formed of limestone-rocks, respecting which there is an idle tradition, that no mouse or rat will live in it, and that its ground is of such a virtue, as to kill vermin although removed for the purpose to any other place. Very far south lies the peninsulated eminence of St Ronan's, joined to the Mainland by a low sand-bank, which, in high tides or gales, is occasionally overflown. The foundations appear of an old chapel dedicated to St Ninian, commonly named Ronan, from the Irish appellation given to the saint of *Ringan*. St Ninian was a Cambrian who zealously preached Christianity in the fifth century to the Britons of the province of Valencia or shire of Galloway. Dr Chalmers conceives, that the chapel might have been founded by some pious Columbans of the sixth century in their visit to Shetland; but this is very doubtful. Both Shetland and Orkney were considered in a pagan state until the year 1195, when Olaus Triguesson, king of Norway, converted the earldom to the true faith at the point of the sword. The account of the country, that the chapel was built by a Dutch captain as the fulfilment of a vow which he had made to the saint for protection in a storm at sea, is much more conjectural than the notion of the learned antiquary whom I have quoted. Little now remains of St Ronan's Chapel, although' it is still used as a burying place. The lower storey of the kirk may be distinctly traced, which having been once vaulted, is supposed to have served for a burying place. The cliffs of St Ronan's are very high, and, with the insulated rocks adjoining, serve as a resort for numerous varieties of gulls, whose nests, when I visited this place, were plundered for the sake of the young birds named scories. I partook of a dinner of them, but found the flesh, as might be expected, strong and fishy. The most southerly islet belonging to the bay of Scalloway is Colsay, which is uninhabited.

Near St Ronan's is a good estate which anciently belonged to the Stewarts of Bigtown, the present representative of whom is John Bruce, Esq. of Simbester. Bigtown was for many years the resort of Scottish traders who trafficked with the natives for salt, or coal-fish, as well as of a Jew who was the great purchaser of the feathers of sea-fowl. On an adjacent promontory named Ireland, once stood a church which was adorned with a lofty steeple. But of three buildings of this kind situated in Ireland, Burra and Tingwall, that were said to have been erected by three Norwegian sisters, it is unfortunate that not one should now remain.*

In sailing north from Bigtown, I passed Maywick, a small open inlet, to the east of which are the extensive dreary scatholds that form the Cliff Hills, where a right of pasturage was long a source of dispute between the proprietors of the islands of Burra and House, and the natives of Coningsburgh on the Mainland. Several pitched battles are said to have

---

* There is a small religious edifice in Orkney, which these kirks of Shetland are said to have much resembled; a specimen, therefore, of the ancient Scandinavian church is given in the Plate of Antiquities that appears in the Appendix of this Work. (See Fig. 17.)

been fought about two centuries and a half ago between the parties; in one of which, the men of Burra and House crossed the Cliff of Sound during the night, and occupied a station among the hills in ambush. In the morning, their wives and daughters, who were instrumental in the plot, dressed themselves in male attire, and launching several yawls made their appearance in the sound as in hostile array. The Coningsburghers, easily deceived by the formidable appearance of this mock armament, came down the hills to attack the boats, when they fell into the snare that had been laid for them, and being fiercely attacked on the rear by the male inhabitants of Burra and House, were for the most part killed or routed. It appears, that the liberty of pasturage on the Cliff Hills continued disputable until about forty years ago, when the late Mr Scott of Scalloway, who acquired a title, by marriage, to the property of the Sinclairs of House, sold or transferred his contested right to the late Mr Bruce of Sumburgh, who owned a considerable estate in Coningsburgh. In order to prevent contentions like these, there are several country acts relative to the rights of the joint scatholders of a parish. Thus it is commanded, "That the bailiff of each parish, with twelve honest men, should annually ride the marches of the parish, betwixt the first of October and the last day of April, or at any other time when required by the scattlers, the penalty of non-performance being Forty pounds Scots: it is also enacted, that none contemptuously pasture upon, rive flaws, cut floss, or cast peats in their neighbour's scattald, under the pain of Ten pounds Scots." In ancient times, a hill or uninclosed pasture ground, was expressed by the term *Hoga*; this is nearly synonymous at the present day with scathold. Whenever, therefore, a liberty was granted, either to pasture cattle or sheep in a hoga or common pasture ground, or even to cast peats within it, the permission was named *Hoga-leave*. The sum paid annually for hoga-leave is very trifling, not amounting for each mark of land to many shillings, except at Bressay, where tenants who cast peat for the town of Lerwick can afford to pay a much greater sum.

After passing the low valley that intersects the Cliff Hills, named *Quarf*, or the Carrying Place,* where boats are dragged across the land from the Western to the Eastern Sea, I visited the low island of Trondra, which is thinly inhabited, and once more came in view of Earl Patrick's ill-fated castle, that, in its last state of habitation, was converted into barracks for the reception of a party of Cromwell's soldiers. My next route led past the upright stone I had before seen in the strath of Tingwall, which my Cicerone, in despite of opposite traditions, conceived to have been erected in commemoration of the scene of a dispute that took place in the year 1391, between Henry Sinclair, Earl of Orkney, and his cousin Malis Sperre, relative to a question that had arisen affecting the right of the former to the Earldom. Torfæus says nothing more than that the rencounter was in Shetland. Malis, and seven of his companions, were killed, while other seven fled in a six-oared boat, and took refuge in Norway. Owing to this event, the government of Orkney was entrusted to other hands, and Henry Sinclair, and his successor, rendered their acknowledgments to King Erie of Norway for Shetland only; but in the year 1434, William Sinclair was reinstated in the undivided possessions of the family.

---

* It was usual with the Greeks to draw boats over necks of land. The Highlanders give to an isthmus or *Quarf* of this kind, the name of *Tarbat*, said to be compounded of Gaelic, terms expressive of its use.

SCALLOWAY TO BIGSETTER VOE.

A little to the north-west of Scalloway, I observed, for the first time, a specimen of the ancient Shetland plough, as it was fixed against the wall of a cottage. This implement of husbandry is of a very ancient construction, being single-stilted, like one that is represented by Olaus Magnus, as common to northern nations. A crooked piece of wood, bent to a right angle, forms the beam of the plough, which has a length of six feet and a height of two feet and a half; the single stilt at the top of it consists of an oak stave seven feet long. Through the lower end of the beam a square hole is cut, for the introduction of a piece of oak about twenty-two inches in length, named the Mereal, to which is affixed the sock and sky. The coulter stands nearly perpendicular to the sock, while a wedge driven below or above the mereal, regulates the depth of the furrow. A slender machine of this sort, which one man may lift with ease, is driven by four oxen abreast. Two yokes, joined by a double rope, are laid on their necks; a large one on the two outermost animals, and a small one on the two innermost. The draught or chain with which their necks are connected to the plough is from eighteen to twenty-four feet long. With this strange instrument two labourers take the field. The holder of the plough stands on the left of the pliable stilt. The driver or *caller* as he is named, goes before the oxen, walking backward; the sound of his whip sets the cattle in motion; the holder of the stilt lies on with his side; the earth is turned over; the work is executed to admiration, until a large stone encounters the coulter, and then crack go the joints of the frame-work. All hands are now pressed into service for repairs, and the plough is again set to rights. A lash of the caller's whip again causes the beasts to resume their tardy pace. Every thing is carried on smoothly until a stiff furrow appears, when another impediment takes place. It is now necessary that the stubborn glebe should be broken down; this is accomplished; the labour of the plough is again resumed, and, by the help of Heaven, is at length happily completed! Such being the operation of this primitive machine, every antiquary must regret that an implement of so precious a description, elucidative of the earliest state of Scandinavian agriculture, is going fast out of use, chiefly owing to the innovating spirit of the Shetland New Agricultural Society. *(See Plate of Antiq. App. Fig. 20.)*

But for turning up land, the plough has been often laid aside, and the ancient slender and long-shafted spade of Shetland, which has a blade a quarter of the breadth of the common garden spade of Scotland, and a convenient projecting piece of wood for the application of the foot, is in much greater requisition, being indeed well enough adapted for the rugged and stony ground of the country. *(See Plate of Antiq. App. Fig. 25.)*

In taking a north-easterly direction near to the head of Catfirth Voe, where we approach thick beds of limestone, a fresh water loch may be observed, that has been celebrated by Torfæus, under the name of Geirhildar-vatn. When Iceland had been accidentally discovered in the ninth century, Floke, a northern pirate, attended by his daughter, went in quest of the country of which he had heard such favourable accounts. The compass was not then known; he therefore took three ravens, which he had consecrated to the gods, seeking, by their direction of flight, the desired land. Landing at Shetland with his daughter, to which place he was directed by the omens that he had consulted, they arrived at a lake, where was a small islet visited by numerous birds, upon which the unfortunate damsel, probably in quest of their eggs, attempted to land, and in her passage was drowned. From the fate which befel her, the lake was named Geirhildar-vatn, of which the modern name of Girlsta was probably a corruption. It is added in the history of Iceland, that the flight of the third raven which Floke let loose, conducted him to his place of destination.

To the south-west of Girlsta, at a distance of a few miles, is Whiteness, where was once a church dedicated to St Olla, and named St Olla's Chair. Here is a beautiful voe which has a course exactly parallel to the long ridges of gneiss, that, running from south-west to north-east, constitute its lofty banks. In this district there is much arable land inclosed. The manure intended for it, which is to be seen at the front of most cottages on the Mainland, is a midden, consisting of dung, of heather that has been cut for litter, of sea-weed and of earth or dry decomposed moss, named *Duff-mould*. This compost, which has been known from the remotest antiquity, is an object of such importance to the Shetlander, that the ill-judged sacrifice which he often makes in order to obtain the ingredient of earth, might be considered as the exaggeration of a traveller, if it were not attested by a committee of the Shetland Agricultural Society, appointed in the year 1818, to adjudge the premiums for a south-east district of the country. They state, that they were concerned to observe the extent to which the pernicious practice, too common all over the country, is carried, of cutting up the uncultivated grounds in the neighbourhood of the principal farms for manure; that it happens unfortunately to be the most improvable ground which is thus sacrificed, and that one man was observed to have destroyed his very town-maills for this purpose, when the earth was not more than two or three inches deep.—Upon the application of the manure it is conveyed in *cassies*, which form an appendage to the klibbars or wooden saddles that are fitted to the backs of the shelties;—though sometimes it is carried to the land by women. Carts are little known in the country.

A walk of a mile to the north-west, leads to the lake of Strom, a fine expanse of water that stretches far to the north, and loses itself among dark mountains of gneiss. In the midst of it is a small holm, on which are the remains of an ancient fortress, where, according to tradition, a son of one of the Earls of Orkney fled, in order to evade the wrath of his father; but meeting with pursuers, he was slain in a contest with them on the strath of Tingwall. In the vicinity of this place, once lived a Shetland gentleman of the name of Sinclair, who, in the year 1530, gallantly headed a number of udallers that composed part of the force which the Governor of Orkney raised in opposition to the designs of the Scottish Government, when, in favour of the Earl of Caithness, it was decreed, that udal rights should be exchanged for feudal servility. In this contest the Earl of Caithness was slain; and in the subsequent reconciliation of the Monarch of Scotland to the udallers, Edward Sinclair of Strom, with thirty companions in arms, received a respite from the King for a nominal term of nineteen years.

To the south of the lake is an inlet of the sea, five miles in extent, that opens into the Bay of Scalloway. Ustaness Voe and the Loch of Strom communicate with each other by means of a small channel, over which there is a rude bridge ; and near this spot, strata of limestone rise into small eminences, contributing, in a great degree, to fertilize the soil. The arable land generally preferred for culture is described as sandy, or composed of a mixture of clay and gravel that approaches to a soft loam ; but often it consists of a black mould resting on clay alone, or on clay and sand. It is usual to give to land a distinction that was no doubt introduced into the country by the Scottish settlers ; that is, into *Infield* and *Outfield*. In Scotland, the land lying near the homestead was kept for successive years in tillage, and under the name of *Infield*, received all the manure, mixed with earth, which the farm afforded. Thus, also in Shetland, many inclosures near the house have been dunged every year, and have been sown in the end of April with bear and oats for more than half a century, without ever lying fallow, or having produced a different kind of grain ; but the Shetlanders have not altogether imitated certain Scottish districts in allowing no manure to any part of the land, but that which was properly *infield*. In Perthshire, for instance, any portion of land which lay in a valley at a distance from the house, and was sufficiently free from stones, was, under the name of *outfield*, alternately kept in corn, and natural ley or weedy wastes, without receiving the smallest return of manure, except that which was afforded by cattle, when it was used for the purpose of folding. But the outfield of the Shetlander, which is often mossy, and seldom drained, has long received each year a portion of dung, mixed with douff-mould, earth, or sea-weed. The ground is slightly harrowed, and is then sown in the end of March or beginning of April with black oats. The dung which has been carried out to the land during the winter is afterwards applied to the surface of the sown ground, and not being incorporated with the soil, wastes away by the action of the sun and rain. During the next season, the outfield lies fallow ; and thus in alternate years it is under tillage and in ley. Sometimes the ground is two years laboured, and lies two years ley. It has been also long customary in the country to adopt in the outfield a mode of marking out beds for oats that resembles the lazy-bed way of Scotland, incidental to the cultivation of potatoes. Moss-earth, sand, &c., are thrown up from an adjacent ditch, and upon this substance oats are sown, which thrive remarkably. In the year 1730, potatoes were introduced for the first time into Shetland, when it became customary to obtain from the infield in alternate years a crop of this vegetable ; and, at the present day, oats, potatoes and bear are not unfrequently produced in succession. Of late years, cabbage have been much less cultivated ; their use as food being superseded by potatoes. Lastly, under the encouragement given by the New Agricultural Society lately founded in Shetland, a complete new system of farming may be in time expected. The attention of the gentlemen of the country is laudably directed to a division of commons, as the groundwork of all agricultural improvements ; but in the mean time, the premiums that are given for the growth of turnips, which are found to succeed remarkably well,—for the breaking out of waste ground,—for the improvement of live stock,—and for the cultivation of artificial grasses,—already promise the most beneficial results. Not long ago leases were unknown; and although annual tenants still constitute by far the greatest portion of land-cultivators, yet much longer terms may in many parts of the country be easily procured.

One of the greatest detriments to the agriculture of Shetland, is the wretched state of the fences. Nevertheless, very ancient laws have existed in the country for the protection of the inclosures destined for cultivated ground. It was ordered that all dikes should be in sufficient repair by the 1st of March, which was reckoned as the time when the labouring began; and should any live stock between this day and the 1st of May tread upon the grounds of others, the penalty for each swine would be 10s Scots; for each sheep 2s; and for each shelty 6s besides payment of damages. After the 1st of May, these penalties were doubled: at the same time, every winter-slap left open, every neglect of closing a grind or wilful act of breaking down, or even scaling a dike, was liable to a fine of 40s Scots. The penalty for swine observed to actually pasture upon the lands or commonty of others, was £10 Scots, besides damages. All these good regulations, which would be highly valued, when agriculture was less oppressed by feudal duties, are now much disregarded, and the imperfect dikes that are constructed of turf or stones, easily yield to the repeated assaults of shelties, sheep or swine.

Near Strom is the Hill of Benyness, which having ascended, I arrived at Wiesdale Voe, the mouth of which is tolerably well sheltered by numerous islets and rocks of limestone, that form excellent grazing holms for cattle. On the west is the house of John Ross, Esq., whose active embarkation in the fishery for cod, by means of decked vessel, much enlivens the scenery of the place; the towering hills of the *Kaim*, which are among the highest in the county, close the prospect. Adjoining Mr Ross's house is Our Lady's Kirk, which, for a century after the abolition of Popery, was, even while in ruins, still visited by the vulgar. It was resorted to in completion of promises made during perilous navigations, or during sickness; "It was much frequented," says Brand, "by women, who, when they desired to marry, went to this church, making their vows, and saying their prayers there, so assuring themselves that God would cause men come in suit of them." The mariner also placed his confidence in the offerings which he might make within the pale of the church, trusting, that they would secure for him a happy voyage. Within these walls the supplicant would light candles, and even when the shrine had been destroyed, would drop money among the ruins, or would parade around the kirk on his bare knees. So great was the temple in repute, that an old smith, living in the vicinity, long found it his interest, after the roof had begun to decay, to attempt its repair, and to preach up the miraculous effects which oblations might produce. Near the pulpit of the church a great quantity of all the different currencies of Shetland has been found, from the guilder down to the stiver. Even at the present day, when the building is almost razed to the ground, the anxious fisherman still occasionally drops a pecuniary offering among its loose fragments.

Tingwall, Whiteness, and Wiesdale, formed, in days of Popery, an archdeaconry. Their union is indeed still perpetuated under the name of a Parish.

In the well-sheltered valley of Wiesdale there is much limestone, which imparts a remarkable degree of fertility to its glebe. The Swedish turnips which grew in the grounds of Mr Ross were of a good size, one of them, which I weighed, being 11 ℔. 8 oz. In this gentleman's garden sycamores seemed to thrive better than in any other place in Shetland. Wiesdale Voe was formerly a port, to which the Orkney men resorted for the purpose of supplying Shetland with grain ; but this country now obtains it from Scotland. Although numerous patches of corn land appear interspersed wherever the traveller turns his eyes, yet it is lamentable to consider the fatality which too often awaits them ; in September heavy gales from the north and north-west may arise which will destroy the crops in a single night. In the year 1792, and for four years afterwards, a disappointment took place in the harvest, which, combined with a great mortality of the horned cattle and sheep, rendered the country almost a desert ; much of the cattle which remained was sold to purchase grain ; the poor, who could not always obtain the fry of the coalfish, were obliged to live on wilks, limpets, and other shellfish. But, to the great credit of the principal landholders, they vied with each other in kindly offices to the poor, in which they were liberally assisted by the British Government. So variable indeed is the climate, that, instead of the crops being in the yard in the middle of September, this event does not often occur before the end of October, or even November. The corn is then cut down with a very small sickle ; the sheaves are put up in small stooks until dry, carried into the cornyard, built in large stacks, taken into the barn when wanted, threshed with a flail, winnowed and dried on kilns.

The best pastures are to be found where limestone prevails. Natural red and white clover, with rye-grass and the *Vicia sepium*, may be observed growing spontaneously in many parts of Shetland. In August, after the expiration of the ling fishery, the natives cut heath, mixed with other plants of the hills, for winter fodder ; at the same time the grass is mown with a small scythe, of a construction peculiar to the country; *(See Plate of Antiq., App. Fig. 23.)* It is then allowed to dry, and is built into stacks. There is one practice, however, which occurs in Wiesdale, that Mr Shirreff, who witnessed it in the Island of Bressay, has deservedly commended. When a moss is but one peat deep, the inhabitants, after obtaining from it their fuel, lay the sods with which the peat was covered in a fine clay bottom, press them down with the feet, and derive from them good crops of grass, or when broken up, good crops of corn.

After ascending an eminence to the west of Wiesdale, I reached a narrow dismal pass named the Skiord, the high hill of Wiesdale appearing above robed in mist, when, for the second time, I came in view of the large irregular Voe of Bigsetter, six miles in length, and from one to two in breadth. The products of the inlet are valuable to the fisherman, on account of the large quantity of shellfish it yields for bait, consisting chiefly of the *Mytilus modiolus* or yeog. The declivity of the high hills surrounding its banks has to boast a tolerable population, and numerous patches of corn land, the marauders of which were the wild pigeons that build among the rocks. Not unfrequently also the grain attracted to it as great a number of larks, linnets, sparrows, redbreasts, wrens or buntings, as I have seen in many districts of Scotland. A kirk has been erected on the west shore, for the administration of the regular Scotch service, and on the opposite banks a small congregation of the sect of Methodists named Haldanites, meet every Sabbath in a little building that constitutes their temple. In skirting along the harbour, the weather was particularly boisterous; numerous slender rills were ambling down the dales to pay their tribute to the voe. These occasionally served to supply some small mill, the presence of which was signified by a low shed of unhewn stones, that stretched across a diminutive streamlet, over which it was possible in many places to stride; compared indeed with a water-mill of Scotland or England, the grinding apparatus of Shetland seemed designed for a race of pigmies.

The millstones are commonly formed of a micaceous gneiss, being from 30 to 36 inches in diameter. Under the frame work by which they are supported, is a sort of horizontal wheel, of the same diameter as the mill-stones named a *Tirl*, which consists of a stout cylindrical post of wood, about 4 feet in length, into which are mortised twelve small float-boards, placed in a slanting direction, or at an oblique angle. It has a pivot at its under end, which runs on a hollowed iron plate, fixed on a beam. A strong iron spindle attached to the upper end of the tirl, passes through a hole in the under millstone, and is firmly wedged in the upper one. A trough conducts the water that falls from the hill upon the feathers of the tirl, at an inclination of 40° or 45°, which, giving motion to the upper millstone, turns it slowly round. To the hopper that surmounts the upper millstone there is a log of wood fastened, which, striking upon the uneven upper surface of the stone, shakes this repository for the corn, and makes it come out, whilst too quick an escape is checked by a device for lessening the size of the aperture. But sometimes there is no hopper at all, and a man patiently feeds the mill with his hand. *(See Plate of Antiq., App. Fig. 2.)*

Such is a description of this exquisite piece of machinery, the invention of which is probably as old as the time of Harold Harfagre. Captain Preston, the author of an old nautical chart of Shetland, was, during his detention on this coast, by shipwreck, shewn a Shetland mill, and was at the same time informed, that it had been for many years a source of dispute between two landed proprietors. The Englishman looked at his Cicerone with surprise, and, significantly eyeing the object of contention, replied, with a sneer, "I can certainly conceive of no dispute which such a structure ought to have reasonably occasioned, —but whether it is a mill or no." There is, however, another sort of grinding apparatus, once used by the English and Scotch, which I saw in a cottage near Bigsetter Voe, that is well known under the name of the *Quern*. A hand-mill of this kind consists of two stones about 21 inches in diameter, that rest on a kind of table. Near the edge of the upper stone, is a handle which the grinder, (generally a female of the house,) seizes and turns round with a sort of centrifugal movement, whilst the left hand is employed in supplying with corn a hole in the centre. The meal then flies outwards, and drops from between the stones on the table, when it is every now and then scraped together and taken away.

This operation was, in former times, much alleviated by the influence of a shrewd and knavish spirit named *Brownie*, who, in return for the attention or neglect he experienced, was known to

---------------------" Sometimes labour in the quern,
And bootless make the breathless housewife churn;
And sometimes make the drink to bear no barm."

In most northern countries, besides Shetland, there was scarcely a family that in former times had not a domestic trow in the house of this description. Mr Douce, in his illustrations of Shakespeare, has shewn, that the Samogitæ, a people formerly inhabiting the shores of the Baltic, who remained idolatrous as late as the 15th century, had a deity named *Putscet*, whom they envoked to live with them, by placing in the barn, every night, a table covered with bread, butter, cheese, and ale. If these were taken away, good fortune was to be expected ; but, if they were left, nothing but bad luck. This spirit is the same as the Goblin-groom of the English, who was an inmate of many houses so late as the 17th century, and would assist in threshing, churning, grinding malt or mustard, and sweeping the house at midnight ; a standing fee being required for him each night, of white-bread, and milk or cream, spread upon a table. A similar tall "lubbar-fiend," who in Shetland was habited in a brown garb of wadmel, used by his influence to ensure a good grinding of corn, a good brewing of ale, a good separation of butter during churning, and protection for corn-stacks against the greatest storm that could blow. In return, therefore, for these benignant offices, it was usual to apply to Brownie's use a sacrificial stone, within which was a small cavity for the reception of a little wort, upon the occasion of every brewing ; or when milk was to be churned, it was necessary that a part should be sprinkled, with the same intent, in every corner of the house. As Brownie was thus an useful kind of inmate, and as the acknowledgments which he required were so moderate, a Shetlander would, in days of Popery, think he had ill spent his money, if he had employed an exorcist to banish the harmless Trow from beneath his roof. There was also another reason for not offering him any disturbance. According to Olaus Magnus, the northern nations regarded domestic spirits of this description, as the souls of men who had given themselves up, during life, to illicit pleasures, and were doomed, as a punishment, to wander about the earth for a certain time, in the peculiar shape that they assumed, and to be bound to mortals in a kind of servitude. It would have been, therefore, an act of opposition to the high decree of Heaven, to refuse the penal labours of such slaves, and, in a temporal point of view, it would have been a sorry description of policy to turn away an useful servant, although an unearthly one, who could be kept at the cheapest of rates. But all such satisfactory arrangements were destroyed, upon the introduction into the country of the Reformed Religion. The divine of the school of Calvinism never affirmed the non-entity of Brownie, but, in accusing him of being a fallen spirit leagued with Satan, maintained that the sacrifices rendered to him were offerings to the devil. It was, therefore, asserted, that a denial of such acknowledgments would clearly confirm the text of scripture, " Resist the devil, and he will flee from you." Thus we are informed by Brand, that a young man " used to brew and sometimes read upon his bible, to whom an old woman in the house said, that Brownie was displeased with that book he read upon, which, if he continued to do, they would get no more service of Brownie ; but he being better instructed from that' book, which was Brownie's eyesore, and the object of his wrath, when he brewed, he would not suffer any sacrifice to be given to Brownie, whereupon the first and second brewings were spilt, and for no use ; though the wort wrought well : yet in a little time it left off working and grew cold ; but of the third browst, or brewing, he had ale very good, though he would not give any sacrifice to Brownie; with whom afterwards they were no more troubled." Another story of the same kind is of a lady in Unst, who refused, on religious grounds, the usual sacrifice to this domestic spirit. The first and second brewings failed, but the third succeeded; and thus when Brownie lost the perquisite, to which he had been so long accustomed, he abandoned the inhospitable house, where his services had so long been faithfully rendered. Yet it may be fairly questioned, if Brand's explanation of the flight of Brownie from the shores of Shetland be of universal application; for when the British Government laid such an exorbitant duty upon malt, as to render it inadmissable into families, the services of the trow, which were chiefly valued during the uncertain operation of brewing, suffered a deterioration, that all the exhortations of the zealous divine could not, with half the success, effect. Taxes, the annoyance even of demons, banished ale from the land, and with it the honest, faithful, neglected Brownie.*

From Bigsetter Voe I again crossed the hills, and arrived at Aithsvoe. In this vicinity some little kelp was burning. A hole, about six feet long and about half the dimensions in breadth, is dug in the earth for the reception of the sea-ware, and, when the ignited matter acquires a glutinous consistence, it is stirred up with a rake, and then allowed to cool.

At Aithsvoe the present Iter is concluded. Nothing, therefore, remains for me at present, but to glance at a few of the domestic habits of the natives, as far as they relate to food. The oats and bear raised by them make a very coarse and ponderous bread, but sometimes the grain is ground by means of a quern, and passed through a sieve with much care, when it is formed into small cakes, very round and thick, named *Broonies*. Often, instead of bread, *kirned milk* is used,—a name given to the curds that fall to the bottom of the churn, after boiling water has been poured into the *bledoe* or butter-milk, for the preparation of bland. Tea is in great request, being taken at all hours of the day. The chief sustenance, however, of the natives is fish, of which the Shetland seas afford a great variety. In former times every dwelling had, adjoining to it, a skeo, which I have described as a building, constructed of stones, with intervals between them, for the admission of the free air. Cod and ling were then caught near the shore, and the best of them being intended for sale, under the name of *stock-fish*, were hung up unsalted, on poles, within a drying house of this kind, that the wind, in issuing through its crevices, might cure them; but as these fish could not always be preserved from putrefaction, they were at first, perhaps from necessity, consumed by families, until a relish for such tainted food would naturally result from their constant introduction at meals. It is probably, then, from this cause, that, though skeos are now in ruins, the love for fish in a semi-putrescent state, named *sour fish*, or *souked fish*, still prevails. Vivda, or unsalted mutton, hung up in their buildings until it was hardened and dried, is no longer known.

But the sillocks, with which every voe swarms, never fail at any time to fill the Shetlander's *buidy* or fishing basket with a meal, while the result of the ling fishery affords

---

* A domestic spirit of this kind was the inmate of the house of Ollaberry, about a century ago. In high gales of wind, that threatened to blow down the corn that was stored up, Brownie was often seen on one side of a stack assisting the husbandmen, who stood on the other side to secure the grain. The good offices of the trow were never increased by extraordinary presents; thus it was a Shetland proverb, when a servant was spoilt by too generous a treatment, to say, that he was like Brownie, who, when a cloak and a hood was given to him, left the house, and did no more good to the donor.

him the means of purchasing flour from Scotland, to compensate for the deficiency of his own crops, which autumnal storms may destroy in a single night. The sources from which the Shetlander derives his support is, indeed, no where so happily illustrated as in the toasts that he gives in his hours of conviviality, the most popular of which is " Death ta da head that wears nae hair ;" or, in less enigmatical words, *Death to the fish*. It was usual about sixty years ago, when a party had been assembled at Johnsmas, a festival held at the time of the ling-fishery, for the principal person of the feast to address his comrades after the following manner : " Men and brethren, lat wis raise a helt. Here's first ta da Glory o' God an da guid o wir ain puir sauls, wir wordy land-maister, an wir lovin meat-mither, helt ta man, death ta fish, an guid growth i' da grund." About Lammas, when from the length of the nights, and the rapidity of the tides, lines were often lost, the convivial sentiment was, " Helt ta man, death ta fish, and detriment ta ne man." But when the natives were about to quit the ling-fishery, and to return home to the harvest, the toast remembered in the cottager's cup was, " God open the mouth of the gray fish,* and haud his hand about da corn."†

These are the chief observations I have to make on the Husbandmen of Shetland. It may be likewise briefly remarked, that, with the exception of the inhabitants of Lerwick, few or no distinct trades are to be found in the thinly inhabited districts of the country; almost every peasant being the fabricator of his own rivlins and shoes, as well as his own tailor, and his own carpenter. The ancient acts of the country, that were directed against commercial imposition, appear, however, to indicate that there was formerly a much greater exercise of separate professions than at the present day. But these laws could little preserve the natives from being defrauded in their transactions with the higher powers of the country; for, as the standard weights of Shetland were regulated by the Bysmer, it was commanded that none should use any instrument of this kind that had not been adjusted by authority. Clandestine means were, therefore, devised, for gradually raising the weights, in order to exact a proportional increase of feu-duties payable to the superior in kind. For a description of the Bysmer, see next page.

---

* By *gray fish*, are meant the fry of the Coal-fish (Piltocks and Sillocks), in contradistinction to ling, coò, tusk, hallibut, haddock, &c. which are called White-fish.

† The interjection that God may *haud his hand about da corn*, implies the wish that the hand of the Diety may be extended to preserve the grain from destructive tempests.

NOTES TO ITER III.

NOTE X. Page 182. OLDEST SHEEP-LAWS OF SHETLAND.

There is a code of sheep laws, preserved in Debes's Description of Feroe, which is dated Opslo, A.D. 1040, being addressed from Hagen, Duke of Norway, and son of King Magnus, to the Bishop of Feroe and Mr Sefvort, Provincial Judge of Shetland, named here *Hetland*.

From the tenor of this sheep-ordinance, it evidently relates to an enclosed state of the country. The laws corrected the grievances that arose from unmarked, stray and wild sheep,—from a clandestine marking of lambs,—from trespasses upon fields or enclosures, —from keeping a superfluous number of sheep-dogs,—and from sheep being injured or destroyed by dogs not properly trained to their office.

NOTE XI. ANCIENT BYSMER OF SHETLAND.

The Bysmer of Shetland, by which is estimated lispunds, has been described with such accuracy by the learned author of the "Grievances of Orkney and Shetland," that I shall give it in his own words. "It is a lever," he remarks, "about three inches diameter; from thence, it gently tapers to the other end, which is about one inch diameter. From the middle, all along this small end, it is marked with small iron pins, at unequal distances corresponding to, and exhibiting the weight of the bodies weighed from one mark to twenty-four, or a lispund. The body or commodity to be weighed, is hung by a hook, in the small end of the bysmer, which is then horizontally suspended by a cord going round it; the weigher still shifting the cord this and that way, till the commodity equiponderates with the gross end of the bysmer, which serves as a counterbalance to it. Thus, the pin nearest the cord, at the time of equilibrium, shews the weight of the commodity in marks." *(See Plate of Antiquities, Appendix, Fig. 22.)*

I may observe, that this instrument for weighing is of the greatest antiquity in Scandinavia and its colonies, being represented in the following plate from Olaus Magnus. (See his Historia de Gentibus Septentrionalibus, lib. 13, cap. 47.)

WEST OF SHETLAND.

"Little know they the fisher's toilsome pain,
   Whose labour with his age, still growing, spends not :
His care and watchings (oft mispent in vain),
   The early morn begins, dark evening ends not.
To foolish men, that think all labour stands
In travel of the feet and tired hands!

Ah wretched fishers! born to hate and strife;
   To others good, but to your rape and spoil.
This is the briefest sum of fisher's life,
   To sweat, to freeze, to watch, to fast, to toil."
                                    PHINEAS FLETCHER.

ISLAND OF MEIKLE ROE.

AT Aiths Voe, well situated for commencing an examination of several districts, I engaged a boat, and sailing to the narrow sound formed by the islands of Papa Little, Vementry and Meikle Roe, landed at the latter place. It would appear that the name of Roe, significant in the ancient Shetland language of Redness, is given to many spots which, in the aspect of their rocks, display this particular tint. Meikle Roe is about three miles in length and two in breadth, being inhabited by scarcely more than a dozen families; its surface is rendered uneven by shapeless crags of granite and greenstone, which are the abodes of the sea-eagle, or by pools that are resorted to by the teal or the raingoose. The shore on the east is low, but on the west its rocks are wrought, by the inroads of the sea, into steep precipices or excavations, that stretch for a considerable distance under ground, being the dark abode of seals. These can only be penetrated in the serenest weather; it was, therefore, unfortunate for my visit, that the murmur of the waves, as they sullenly broke on the sides of the caverns, might be heard at some little distance from the coast, in forbiddance of the gloomy pleasure of exploring these dismal recesses. After several ineffectual attempts to struggle through passages beset on each side by white breakers, that burst with loud commotion over disjointed rocks, our unsteady yawl was at length safely steered into what appeared the gloomy mouth of a cave: but we had not rowed many yards, when, emerging from a black and shady vault, we found ourselves floating upon a narrow canal-shaped basin about twenty feet in width, that was completely open to the sky; and at the same time, the full light of the sun burst upon us in its meridian splendour. The pellucid water of this retired shelter, undisturbed by a single ripple, beautifully reflected the lofty perpendicular walls of granite, through which it extended in a straight course for a considerable distance: the channel, resembling, in the undeviating regularity of its form, some stupendous work of human ingenuity, where the solid rock had been pierced so as to form a deep secure cove. But Nature soon appeared to be the sole engineer of this wellwrought excavation: it was the result of atmospheric elements, acting for an incalculable number of years upon the soft and mouldering materials of a dike or vein of granite, enclosed within a matrix of the same substance, but of a much firmer texture.

A narrow sound bounds the north of Meikle Roe, being so closed in by the land that about seven or eight years ago a Spanish vessel, which was driven by force of tempest upon this horrid part of the coast, could not see the channel though close to its mouth, and went to pieces, when the exertion to steer the ship but a few yards to the south of the fatal rock on which she split, would have conducted her safely into a deep confined basin, that is calm in the most stormy weather.

I now prepared to visit the parish of Northmavine, off the shores of which the greatest quantity of ling is caught; but as I shall have occasion, in adverting to the circumstances that gave rise to the landed tenures of the country, strangely involved in its fisheries, slightly to notice the ancient Dutch herring fishery that was prosecuted on the outside of this coast, I shall take this opportunity of giving a concise view of its history.

HISTORY OF THE DUTCH HERRING FISHERY OF SHETLAND.

The herring fishery of Shetland carried on by the Dutch, was in ancient times an undertaking of the greatest national importance. Near the close of the 15th century, the success of this people induced the Scotch to take into serious consideration the propriety of embarking in the same pursuit; but the design was not carried into execution. In the year 1633, there were so many as 1500 Dutch herring busses, each of 80 tons burden, employed on this coast, with 20 armed ships carrying 30 guns each, and a fleet of dogger-boats to the number of about 400, each of 60 tons burden. But not many years had elapsed in the same century, before the number of busses that visited Shetland amounted to 2200. Owing, however, to wars, and other causes, a diminution took place ; and, at the close of the 17th century, only 500 or 600 busses visited the country. In the year 1702, the French burned 150 of these vessels in Bressay Sound ; and for several years following, no more appeared than 300 or 400. In the year 1774, the number of Dutch vessels only amounted to 200 ; but there were as many at the same time belonging to the Danes, the Prussians, the French, and the Flemings ; the English had also two vessels, and the Scotch one. The Dutch fishery off the coast of Shetland, has since continued to diminish in extent, has been often interrupted, and at present scarcely deserves a name.

The busses employed in the herring fishing, sailed from Holland about the 10th or the 15th of June, in order, if possible, to rendezvous a few days in Bressay Sound. The doggers attached to them, named also Jaggers or Yaggers, were swifter sailers, being intended to run home with the herrings first caught. There were also a few armed vessels, named Convoyers, sent out with the fleet, which, besides being fitted up as hospitals for the sick, carried with them supernumerary hands, carpenters, and materials for fishing of all descriptions, in order to give assistance to busses in case of losses or accidents. In the year 1774, two convoyers arrived with the fleet, with the intent that one of them should always attend the fishing, while the other should be stationed at Bressay Sound, and that they should thus alternately change situations every fortnight.

It was during the time when the busses were detained at Bressay Sound, that the Shetlander anticipated, from his commercial intercourse with them, a great means by which his family would be enabled to support themselves during the year ; and, accordingly, numbers of stockings, gloves, night-caps and rugs, were previously manufactured, in expectation of the annual fair that was then held in Lerwick. A great employment was at the same time given to boatmen : for, as none of the busses brought with them boats, each was attended, when lying in the Sound, by a yawl. The quantity of fresh meat required by the Dutch was so great, that during the fishing season provisions were three times as dear as in Orkney. When Mr Low visited Lerwick in the year 1774, he described the fair as a scene of uncommon bustle ; the country people were very smart in making bargains, using as many Dutch and Norwegian words as served their purpose of buying and selling ; but as for the Dutch language they spoke it with great fluency. The Foreigners paid money for every thing. A scathold behind the town was crowded with shelties, which were let out for the amusement of the Dutch at the rate of a stiver a mile ; this being a kind of exercise prescribed by their medical men, as useful to them after having been long confined on shipboard.

On the 23d of June, (St John's Mass), the Dutch would set sail from Bressay Sound to the fishery, but the Prussians, the French, and the Flemings would leave it six days sooner, —which practice was much reprobated as breaking the shoal of herrings, and causing them to fly towards the shore ; it was even said, that if any of them were caught a week sooner than the 24th, they would be unfit for curing. In the beginning of the season, the Dutch fished off the middle of Shetland, but as the season advanced, they followed the herrings southward, discontinuing in later years to visit the Yarmouth banks, and fishing no farther than Buchan Ness. Mr Low describes the system that was pursued in the following manner: "The jaggers or doggers (from 30 to 35 in number), are numbered 1st, 2d, 3d, 4th, &c., and if the first jagger can get ten barrels among the fleet the first night, she proceeds home immediately, when nothing is more common than to sell these herrings for £50 per barrel, as every individual, almost, in the eastern countries look on the first fruits of this fishery as medicine. When the earliest jagger arrives, a present of her cargo is immediately sent to the Prince of Orange, and then every one who can may purchase. The first three jaggers go to Holland, a fourth to Hamburgh, the others sail as they get cargoes, the last being obliged (for they are all freighted vessels), to stay on the coast till the 15th July, if she does not get a full loading. Every one has her station; and though the fishing busses belong to different companies, yet in dispatching the jaggers, they take from every buss what herring she has got, and account to each other at home, as they are sold. After the jaggers are all dispatched, the busses continue fishing till they make up cargoes."* The narrator speaks, at the same time, of the remarkable cleanliness of the Dutch, and of the national encouragement given to the fisheries, by rendering all provisions and materials used for them duty free, and by bounties paid for the first herrings caught.

Such are the particulars relative to the annual visits that the Dutch formerly paid to these shores. The commercial intercourse resulting from them, greatly assisted the Shetlanders in struggling for a bare subsistence, when the weights and measures of their country had been clandestinely raised by the hand of power to more than twice their ancient standard, for the purpose of exacting, in the same proportion, the rent, scat, wattle, and feudal duties paid in kind to a superior.

In the year 1750, the British Government first directed their attention to the herring fishery; and a company incorporated in the same year, entitled, *The Free British white Herring Company*, fitted out vessels that visited the Shetland coasts. They were, by means of bounties, so feebly encouraged by the British Government, that the twenty busses which they at first owned, gradually dwindled to eight,—at which number they stood for several years, and the undertaking was eventually given up, after the loss of half a million of money Sterling. Lately, the herring fishery of Britain has revived under much greater encouragement, but it is generally conducted off more southerly coasts of Britain than those of Shetland. Two or three vessels are, I believe, fitted out for the purpose from Lerwick; but the herring fishery is by no means a favourite pursuit in the country. "We have hitherto," says a Shetland landholder, in a letter addressed to the Highland Society, "considered it as beyond our reach, as precarious, and requiring a great capital in ships, nets, cash and salt, than we could afford."

MAVIS GRIND TO FEIDELAND.

I again crossed the narrow ridge of land named Brae, that separates Busta Voe from

---

* From Mr Low's MS. Tour through Orkney and Shetland, much of my information on the Dutch herring fishery of the last century is derived. See also Brand's, Sir Robert Sibbald's, and Mr Gifford's, Descriptions of Shetland.

Soulam Voe, where were anciently erected the booths of foreign merchants, when they carried on a traffick with the natives for ling. The situation was very central, readily communicating with the North Isles of Shetland, and, by an isthmus only one hundred yards broad, named Mavis Grind, with the large peninsulated district of Northmavine. From the 1st of May to the 1st of August (old style), vessels freighted with goods for barter were constantly arriving in the country from Hamburgh, Lubeck, Bremen, Denmark, and more latterly from Scotland and England. The merchants, upon landing, obtained either booths ready constructed, or the privilege of erecting them upon some convenient site of ground, for which they paid the landed proprietors of Shetland a most exorbitant rate. They then stored these buildings with a variety of articles for sale or barter, such as hooks, lines, herring-nets, several descriptions of corn and flour, a kind of wheaten bread named Cringel-bread, salt, fruits of all kinds, mead, strong beer, various sorts of distilled spirits, particularly one named *Corn-waters*, coarse hempen cloth, together with fine linens, muslins, and other merchandise. At the same time, the natives got ready their yawls, which were then so small that none contained more than three or four men, and laid their lines for ling, cod, or tusk, in the voes, or within the distance of two or three leagues. They then generally brought these fish for barter to the doors of the booths in a wet state, though sometimes, under the name of Stock-fish, they were previously dried in skeos. Other articles which were disposed of to the strangers, comprised stockings, wadmel, horses, cows, sheep, seals' skins, otters' skins, butter, and oil that had been extracted from the livers of fish. Booths were also opened in other parts of the country, particularly at Unst, Yell, Sumburgh, and Hillswick; but when, in the beginning of the last century, various acts of Parliament were framed, prohibiting the importing of foreign salt, except in British vessels, and encouraging, by bounties, the exportation of fish cured at home, foreigners gradually left the ling-fishery of Shetland to its own resources.

After passing Mavis Grind, I coasted along the sloping shores of Soulam Voe, covered by a deep moss, and arrived at the Peninsula of Glus, divided from the Mainland by a narrow low bank of sand, named an *Air*. A sweeping shower of rain compelled me to seek for shelter in the first habitation that I could find. The owner of it having been caught by the same tempest, had just retired to bed indisposed; but his sister, on seeing that I was a stranger (for this character needed no further introduction on the hospitable soil of Thule), politely stept forward and offered me every accommodation which the mansion could afford,—an invitation which, to a rain-drenched traveller, could not but be acceptable. A blazing peat-fire, and an excellent dish of trout fresh from the lakes of Roeness Hill, soon made me forget the late pelting of the storm. Shetland is, in point of hospitality, what England was several centuries ago,—what the Hebrides were much later. It is often with regret observed, that hospitality diminishes with an increased population. Why should it not? A man may make his house an occasional solace to a scanty collection of inhabitants, but the more frequent demands of the same sort that would accrue from increasing villages or towns, would no longer render his house sacred to the duties of domestic retirement, but would convert it into a public inn.

On the following morning, I was welcomed by the gentleman of the house, and among the dainties with which our breakfast-table was supplied, a dish composed of small quarters of lamb, daintily carbonadoed, and of a most exquisite flavour, was pre-eminent ; their size was what might have been expected from the fleecy progeny of Shetland, not one of them being much more than twice the size of the limb of a rabbit.   The morning being fine, my kind entertainer assisted me in my journey by a passage in his yawl, which was bound to the foot of Roeness Hill, where he was meditating, among the lakes of that wild region, a fishing excursion ; and to the same place I was tempted to accompany him with geological views. After sailing along the dull line of coast that is opposite to Glus Voe, we reached the remains of an ancient church and a town, known by the name of Ollaberry. This was a situation that, in the commencement and middle of the last century, formed a convenient residence for a few gentlemen of Shetland, when, by the cessation of the periodical visits of Hamburgh traders, and the decline of the Dutch herring-fishery, they were obliged themselves to turn exporters of fish. The country had long enjoyed a successful traffic with the Dutch, by selling them stockings and fresh provisions ; nor was the commercial intercourse less lucrative than subsisted with those foreigners who annually set up booths, and stocked them with the various commodities that the Shetlanders required, taking in exchange ling, cod, and tusk, which they cured. But owing to the various feudal impositions of the country, conjoined with the fraudulent increase of its weights and measures, attributable to the Stewarts, Earls of Orkney, and the rapacious farmers of the Crown revenues, which had eventually more than doubled the amount of the lispund, it was almost impossible that any resources of commerce could afford the tenant the means of a tolerable subsistence. When, therefore, the landlords saw that the herring-fishery was dwindling away, and that the foreigners who traded for ling were, by the new powers intrusted to custom-house officers, about to leave the country, nothing but ruin threatened them, unless they would avail themselves of the encouragement given by successive acts of Parliament, towards the promotion of the British fisheries. Accordingly, they were compelled, in their own defence, to be the proper successors of the foreign merchants, who had, for the uninterrupted period of two centuries, been the chief supporters of the Shetland fishermen.

After passing the small inlet of Quayfiord, we reached the spacious harbour of Colafiord, and at the north-west angle of it landed at the foot of a large hill of granite, near to which is an accumulation of large stones, bearing the form of a sepulchral tumulus, and around it a circle of considerable extent. There is a monstrous story told concerning it,— as that a giant proposing to build a bridge over the voe, brought these rude materials intended for the structure in a *maisey ;* and about a mile to the northward, there is a steep ridge of rocks named the Biorgs, on the summit of which is a rude inclosure, styled the Giant's Garden, where he secured the cattle and other property that he had acquired by plunder. But the inhabitants contrived, either by force or stratagem, to throw him over the precipice, when he was buried between two large upright stones, still existing, that are set up at a distance of several yards from each other.

In tracing the burn of Roer-water, we arrived in our ascent at an immense barren and trackless wilderness of red granitic rocks, where the apparent disturbance, induced by the penetration into the mass of a large dike of greenstone, was exhibited in the deep hollows of a chain of lakes. Of these the largest is Roer-water, an untroubled and limpid pool, contained in an irregular basin of more than two miles in circumference, and abounding with fine trout. The holms with which it is studded are peopled with gulls and wild ducks, but on one of them the sea-eagle has long built its nest. In a southerly direction, the eye might trace the gradual ascent to the round summit of Roeness Hill, which was reflected into various tints and shades. The rangers of this desert tract were the small sheep of the country, regarded here as a kind of *feræ naturæ*, that have long defied the celerity of the had-dog. I now became well acquainted with the companion of my journey, and was surprised to find, in this retired inhabitant of the Shetland hills, one who had been so great atraveller, that it might be said of him, "mores hominum multorum vidit et urbes,"--one who had visited far distant tropical climates,--who had enjoyed the polished societies of the principal capitals of Europe. While he was engaged in angling, I set off alone in a north-westerly direction, to explore the nature of these solitary rocks. Light wreaths of mist moved gently over the dreary waste, while the deepest silence prevailed, except when interrupted by the plaintive note of the plover, or the shrill cry of the whimbrel, whose haunts I had invaded. At length appeared in view a vast range of impendent cliffs, extending for a distance of ten miles, and worn by the action of a turbulent sea into a thousand fantastic forms. Insulated rocks were whitened with innumerable flocks of sea-fowl; and at their base were hollow caverns, the domicil of seals and otters. Some hundred feet below me, the billows of the Atlantic broke with tremendous roar, being unchecked by any land intervening between America and the western banks of Roeness. In returning, the sun shone bright, and I retraced my course along the chain of lakes, which, flowing with silvery whiteness among rugged and dreary crags, reflected every object near them; sky, rocks and heath limited the horizon; no marks of the labour of man appeared, but tranquility pervaded the scene. At length I descried my friend busily ruminating with his angling rod in his hand on the bleak banks of Roer-water, and, in allusion to the wild scene before him, lamenting his hard destiny, which had compelled him to terminate his days, a mere hermit as he named himself, in the vile climate of Thule. His dejection he explained as that of Jacques: "It is a melancholy of mine own, compounded of many simples, extracted from many objects, and indeed the sundry contemplation of my travels, in which my often rumination wraps me in a most humorous sadness." I could have replied to him even as Shakespeare's misanthrope was answered: "A traveller! by my faith you have great reason to be sad; to have seen much, and to have nothing, is to have rich eyes and poor hands." The hermit's meditations were, however, soon interrupted by the announcement of the repast that was prepared. A natural table of granite, upon which a white cloth was laid, displayed the attractions of an excellent cold collation. In the mean time, a vessel, filled with the limpid water of the lake, was simmering over a boiling apparatus brought from Vienna. The regale of cold fowls and lamb which followed, washed down with Cape Madeira, and the luxury after it of hot punch, was mountain cheer of the most unexpected kind.

After retracing my steps to the shores of Colafiord Voe, I arrived at Lochend, where I was received with much hospitality by Mr Hoseason, and pursuing from thence a course parallel to the mural ridge of rocks named the Biergs, I arrived at North Roe, where I met with a similar welcome at the house of Mr Sinclair. An extensive ling fishery is carried on in this district, the usual mode of prosecuting it being through the medium of tenants. The origin of the tenures that involve the obligation to fish for landlords, may be traced to a date a little preceding the middle of the last century. When the foreign merchants who had almost exclusively conducted the Shetland ling fishery for nearly two centuries, had left these shores, in consequence of the bounties granted for the exportation of fish from Great Britain, occasional companies of Scotch and English merchants next appeared. But, as I have before had occasion to observe, the chief successors of the foreigners were the landholders themselves, who cured and exported ling, chiefly with a view to procure for their tenants the only means that they possessed, of paying their rents. They had not, however, been long engaged in their new occupation, before the foreign markets at Hamburgh and Bremen, from some unexplained cause, began to fail; and the utmost commercial exertions of landholders could not ward off the distress of the peasantry, who were reduced to the most abject state of penury. Consequently, when in the course of a few years, through the means of a Greenock and London company, conjoined with the stimulus of a more advantageous bounty offered by the British Grovernment, a renewal of the exportation of ling was meditated, and when it was intended that the markets of Portugal, and those of Barcelona and Alicant should be first tried, a new embarrassment arose,—the tenants were totally incapacitated by their distresses from purchasing the boats and lines necessary for the fishery, and unless sums sufficient for the purpose could be advanced by the landlord, the attempt to renew the ling fishery must have proved abortive. Under such novel circumstances, then, it was found necessary to introduce into landed tenures, a condition of a very remarkable kind. The landlord allowed his yearly tenant to be in debt to him for the boats and fishing lines necessary for the taking of ling, but required from him the obligation, that all the fish which he might take during the customary season, should be sold to him at a stipulated rate. This complicated relation of landlord and tenant has ever since prevailed in the country.

From the spacious and open bay of North Roe, I proceeded northwards, but, on setting out, a heavy rain came on, which obliged me to take shelter in the house of a poor woman, who was contenting herself with a humble repast of potatoes, and the scanty nutriment that could be picked off from the rig or back-bone of a cod or ling, which had been separated in the process of curing. This was a sort of fare, that, in the language of Pennant, might rather be called a permission to exist, than a support of vigour. On the north of the parish of Northmavine, the low hilly ridges, formed by the sea into deep fissures or caverns, terminate in a line of ragged coast, agreeably diversified by a long narrow peninsula of green land jutting out far into the Northern Ocean, which is named Fiedeland, an appellation of true Scandinavian origin, that is explained by Debes, in his description of Feroe. He observes, that where grass is found so abundant and juicy, that oxen feed thereon both winter and summer, such places are named *Fiedelands;* and it is very remarkable, he adds, that where there are any Fiedelands, they invariably turn to the north-east and north. Every where the coast is awfully wild, the peninsula is broken on each side into steep precipices, exhibiting now and then a gaping chasm, through which the sea struggles, while numerous stacks rise from the surface of a turbulent ocean,—the waves beating around them in angry and tumultuous roar. This is a great station for the ling fishery, which commences in the middle of May, and ends on the 12th of August. When any fishermen resort, for the first time, to a convenient place of this kind, they are allowed by the law to build for themselves huts, on any site which may be uninclosed, uncultivated, and at a distance of not more than 100 yards from the high water-mark. These are constructed of rude stones, without any cement, being made no larger than is sufficient to contain a six-oared boat's crew. The men form the roof of thin pieces of wood, on which they lay turf;—they then strew a little straw upon the ground, and snatch from their severe labours a short repose. On the narrow isthmus of low marshy land, that connects the peninsula of Feideland to the Mainland, is interspersed, with all the disorder of a gypsey encampment, a number of these savage huts named *summer lodges*, and in the centre of them is a substantial booth, used by a factor for curing fish. Here I met with excellent accommodation, owing to the kindness of Mr Hoseason, who had sent from his house at Lochend every refreshment I might need, together with a comfortable bed for the evening. Feideland is a place possessing no little interest; a remarkable busy scene is presented by the numerous crews sailing to the Haaf, or returning from it laden with fish; some men are busily engaged in weighing the stock of ling, cod and tusk, as it is brought in to the factors; others in spreading their lines on the rocks to dry, or in cooking victuals for their comrades who may be employed on the haddock grounds, or in brushing, splitting and salting the fish, that are brought to the door of the booth. But to the naturalist, Feideland presents attractions of no mean kind; the numerous rare marine productions that are continually drawn up by the lines of the fishermen, which a small perquisite might induce them to preserve and bring to the shore, would richly repay him for lingering several days in such a station.—*(See Sketch of Fiedeland, Plate 5.)*

I shall now take an opportunity of giving an account of the Ling Fishery, as it is prosecuted at

THE HAAF.

The *Haaf* is a name applied to any fishing-ground on the outside of the coast, where ling, cod, or tusk may be caught. Not much above a century ago, the fishery for ling and cod was prosecuted much nearer shore than it is now, and fishing places designated *Raiths*, were pointed out by certain land-marks called Meiths, so that every one knew his own raith, and any undue encroachment upon it was considered no less illegal and actionable, than if it had been upon a landed inclosure. The fishermen, however, at the present day, find it their interest to seek for ling at a much greater distance, even to the extent of thirty or forty miles.

The men employed at the Haaf are from 18 years of age and upwards. Six tenants join in a boat, their landlords importing for them frames ready modelled and cut out in

Norway,* which, when put together, form a yawl of six oars, from 18 to 19 feet in keel, and six in beam; it is also furnished with a square sail.†

On the 25th of May, or on the 1st of June, the fishermen repair to their several stations. They either endeavour, with rod and line, to procure for bait the fry of the coalfish, of the age of 12 months, named Piltocks, or they obtain at the ebb mussels and limpets; and then going out to sea six miles or more, lay their lines for haddocks, and after obtaining a sufficient supply of these fish, reserve them for bait.

The Fiedeland Haaf being 30 or 40 miles from land, the fishermen endeavour to leave their station in the morning of one day, so as to be enabled to return in the course of the day following. And if, owing to boisterous weather, they have suffered long detention in their lodges, the first boat that is launched, induces every weather-bound crew to imitate the example; it is, therefore, no unusual circumstance to see, in a fleet of yawls, all sails set, and all oars plied nearly at the same instant of time. Each boat, in the first turn that it makes, observes the course of the sun,‡ and then strives to be the first which shall arrive at the fishing station.

Some few of the fishermen, during their voyage, superstitiously forbear to mention in any other name than one that is Norse, or in some arbitrary word of their own coinage, substituted for it, various objects, such, for instance, as a knife, a church, the clergyman, the devil, or a cat. When after a tug of 30 or 40 miles, the crew has arrived at the Haaf, they prepare to set their *tows*, which is the name they designate the lines by that are fitted with ling hooks. Forty-five or fifty fathoms of tows constitute a *bught*, and each bught is fitted with from nine to fourteen hooks. It is usual to call twenty bughts a *packie*, and the whole of the packies that a boat carries is a *fleet of tows*. Thus, while a boat in the south or east of Shetland carries only two or three packies, a fleet of tows used on the Feideland Haaf, amounts to no less than six, these being baited with seldom less than twelve hundred hooks, provided with three buoys, and extending to a distance of from 5000 to 6000 fathoms.

The depth at which ling are fished for varies from 50 to 100 fathoms. In setting the tows, one man cuts the fish used for bait into pieces, two men bait and set the lines, and the remaining three or four row the boat. They sink at certain distances, what they call *Cappie-stanes*, the first that is let down being called the *Steeth*. These keep the tows properly fixed to the ground. When all this labour is finished, which, in moderate weather, requires three or four hours, and when the last buoy has floated, the fishermen rest for

---

* A friend of mine has informed me, that the price of boats has been almost tripled of late years, by a most unjust and oppressive mode of levying the duties on importations, at so much for each piece of wood, however small, of which the boat consists, before it is put together. He adds, that nothing but dire necessity could induce the poor people to purchase materials at such prices. A boat is said to cost £20. I may add, that the Agricultural Society of Shetland has properly petitioned for a reduction of the duties upon wood.

† Boats of this size are, says Mr Shirreff, 20 to 24 feet from stem to stern, the depth 2¼ feet to 2½. Each oar is from 10 to 14 feet long, and the sail 15½ feet deep, by 12 broad at the top, and 14 at the bottom.

‡ This is a superstition not peculiar to either Celtic or Scandinavian nations. Sir Walter Scott has observed, that the Highlanders, in making the *Deasil*, a sort of benediction which they bestow in walking round the party to be propitiated, always observe the course of the sun. And witches, on the other hand, make their circles *widdershins*, as the Scottish dialect expresses it (*widder-sins* Germ.), or in opposition to the course of the sun. Dr Henderson again observes, that in Iceland the altar is always left by turning to the right, or sunways.

nearly two hours, and take their scanty sustenance; but it is lamentable to think, that their poverty allows them nothing more than oat-meal bread, and a few gallons of water. Their severe labours have never yet excited the commiseration of the British Government; for, owing to the excessive duty on spirits, they can rarely afford to carry with them the smallest supply of whisky.

At length, one man, by means of the buoy-rope, undertakes to haul up the tows,—another extricates the fish from the hooks and throws them in a place near the stern, named the shot,—a third guts them and deposits their livers and heads in the middle of the boat. Along with the ling that is caught, there is a much less quantity of cod and of the Gradus Brosme or tusk; these are all valuable acquisitions. Six to ten wet lings are about a hundred weight, and hence six or seven score of fish are reckoned a decent haul —fifteen or sixteen a very good one,—twenty scores of ling are rarely caught, but in such a case, garbage, heads, and small fish are all thrown overboard, nor can these lighten the boat so much as that she will not appear, according to the phrase of the fishermen, just *lippering* with the water. The skate and halibut which may be taken, are reserved to supply the tables of the fishermen. That formidable looking fish, the stone-biter, (Anarchicus Lupus), is also esteemed good eating. When all the tows are heaved up, they are deposited in the bow of the boats.

If the weather be moderate, a crew does not need to be detained at the Fiedeland Haaf more than a day and a half. But too often a gale comes on,—the men are reluctant to cut their lines, and the most dreadful consequences ensue. About two years ago Mr Watson, the respectable minister of Northmavine, communicated to the editor of an Edinburgh paper a striking instance of the misfortunes to which the fishermen are liable. In speaking of a number of boats that went off to the Haaf, he remarked, that "about the time they were laying their lines, it blew strong from the south-east, so that it was with much difficulty they could haul them in again. The storm increased and blew off land; two boats particularly, were in great distress; they having lost their sails, and being quite worn out with fatigue, were able to do very little for their own safety. Luckily the wind shifted to the westward, and on the third day the crews all reached land, completely exhausted with hunger and labour, having had nothing but a very little bread and some water. Two of the men, one in each of the boats which suffered most, died before they came to land, and the rest were not able to walk to their houses without assistance."* In my journey through Shetland, I have, indeed, heard too many females lamenting the loss of a husband or of a son at the distant Haaf. The dangers there encountered are the frequent theme of the Shetlander's conversation, and his recital of them beguiles the tedious hours of a long winter's evening. One of these stories I shall venture to give in all its native rudeness and prolixity, as it was collected by a friend of mine from the recital of a Fiedeland fisherman. It possesses little or no interest as a mere narrative, but it may afford a tolerable specimen of the modern Shetland dialect.

---

* Mr Watson remarks, that " since the smuggling has ceased, and the spirits are so dear, the boats cannot afford to take out with them a drop to refresh them in the heat, or to cheer them in the wet. It would be a good deed in Government to allow them a small quanity of rum per man, duty free, in the same manner as in the navy, and such a boon would be most gratefully received, and not in *many* cases abused."

Account of a Voyage to the Haaf, as given by a Fisherman at Feideland in Northmavine.

Mony a foul dae hae I seen at da Haaf; bit I tink *Martinabullimus*[1] dae *fearnyear*[2] wis da warst dae I ever saw. He wis a bonny morning, but a grit lift i' da sea and a hantle o' brak. So I said to wir men, we hae a guid *nebert*[3] o' haddicks, he's bonny wather, and I tink we'll try da deep watter. So we gat wir tows and *capistanes*[4] into the boat, and we set aff, and we row'd oot upon him till we sank a' da laigh land, and dan we began and *laid fram*,[5] and whan we *cuist wir ooter bow*,[6] de'el a stane o' Shetland did we see, except da tap o' Roeness hill and da Pobies o' Unst. *Noo he beguid ta gro frae the sud east.*[7]—So whan we had sitten a while, we tuik wir *bow*[8] and began ta *hail*;[9] and, faith, before we gat in ee packie o' tows, four men cood doe nae mair den *keep da tow at da kaib*.[10] We gat *tw'ar'-tree*[11] fish *f'ra'dat*,[12] and at last sic a grit weight cam upo' da line, dat it tuik a' mi strent to hail, and whan it cam to da *wayl*,[13] what wis it bit a grit dayvel of a skate. So I said ta Tammy, dam her, cut here awa, wha's geean ta row under her sic a dae? So he tuik da *skuin*[14] and *sneed da tombe*.[15] And at last we got in wir tows, and, faith, we'd gotten a braw puckle o' fish. Noo, says I, lads, i' God's name, *fit da mast and swift da sail*,[16] da east tide is running, and we'll sail wast be sooth upon him. So I guid i' the starn, and just as we gae sail, he made a watter aff o' da fore kaib, and when he brook, he took *Hackie*[17] aff o' da *skair taft*,[18] and laid him i' da shott. Dan I cried to *Gibbie*,[19] for God's sake to strik da head oot o' da drink kig and *ouse*[20] da boat; da watter wis up at da *fasta bands*,[21] bit wi' God's help we gat her *toom'd*[22] before anither watter cam. Whan the east tide ran aff, noo said I, lads, we'll tak doon da sail an row in upon him. So we did sae,—and whan da wast tide made, we gae sail agin and ran east upon him, and faith we lay upo' Vallyfield in Unst, and we wrought on rowing an' sailing till, by God's Providence, we gat ashore about aught o'clock at night. O man, dat wis a foul dae!

In the foregoing specimen of the modern Shetland dialect, a curious circumstance is the omission of the neuter pronoun *it*, and the personification of every object by the words *he* and *she*. Although some Scottish phrases are evidently introduced into the language, yet they are delivered with an acute pronunciation and accent resembling no provincial dialect of Britain that I have ever heard, being no doubt referable to a Norwegian origin.

SAND VOE TO ROENESS VOE.

The small tract of country between Feideland and Sand Voe possesses not the least interest. Its bleak coast to the west affords a refuge for seals and otters, and its forlorn

---

1 Festum St Martini Bullientis?
2 Last year.
3 A sufficient quantity of bait.
4 Stones used for sinking the lines or tows.
5 Laid their lines to sea-ward.
6 Threw their last or outer buoy.
7 It began to blow an increasing breeze from the south-east.
8 Buoy.
9 Haul.
10 Keep the lines at the thowl on which they rest in hauling.
11 Two or three.
12 For all that.
13 Gunwale of the boat.
14 Knife.
15 Cut the line to which the hook is attached.
16 Put up the mast and reef the sail.
17 Hercules.
18 The aftermost thwart but one.
19 Gilbert.
20 Bale.
21 Pieces of wood that cross the boat to strengthen it under the thwarts.
22 Emptied.

inland tracts for mountain sheep. Sand Voe is a channel hemmed in with irregular ridge-shaped hills, which appear broken into many various shapes, while they stretch so far into the land as almost to meet the inlet of North Roe, and to intersect with it the northern district of Northmavine. At Roer Mill, Mr Sinclair's factor receives and cures the fish that are obtained at Uyea Haaf. Leaving Sand Voe to the east, a desart range of precipices displayed itself on the northern coast, backed by the ruddy eminence of Roeness. At Uyea, the north-westerly angle of Northmavine, there is a large verdant holm, that affords one of the richest pastures for cattle which is to be found in the country; and on the mainland adjoining to it, a number of fishermen have erected their rude summer lodges. While the fishing season lasts, these men repair to their station every Monday morning, and are employed until the Friday or Saturday following. During this period they have but few hours for rest. On the return of a boat from the Haaf, the fishermen are first engaged in spreading out their tows to dry; then a part of the men catch piltocks with a rod and line, or procure other kinds of bait at a distance from shore,—while others again mend the tows, and cook victuals for the next day's voyage to the Haaf. Owing to all these successive and rapid demands on the time of a crew, their sleep must be very trifling, not exceeding, as is supposed, two or three hours in the twenty-four. When piltocks and haddocks cannot be procured for bait, which is a rare circumstance, halibut, cod, tusk, and even ling are substituted.

I sailed from Uyea to Roeness Voe, along the range of vast impending cliffs of granite open to the Atlantic, that form the western coast of Northmavine. The remarkable invasion of a dike of greenstone, which is fantastically displayed in a natural section of the mountain of Roeness,—the subordinate inequality of lesser crags that have been separated by encroachments of the sea,—the numberless seals that bask on low ledges, within dark caverns, or that follow the boat, eyeing it with evident marks of curiosity,—the stacks that boldly rise from the expanse of the ocean, together with the distant skerry of Ossa, inhabited by the greater gulls,—these are the objects which form the interesting display of coast and mountain scenery on the west of Northmavine. I at length arrived at Roeness Voe, a considerable inlet, seven miles in extent, which, with Quayfirth Voe, nearly divides in two the parish of Northmavine. To the north it opens into the sea; but as it winds in its inland course round the steep hill of Roeness, it is closed in by the land, and expanded like a lake. On the south of the Voe there is a cottage or two, with a few temporary huts, built for the accommodation of the natives employed during the summer in the deep water fishery. Here, also, may be seen a solitary knoll, that commemorates an event which took place in the reign of Charles II., when a Dutch sixty-gun ship came into this estuary, to harbour in it during the winter. England being then at war with Holland, an express was sent by the Shetlanders to the British Government, who dispatched two frigates to Roeness Voe. They there met with the enemy's vessel, an engagement took place, and after a severe contest she was captured. A number of the Hollanders being killed, their bodies were interred at a place that is still named the Dutchman's Knoll.

From the Voe I ascended Roeness Hill by a very steep side. Its surface abounds with several alpine plants. Its height, which is the most considerable in Shetland, has been estimated at 1447 feet. To the north there was nothing in view but the red barren scalp of a mountain of granite, affording in its hollows a receptacle for deep pools of water,— except a woodless tract, the haunt of wild mountain sheep,—the prospect being closed by the northern sea and the skerries of Feideland. On my right was the wide estuary of Yell Sound, with its rocky promontories, and the long parallel ranges of mountain summits and intermediate hollows that distinguish the Island of Yell. In an opposite direction, where the western waves murmured at the foot of the mountain, the eye might roam over the wide domain of the Atlantic. The immense bay of St Magnus lay to the south, with its several estuaries and swelling shores, the bold island of Foula being in distant perspective. But to the south-east Thule has assumed her wildest dress,—she has decorated this vast collection of leafless mountains,—this assemblage of rocks piled upon rocks, of different shapes and elevations,—with thickly-studded lakes and voes, and with the habitations of men, all in their rudest form. On the highest part of Roeness Hill, stands a watch-tower of a circular shape, composed of rude uncemented stones of granite, and capable of containing within it about six people:—it is doubtful, however, if the appearance it presents is that of its original form. The fishermen are careful in preserving it entire, since it is found an useful land-mark at sea.

FISHING-TENURES OF SHETLAND.

When at Roeness Voe, I was obliged, before I could pursue my tour, to set off for Colafiord, half a mile distant, and from thence to cross Yell Sound. At the south-west angle of Yell, the crew of a six-oared boat had come in from the Fiedeland Haaf, having in bad weather lost the fleet of tows that they had laid, the value of which was estimated at a sum exceeding twenty pounds. Thus were gone at one stroke the profits of the year; the poor fellows would be even indebted to their masters, and a season or two must pass over their heads, before they would be enabled to recover themselves from their misfortune. I shall never forget the looks of despair that the men expressed, when they had to relate their story,- how the hopes of supporting their family with independence were thus blighted. An adject dependence is the consequence that ensues from the state of tenures in Shetland. The landlord lets his land for one year only, in consideration of a certain rate that was regulated by the ancient rental of Shetland; he undertakes, at the same time, to advance a tenant the articles necessary for the ling-fishery, such as boats and lines, requiring from him the same profit that a buyer would expect from a seller; but in lieu of all these offers, the tenant must enter into an obligation to deliver the fish which he takes at a stipulated price. A system such as this cannot but be objectionable; it had its origin in the debased political state of the country, which was occasioned by the fraudulent doubling of its weights and measures, and by excessive feudal exactions, all of which are attributable to the number of mesne lords and farmers of the Crown-revenues, that in ancient times ravaged Orkney and Shetland. These oppressions so impoverished the peasantry, that upon the revival of the ling-fishery, their landlords were obliged to furnish them on trust, with boats and lines necessary for carrying on the business. This advance became ever afterwards involved in the system of Shetland tenures; and, for the cause stated, it ought to be criticised with much lenity. That it opens a wide field for oppression, against the temptation of which no country, where human passions prevail, is proof, it would be absurd to deny. An unfavourable state of the weather occurring throughout the short summer season in which the fishermen repair to the Haaf, or a loss of lines or boats, may oblige the tenant to become a debtor to his landlord, and actuated under these circumstances, by a threat of distrain or ejectment, he may assent to any slavish conditions which a task-master may choose to dictate. These are certainly very possible results that must arise from such a system, and whether, under the fear of them, the moral character of the Shetland tenant has not been in some degree debased, and his stimulus to exertion checked, I shall leave for those to determine, who are better acquainted than myself with the internal state of the country. The late Mr Cheyne of Tanwick, however, who was both a considerable landholder himself and a tacksman, made his dependents forget the power that the tenures of the country threw into his hands; he attended to their wants, and encouraged their exertions in so many different ways, that he had the satisfaction, before he died, of seeing the tenants under his influence pre-eminent in the country as an industrious, enterprising, and contented race of people. His example, also, has been imitated with success by other gentlemen in Northmavine. But this circumstance argues little in favour of the tenures of Shetland. A people may flourish under a good king, though the system of the government be arbitrary; but the system is not to be defended on this account, since a successor may rule with a rod of iron. It is, however, creditable to the present race of Shetland landlords, that they are fully sensible of the advantages to be derived from letting land at a definite price, independent of the obligation of fishing, and of paying tenants a regular price for their fish, that may correspond with the fluctuations of the market. Yet, after all, the introduction of any new description of tenures must be necessarily a slow process; for I have frequently had opportunies of seeing, that the objection against it chiefly arises on the part of the tenants themselves, who, though familiarized all their lifetime to a system which they are conscious is a bad one, are, notwithstanding, unwilling to exchange it for one of which they have had no experience. It was long ago remarked by a writer, strenuous for the support of the present state of Shetland tenures, that the fishermen were so poor that they durst not fish for themselves, fearing, that if they were deprived of the support of their landlords, they should perish for want. This assertion affords the best argument that can be produced for the necessity of a change of system. A sense of dependency in the human mind, is too often the forerunner of an inactive and unadventurous state of poverty.

It is very unfortunate for the tenants, and must be annoying to the feelings of the respectable ministers of Shetland, that the teinds are drawn in kind.* These are, for the most part, farmed by tacksmen, who exact for every milch-cow from two to four marks of butter; for each sheep under the number of thirty 1d or 2d per head, or for thirty head one mark of butter and three marks of wool; for each six-oared boat 1½ cwt. wet fish; for

---

* The penalty of concealing teinds was, by an ancient act of the country, £10 Scots.

each four-oared boat 1 cwt.; for each mark of land three quarters of a can or gallon of oil, and from three to four marks of butter. Such are sums disbursed by the Shetland fisherman to the church; but to his immediate landlord, or to his superior, he owes scatt, landtax, land-maills, wattle, ox-money and sheep-money, three days service (the same being due to the clergyman,) *poultry fowls* (similar to the Scotch canage), school-penny and hawkhens.

The complicated system of Shetland tenures, has been complained of as giving an illegal encouragement to a number of clandestine traders in fish. Thus, when a needy tenant was obliged to sell his landlord all the ling, cod, or tusk that he caught, at a certain rate for each fish, he was tempted to violate this contract, by privately disposing of them, often at a better price, to private dealers. The landlord could not always detect this fraud, but in order to prevent the largest of the ling or cod from disappearing, he paid his tenant a certain sum, reckoned by the weight of the fish.

I engaged the boat that had been so unfortunate as to lose its lines, to convey me across Yell Sound. A sudden squall came on, which, conspiring with the rousts of the channel, gave me a complete wetting; but landing at Glus Air late in the evening, every accommodation was kindly provided for me by Mr Henderson of Bardister. On the next morning I proceeded west, mounted on a shelty, over the soft scatholds of the country, frequently slackening the reins, and allowing the animal to exert the particular sagacity for which he is celebrated, by chusing for himself the firmest road:—I was not deceived in him, for, after little hesitation or floundering, he soon arrived with me safe at

HILLSWICK.

The Ness of Hillswick is a bold, narrow headland, two miles in length, and not exceeding half a mile in breadth, being joined to the Mainland by a narrow isthmus; it is broken on the west and south into steep cliffs, the easterly banks sloping gradually towards the shore. On the north-east, there is a small bay, containing good anchorage for vessels, and the isthmus has to boast of a parish kirk, and two well built houses. The largest mansion is occupied by Messrs Cheyne, having warehouses and cellars attached to it, and before the door a spacious beach of stones cast up from the sea, which in this country, is particularly valuable for drying fish. On the east of the Ness, a narrow stripe of land stretches out that is named the Taing of Torness. The word Taing expresses the character of the low projecting cape; and as for *Torness*, the antiquary is at perfect liberty to suppose it a corruption of *Thors Ness*. As we approach the south of the Ness, it is impossible to withhold our astonishment at the immense veins of red porphyry ramifying among dark strata of gneiss, and distorting them in the most remarkable manner. The Huttonian would regard such veins as flung up by some internal convulsion; but they rather suggest the comparison made by a French geologist, in the true spirit of petromania, "of a sea consolidated in a storm, the violence of which may still be seen in its petrified waves. In doubling the headland, I arrived at the Stack of Sound, where strata of gneiss and hornblende presented the most picturesque distorsions that can well be imagined; and farther to the north-west, perpendicular cliffs arose, shewing an endless variety of bold advancing promonotories and deep indentations or gios; but at the most westerly point of the Ness, the sublimity of the scene was complete. The sun shone in full splendour, and beamed on certain tall stacks, issuing from ocean's depths like sea-encompassed towers. On this account, they have had the same Scandinavian name given to them, which similar shaped rocks still bear in Feroe, of Drenge or Drongs. They present a variety of shapes as they are seen from different parts at sea, having been oftened likened to a small fleet of vessels with spread sails. Nearer the shore, the sea struggles through a cluster of other crags, which in some places rise in large masses above its surface, and in others, appear through the transparency of the stream, shelving to a fathomless depth. On the west, the Ness, which is exposed to the fury of the western ocean, is advanced into a lofty eminence; and near the summit of it, a red unhewn obelisk of granite, mantled with grey moss, being the memorial of far remote times, shews its venerable head. *(See Plate IV.)*

The curing and drying of fish taken at the Stenness Haaf, is conducted at Hillswick with great regularity, a bell ringing for the cessation and resumption of labour. When a boat comes on shore, the ling, cod and tusk that have been taken at the Haaf, are in a gutted state, and with their heads taken off, delivered by weight to the factor. A *splitter*, as he is called, then, with a large knife, cuts a fish open from the head to the tail, and takes out half the back bone next the head; he now hands it over to the *washer*, who, with a heath brush, and the assistance of the sea water, clears away every particle of blood. When all the fish are in this way split and washed, they are allowed to drain; after which comes the *salter*, who places at the bottom of a large wooden vat a stratum of salt, and over it one of fish with the skin-side undermost, until the chest is filled with alternating layers, and above all are laid heavy stones to keep the fish under the pickle. After remaining in the vat some days, they are taken out, well washed and brushed in a direction from the shoulder to the tail, and put up in small heaps called *clamps*, in order to allow the water to drain off. The fish are next spread out with the skin-side undermost, and exposed to the action of the sun, on a beach composed of round stones, where they are again *clamped*, and thus alternately spread out, turned and disposed into piles of a gradually increasing size, until dry. They are afterwards built into a large stack named a *steeple;* and, for the sake of equal pressure, the steeple is again taken down and rebuilt, by which means the fish that were the uppermost in one steeple, are the undermost in another. When the drying, or *pining*, as it is called, has been completed, which is indicated by a white efflorescence appearing on the surface named the *bloom*, the fish are transported to a dry cellar lined with wood, and there piled up closely, or shipped off immediately to a market. A well cured fish is said to be of a greenish-white colour, and when held in the light is translucent.

While I was at Hillswick, a sloop came into the harbour, belonging to Mr Gifford of Busta, loaded with fish, which had been taken from a cod-bank recently discovered to the west of Foula.* Mr Stevenson, whose knowledge of this coast is very extensive, considered

---

* Aware of the importance of the discovery in a national point of view, I omitted no opportunity afforded me to procure every information in my power, with regard to its situation, extent, and productiveness; and a very brief account of the result of my inquiry was communicated to the public in January 1819, and a more full one afterwards throught the medium of the Edinburgh Philosophical Journal. The testimonies which I obtained from various individuals, only disagreed on subordinate points.

it of such importance, as to propose for it the name, which I shall follow him in adopting, of

THE REGENT'S FISHING BANK.

This cod-bank has been described to me as having a breadth averaging from fifteen to twenty miles,—as commencing from the west of Westray, in Orkney, and as having been traced in a direction nearly N. by W., until Foula appears to the east, or even south-east; but it is very doubtful if its extent be known. The depth of the water on the bank is estimated from 30 to 50 fathoms; its surface being in some places rocky, and in others sandy; it is also covered with buckies, mussels, and razor-fish.

In connection with the history of this bank, it may not be uninteresting to learn if it was really known to those nations who cannot be accused of a supineness in the prosecution of their fisheries, and, for this purpose, my inquiries will be directed to the Dutch, who, for nearly three centuries, have been the principal fishers frequenting the coast of Shetland. Captain Smith, who, in the year 1633, by order of the Earl of Pembroke, and the British Fishery Company of London, visited Shetland, saw 1500 sail of busses, of 80 tons each, taking herrings on this coast, and with them, as he adds, "a small fleet of dogger-boats, which were of the burden of 60 tons and upward, which did fish only with hooks and lines for ling and cod. Many of these boats and busses came in to several havens or sounds, to fit and trim themselves. One thing was observable, that within eight or ten days after the dogger-boats went to sea, they came into the sound again so full laden as they could swim. The certain number of dogger-boats I could not learn, but the general report was about 400." In Sir Robert Sibbald's description of Shetland, written A.D. 1711, we learn "that the Dutch employed hundreds of doggers for the taking of cod."

But in the year 1774, the mode of prosecuting the cod fishery was witnessed and accurately described by Mr Low, from whose manuscript tour in Shetland I shall make the following transcript. "Besides the herring busses, the Dutch have doggers on the cod fishery. These are going and coming from early spring, through the whole summer. They are fitted out in this manner,—the owner of the dogger lays in provisions, salt and casks, which are paid for out of the first returns of the voyage; about a fourth of what remains is the property of the owner of the dogger, and the remainder is divided among the crew. Each dogger has ten men and two boys, the half of whom sleep while the others are employed in fishing. As soon as they catch a cod, they cut its throat, and soon after lay it in salt; every man salting and packing his own barrel. When these fishermen come first on the coast, they use the lesser lamprey for bait, kept alive in fresh-water wells on board, and continually stirred (which is done by the boys) while in harbours, to keep them in motion, otherwise they immediately die; but at sea this is done by the motion of the ship. They prefer this kind of bait to all others for a cod, but when there is a failure of it, each of the doggers is provided with eight herring nets, for catching herring after the month of June comes on. To hinder the too rapid motion of the vessel, which would prevent their lines from taking the bottom, each has what is called a drove-sail, or one which hangs under water, and effectually stops her way, and they can then pursue their business at leisure."

It was long after the departure of the Dutch from the Shetland coast, that the cod fishery, by means of decked vessels, was languidly revived. About ten or twelve years since, a few vessels, from 6 to 35 tons burthen, and carrying from six to eight hands, first prosecuted a fishery for cod off the coasts of Shetland, using hand lines, baited with two or three hooks. They seldom went farther to look for fish than the immediate neighbourhood of Foula or Fair Isle; their search was highly desultory, and their success proportionably uncertain; it rarely happened that vessels of only 10 to 30 tons, after being employed a week in fishing, returned to their several harbours, like the Dutch doggers described by Smith, "so full laden as they could swim." For this reason, I am strongly inclined to suspect that the bank was, two centuries ago, well known to Holland, and that the knowledge of it was either carefully withheld from this nation in particular, or, which is more probable, regarded by us with such an indifference, that when the Dutch left these shores, it was soon forgotten that such a bank existed. It, however, appears from the testimony of Mr Low, in his Fauna Oreadensis, that a bank lying to the north-west of the Burgh of Birsay was well known in Orkney; but that it extended to the west of Foula, and perhaps much farther north, was a circumstance undiscovered. "The cod-fish," he remarks, "is found in swarms on the banks all round the coasts, but is very little sought after. Of old this was not the case. Merchants from the south had their factors here, and many fish were yearly made and transported from these isles. Now all is sunk in idolence and sloth." Additional evidence relating to an accidental visit to the bank, has been politely given me by Mr Sheriff Duncan of Lerwick. "I recollect," he remarks, "that a vessel came into Bressay Sound several years ago, with her decks filled with cod. I was told by the master of the vessel, that they had been caught to the northward of the Orkneys, during two or three hours of a calm. The master must therefore have been upon the bank when he fell in with the fish, since it stretches round the northward of these islands." Mr Neill, also, in his Tour through Orkney and Shetland, during the summer of 1804, has the following observations on the fishery of the north of Orkney, which no doubt took place on the southerly commencement of the cod-bank of Shetland, now named the Regent's Fishing Bank. "We weighed anchor," he states, "in the afternoon, and got under way with a gentle breeze. The sailors being provided with strong lines, we here lay to, and fished for cod and haddock. So abundant were all kinds of fish in this place, that in an hour our deck was strewed with about fifty fine firm cod-fish, besides some haddocks of a large size. This was not two miles distant from Papa Westray; *yet we saw no boat engaged in this rich fishery!* How supine is such conduct."—With regard to the recent discovery of the Regent's Fishing Bank, it is I believe attributed to some of the vessels latest engaged in the cod fishing.* From that time, the average quantity of cod, annually taken, has much increased.

The obstacles incidental to the present mode of conducting the fishery, chiefly refer to a supply of bait. That which is used by the Shetland fishermen, consists of the *Mytilus modiolus* or *yoags*, of a large species of whelk, and other shell-fish common to almost every

---

* The discovery of it is claimed by three or more parties; to whom it is properly due, I know not.

northern coast. These are abundantly found in the numerous voes of the country. But it unfortunately happens, that when vessels run short of bait, they are obliged to quit the fishing bank with all expedition, and thus sustain a serious loss, which, as Mr Low has shewn, was not the case when the Dutch prosecuted the fishery, who depended for their first supply of bait upon the lampreys that they brought with them from their own coasts; and afterwards upon their nets which they spread out to take herring for the same purpose.

It has been always supposed that the cod prepared in Shetland will maintain its preeminence over that of other places. The Newfoundland fishermen are described as exposing their fish, after it has been salted, on standing flakes, made by a slight wattle, and supported by poles often 20 feet from the ground. But the humidity is not near so well extracted from the fish as when, according to the Shetland method, they are carefully laid out upon dry beaches, the stones of which have been, during winter, exposed to the abrading action of the ocean, and are thus cleared from vegetable and animal matter.

The discovery of the cod-bank has already proved of great importance to the country. Employment has been given to many seamen, and an opportunity has been afforded them, by purchasing small shares of vessels manned by themselves, of investing, to the greatest advantage, the profits of their severe labours in remoter climates.* When we also take into consideration, the improved state of our coasting navigation, it may justify the expectation, that, from this northern source, an economical and nutritious food may eventually come within the reach of the populous districts of our manufacturing counties, the alleviation of whose wants has always actively engaged the attention of the most enlightened of our countrymen.

HELGA WATER.

A mile or two to the north west of Hillswick, among the hills, is a very small pool named Helga Water, or the Water of Health. The reverence that was anciently paid to lakes or wells for their supposed sanative virtues, forms a striking feature of the early supersition of Orkney and Shetland. It was probably derived from the dry and parched countries of the east, being early perpetuated by the Asiatic followers of Odin, in connection with the bubbling streams that issue from the less arid soil in Europe; or probably the Scandinavians might have copied the supersition from the Celts, who paid homage to a peculiar god that presided over all the waters, under the name of Niord or Neith. In Shetland he was recognised by the name of the *Shoopiltee*. While the Romans confined the dominion of Neptune to the seas, and gave the guardianship of wells and fountains to Nymphs, in honour of whom they instituted certain festivals named Fontinalia, the water-god of the Celtic and Teutonic tribes had not only a controul over the sea, but over all rivers, lakes, brooks, and springs. *Neckar* (as the deity was named in the north of Europe) was wont to assume the form of various animals, also of a horseman, or of a man in a boat.

---

* It is worthy of remark, that several of the vessels which have fished this season, have, for their joint proprietors, sailors who have saved a little money in the navy or in the Greenland fishery. In Scalloway, a company of this deserving class of people were highly successful in the prosecution of their new object.

In Orkney, the same spirit, under a different appellation, had something of a human shape, though inclined to the nature of a horse, and was decked with fuci and other productions of the sea:* in Shetland, he took the decided form of a shelty, making his most frequent haunts near water-mills, but when observed, hastily withdrawing himself into a burn, or vanishing in a flash of fire.

This deity, or water-trow, is the same to whom the Edda recommends the offering of a prayer for success in navigation, hunting and fishing, since he gives to his votaries treasures, and even kingdoms. The inhabitants of Lewis formerly sacrificed to him, in the hopes that he would send them plenty of sea-ware, for the purpose of enriching their ground. But although he figures away with the northern mythologists as the ruler of winds, of waves, and of fire, his goodness was ever considered no less uncertain than the deceitful elements over which he had command. The Scandinavians, therefore, denied that he was of the true lineage of the gods, but deemed it prudent that some token of submission, though it might be of the smallest value, should be made to him on account of his power. In St Kilda, it consisted of shells, pebbles, worn-out rags, pins, rusty nails, or some mean description of currency. The Lewismen, with more liberality, cast into the sea, at Hallowtide, a cup of good ale. In Unst, it was customary to repair to the head of a stream, named Yelaburn, or the Burn of Health, and to throw, as an acknowledgment to the water-god, three stones on an adjoining site of ground. The pool of Helga Water also appears to have been formerly visited by the natives with superstitious views, and with perhaps the same mysterious ceremonies that were used from time immemorial in Orkney, such as walking round it in the course of the sun, observing strict silence in their perambulations, taking up water in their hands, and casting it on their heads. But when Christianity was introduced into the country, and when the priests found it impossible to root from the people their ancient Pagan customs, it is not unlikely that they took away the government of this pool from a water-deity, and gave it to some favourite saint. Thus there is a rude stone, with a small cavity in it, probably a natural one, that held water, which might have been sanctified with Christian ceremony, in order to repay the pilgrimage made to it by the zealous imbiber.

The water deity of the Celts and Teutones was ever regarded with great alarm. It was a popular superstition, that when a person fell into the water, the lips of this god were applied to his nostrils, and through such a conveyance his blood was sucked out; hence the redness that appears in the face of drowned persons. On account, therefore, of these destructive propensities, a Teutonic name was awarded to him of Nocka, Nickur, or Necker, answering to the Latin *necare*, and giving origin, as many profound antiquarians have supposed, to the name of *Old Nick*, that the English have so long applied to the devil. In Scotland, the appearance of this demoniacal Neptune is always considered as a prognostication of the swelling of rivers, and of deaths taking place from drowning; it is then that he

---

* In Ben's Description of Orkney, written A.D. 1529, the god is thus described: "Initus est algis marinis toto corpore, similis est pullo equino convoluto pilis, membrum habet simile equino et testiculos magnos." An exquisite story is at the same time told of the addresses which he paid to a female of Stronsay: "Mulier illic erat formosa maritata colono forti; ipsa verebatur spiritu maximo, invito marito, concubantibus in uno thoro, et naturaliter concubuit cum muliere ut videbatur. Mulier tandem macera facta est præ dolore. Hortatus sum ut vacaret precatione eleemosyna et jejunio quod et fecit; durante anno siccine turbata est."—Barry's Orkney, p. 435.

comes under various shapes, such as the river-horse, or the bull of the waters. In Shetland, the same deity, the Shoopiltee, assumes the form of a beautiful shelty, inviting some one to mount him, when he immediately runs into the sea and drowns his rider.

When the warlocks of Shetland communed with various demons, known by the name of Sea-trows and Land-trows, the beneficial acquaintance of an unearthly nature would be made with the Shoopiltee. John Sutherland, for instance, of Papa Stour, who, not half a century ago, was accustomed, at the distant Haaf, to haul up, whenever he was hungry, a cod ready dressed, was perhaps indebted to his friendship with this water-trow, for his demoniacal repast.

TANGWICK TO ROENESS VOE.

Tangwick, lying to the west of Hillswick, was, when I visited it, the residence of Mr Cheyne, the representative of an ancient respectable family that settled in Shetland from Aberdeenshire.* The shores near Tangwick are low; farther to the west, as we approach Stenness, Dorcholm rises from the surface of the sea, hollowed out on the west by the incessant action of the waves and atmospheric elements, into a spacious arch 70 feet high. The holm is visited by the black and white gull, the puffin *(Alca Arctica)*, and the kittywake. Farther west, dark reddish rocks of secondary porphyry are formed by the sea into steep cliffs, and on approaching Stenness, a considerable number of the rude lodges of fishermen, overtopped with a factor's booth, rise above the black crags that line the coast. The Isle of Stenness, and the Skerry of Eshaness, appear at a short distance, exposed to the uncontrolled fury of the Western Ocean. The isle presents a scene of unequalled desolation. In stormy winters, huge blocks of stones are overturned, or are removed far from their native beds, and hurried up a slight acclivity to a distance almost incredible. In the winter of 1802, a tabular-shaped mass, 8 feet 2 inches by 7 feet, and 5 feet 1 inch thick, was dislodged from its bed, and removed to a distance of from 80 to 90 feet. I measured the recent bed from which a block had been carried away the preceding winter (A.D. 1818), and found it to be 17½ feet by 7 feet, and the depth 2 feet 8 inches. The removed mass had been borne to a distance of 30 feet, when it was shivered into thirteen or more lesser fragments, some of which were carried still farther, from 30 to 120 feet. A block 9 feet 2 inches by 6½ feet, and 4 feet thick, was hurried up the acclivity to a distance of 150 feet. Such is the devastation that has taken place amidst this wreck of nature. Close to the Isle of Stenness is the Skerry of Eshaness, formidably rising from the sea, and shewing on its westerly side a steep precipice, against which all the force of the Atlantic seems to have been expended: it affords a refuge for myriads of kittiwakes, whose shrill cries, mingling with the dashing of the waters, wildly accord with the terrific scene that is presented on every side.

---

* This gentleman, since I left Shetland, died at a very advanced age. His memory will ever be held dear in the country, for the judicious and kind treatment he shewed to his tenantry, and for the proof that he established of the effects which a liberal treatment to dependents might have in increasing their active and industrious spirit; the result having been alike beneficial to both landlord and tenant.

TANGWICK TO ROENESS VOE.

The fishing station of Stenness is occupied by the tenants of Messrs Cheyne, who, from the liberal manner in which they are treated, bear the character of being the best fishermen in the country. About seventy boats are annually employed at the Stenness Haaf. It is computed, that between the middle of May and the 12th of August, when the ling fishery ceases, a boat makes about eighteen trips to the Haaf. Most of the ling, cod, and tusk that are cured in Northmavine go to Ireland ; other markets are found for them by Scottish and English merchants, in Barcelona, Lisbon, Ancona, and Hamburgh. The dangers that the boats run at the Haaf have often suggested the expediency of employing small decked vessels for the fishery. Accordingly, there was an undertaking of this kind set on foot about half a century ago, but it was in every respect ill managed, and failed.

Leaving Eshaness, where may be observed an immense block of granite, not less than three yards in diameter, thrown up by the sea, I pursued my way north, along a high gradually ascending ridge that impends the ocean, which is covered by the finest and softest sward that ever refreshed the tired feet of the traveller, being frequently resorted to by the inhabitants of Northmavine, on a fine Sabbath evening, as a sort of promenade. The verdure that embroiders this proud bank, on which numerous sheep continually feed, pleasingly harmonizes, on a calm day, with the glassy surface of the wide Atlantic ; nor is the pleasure less perfect, when the smooth coating of so luxuriant a green turf is contrasted with the naked red crags that form the precipice below, whitened with the spray of the breakers which continually dash against them with angry roaring. The rich surface of pasture that thus gradually shelves from the elevated ridge of the coast, bears the name of the Villans of Ure ;—and well might we apply to this favoured spot of Thule, the compliment that has been often paid to some rich vale of England,—" Fairies joy in its soil." After a distance of three miles, this gladdening prospect of fertility is suddenly closed with the harsher features that Hialtland usually wears. Near the mountain lake of Houland, where a burgh built on a holm close to its shore displays its mouldering walls, the coast resumes its wild aspect.

A large cavernous aperture, ninety feet wide, shows the commencement of two contiguous immense perforations, named the Holes of Scraada, where, in one of them that runs 250 feet into the land, the sea flows to its utmost extremity. Each has an opening at a distance from the ocean, by which the light of the sun is partially admitted. Farther north, other ravages of the ocean are displayed. A mass of rock, the average dimensions of which may perhaps be rated at twelve or thirteen feet square, and four and a half or five feet in thickness, was first moved from its bed, about 50 years ago, to a distance of thirty feet, and has since been twice turned over. But the most sublime scene is where a mural pile of porphyry, escaping the process of disintegration that is devastating the coast, appears to have been left as a sort of rampart against the inroads of the ocean ;—the Atlantic, when provoked by wintry gales, batters against it with all the force of real artillery,—the waves having in their repeated assaults forced for themselves an entrance. This breach, named the Grind of the Navir, is widened every winter by the overwhelming surge, that, finding a passage through it, separates large stones from its side, and forces them to a distance of no less than 180 feet. In two or three spots, the fragments which have been detached are brought together in immense heaps, that appear as an accumulation of cubical masses, the product of some quarry. *(See Plate V.)*

From Navir I returned to Tangwick, with the intent to pursue my journey the following day farther north, to Roeness Voe, and in my way passed Cross Kirk, now almost erased to the ground, which was one of the most famous kirks in Shetland. Orkney and Shetland were very late in embracing the tenets of Christianity. The first person commissioned by Olaus, King of Norway, to baptize the pagans of Hialtland, was Sigismund Bretteson, a hero of Feroe, whom the Scalds, in marvellous stories of his prowess, have celebrated in their songs. But the light of Christianity was at first feebly opposed to the phantoms of the Scandinavian mythology. The temples at Unst and at other places dedicated to Odin, or to Thor, long retained their influence over the popular mind. In Orkney, it was customary, even in the last century, for lovers to meet within the large circle of stones that had been in the earliest times dedicated to the chief of the Scandinavian gods. Through a large hole in one of the pillars, the hands of the contracting parties were joined, and the faith they plighted was named the promise of Odin, to violate which was infamous. The chief Christian Saint of Orkney and Shetland was Magnus, once partaker, in the 13th century, with Hacon, his cousin, in the earldom of Orkney. He was a meek ruler, worthy a throne in the period of the Millenium, since he refused to fight against men from whom he had received no injury. Hacon was his deadly foe, and Magnus, attended with unarmed men of peace, went to meet him, by appointment, in an island of Orkney, hoping for conciliation, while Hacon repaired thither, with warriors well accoutred, and instantly doomed his cousin to death. Vainly did the pious Magnus entreat that his adversary would not by such an act lose the protection of heaven—recommending him to pronounce a sentence of banishment—of imprisonment for life, conjoined even with the mutilation of limbs, or the privation of sight,—any thing, rather than take away an innocent life. Hacon was inexorable; his victim then, with all the fortitude of a martyr, bent forward his head, and an executioner cut it off at a single blow. After his death, he was sainted by the Pope; a grand cathedral was dedicated to him in Kirkwall, and numbers repaired to his tomb, where, with the assistance of proper oblations and ceremonies, they were cured of their diseases.*

All the ecclesiastical buildings of Shetland appear to have been devoid of the least show and ornament, the ingenuity of the architect extending little farther than in constructing a round vaulted roof. The pointed arch, the pinnacled buttress, or the rich stone canopy, never dignified the chapels of humble Hialtland. The number of them, however, was remarkably great. The parish of Yell, for instance, boasted twenty chapels, when only two or three are used at the present day. Many of these buildings may be attributed to wealthy udallers, who generally had a private oratory contiguous to their dwellings; others were erected by foreign seamen, in fulfilment of their vows to some tutelar saint, who had been miraculously preserved on these dreaded shores from shipwreck or from death. They

---

* Among those in Hialtland who were miraculously healed by the interference of the Saint, the names are recorded in the Orkneyinga Saga of Bergfinr, Amundi Illhugason, Sigurdr Tandrasonn of Dale, Thorbiorn Olafson, Sigridr daughter of Sigurdar of Sanud, Sigridr daughter of Arnfridar of Unustadir, and Sigridr of Aumstr.

were variously dedicated to Our Lady, to St Olla, to St Magnus, to St Lawrence, to St John, to St Paul, or to St Sineva.

Orkney and Shetland were late in receiving the Reformed Religion; and when at length it was ungraciously introduced by such an unworthy professor of it as Lord Robert Stewart, the cidevant Abbot of Holyrood, no wonder that it should be necessary, at a very late period, to issue out acts in Kirkwall, forbidding, under severe penalties, all idolatry, such as walks and pilgrimages. In the commencement of the last century, many Romish Festivals were still preserved, particularly those of Halloween, of St John's Mass, or of Whitsuntide. The people had their fasts, in which they eat fish, or, in conformity with an ancient church decree, they indulged themselves with the flesh of seals, which was admitted as a lawful substitute, whenever it could be proved, that these animals, in having been pursued, had betaken themselves for safety to sea, in preference to dry land. But the greatest complaint that the clergymen of the Reformed Religion had to make against their parishioners, was for their labour in preserving the old chapels that had been dedicated to particular saints, or had been connected with the solemnization of Catholic Festivals, that were held in abhorrence by the minister of the New Light. They were resorted to so late as the beginning of the last century, upon every Easter Sunday, or during Lent. It was therefore recommended, that, in order to purify these northern islands from the sour dregs of Popish superstition and idolatry, all the old chapels should be rased, which might prove as the taking away of a nest egg. Cross-Kirk in Northmavine had been one of the most noted edifices in Shetland, for the superstitious reverence that was long paid to its vacant walls. The devotee cast among the ruins of the church, as a religious offering, a small image of silver, representing any particular part of his body, that might be afflicted with illness:— a recovery was then fully anticipated. Even the shell-snails that infested the walls, were supposed to be possessed of particular healing powers;—they were dried, pulverised and administered for the cure of jaundice. It was customary, long after the abolition of Popery, to walk at Candlesmas to the chapel, in the dead of night, with lighted candles; this being the ceremony used in memory of Christ, the Spiritual Light. The tapers thus solemnised, would, no doubt, be converted to the popular use which their well known virtues throughout all Christendom have from time immemorial suggested; they would be lighted up whenever thunder was heard, or the malevolence of demons was apprehended. But at length came Mr Hercules Sinclair, minister of Northmavine, mighty and fervent in zeal against all idolatry, who, by rasing Cross-Kirk to the ground, succeeded, as Brand supposed, in making the people of Northmavine more civilised than the rest of their neighbours. The crews of the numerous French privateers, also, who, a century ago, landed in different parts of the country, were coadjutors in so holy a work. They found the old chapels very convenient, in a country like Shetland destitute of trees, for affording them a supply of fire-wood, and, therefore, readily assisted in the pious labour of demolition.

There is a gravestone in Cross-Kirk which I overlooked, that contains a Runic inscription. The copy of it, for which I am indebted to the MS. Tour of the late Mr Low, appears in the Plate of Antiquities, at the end of this work.

After again visiting Navir, I arrived at Hamna Voe, a small but safe harbour, that extends a mile and a half into the land, where the Messrs Cheyne have a factor's booth for the curing of ling; here also are a few fishing-lodges. The remains of three upright stones denote *The Giant's Grave*, respecting which tradition is silent. It is said, that an ancient weapon was found in this vicinity, which, by the Antiquaries of Edinburgh, was pronounced to be a Roman Pugio. But the shores of Hamna Voe deserves the most particular notice, for giving birth to a native practitioner of medicine, who well deserves the erection of a monument to his name, for his successful treatment of the small-pox. This disease, which in its dreaded visits, had periodically appeared once in about twenty years, committed great ravages in Shetland. Brand was told a centuary ago, that upon its occurrence, a third of the inhabitants had died of this complaint. Mr Bruce of Urie estimated the number, forty years ago, at a sixth. Not very long ago started up a successful inoculator for variola, in the person of John Williamson of Hamna Voe, who, without recommending that any medicines should be given as preparatory to the infection, or even during its progress, proposed to use matter that had been deprived of its virulence, by being first dried in peat-smoke,--then covered with camphor,--buried in the earth, and retained in this situation for so long a period as seven or eight years. In the application of it, he carefully raised with a knife, a very little of the outer skin of the arm, so that no blood should follow, and insinuated beneath it, the smallest possible portion of the virus, healing the wound with a common cabbage leaf. It was confidently maintained by the Reverend Mr Dishington of Yell, who published this account, that several thousand persons were thus inoculated, without the loss of a single patient; and that there was not an instance in which the infection had not taken place, and made its appearance at the usual time.

The large tract of country that lies between Hamna Voe and Roeness Voe is devoid of the smallest degree of interest. Its banks are indented by the sea into numerous gios; and its hills are long, irregular, bleak and uninhabited. From Roeness Voe I returned to Hillswick, with the intention to take my leave of Northmavine; not, however, without feeling the deepest obligations to Messrs Cheyne, for the unremitting attention paid me, during the long period that I was employed in examining the geology of the parish.

HILLSWICK TO MAVIS GRIND.

From Hillswick Ness to Mavis Grind, a distance of eight miles, a wild tract of hills is exhibited, not gentle in their ascent, but broken into numerous small craggy eminences, thinly inhabited. Every height we ascend shews some new mountain lake, or on the coast some deep indentation and extensive voe winding far into the land. Near Magnussetter Voe, appears the small holm of Eagleshaw, where a perpendicular vein of greenstone, softer than the included mass of the same kind within which it is contained, has yielded to a process of disintegration, so as to convey the idea of a deep rent, dividing the island into two unequal parts. This appearance has given birth to a monstrous tale. The two sons of a deceased udaller, in sharing their father's money between them, made use of a cylindrical wooden vessel, named a *cog*, which, being unequally divided within, by means of a transverse piece of wood, formed, when turned on one end, double the measure that it was when resting on the opposite margin. The younger son was blind, and the elder, in dealing out the respective shares, clandestinely contrived to fill the greater measure for himself, and the smaller one for his brother. "You have now your share of the money," said the heir whose eyes were perfect. "I doubt it," said the blind one, "and may the Lord divide Eagleshaw to-morrow as you have divided the money to-day." The defrauded son had his wish. After a horrible night of thunder and lightning, the island was found in the morning split across by a deep rent into two parts, one of which was just twice the size of the other.

Arriving at Mavis Grind, I took my leave of Northmavine, a parish inhabited by an honest, enterprising, industrious, and civil people; which is saying much, considering the fate that has attended the provisions made by the country for the preservation of morals. During the seventeenth century, whenever the ranselmen heard that there was any discord or unbecoming carriage between husband and wife, parent and child, master and servant, or any quarrels or scolding, he entered the house of the parties offending, rebuked them, and, if his advice was unheeded, made a report of the domestic irregularity to the Bailiff.* Yet strange to say, the landholders, in the year 1725, did not think the acts that concerned domestic morals half strict enough; they accused the country, at the same time, of all manner of vices, as Sabbath-breaking, cursing, lying, fornication, malice, covetousness, drunkenness, and abominable feuds between husband and wife. These they referred to a neglect of religion and education, a fulness of bread, indifference of the civil officers and ministers to their duty, and early marriages without means of subsistence. They complained that Shetland was in a difficulty for the want of servants, which they conceived was owing to the poverty of masters, who, on that account, could not afford to give their dependents proper instruction. For all these reasons, they formed the ranselmen and elders of each district into a society, for the regulation of servants and the reformation of manners, with the power of inflicting penalties for offences; three of their number being a quorum. The officious and consequential ranselman could now boast additional and most extraordinary powers: he could settle, with two of his compeers, every dispute between master and servant; he could determine the number and character of those who ought to be kept; he could dismiss from a house any dependent whose services he conceived were superfluous, or he could transfer him to another family, who were in greater want of an assistant. The ranselman could dictate to the poor father of a family, how many children he might retain in his house for the purpose of assisting age and weakness; or he could prevent any servant after having left his place, from engaging himself elsewhere, without a certificate of proper conduct from the society for the reformation of manners; he could,

---

* This judge, when charges of scolding or abusive language came before him, had the power of punishing it with a penalty of £3 Scots, or of treating the delinquent more severely, if a perpetual scold.

lastly, prevent any stranger from being employed without a testimonial in his favour from the elders and ranselmen of his own parish.

It is almost useless to inquire what must be the fate of such inquisitorial functions. The society for the reformation of manners, as well as the ancient ranselman, gradually fell into contempt. Under such circumstances, a complete laxity of morals must have ensued, if the clergymen of the country had not availed themselves of the opportunity afforded them of exercising their own proper province,—of succeeding to the duty of correcting domestic immoralities, which had been improperly entrusted to a civil officer. The increased influence which the minister has since possessed, appears, however, to have been in no small degree strengthened by kirk-sessions, and by the heavy penalties of the ancient country acts denounced against such offences as profane cursing and swearing, violations of the Sabbath, or the refusal of a householder to afford his family instructions in religion and morality. But this ascendancy, as I have had frequent occasion to witness, has been no less maintained by the attention that the pastor pays to his parishioners, in giving them solace or assistance, during hours of distress or sickness. The reverence with which he is consequently held among the people, of whom he is a real guardian, has rendered the occasional public censures which he bestows, a punishment of the most dreaded kind, and highly effective among detached islands, that, from the frequent absence of landed possessors of civil rank, cannot be otherwise under proper controul. I have, indeed, no where seen more discreet and orderly parishioners than are to be found in Shetland.*

The cause of education has never met with liberal encouragement in Shetland. A century ago, there was not even a school for the wealthier classes, "whereby," said Brand, "many promising and pregnant ingenys were lost;" but shortly afterwards, the poor were taught by a master sent over by the Society for the Propagation of Christian Knowledge. In the year 1724, the landholders of the country met and established a school in each parish, obliging parents, under a heavy penalty, to send their children thither. Afterwards, for a long period, the education of the poor was again neglected. At the present day, however, many schools are established in different parts of the country, although some of them appear to be ill attended.

The manner in which the poor are supported merits particular notice. In early times, it was a particular duty of the ranselman to see that there were no vagrant or idle persons in his quarter or district, and he was empowered to order them to service, or to award them punishment. But in cases of real poverty, a mode was adopted, that still prevails. At the present day a parish is divided into a certain number of parts, named Quarters, to each of which the support of a definite number of poor is entrusted. Every householder receives a pauper into his family for a limited number of days and nights, proportional to the amount of the marks of land that he occupies. Thus the poor are continually transferred from house to house. There are also weekly collections and contributions at each sacrament

---

* Twelve ministers constitute the Presbytery of Shetland, and to each of them is entrusted two or three kirks. Their church discipline in kirk-sessions, is constituted by elders, and they send up yearly one of their members as a commissioner to the General Assembly of Scotland. At first, the Presbytery had the power of presentations, but, by the act of Queen Anne restoring patronage, it is devolved to the superior of the country, his choice of ministers to vacant kirks being confirmed by a popular call.

week, from which source raiment is procured for the indigent, or their funeral-expences defrayed. When children have lost their parents, their support is entrusted to some family, the expence of it being defrayed until they are ten years of age, when they are considered as belonging to the house in which they were reared. The extraordinary calamities of individuals are provided for by special collections.

AITHSVOE TO CLOUSETTER.

I again arrived at Aithsvoe, and after visiting Papa Little, inhabited by one or two families, crossed over to the island of Vementry. In this single spot, not more than three miles in length, all the varieties of a Shetland landscape are exhibited,—the fissured cliff, the barren crag or knoll, on which few tufts of vegetation hang,—the low, fertile grassy patch, or the still and dark mountain lake,—the rocky gio deeply indenting the coast, the bold promontory jutting out far into the sea, or the long-winding voe. Vementry is in so many places intersected by its inlets, that Mr Dickson, the intelligent Scottish farmer who occupies the island, has by short dikes from sea to sea, formed many inclosures, convenient for pasturing in them black cattle or sheep. A lofty hill of granite rises on the north, where may be traced the foundation-stones of a round watch-tower, about 15 feet in diameter, containing within it an irregular cavity, that is entered by a strait passage about two feet long and one broad, being narrow near the entrance, but widening out at its opposite extremity:—the length of its internal cavity is ten feet; its narrowest width five, and its greatest ten feet; it appears to have been roofed with large flat pieces of granite. The cavity was probably intended for containing the peat or fuel necessary for lighting a fire to give an alarm in case of invasion. We read in early Orcadian Annals, of a spy being landed on Fair-Isle, who was commissioned to secretly drench the wood with water, which was stored up for the purpose of being kindled, whenever an enemy appeared off the coast. Mr Pennant has remarked, in his Notice of the Shetland Isles, that the Norwegians had anciently their *ward-madher*, or watch-man, a sort of centinel who stood on the top of a Vord Hill, and challenged all that came in sight. In Orkney, so late as the 17th century, it was ordered, that every bailiff should, in his respective district, have a signal of this kind, and that when a blaze was seen on Whiteford Hill, each should fire the beacon of his own watch.

In returning to Aithsvoe, I was induced to ascend the lofty eminence of Scallowfield, from which the prospect is in most directions confined, except on the west, where a succession of barren and naked eminences arose, while the waters of distant lakes appeared more than usually dark and gloomy. This was the district I was now about to visit; but to explore the strata of such a wild tract, the geognost ought to be endowed with a more than common share of petromania:—

> " And hither to approach he will not dare,
> Where deserts, rocks, and hills no succour give,

"Where desolation and no comforts are,
Where few can do no good, many not live.
Besides, we have the ocean to prepare
Some other place if this should not relieve."

I proceeded to the hill of Aithsness, where a greater quantity of bog iron-ore occurs than is often to be seen in the country, and became the *opgester* or inmate of a farmer of that place. His house was situated on the south side of the hill of Aithsness, upon the brow of the acclivity. A steep brown hill rose to the north, washed at its base by a transparent pool. The farm-house was built of the rough unhewn stones of the country; much green outfield, well cultivated, appearing in various patches along the valley. Stone-dikes ran around the dwelling in a zig-zag direction, enclosing it like so many outworks of a fortification. On a small adjoining eminence were the remains of a skeo, where was once prepared the blown fish and vivda that furnished a delicious repast for the ancient udaller. Before the door were placed a few stepping stones, somewhat difficult to trace, and intended to prevent a plunge, knee-deep, into the immense bed of compost that lay reeking all around. The visitor, after entering a dark and gloomy byre which forms a part of the tenement, after grazing the heels of the cows on the left of him, and feeling carefully along the surface of a partition to his right, may detect the latch of a door that leads to a spacious apartment containing a fire-place in the middle of it, — where the floor is of clay, — where the walls are thickly coated over with soot, — where are two long forms, on which the servants of each sex are seated, the mistress of the house being distinguished by a high and separate chair, where, in one coner, is a favourite calf quietly regaling itself with a bowl of milk, — and where are two or three surly had-dogs stretched on the hearth, perfectly happy in the society of a miraculous quantity of cocks, hens, and chickens, a sow and a playful litter of young ones. A rude partition divides, from the main room, a small private apartment, including within the recesses of its walls two or three press beds. The state dormitory, however, reserved for the opgester, is reached by scaling a wooden ladder, on each side of which are stored barrels of meal or oats, dusty tows, fishing-nets, sillock-rods, and various kinds of hand-lines; the middle of the room being reserved for a curtainless bed. There may the inmate, after commending himself to the guardianship of all good spirits, consign himself to repose, and rise in the morning cheered by the unobstructed rays of the sun, that light the room from an open fissure in the roof.

West from Aithsness is Uyea Sound, a channel two miles and a half in extent, which, in its tortuous course, winds around the extended base of the island of Vementry, often gliding through the straitened confines of protruding capes, or emerging in a proud sweep, so as at length to join the wide expanse of the Bay of St Magnus. These shores afford numerous coverts for sea-otters, whose skins were once in great requisition as an article of commerce by the Hamburghers. Their food, which they collect from the sea, principally consists of the conger eel. At Sonsoness, the winding voes and clear lakes of Clousetter, are wildly disordered by the irregular encroachments of the hills among which they run. Nature, from mere rocks and water, without the assistance of a single tree, has presented ceaseless varieties of interesting scenery. Nunsburgh, a bold eminence, rises to the west of Clousetter; the fortalice which gives rise to its name, being almost wholly rased. From this hill, I was compelled, by a heavy shower of hail and rain, attended with lightning uncommonly vivid, and loud thunder that rolled awfully among the hills, hastily to cross the channel of Onzie Firth, and seek for shelter until the weather cleared, at a cottage near Brindaster. Along this part of the coast, several wretched dwellings are interspersed, where a melancholy want of cleanliness prevails, which is a too general characteristic of the hovels of Thule. The fairies of the hills, numerous as they are, have never inculcated among the peasants those notions of cleanliness, that in early times recommended them to the notable English housewife:

> " Within one of these rounds was to be seen,
> A hillock rise, where oft the Fairie Queen
> At twilight sate, and did command her elves
> To pinch those maids that had not swept their shelves."

ONZIE FIRTH TO NORBAY.

The aspect of this part of Aithsting is of the most rugged description. From the surface of Onzie Firth, low rocks and dangerous shoals arise, while on each side oozy pools or creeks, replenished every tide, named *vaddles*, find for themselves channels among irregular brown hills of heath.

During the preceding winter a fever had raged in the cottages of this place, and owing to their construction, by which air was too much excluded, the disease proved fatal to many. In some instances, every member of a family would be attacked with Typhus; and as the dread of the contagion that prevailed in the country was very great, the attendance which a sickbed demanded could not be obtained from neighbours.* The situation of a family thus left without succour to linger or perish, is too painful to contemplate. That cases of this sort have too often occurred, I had the opportunity of learning. Nor is the assistance of a medical man always to be obtained, for when patients do not live on the Mainland, but in detached islands, ferries must be crossed, upon which no boat in winter could with the least chance of safety venture. It would, on all these accounts, be an act of great humanity, if, on the recurrence of fever, a few well aired rooms could be economically fitted up, and provided with a nurse or two, to which patients of this kind might be removed. The expence to a parish in procuring attendance and rooms of this kind would be so trifling, as not to merit the smallest degree of notice, when contemplated in reference to the great service which it might render. In the report of the Agricultural Society of Shetland, it appears that Mr Spence and Dr Scott, two eminent medical gentlemen in Lerwick, had formed a plan for the establishment of a Public Dispensary. Nowhere would such an institution be more useful than in Shetland, particularly if its effects could be extended to

---

* In an island that I visited, the groans of a man attacked with an inflammation in the bowels, had attracted many neighbours round the house. But as the poor fellow lived in a dwelling where fever had recently raged, no one would come within a hundred yards of it. I was detained in the cottage some time in detracting from the man a quantity of blood, and in coming out of it, was myself in great danger of being shunned, from the fear of the infection which I might spread through the vicinity.

the distant extremities of the country. If it were not indeed for the friendly offices of ministers of parishes, or the principal heritors of the country, who are in the habit of distributing medicines gratis, the poor inhabitants would be still more distressed.

In Shetland there are several native popular medicines. Scurvy grass, for instance, is used in cutaneous complaints, butter-milk in dropsy, the shells of whelks calcined and pounded for dyspepsia, and a variety of steatite named in the country *kleber*, for excoriations. But the mode of letting blood, known from time immemorial, deserves the most particular notice. When the native chirurgeon is called in, he first bathes the part from which the detraction is to be made, with warm water, and then draws forth his cupping machine, which consists of nothing more than the upper part of a ram's horn perforated at the top, and bound round with a soft piece of cotton or woollen rag. In applying it to the skin, he sucks out a little of the included air, takes off the horn, makes upon the surface of the part that has thus been gently raised six or seven slight incisions, again fixes the cupping instrument, freely draws out the air by the reapplication of his lips to it, and, either by insinuating his tongue within the perforation, or by twisting round it a piece of leather or bladder, prevents the ingress of fresh air. He next uses coarse cloths, wrung out with warm water, to stimulate the flowing of the blood, and when the horn is half filled, it leaves the skin and falls down. The same process is repeated several times, until a sufficient depletion has been made. It is worthy of remark, that the African negroes, described by Park, have a similar mode of cupping; but I should pay an undeserved affront to the natives of Thule, by adding, that, on the theory of a philosopher, who maintains that the manners of an uncultivated people are in all periods and countries the same, such a coincidence ought to have been expected.*

In so variable a climate as that of Shetland, Phthisis pulmonalis, pneumonia, croup, and scrofula, are, as we might expect, very frequent. There is a great variety of cutaneous complaints, tinea capitis being the most common. Sibbens, a disease hitherto ill defined, I saw occasionally. Brand describes a leprosy that was very prevalent about a century ago, indicated, as he says, "by the hairs falling from the eye-brows, and the nose falling in." It was considered as infectious, and huts were erected for the reception of the lepers, in order that they might be separated from the rest of the community. Owing to some peculiarity of food, conjoined with the nature of the climate, dyspepsia and liver complaints are very common. If, however, the reports of instances of great longevity are to be depended upon, as they appear in Buchanan's history, or in the statistical accounts of different parishes that have been published, several remarkable ages appear from 90 to 105, and even 120. A native of Walls, of the name of Laurence, is said at the age of 100 to have married a wife, and when 140 years old to have gone out to sea in his little boat. But Brand, the honest missionary, heard of a case far more wonderful;—of a man of the name of Tairville, who lived 180 years, and during all this time never drank beer or ale. He was descended from a family remarkable for their longevity, his father having attained even a greater age than himself.

---

* This native cupping instrument of Shetland, has been well described by Dr Copland in his Disputatio Medica Inauguralis de Rheumatismo, (A.D. 1815), where the effectiveness of this mode of detracting blood is spoken of with much commendation. Dr Scott of Lerwick, who politely presented me with an instrument of this kind, entertains the same sentiment respecting it.

From Onzie Firth, I ascended a high promontory, name the Neing of Brindaster, beset with dangerous islets and stacks, which have too often proved fatal to vessels that have been driven on this insidious shore. The rapacity exercised on such occasions by the natives of this wild district has been often reprobated. Their distant Scandinavian progenitors were little addicted to the vile practice of plundering wrecks. "The Norwegians," says Pennant, "stationed on a ward hill an officer, whom they named a *Gackman*, who was appointed to give notice if he saw a ship in distress; and," adds the same writer, "he was allowed a large horn of generous liquor, which he had always by him, to keep up his spirits." Earl Patrick Stewart, however, issued forth an edict, the most cruel that perhaps ever entered into the code of any despot, imposing a personal punishment, and a fine, the amount of which depended on his own pleasure, upon any one who should be found giving relief to vessels distressed by tempest. It is by no means improbable that so barbarous an edict, thus publicly proclaimed, should have been one of the first causes that produced that insensibility to the crime of stealing from a wreck, which has been transmitted through successive generations to the present sons of Thule. Not long before I visited Onzie Firth, a vessel was stranded in the vicinity. The vultures of the coast immediately flocked to the spot; the master loudly remonstrated against the object of the visit, and maintained that the vessel could be got off: the Shetlanders, on the contrary, as a justification for their meditated plunder, asserted that she came under their peculiar definition of a *wreck*. A scuffle ensued; when the captain, overpowered by numbers, was threatened with death, if he opposed the views of the savage and rapacious multitude by whom he was surrounded. But if the pillage from vessels driven on these shores be reconciled to a Shetlander's conscience as a *god-send*, or, if the pilfering of sheep out of a scathold be considered by him as not belonging to the prohibition contained in the eighth article of the Decalogue, it would be an injustice to his character not to state, that against other temptations to dishonesty, he is proof to a remarkable degree.* It is, in fact, from the earliest period of youth that the Shetlander is taught to regard an attack upon a wreck as no less commendable than was piracy to the ancient Scandinavian sea-kings, one of whom has, by a northern Scald, been thus lauded:

<blockquote>
Tolf vetra nam   At twelve years began
Tyggi at heria.   The king to plunder.
</blockquote>

It is doubtful in what manner the ancient Scandinavian inhabitants of Shetland reimbursed themselves for their exertions to save lives or property when a ship was in danger; but there can be no doubt, that when Earl Patrick became superior of the country, he divided a wreck in the manner most agreeable to him, and without reference to any existing law. When Shetland, however, was in a more settled state, it was ordered that a third of the ship and cargo which might go ashore, should accrue to the proprietor of the ground; a

---

* Not two miles from Onzie Firth, the contents of my trunks, owing to the loss of my keys, were indiscriminately exposed, in a small house, to more than a score of eyes, for several days together, but I was perfectly easy with regard to the safety of my property; nor was I in this, or any other instance of the like kind, deceived in the confidence I had placed in the cottagers of Shetland.

third to the salvers, and a third to the owner ; or in default of claim within the year, to the King.* When the Earl of Morton, was invested with the rights of Admiralty, he, with a great sense of justice, refused to give the proprietor of the ground any greater allowance than was necessary for the damage that he sustained,—this being awarded to him by a Court of Admiralty, as a kind of premium ; at the same time, salvages were rated according to the trouble and charge that had been incurred. I understand, that, at the present day, there is an Admiralty Court empowered to judge all circumstances regarding the wrecks of Shetland, which consists of a judge, a clerk, and a procurator-fiscal. When a wreck happens, and none of the marines are saved, it is the duty of the procurator-fiscal to state the circumstances to the judge, who appoints a person to take charge of what part of the property may remain, to sell it, and publicly to advertise that the proceeds are lodged in court, until an owner appears ; and if, after the lapse of a year and a day, no claim be made, the property devolves to the Admiral.

Burrafiord, an open bay, lies to the west of the Neing, affording no shelter for vessels, containing sunken rocks, and beset on each side by dangerous rocky crags. A burgh, situated in a holm, gives its name to the inlet. This building of uncemented stones has a single wall 13 feet thick, with eleven small round apartments, each of the diameter of 5 feet, which were entered from within the internal area of the burgh ; the roofs of them were not vaulted, but formed of stones, that, projecting over each other, drew to a point. The area included within the fort, was 31 feet. The burgh was well protected by the sea on all sides. *(See Plate of Antiq. Append. Fig. 13.)*

When visiting this Voe, I was, by the extreme lateness of the evening, under the necessity of availing myself of the custom of the country, when a stranger is perplexed for a lodging, which was to seek for hospitality in the nearest convenient house on my way. My boatman led me to a small creek, at the head of Burrafiord, where the setting sun brightened into a fine purple, a wild intermixture of crag and lake. The smoke arose from a low house, built of unhewn stones, after the most ancient fashion of the country ;—it was the *Head Buil* or Manor-house of a small landed possessor of Aithsting, named the Laird of Fogrigate. On opening the door, I passed through a double range of servants of both sexes, who occupied forms disposed along each side of the room, and made suitable obeisance to the *hoy saedet* or high seat of the house, filled by the laird himself, with all the patriarchal dignity worthy that primitive state of manners described in an ancient poem of the 8th century.

Ipse insedit	Meir settizt hann
Medio scamno	Middra fletia
Ad utrumque latus	Enn a' hlid hvara
familia domus	hión salkynna.
	Rigs-Mal.
	Song of King Eric.

---

* This law I was taught three miles west of Onzie Firth. A little girl was tempted, with the offer of a shilling, to take a mile's walk, and find an umbrella for me that I had left on the shore of Kilista Voe. She soon brought it back, with an intimation from her father, that, according to the law of the country, she was entitled to a third of its value for salvage. I next expected a similar demand of a third of this *wreck* from the proprietor of the ground, but the claim was graciously waved.

Native Shetland ale was introduced, which was the first I had tasted in the country. It was not many days old, and had such a pleasant briskness in it that it might have been seasoned with the tops of heather, after the recipe, as learned Antiquaries would tell us, of Pictish Ale. But there was no other ingredient in it except malt;—it was, as an Englishman in Henry the Eighth's time would have said, "As good as the King's ale, for it contained neither hops nor brimstone."* The room to which I was shewn for repose, served the double purpose of being a dormitory for the opgester, and a granary for the family. A quantity of straw was strewed on the floor, and upon this was laid a sufficient number of *kiverins* and blankets, with clean white sheets. The morning was announced by the grinding of the quern. Breakfast was got ready; my trunks furnished me with tea and sugar, and to a thrifty female I was indebted for cakes:—

Protulit tum Edda	Tha tór Edda
Conspectum cinere panem	Okunn leif
Ponderosum et crassum	Thúngann oi thyckvann
Plenum furfuribus.	thrúnginn sádum.
	Song of King Eric.

There are in the vicinity of Burrafiord, a number of families of the name of Doule, descended, as it is said, from a soldier of the clan of M'Dougal (hence the corruption of Doule), who coming over with a party of soldiers in the pay of Cromwell, that garrisoned Scalloway Castle, eventually settled in this secluded district. It was very easy, not many years ago, to know all the native inhabitants of Shetland, since they distinguished themselves from later settlers by retaining in their names the use of patronymics. Thus, if the father's name was William, or Magnus, the son's would be John Williamson, or William Magnusson; and, in the old records of the country, it appears that the names of daughters were subjected to the same rule; there were, for instance, in ancient deeds, such appellations as Madda Scuddadaughter, and Freia Erasmusdaughter.

There is a good estuary on the west of Burrafiord, named Keilester Voe. All this part of the country is rocky and unproductive, yet not lacking cottages and inhabitants, each of the poorest description. Marriages take place, and housekeeping is begun, with little concern for the future. This was attempted to be remedied so early as the year 1680, by a law that might have been dictated by Malthus himself. Every person who had not forty pounds of free gear, or some lawful trade, was forbidden to marry; and none were allowed, under the penalty of ten pounds Scots, to set them house or land. It was formerly the custom for a young married couple to beg from each of their neighbours a supply of domestic articles, as a set-up for housekeeping, but this plan was obviated, by rendering it liable to the rigour of a law that punished with the stocks and juggs all tiggers [or beggars] of wool, corn, fish, &c. whoever they might be, and that inflicted the penalty of ten pounds Scots to any one who might grant them service or hospitality.

---

* In the time of Henry VI. an information was exhibited against a person for putting an unwholesome weed called *An Hopp* into his brewing; and it was a positive order issued to the brewers of Henry the Eighth's household, that there should be neither hops nor brimstone in the King's ale.

The parish of Sandness terminates on the west part of the coast, where is exposed a large valley, that is enriched with several patches of good corn land, and that may boast houses and cottages of a neater appearance than usual, as well as a good parish kirk. It is watered by one or two fresh-water lakes, the largest of which contains a holm, the aviary for myriads of gulls. The high hill of Sandness rises to the south, amidst fogs and vapours. The north of the valley is sheltered by an elevated ridge of land gradually ascending from it; and on attaining the summit of this steep, which is clothed by Nature in her best robe of green, crumbling perpendicular cliffs appear beneath, impendent over a sandy shore; an uninterrupted view is at the same time commanded of the Bay of St Magnus, where, amidst projecting and receding mountains, Roeness Hill towers above the whole. Mr Low was shewn a stone fixed in the wall of the parish kirk of Sandness, of so old a date as to require for its interpretation an antiquary possessed of the accomplishments of a northern hero, who was versed in the knowledge of the newer as well as of the older Runic characters.

En Konr natu minimus
Novit Runas,
Antiquas Runas,
et sui temporis Runas.

Enn Konr vngr
Kunni runar
Ae finn runar
Oc alldr runar.
Song of King Eric.

Mr Pennant, who has shewn a drawing made by Mr Low of this inscription, conceived it to be of a date not later than the tenth or eleventh century. It was one of the commands of Odin, that over the graves of the great, huge heaps of earth should be raised, but that over those who had performed signal achievements, high stones should be erected, inscribed with Runic characters, which ever commanded in Scandinavia a superstitious awe. To add, therefore, to the sanctity of an early Christian Church, the relic of this kind existing in Sandness might have been removed within its pale. It certainly, as Mr Low has asserted, commanded, so late as the last century, a mysterious sort of regard, though unconnected with any tradition relative to its use or origin. In the same period, some relic appeared of the ancient mode in which a respect to Pagan sepultures was testified. "It was usual," said a minister of Unst, "when any one met a funeral, to lift up three clods, and to throw them, one by one, after the corpse."

I was surprised to observe, that, in the kirk-yard of Sandness, no less than in other burying places of Shetland, few or no sepulchral stones should be set up to record the names or virtues of those who were sleeping with their fathers. But, in this neglect, there was much true philosophy:

"Where will you have your virtuous name safe laid,
In gorgeous tombs, in sacred cells secure?
Do you not see those prostrate heaps betray'd
Your father's bones, and could not keep them sure?
And will you trust deceitful stones fair laid,
And think they will be to your honour truer?

> No, no; unsparing time will proudly send
> A warrant unto wrath, that with one frown
> Will all these mock'ries of vain glory rend,
> And make them (as before) ungrac'd, unknown;
> Poor idle honours, that can ill defend
> Your memories, that cannot keep their own."
> DANIEL'S *Musophilus*.

It certainly appears, that while among the Scandinavian inhabitants of Shetland, there are more scanty honorary observances paid to the dead than are preserved by the descendants of Celtic tribes, the superstitious notions entertained on the subject of death are no less few. Second sight has been claimed by none except by a family which is not Norwegian, the representative of whom was always supposed to be gifted by a power of foretelling the time of his own decease.* *Ganfers* or ghosts are, however, very commonly seen, particularly by the sagacious shelty. When a medical gentleman, of the last century, was returning home from visiting a female whom he had left—at least alive, the shelty on which he rode suddenly began to snort and gallop; and on looking behind him to see the cause of the alarm, he saw the spectered form of the patient he had visited, and soon afterwards heard of her death, which took place at the exact time when she took it in her head to frighten the shelty and his rider. There is also a popular belief among the lower class, that if two infants who have got no teeth, meet in the same room, one of them will immediately afterwards die. When a death takes place, there are few or no popular customs observed relating to it, differing from the most familiar ones in Scotland; a plate, as in that country, is set on the body containing salt, the reason for which ceremony it is difficult to explain, unless we admit the force of what a learned expounder has remarked, that "the Devil loveth no salt to his meat, for that is a sign of eternity, and used by God's commandment in all sacrifices."

PAPA STOUR.

I now prepared to set off for Papa Stour, an island deriving its name from certain Irish Papae or Priests, who, in the earliest period of Christianity, either sought in Ireland, as well as in the islands to the north of Britain, places of refuge during some commotion in their country, or came over to propagate the Gospel. In Shetland, three islands bear the name of Papa, the largest of them being named Papa Stour, or the Great Papa.†

The sail from Norbay to Papa Stour is across a very troubled channel, where there is an opposition of tides, occasioned by the meeting of one current that sets into the Bay of St

---

* The last head of this family exercised such a power when he happened to be in a large party of company. He suddenly looked grave, and on being questioned as to the cause of his seriousness, declared that in a fortnight his spirit would be hovering over them in the air. The death took place at the time foretold, as an event, *of course*.

† In the diploma given in Wallace's Orkney, dated A.D. 1406, in order to ascertain the right of William Sinclair to the Earldom of Orkney, there is a very obscure tradition, scarcely deserving the notice bestowed upon it by Antiquaries, on the subject of two nations named the Peti and Papae, who were utterly destroyed by Harold Harfagre. The Papae were the Irish priests; but by the Peti, a race of Picts is understood,—this name being indiscriminately given by the Scotch in the 15th century, to any description of early tribes or nations of whom they had but indistinct traditions. Northern historians assure us, that the people whom Harold subdued were Norwegian pirates.

Magnus, and another into Papa Sound. Houseavoe is indicated at a distance by a plain well-built white house,—by several cottages that line its shores, and by an uninterrupted line of rich arable land. The evening was calm, and so transparent was the water, that our yawl appeared suspended in mid-air, over meadows of yellow, green, or red tangle, glistening with the white shells that clung to their fibres. From the surface of the waters started up red barren stacks of porphyry, scooped by the attrition of the sea into a hundred shapes. One of these insulated rocks, named *Frau-a-Stack*, or the Lady's Stack,—accessible to none but the best of climbers, is crowned on the summit by the remains of a small building, that was originally built by a Norwegian Lady, to preserve herself from the solicitations of suitors, when she had entered into a vow of pure celibacy. The ascent to the house was considered almost unsurmountable, except by the help of ropes. But a dauntless lover, an udaller from Islesburgh, contrived in the dark secrecy of evening to scale the stack, and, after the first surprise was overcome, so far ingratiated himself in the fair devotee's affection, that, in a fatal hour, she was induced

"To trust the opportunity of night,
And the ill counsel of a desart place,
With the rich worth of her virginity."

When the consequence of the Lady's *faux pas* could no longer be concealed, Frau-a-Stack became the scoff of the island, and was deserted by its fair and frail tenant. The house was soon afterwards unroofed and reduced to ruin, in contempt of the vow of chastity that had been broken.*

Another insulated rock rises above the surface of the water, which the sea has worn into long winding caverns. The boat in which I sailed entered a vault involved in gloom, when, after turning an angle, the water began to glitter as if it contained in it different gems, and suddenly a burst of day-light broke in upon us, through an irregular opening at the top of the cave. This perforation, not more than twenty yards in its greatest dimensions, served to light up the entrance to a dark and vaulted den, through which the ripples of the swelling tide were, in their passage, converted by Echo, into low and distant murmurs.

The coast on the south and west of Papa Stour continued to be wild and rugged, where, from low projecting ledges that impended over the sea, the Shetlander might be seen angling for his nightly meal of sillocks :—

"About his head a rocky canopy,
And craggy hangings round a shadow threw,
Rebutting Phœbus' parching fervency ;
Into his bosom zephyr softly flew,
Hard by his feet the sea came waving by,
The while to seas and rocks (poor swain) he sang ;
The while to seas and rocks ans'ring loud echoes rang."

---

* Another tradition is, that an udaller confined his daughter in this rock, in order to prevent her from listening to the solicitations of a favoured suitor; but Love soon scaled the beetling cliff, when the same consequences ensued which befel the Norwegian lady.—I may add, that, steep as the cliff is, it has been scaled by several inhabitants of Papa, and even by a young lady dwelling in the island, who ascended it without the help of a rope.

An inlet, named Hamna Voe, rather difficult of access, affords a secure harbour for vessels. To the north of it high cliffs succeed, which are shaped by the water of the sea into a continual recurrence of excavations. The most remarkable of these is Christie's Hole, which, when surveyed from the summit of a cliff, appears a cavity of some hundred feet deep, and about 120 feet in length, being situated at a distance of 180 feet from the sea. It can be explored by means of a boat,—a labour that is only to be accomplished in the calmest weather. A large arch first presents itself, and, after rowing through dark vaults, the light of the sun bursts in from the lofty opening above;—here the water is said to be several fathoms in depth. The boat then pursues its gloomy course through another extensive perforation, which at length expands into an immense cavern, where the light of the sun is wholly excluded. In the innermost recesses there is a steep beach, which terminates in small dens, where the larger seals and Haaf fish couple, and where the females produce their young and suckle them, until they are able to accompany their dams to sea.

It is customary for two boats' crews of the island of Papa to go to this place, at certain seasons of the year, armed with thick clubs, and well provided with candles. They attack the seals with their weapons, stun them by a blow on the head, and, in this state of insensibility, put them to death. The animals boldly step forward in defence of their young; they face their destroyers, and with their teeth often wrench the clubs out of their enemies' hands. But the attempt is vain; the walls of these gloomy recesses are stained with their blood, and numbers of dead victims are carried off by the boats.

On the north-west of the island, Lyra Skerry, Fugloe Skerry, and other insulated rocks and stacks, rise boldly out of the sea, richly clothed on their summits with stripes of green turf, but presenting perpendicular sides, and entrances into dark caverns, that resemble the vaulted arches of some Gothic crypt. In Lyra Skerry, so named from the multitudes of lyres, or puffins, by which it is frequented, there is a perforation throughout its whole breadth; yet so violent are the currents that force their way through it, that a passage is forbidden to the explorer, except when the ocean shews no sterner wrinkles than are to be found on the surface of some sheltered lake. These stacks are covered with gulls and other sea-birds, but on one of them the sea-eagle has long fixed its aerie. Such is the coast of Papa Stour, which receives additional beauty when the glaring tint of its red rocks has a sombre hue imparted to it by the shades of a declining sun. Nor can there be any greater satisfaction experienced than in viewing this interesting scenery at an hour so late that the smoke of the cottage has become extinct. The twilight of this northern latitude has little of the demureness under which it appears in the south, and a summer's midnight in Thule shews so bright an aspect, that the evening and the morning seem, in the words of a poet, "to melt into each other."

Leaving the north coast of the island, and passing Culia Voe, I arrived at another islet, named Ollas Voe, where there is a factor's booth for curing fish belonging to Mr Gideon Henderson. Two sloops had just arrived from the cod-fishery. The skipper of one of them obstinately persisted in looking for fish in the places to which vessels had been previously accustomed to resort. The other master, who, having formerly belonged to the Royal Navy, was accustomed to adventure, boldly steered at a considerable distance from land to the newly discovered fishing-bank, on which other vessels appeared to have been profitably engaged. The consequent difference of success in each vessel was remarkable. Whilst sympathising in the disappointment which the proprietor experienced in the empty hold of the first sloop which came into the harbour, the subsequent entrance of the other, rich with the product of the new bank, amply compensated for the failure of the less adventurous crew. In returning to Housea Voe, I observed at North House the gateway of an old mansion that belonged to the Mouats of Bauquhally, in Banffshire, where might be traced the armorial bearings of the family, with the inscription "*Monte Alto.*" The kirk, a neat structure, and not very old, is situated near the centre of the island. A merchant, from Holland, gave to it, about a century ago, a bell, a silver cup for the administration of the sacrament, and a curious copper bason for holding water in baptisms, on which appeared several religious emblems. I did not see a stone in the kirk, conceived by Brand to have been the grave-stone of a man of note, but, by another visitant, to been an ancient ship-anchor.

I had at length finished my survey of the Island of Papa Stour, having been hospitably entertained during my stay at the house of Mr Henderson. Among the dainties of a Shetland gentleman's table, the Tusk-fish must be always considered pre-eminent; it is in truth the most delicious of the Gadus species, and Thule no less deserves a pilgrimage to it from the epicure on account of this dish, than Plymouth, for the sake of eating John Dories. Another favourite Shetland dainty is known by the name of *Cropping moggies*, consisting of the liver of the cod mixed with flour and spice, and boiled in the fish's stomach; this preparation, when met with at the houses of the more opulent inhabitants, is excellent;—in the plainer form of *livered moggies*, the flour and spice being absent, it regales the fishermen at their summer lodges. The ancient Scandinavian beverage of *Bland*, prepared from the serum of milk, is met with at almost every house. There is a great variety of shell-fish to be found in Shetland, that might add to the varieties of a table, particularly lobsters, which occur in abundance near Papa Stour, but none of these are very favourite kinds of food.

FESTIVITIES OF SHETLAND.

Papa Stour is the only island in the country where the ancient Norwegian amusement of the *sword-dance* has been preserved, and where it still continues, in Thule, to beguile the tediousness of a long winter's evening. At the shortest day, the sun is not more than five hours and a quarter above the horizon.[*] To dissipate, therefore, the graver phantoms of the night, the careless Shetlander spends, in the conviviality of an assembled party, the hard earnings which he has received for his summer's labours on the seas of Greenland, and it is then that he invokes the spirit of conviviality,

" Whose beauty gilds the more than midnight darkness,
And makes it grateful as the dawn of day."

---

[*] It has been remarked by Mr Mouat, in his Letter to the Highland Society, that the sun is 5 hours and 25 minutes above the horizon, but owing to refraction, the daylight is, in clear weather, prolonged to about 7 hours and a half.

When the ancient udaller gave an entertainment, it was open to the whole country; but strangers from the south, with more rigid notions of economy, corrected the generous custom, by rendering such feasts liable to the scrutinizing influence of the Ranselman or bailiff, who was empowered to levy a fine to the amount of forty shillings Scots upon any one who came to feasts uninvited. Marriages also, which are chiefly contracted during the winter, serve to draw together a large party, who, not many years ago, used to meet on the night before the solemnity took place. It was then usual for the bridegroom to have his feet formally washed in water by his men, though in wealthy houses wine was used for the purpose. A ring was thrown into the tub,—a scramble for it ensued, the finder being the person who would be first married. On the eve before the marriage, the bride and bridegroom were not allowed to sleep under the same roof; and on the wedding-night, the bridegroom's men endeavoured to steal the bride from her maidens, and a similar design on the bridegroom was made by the bride's maids,—kisses being the usual forfeiture exacted from the negligent party. Last of all took place the throwing of the stocking, and, as an old writer styles such kind of amusements, "many other pretty sorceries." The bride, when in bed, threw the stocking of her right foot over her left shoulder, and the individual on whom it fell, was predicted to be the first who should be married. Many of these customs are, however, at the present day, much laid aside; but there is a sport still retained on occasions of festivity, that deserves particular notice.

A martial dance was practised by many early nations, as by the Germans and the Gauls; it was also known to the Curetes or Priests of Cybele. Olaus Magnus, in his account of the manners of the Northmen, describes an ancient military dance as being common to them, which from the illustration he has given of it in a plate, seems to have been achieved by six persons. It was accompanied by a pipe and song,—the music being at first slow, and gradually encreasing in celerity. The dancers held their swords, which were sheathed, in an erect position,—they then danced a triple round,—released their blades from the scabbards,—held them erect,—repeated the triple round,—grasped the hilts and points of each others swords, and extending them, moved gently round,—changed their order, and threw themselves into the figure of a hexagon, named a *rose*. They again, by drawing back and raising their swords, destroyed the figure which they had made, in order that over the head of each other a four-squared rose might be formed. Lastly, they forcibly rattled together the sides of their swords, and by a retrograde movement ended their sport.

The sword-dance performed by the Curetes of Papa Stour, is not unlike that described by Olaus Magnus; but since the residence of Scottish settlers in the country, it has sustained some modification, by being rendered the sequel to a sort of drama performed by seven men, in the characters of the Seven Champions of Christendom. In this state, therefore, it will now be noticed.

We shall suppose Yule to be arrived, which is always announced at break of day by the fiddles striking up the *Day-dawn*, an ancient Norwegian tune, that, being associated with gaiety and festivity, is never heard without emotions of delight. As the evening approaches, piles of turf are lighted up in the apartment where wassail is to be kept; young and old of each sex make their appearance, and, after the whisky has gone liberally round, it is announced that the sword-dancers are making their appearance;

"The actors are at hand, and, by their show,
You shall know all that you are like to know."

The company then seat themselves on the forms, tubs, beds, and benches, that serve the place of chairs, leaving a large space in the middle of the room for the exhibition. The fiddle strike up a Norn melody, and at the sound of it a warrior enters in the character of St George, or the master of Seven Champions of Christendom, a white hempen shirt being thrown over his clothes, intended to represent the ancient shirt of mail that the Northman wore, and a formidable looking sword being girt to his side, constructed from the iron-hoop of a barrel. St George then stalks forward and makes his bow, the music ceasing while he delivers his

PROLOGUE.

"Brave gentles all within this bow'r,   if ye delight in any sport,
Come see me dance upon this floor :—   you, minstrel man, play me a porte."*

The Minstrel strikes up: the master bows and dances.

"Now have I danced with heart and hand,   brave gentles all, as you may see;
For I've been tried in many a land,   in Britain, France, Spain, Italy.
I have been tried with this good sword of steel, yet never did a man yet make me yield."

Draws his sword, flourishes it, and returns it to his side.

"For in my body there is strength,   as by my manhood may be seen :
And I, with this good sword of length,   in perils oftentimes have been.
And over champions was 1 king,   and, by the strength of this right hand,
Once on a day I killed fifteen,   and left them dead upon the land.
Therefore, brave minstrel, do not care,   to play to me a porte most light,
That I no longer may forbear   to dance in all these gentles' sight !"

The Master then bows, and, while the music plays, again dances; and thus, after having "rid his prologue like a rough colt, knowing not the stop,"—he gives notice of the further entertainment that is intended.

"Brave gentles all be not afraid,   although my sight makes you abas'd,
That with me have six champions stay'd,   whom by my manhood I have rais'd.
For since I've danc'd, I think it best   to call my brethren in your sight,
That I may have a little rest,   that they may dance with all their might;

---

* In the 1st volume of the Edinburgh Antiquarian Transactions, p. 486, I find it remarked, that "to the wandering barpers we are indebted for that species of music which is now scarcely known,—I mean *the Port*. Almost every great family had *a port*, that went by the name of the family. Of the few that are still preserved, are Port Lennox, Port Gordon, Port Seton, and Port Athole, which are all of them excellent in their kind. The Port is not of the martial strain of the *march*, as some have conjectured; those above-named being all in the plaintive strain, and modulated for the harp."

And shake their swords of steel so stout, and shew their main strength on this floor,
For we shall have another bout, before we pass out of this bow'r.
Therefore, brave Minstrel, do not care to play to me a porte most light,
That I no longer may forbear to dance in all these gentles' sight."

The Minstrel obeys;—the Master again dances, and then, with much polite discretion, introduces into the room six formidable looking knights, each with a white shirt over his clothes in the place of a shirt of mail, and a good sword girt to his side, their respective names and deeds being announced in well set verse.

"Stout James of Spain, come in our sight, thine acts are known full well indeed,
And champion Dennis, a French knight who shews net either fear or dread.
And David, a brave Welshman born, descended of right noble blood,
And Patrick, too, who blew the horn, an Irish warrior, in the wood.
Of Italy, brave Anthony the good, and Andrew, of fair Scotland knight;—
St George of England here indeed! who to the Jews wrought mickle spite;
Away with this!—Lets come to sport,— since that ye have a mind to war,—
Since that ye have this bargain sought, come let us fight and do not fear.
Therefore, brave Minstrel, do not care to play to me a porte most light,
That I no longer may forbear to dance in all these gentles' sight."

The Master, after shewing his brethren a specimen of the sort of *pas seul* that they will be required to exhibit before the company, draws his sword, and addresses all the Knights in succession.

"Stout James of Spain, both tried and stour, thine acts are known full well indeed,
Present thyself upon the floor and shew not either fear or dread;
Count not on favour for thy meed, since of thy acts thou hast been sure;—
Brave James of Spain, I shall thee lead, to prove thy manhood on the floor!"

James of Spain draws his sword, and on the fiddle being heard, he proves his manhood on the floor by a *pas seul*.

"Stout champion Dennis, a tried knight, as by thy manhood may be seen,
Present thyself here in our sight, thou true French knight that bold hast been;—
Since thou such valiant acts hast done, come let us see some of them now;—
With courtesy, thou brave French knight, draw out thy sword of noble hue."

The Minstrel strikes up; Dennis draws his sword and dances.

"Brave David, a bow must string, and big with awe,
    Set up a wand upon a stand,
And *that* brave David will cleave in twa."

David draws and dances.

"Here is, I think, an Irish knight, to prove himself a valiant man,
Who has not either fear or fright!— Let Patrick dance, then, if he can."

Patrick draws and dances.

SWORD-DANCE.

"Thou stout Italian, come thou here ;   thy name is Anthony most stout,
Draw out thy sword that is most clear,   and fight thou without dread or doubt.
Thy leg shake! bow thy neck thou lout!   some courtesy shew on this floor,
For we shall have another bout   before we pass out of this bow'r."

Anthony draws and dances.

"Thou kindly Scotsman, come thou here;   Andrew's thy name of Scottish land!
Draw out thy sword that is most clear,   and by the strength of thy right hand,
Fight for thy king with all thy heart,   fight to confirm his loyal band,
Make all his enemies to smart,   and leave them dead upon the land."

Andrew draws and dances.

  The Minstrel now flourishes his bow with spirit, and the sword dance commences. The Master gives a signal to his brethren, who stand in rank with their swords reclined on on their right shoulders, while he dances a *pas seul*. He then strikes the sword of James of Spain, who moves out of line, dances and strikes the sword of Dennis; then Dennis sports a toe on the floor, and in the same manner brings David out of line, and thus each champion is successively made to caper about the room.

  The Champions then extend their swords out at full length, when each of them is seen to grasp his own sword with his right hand, and the point of his left hand neighbour's sword with his left hand; and being thus formed into a circle, *hilt and point*, as it is named, they dance a double roundel.

  The Champions hold their swords in a vaulted direction, and, headed by the Master, successively pass under them; they then jump over their swords;—this movement bringing the weapons into a cross position, from which they are released by each dancer passing under his right hand sword. A single roundel, hilt and point, is then performed as before.

  The roundel is interrupted by the Master, who runs under the sword of his right hand, and then jumps over it backwards; his Brethren successively do the same. The Master then passes under his right hand sword, and is followed in this movement by the rest. Thus they continue to dance, until a signal is given by their Director, when they form into a circle, swords tended, and grasping hilt and point as before. After a roundel has been danced, the Champions jump over their right hand sword, by which means their back is to the circle, and their hands across their backs, and in this form they dance round until the Master calls "loose!" They then respectively pass under their right hand swords, and are in a circle as before.

  The Master now lays down his own sword, and seizing hold of the point of James's sword, turns himself, James, and the rest of the champions, into a clue, and the swords being held in a vaulted position, he passes under them, and thus removes out of the circle, being followed in the same manner by the other Knights. A repetition of all, or part of the movements already described, then ensues.

  The Master and his Brethren, in the next place, throw themselves into a circle, each holding his arms across his breast, and with their swords, form a figure intended to represent a shield; this being so compact, that each Champion alternately dances with it upon his head. The shield is then laid down upon the floor, when each Knight, laying hold of the hilt and point which he before held, and placing his arms across his breast, extricates his sword from the shield, by a figure directly opposite to that by which it had been formed.

This movement finishes the Sword-dance. The Master then gravely steps forward and delivers the following

EPILOGUE.

Mars does rule, he bends his brows,   he makes us all aghast ;
After the few hours we stay here,   Venus will rule at last.
Farewell, farewell, brave gentles all,   that herein do remain,
I wish you health and happiness   till I return again.

The whole of the champions then repeat the last verse.

Farewell, farewell, brave gentles all,   that herein do remain,
We wish you health and happiness   till we return again.*

When in frolics and dances, the prophecy of St George has been fulfilled, that "Venus would rule at last," it is not unusual to hear of the announcement of the *guisards*. A number of men enter the room dressed in a fantastic manner, their inner clothes being concealed by a white shirt as a surtout, which is confined, at the waistband, by a short petticoat formed of loose straw, that reaches to the knee. The whole are under the controul of a director, named a *scudler*,† who is distinguished from his comrades by a very high straw cap, the top of which is ornamented with ribbons. He is the proper *arbiter elegentiarum* of his party, regulating their movements, and the order in which they should alternately dance with the females assembled. The amusement thus afforded is the same that may be found in any politer masquerade, since it depends upon the guisards being able to conceal from the company who they are.‡

The great delight, however, of the ancient udaller's convivial hours was in the recitation of Norwegian ballads. Shetland was, from time immemorial, celebrated for its native poets. Ronald, Earl of Orkney, being in the year 1151 shipwrecked near Gulberswick, was visited by two poets, Oddi Glumson the Little, and Armodr. The Earl, who composed verses himself with great fluency and elegance, found them so well skilled in the same art, that he received them among the number of his retainers, and took them with him on his travels to the Holy Land. On the occasion of a public feast, he gave to Armodr, as an acknowledgment for his poetic talents, a golden spear. Not longer ago than seventy years, a number of popular historic ballads existed in Shetland, the last person who

---

* The words of this drama are taken from an official *prompt-book*, for which I am indebted to a lady of the island ; a few glaring interpolations have been omitted, and the words have been corrected according to other recitations.

† An ancient Shetland name given to the pilot of a Scuda or twelve-oared boat.

‡ The custom of paying visits to parties under the disguise of a mask, is delineated in a plate given in Olaus Magnus's History of the Northern Nations. See Olaus Magnus, *di Gentibus Septentrionalibus*. Lib. xiii., cap. 43.

could recite them being William Henry, a farmer of Guttorm, in the island of Foula, who was visited in the year 1774 by Mr Low. "I do not remember," says this tourist, in a letter to Mr George Paton of Edinburgh, preserved in the Advocates' Library, "if I left you a copy of a Norse ballad. I wish you would try if Dr Percy could make any thing of it. If you have no copy, I shall send an exact one, though I cannot depend on the orthography, as I wrote it from an honest country man's mouth, who could neither read nor write, but had the most retentive memory I ever heard of. He, I am afraid, is by this time dead, as he was then old and much decayed; but, when I saw him, he was so much pleased with my curiosity,—and now and then a dram of gin,—that he repeated and sang the whole day." Some kinds of poetry, as the historical ballads and romances, which William Henry could recite, were, as he stated, never sung but on a winter's evening at the fire-side. The subject of one of them, as explained by this aged and last minstrel of Hialtland, was

The Strife of the Earl of Orkney, on account of his Marriage with the King of Norway's daughter.

Hildina, the daughter of the King of Norway, was beloved by Hiluge, a courtier, whose pretensions to her hand, though supported by the approval of the Crown, she discouraged. While this Sovereign, accompanied by his favourite, was engaged in a distant war with some northern potentate, one of the Earls of Orkney, in his rambles on the coast on Norway, met with the fair Princess, and became enamoured of her charms. Nor did his accomplishments obtain for him less favour in the lady's eyes, as she eventually gave her hand to this new lover, and fled with him to the shores of Orkney, in order to avoid the wrath of her sire. When the King, on returning from the wars, had learned what had happened, the daring presumption of the Earl, in obtaining an unsanctioned alliance with the Crown, exasperated him to the greatest degree; while Hiluge felt no less wounded under the poignancy of slighted love. Both were impatient to gratify their revengeful feelings, and, for this purpose, set sail with a strong force, and landed at Orkney. By the persuasion of Hildina, the Earl met her father unarmed, and, throwing himself upon his mercy, eloquently besought from him a reconcilement to the nuptials. The monarch's affection for his daughter, which nothing could wholly subdue, made him relent; but no sooner had his son-in-law left him, to communicate the joyful result of the conference to his spouse, than the courtier, by resorting to all the artful means he could devise, by reminding the King of the affront committed against the royal dignity, succeeded in inducing him to recal his promise of forgiveness. Nothing, then, could prevent the dispute from being decided by the sword alone. Hiluge and the Earl met arm to arm; their combat was desperate, but the contest proved fatal to Orkney's chief, who was cleft to the earth by his fierce and overwhelming adversary. The victor cut off the head of the unfortunate bridegroom, and, bearing away this dreadful signal of his triumph, threw it, bedewed with blood, at Hildina's feet, accompanying the brutal act with the most sarcastic reproaches. The lady, after recovering from the horror with which she was struck at the sight, felt her injured pride return, and told the destroyer, that great as was her affliction for the loss of her husband, the feeling was subordinate to the impatience that she felt under the cruel insult with which her feelings had been mocked. Hildina being compelled to return with her royal father to Norway, was again sought for in marriage by Hiluge, the renewed suit being importunately seconded by the king. The lady thus beset, gave a reluctant consent, requesting, as the slightest of acknowledgments for her concession, that she might be allowed to fill the goblets with wine at her wedding-dinner. A boon so humble was readily granted. The bridal party was assembled, the marriage was solemnized, the banquet prepared, and Hildina, after having secretly drugged the wine that was to be used, poured it into the cups, and presented it to her guests;—its narcotic qualities soon threw the company into a deep slumber, and the lady then began to execute the work of deadly vengeance she had meditated. She first ordered her sleeping father to be conveyed out of the house to a place of safety, and, seizing a lighted brand, set the mansion in flames, and invested it with her dependents to prevent escape. Hiluge, roused by the blaze, saw the treachery, and piteously cried out for mercy. Hildina heard with horrid delight his supplication, and, bitterly returning the taunts he had used while throwing her husband's head at her feet, left the wretched courtier to perish in the flames.*

It was not many years before Mr Low's visit to Shetland in the 1774, that numerous songs, under the name of *Visecks*, formed the accompaniment to dances that would amuse a festival party during a long winter's evening. When the corn-waters of Hamburgh had gone merrily round, the tables labouring, at the same time, under the weight of skeo-dried vivda, sillocks, gammon, and reeked trout,—when the *gue*, an ancient two-stringed violin of the country, was aiding the conviviality of Yule, then would a number of the happy sons and daughters of Hialtland take each other by the hand, and while one of them sang a Norn viseck, they would perform a circular dance, their steps continually changing with the tune. In the middle of the last century, little of the Norwegian language remained in the country, and these visecks being soon lost, they were followed, as a clergyman of Unst informed Mr Low, by playing at cards all night, by drinking Hamburgh waters, and by Scotch dances. The reel, upon being introduced, became highly popular, and a few original melodies adapted to it, were composed by native musicians of Shetland, the most popular of which was the Foula Reel. To this tune a song was afterwards adapted, named the Shaalds of Foula, bearing allusion to a profitable fishery for cod that was long conducted upon those *shaalds* or shoals. The words sufficiently express the freedom with which the cottager spent in the conviviality of a winter, the hard-earned savings of a summer, in the perilous fishery of the haaf.

Weel, since, we are welcome to Yule,	up wi't Lightfoot, link it awa', boys;
Send for a fiddler, play up Foula reel,	we'll skip as light as a maw, boys.

Chorus.

The Shaalds of Foula will pay for a',	up wi't Lightfoot, link it awa', boys;
The Shaalds of Foula will pay for a',	the Shaalds will pay for a', boys.

---

* For an account of the original of this romance, see Note 12, Iter IV.

The Awens are amang the cows in the byre,   up wi't Lightfoot, link it awa', boys;
Link up the pot, and put on a gude fire,   we'll sit till cocks do craw, hoys.
                    The Shaalds of Foula, &c.

Now for a light and a pot of gude beer,   up wi't Lightfoot, link it awa', boys;
We'll drink a gude fishing against the next year,   and the Shaalds will pay for a', boys.
                    The Shaalds of Foula, &c.

VE SKERRIES.

(Including an account of the Superstitions of the Shetland Seas.)

With the intention of visiting the Ve Skerries, I passed several low rocks lying a little below the surface of the water. Inequalities of this kind, named in Shetland *Baas*, and in Feroe Boffves, which interrupt the currents of tide, and raise immense high waves that break, may be found at various depths, some of them having upon them as much as twenty fathoms of water. When the sea is disturbed, the breaking is repeated a few times, said to not exceed seven, and before it recommences, a long interval of stillness succeeds. It is a popular opinion, that the breaking of a Baa may be induced by hot weather;—that when it takes place in calm weather, an approaching storm is indicated, and that though a Baa appear perfectly still, if a boat approach or go over the place where it lies, a breaking, often fatal to the crew, immediately ensues.* Debes notices the latter circumstance, and with much ingenuity supposes, that a magnetic sympathy possessed by the hidden rock, attracts the iron of the boat, which the shallow water, in its magnetic antipathy, "not being able to endure, riseth itself." I have been assured that the Shetlanders, whose imaginations have conceived of strange wonders in the seas, entertain similar notions of the existence of submarine magnetic rocks. The opinions, indeed, which they entertained during the last century, and which are scarcely forgotten at the present day, of the ocean, or of its inhabitants, have all the wildness in them of the popular notions existing on the same subject among Norwegian fishermen, and are still blended with the mythology of the north. Formerly, whenever a crew at the Haaf met with some immense and unusual visitant of the seas, as a finner,† a grampus or a porpoise, it was converted by them into a sea-trow.‡ The kraken or horven, which appears like a floating island, sending forth tentacula as high as the masts of a ship,§ and the great sea-snake with his formidable mane,‖ are monsters that have

---

* There is a rock near Mavis Grind, named Tairville's Baa, connected with the name of an ancient Norwegian settler, who slew in a deul, fought at Papa Stour, a gentleman of rank, and resistedall the attempts that were made to bring him to a trial for the act, living by depredations in the country. He is said to have perished in a boat with many of his sons, on the Baa that bears his name. Mr Low was shewn in Papa Stour a circular inclosure of stones, where the duel alluded to was said to have been fought.

† The Finner of Shetland may consist of the Balaenoptera gibbar, the Jubartes or Rorqual of La Cepede. One of the latter kind was killed in Balta Sound, A.D. 1817.

‡ Brand describes certain sea-trows as great rolling creatures tumbling in the water. Some of them, adds the same author, come among the fishermen's nets, break them and take them away.

§ A few years since, an affidavit was taken by a Justice of the Peace in Shetland, relative to a monster of this kind, that was seen at a distance from the shore off the island of Burra. It appeared, said the men, like the hull of a large ship, but on approaching it nearer, they saw that it was infinitely larger, and resembled the back of a monster. It is also said, that part of the remains of a dead kraken were found about 70 years ago driven to the mouth of a large cave in the island of Meikle Roe.

‖ The existence of the sea-snake,—a monster fifty-five feet long, is placed beyond a doubt, by the animal that was thrown on

been occasionally recognised, and their occurrence is much connected with the demonology of the Shetland seas. If we could, indeed, conjure up all the creatures that either do actually exist, or only live in the imagination of the natives, an hideous host of monsters would present themselves in array.

> "Most ugly shapes and horrible aspects,
> Such as Dame Nature's self mote feare to see,
> Or shame that ever should so fowle defects
> From her most cunning hand, escaped bee,
> All dreadful portraicts of deformitee."

The appearance assumed by the malevolent Neptune of the Shetlanders, named the Shoopiltee,* bear a complete or near resemblance to that of a horse. Of mermen and merwoman, many strange stories are told. Beneath the depths of the ocean, an atmosphere exists adapted to the respiring organs of certain beings, resembling, in form, the human race, who are possessed of surpassing beauty, of limited supernatural powers, and liable to the incident of death. They dwell in a wide territory of the globe far below the region of fishes, over which the sea, like the cloudy canopy of our sky, loftily rolls, and they possess habitations constructed of the pearly and coral-line productions of the ocean.† Having lungs not adapted to a watery medium, but to the nature of atmospheric air, it would be impossible for them to pass through the volume of waters that intervenes between the submarine and subra-marine world, if it were not for the extraordinary power that they inherit, of entering the skin of some animal capable of existing in the sea, which they are enabled to occupy by a sort of demoniacal possession. One shape that they put on, is that of an animal human above the waste, yet terminating below in the tail and fins of a fish, but the most favourite form is of the larger seal or Haaf-fish; for, in possessing an amphibious nature, they are enabled not only to exist in the ocean, but to land on some rock, where they frequently lighten themselves of their sea-dress, resume their proper shape, and with much curiosity examine the nature of the upper world belonging to the human race. Unfortunately, however, each merman or merwoman, possess but one skin, enabling the individual to ascend the seas, and if, on visiting the abode of man, the garb should be lost, the hapless being must unavoidably become an inhabitant of our earth.

I effected a landing, not without considerable difficulty, on one of the low rocks that

---

shore in Orkney, the vertebrae of which are to be seen in the Edinburgh Museum. The faith in the Edda of the great serpent that Thor fished for, did not, as Dr Percy conceives, give rise to the notion of the sea-snake, but a real sea-snake was the foundation of the fable. I have heard, in Shetland, of a sea-serpent being seen off the Isle of Stennes, Vailey Island, and Dunrossness.

* Sir Robert Sibbald says, that the Shetlanders "sometimes catch with their nets and hooks Tritons, they call them *Shoupiltins*." This account does not agree with the superstition of the present day. There is only one shoupiltin or shnupiltee, whose character is that of Nickur, the demoniacal Neptune of the North of Europe.

† I could obtain little satisfaction from the Shetlanders relative to the nature of the country beneath the sea; but a native of the Isle of Man once visited it by means of a diving-bell, that drew after it a rope double the distance of the moon from the earth. After passing the region of fishes, he descended into a serene atmosphere, and at length arrived at the bottom of the submarine world, which was paved with coral and unknown shining pebbles, where were large streets and squares on every side, pyramids of crystal, and buildings of mother of pearl. The interior of the houses boasted walls of jasper, floors of diamonds, topazes, and other precious stones, chairs and tables of amber, and comely mermen and pretty mermaids for inhabitants, who were greatly alarmed at the sight of the diving-bell and its occupant.—See Waldron's Isle of Man, and Sir Walter Scott's Minstrelsy of the Scottish Border, vol. iii, p. 300.

forms a part of the Skerries, seven or eight miles north-west of Papa Stour. This is a dangerous reef for vessels,—the sea around being agitated by opposite tides, while in the winter it is so washed over with the waves as to be scarcely visible. From the shelving crags of these Skerries, numerous large seals sought their safety in the ocean, while others less timorous, drew near the boat and gazed at us with attention; but these might have been the disguised submarine inhabitants of ocean's depths,—philosophers, perhaps, in their own world, availing themselves of the opportunity of examining the geognosy of our portion of the earth's crust, and the external characters and habits of the Homo Sapiens of supra-marine systematic writers. The Ve Skerries are, according to popular belief, the particular retreat of the fair sons and daughters of the sea, where they are defended by a raging surf, that continually beats around them, from the obtrusive gaze and interference of mortals; where they release themselves from the skins within which they are inthralled, and, assuming the most exquisite human forms that ever were opposed to earthly eyes, inhale the upper atmosphere destined for the human race, and, by the moon's bright beams, enjoy their midnight revels.

As the green-haired denizens of the ocean are mortal, the visits that they pay the upper world are not always unattended with peril. On the authority of Brand, it appears, that in making their way through the ocean, there was much danger in their being entangled among the meshes spread out for taking herring; in which case they were certain to obtain a sound beating from the fishermen. It often happened, therefore, that they would contrive to break through the nets, or to the vexation of the Shetlanders, bear them away. Sometimes, however, a more disastrous fate attended these beings. A damsel, who, in swimming through the intermediate expanse of the ocean, had assumed the peculiar half-fishy form under which a mermaid in her disguise very frequently appears, was caught by a ling hook that had been laid, which, from the narrative of Brand, appears to have entered her chin, and come out at her upper lip. When she was brought to the side of the boat, one of the crew fearing that her appearance denoted mischief, took out his knife, and stabbed her to the heart;—the luckless mermaiden fell backwards, emitted a mournful cry, and disappeared for ever. The murderer never afterwards prospered in his affairs, but, until his death, was haunted by an old merman, who continually upbraided him with the crime he had committed. But the greatest danger to which these rangers of the sea seem liable, are, from the mortal hurts that they receive, upon taking on themselves the form of the larger seals or Haaf-fish; for when shot under this shape, the blood no sooner issues forth from the wound, and mixes with the ocean's brine, than it possesses the supernatural power of causing an awful swell and break of the sea, in the vicinity of the spot where the victim, from a sense of the pain inflicted, has been seen to dive. On the Ve Skerries, the inhabitants of submarine depths are liable to considerable peril, whenever the natives of Papa Stour repair thither, at certain times of the year, for the purpose of attacking the seals, as they lie in the hollow of a certain crag. A story is told of a boat's crew that landed with this design at one of the Stacks;—they stunned a number of these animals, and, in this state, stripped them of their skins, with the fat attached to them,—left the carcases on the rock, and were about to set off for the shore of Papa Stour, when such a tremendous swell arose, that every one flew quickly to the boat, and were successful in entering it, except one man, who had imprudently lingered behind. The crew were unwilling to leave a companion to perish on the skerries, but the surge increased so fast, that after many unsuccessful attempts to bring the boat close in to the stack the unfortunate wight was left to his fate. A stormy night came on, and the deserted Shetlander saw no prospect before him, but of perishing with cold and hunger, or of being washed into the sea by the breakers which threatened to dash over the rocks. At length, he perceived many of the seals, who, in their flight, had escaped the attack of the boatmen ;—they approached the skerry, disrobed themselves of their amphibious hides, and appeared like the sons and daughters of the ocean. Their first object was to assist in the recovery of their friends, who, having been stunned by clubs, had, in this state, been deprived of their skins. When the flead animal had regained their sensibility, they assumed their proper form of mermen or merwomen, and began to lament in a mournful lay, wildly accompanied by the storm that was raging around, the loss of their sea-dress, which would prevent them from again enjoying their native azure atmosphere, and coral mansions that lay below the deep waters of the Atlantic. But their chief lamentation was for Ollavitinus, the son of Gioga, who, having been striped of his seal's-skin, would be for ever parted from his co-mate, and condemned to be an outcast inhabitant of the upper world. Their song was at length broken off, by observing one of their enemies viewing, with shivering limbs and looks of comfortless despair, the wild waves that dashed over the stack. Gioga immediately conceived the idea of rendering subservient to the advantage of her son the perilous situation of the man. She addressed him with mildness, proposing to carry him safe on her back across the sea to Papa Stour, on condition of receiving the seal-skin of Ollavitinus. A bargain was struck, and Gioga clad herself in her amphibious garb ; but the Shetlander, alarmed at the sight of the stormy main that he was to ride through, prudently begged leave of the matron, for his better preservation, that he might be allowed to cut a few holes in her shoulders and flanks, in order to procure, between the skin and the flesh, a better fastening for his hands and feet. The request being complied with, the man grasped the neck of the seal, and committing himself to her care, she landed him safely at Acres Gio in Papa Stour ; from which place he immediately repaired to a skeo at Hamna Voe, where the skin was deposited, and honourably fulfilled his part of the contract, by affording Gioga the means whereby her son could again revisit the ethereal space over which the sea spread its green mantle.*

Sometimes mermen and merwomen have formed connubial attachments with the human race.† A story is told of an inhabitant of Unst, who, in walking on the sandy margin of a voe, saw a number of these beings dancing by moonlight, and several seal-skins strewed beside them on the ground. At his approach they immediately fled to secure their garbs, and taking upon themselves the form of seals, plunged immediately into the sea. But as the Shetlander perceived that one skin lay close to his feet, he snatched it up, bore

* There is a story that perhaps proceeds from a superstition nearly like this, to be found in the Illustrations of Northern Antiquities, which is derived from the Wilkina Saga. Some merwomen, in going to the Rhine to sport, take off their clothes, and lay them at the water's edge. These are seized by a warrior, who will not restore them but on certain conditions.

† It is said in Ben's Description of Stronsay in Orkney, written A.D. 1529, " Monstri maxinii nomine Troices (trows), sæpissime coeunt cum mulieribus illic colentibus." The belief in such attachments is popular in many countries.

it swiftly away, and placed it in concealment. On returning to the shore, he met the fairest damsel that was ever gazed upon by mortal eyes, lamenting the robbery, by which she should become an exile from her submarine friends, and a tenant of the upper world. Vainly she implored the restitution of her property; the man had drunk deeply of love, and was inexorable,— but offered her protection beneath his roof as his betrothed spouse. The mer lady, perceiving that she must become an inhabitant of the earth, found that she could not do better than accept of the offer. This strange connubial attachment subsisted for many years, and several children were the fruits of it, who retained no farther marks of their origin than in the resemblance which a sort of web between their fingers, and a particular bend of their hands, bore to the fore feet of a seal,—this peculiarity being possessed by the descendants of the family at the present day. The Shetlander's love for his merwife was unbounded; but his affection was coldly returned. The lady would often steal alone to the desert strand, and on a signal being given, a large seal would make his appearance, with whom she would hold, in an unknown tongue, an anxious conference. Years had thus glided away, when it happened that one of the children, in the course of his play, found concealed beneath a stack of corn a seal's skin, and, delighted with the prize, ran with it to his mother. Her eyes glistened with rapture,—she gazed upon it as her own,—as the means by which she could pass through the ocean that led to her native home,— she burst forth into an ecstacy of joy, which was only moderated when she beheld her children, whom she was now about to leave, and, after hastily embracing them, fled with all speed towards the sea-side. The husband immediately returned,—learned the discovery that had taken place, ran to overtake his wife, but only arrived in time to see her transformation of shape completed, to see her, in the form of a seal, bound from the ledge of a rock into the sea. The large animal of the same kind with whom she had held a secret converse soon appeared, and evidently congratulated her, in the most tender manner, on her escape. But, before she dived to unknown depths, she cast a parting glance at the wretched Shetlander, whose despairing looks excited in her breast a few transient feelings of commiseration. "Farewell," said she to him, "and may all good attend you. I loved you very well when I resided upon earth, but I always loved my first husband much better."

These inhabitants of a submarine world were, in the later periods of Christianity, regarded as fallen angels, who were compelled to take refuge in the seas: They had, therefore, the name of Sea-Trows given to them, as belonging to the dominion of the Prince of Darkness. Brand appears to have confirmed this view, by assenting, to the opinion of the sailors, that it was the devil, who in the shape of great rolling creatures, broke their nets; adding; "It seems to be more than probable that evil spirits frequent both land and sea."

SANDNESS TO VAILEY.

In an inland course from Sandness, on the Mainland, to Vailey, there is not a single habitation; hills, that afford receptacles for numerous lochs, and covered with a thick brown moss, are surmounted by higher rising heaths, which present a barren and bleak picture of more than usual wildness. Along the coast, which is broken into steep precipices and gios, there are several patches of cultivation. On the rocks of Deepdale, a ship freighted with timber had recently gone into pieces; the few individuals, whose lives were saved, having effected their escape, by being thrown upon a frightful cliff, which, in a dark night, they contrived to scale, and in the morning reached the small town of Dale. As soon as they related their story, every boat in the vicinity was launched, for the sake of plunder.

At Vailey, a more enlivened prospect is presented, from the many voes which lead into the sound, and from its populous and well cultivated shores. The island, on which a handsome house is built, is the residence of John Scott, Esq., the proprietor. There are several burghs in this vicinity, one of which is situated on a holm at the loch of Burroland, having a double concentric wall, with ditches that were filled with water from the loch, and communicating with the shore, by means of stepping stones. I found in this vicinity some tenants who had been released from the obligation of fishing. They sold their fish to *Yaggers*, by which cant phrase, derived from the vessels that attended the Dutch busses and took home the first herrings, an enterprising set of young men were originally designated, who, having few or no boats themselves employed at the Haaf, purchased fish from the natives at a higher price than that which landlords paid. There was an old tradition respecting Vailey, that neither cat nor mice would live in it, and, as a cat was seen there, about a century ago, at the time a gentleman was afflicted with illness, it was judged that the creature could be nothing but a noted witch of the vicinity in disguise. On the popular notions entertained at present, and more particularly in the last two centuries, respecting the witchcraft of Shetland, I have hitherto said nothing, and this task I shall fulfil on the present occasion.

WITCHCRAFT OF SHETLAND.

Magic was originally sanctioned in Scandinavia by Odin, and, during the Pagan state of Orkney and Shetland, was practised by individuals of the highest rank. The mother of Thorfin, Earl of Orkney, who lived in the 11th century, gave to her son a standard, embroidered with the signal of a raven, telling him, that if the fates had intended he should have lived for ever, she would have nursed him much longer in his cradle; but that life was finished more honourably with glory, than lengthened out with dishonour;—that although the standard on which she had expended all her magic art portended victory to him before it was carried, yet it might bring death to the bearer. The females who, in Scandinavia, or its colonies, had most distinguished themselves in the art of divination, were deified after their decease, under the name of Nornies, or Destinies; and it was supposed, that upon the completion of their apotheosis, they had the power of controlling human events. Urda the past, Verdandi the present, and Skulda the future, mounted swift horses, and with drawn swords travelled through the air and over the seas, in order to select the particular mortals who were to die in battle, and to conduct them to Valhalla:—they were the handmaids of Odin, and dwelt in a beautiful city. But Nornies of a subordinate character lived in caves; some of them were descended from the gods, some from genii, and others from the malignant dwarfs. They assisted at the birth of children, and determined their fate and age: the Nornies of good origin dispensing riches and honour; and the Nornies of wicked descent dooming certain individuals to poverty and infamy, or to death in the flower of life.

The esteem in which the Pagan professors of magic were held, was first diminished upon the introduction of Christianity, when it was far from being believed that the deities of the Edda were fabulous beings, but that they were fallen angels in league with the Prince of Darkness, who, until the appearance of our Saviour, had been allowed to range on the earth uncontrolled, and to involve the world in spiritual darkness and delusion. It was then supposed, that witches and warlocks, by a compact with Satan himself, were enabled to command the assistance of the demons of the Pagans, who, having been driven from Heaven, took shelter in caverns, seas, and lakes, or became the drudging domestic spirits of particular families. An opinion precisely similar was entertained among the early Reformers of the Christian Church.

The forms in which the demons appeared, with whom the magicians of Shetland communed, were often those which had been familiar to Pagan times. The raven, for instance, whose language the ancient diviner boasted he could understand,* had a supernatural knowledge of the secret affairs of men, and the hidden things of Nature. Odin had always in attendance two ravens, who would sit upon his shoulders,—who would fly the world over, and, at dinner time, return, for the purpose of whispering in his ears all the occurrences they had either heard or seen. In like manner, a witch of Shetland, who, in the middle of the 17th century, held converse with the Prince of Darkness, was seen going to and from Brecon to Hillswick, while the devils, who were her familiars, appeared to her in the likeness of two corhies, that hopped on each side of her all the way. As this appearance was maintained to be contrary to the nature of wild fowls, it formed one of the charges against the unhappy woman, for which she was condemned to be worried and burnt at a stake. It was also customary for a familiar to appear under the form of a cat; and sometimes he put on a human shape, as when, about fifty years ago, he assisted the wife of a warlock in Papa Stour to delve, during the time that her husband was engaged at the Haaf. As soon as the devil had abandoned a Shetland witch, he was seen under the shape of a fiery ball. Sinclair, in his Invisible World Discovered, assures us, that when Helen Stewart and her daughter were brought to the gibbet to be burned, the poor girl was so stupified that she was thought to be then possessed by Satan; for after she had hung some little time at the gibbet, a black pitchy ball foamed out of her mouth, which, after the fire was kindled, grew to the bigness of a walnut, and then flew up like squibs into the air,—this being a visible sign that the devil was gone out of her.

---

* The supernatural powers that were the boast of the ancient Scandinavian magicians, are thus recited in the song of King Eric:

<ul style="list-style:none">
<li>Intellexit quid garriant aves,</li>
<li>potuit ignem restinguere,</li>
<li>fluctus compescere,</li>
<li>dolores lenire.</li>
</ul>

<ul style="list-style:none">
<li>Klok nam fugla</li>
<li>kyrra elda</li>
<li>saeva oc svefia</li>
<li>sorgir laegia.</li>
</ul>

WITCHCRAFT.

The chief means by which the devilry of a Shetland witch or warlock was accomplished, appears to have been by an evil eye or an evil tongue. It was said of Marion Pardon, who suffered in the year 1645, that she was all her days a wicked, devilish, fearful and abominable curser, and that whenever she cursed those whom she wished evil, every evil, sickness, harm, and death, followed thereupon;—she cursed Janet Robinson and, accordingly, showers of pains and fits fell upon the victim. Nor was her eye less baneful; she looked upon a cow, and it "crapped togidder till no lyfe was leukit for her." It may be remarked, however, that the notion of an evil eye or tongue having the power to hurt, was not confined in Shetland to the professors of magic, but was attributed to any enemy who might look maliciously at a neighbour's person and property, or might bestow upon them a curse.* A superstition of this kind was not unknown to the ancient Romans, the Turks, the modern Egyptians, and many of the Celtic tribes. The influence of an evil eye was also supposed to be in a more intense degree blasting, when any one was beheld in glory and triumph. There is, again, in Shetland, another modification of the superstition, resembling one which may be found described in Lupton's Book of Notable Things, on the authority of Gellius, that "There are in Africk families of men, who, if they chance exceedingly to praise fair trees, pure seeds, goodly children, excellent horses, fair and well-looking cattle, soon after they will wither and pine away and so dye." In like manner, Mr Low was informed in Shetland, by a minister, that, "if you praise their children, or call them fat, they think you their worst enemy, and that such children are certainly doomed to die. Nor must any be praised upon which these poor people set a value."

The Shetland witch delighted in imitating a practice to which Brownie, the well known domestic spirit, was addicted; for whenever sacrifices were not the regular pay of the goblin's drudgery, the brewing was spoiled, which was named "Taking away the profit from the malt." Accordingly, she has long been notorious for gratifying her revenge or malevolence, in depriving her neighbours of the profits of their rooms, lands, corn, grass, butter, cattle and wool. In an indictment against Marion Pardon of Hillswick, she was charged with attempting to take away the profit of some bear belonging to Edward Halcro, when he was dichting it to steep for malt; with marring and undoing two whole makings of the same bear, and with taking away the profit of Andro Erasmusson's kine for thirteen days.†

The witch of Shetland had, like Odin, the great father of Scandinavian magic, the power of undergoing a transmutation of shape resembling various animals. Marion Pardon of Hillswick, conceived a malice against the crew of a fishing-boat, and, transforming herself into the likeness of a *pellack-whale* or porpoise, upset a fishing-boat. She was convicted of the crime by the confession of another witch, and by the well-known test of the *bahr-recht*, or law of the bier; for being commanded, along with Swene, her husband, to lay hands on two of the dead bodies that were found, one of them bled at the *craig-bane*, and another in the head and fingers, "guishing out bluid thereat, to the great admiration of the beholders, and

---

* Mr Low remarked of the Orkney natives, that there were not a few instances of their falling ill upon being cursed by an enemy.

† A similar superstition prevailed in Orkney. Elspet Smith, in the year 1672, complained to the minister and elders of Hoy, that Marion Mangie had falsely accused her of witchcraft, in saying, "That she sent for ane pynt of aile from her, and did thereby take awa the fruit and fusion of ane dyssen of pynts or thereby, that remained in the vessel."

revelation of the judgment of the Almightie." On this irrefragable proof of murder, admitted, as the indictment expressed, not only in this country but likewise in most foreign kingdoms, the unfortunate woman was executed.

It was usual with the Shetland dealers in sorcery, like the ancient magicians of Scandinavia, to use incantations. "I know a song," said Odin, "of such virtue, that were I caught in a storm I can hush the winds, and render the air perfectly calm." But the warlocks and witches of Thule used, by the same means, to raise tempests, the lay being accompanied by some simple process, that denoted the advancement that was made towards the attainment of the malevolent object. About fifty years ago, a woman, of the parish of Dunrossness, known to have a deadly enmity against a boat's crew that had set off for the Haaf, took a wooden bason, named a *cap*, and allowed it to float on the surface of a tub of water; then, to avoid exciting a suspicion of her devilry, she went on with her usual domestic labours, and, as if to lighten the burden of them, sang an old Norse ditty. After a verse or two had been recited, she sent a child to the tub, and bade him tell her if the cap was *whummilled*, or turned upside down. Her orders were obeyed, and intelligence were soon brought to her, that the water was beginning to be agitated, but that the bowl was afloat. She then continued her incantation, and once more broke it off, by requesting the child to go again to the tub, and let her know if the cap was whumnilled. The little messenger soon returned with the news that there was a strange swell in the water, which caused the bowl to be sadly tossed about. The witch then sang still more loudly, and, for the third time, sent the child to the tub to report the state of the bason, who immediately hastened back with the information that the water was frightfully troubled, and that the cap was whummilled. The enchantress, with an air of malignant satisfaction, then ceased her song, and said, "The Turn is done." On the same day, news came that a fishing yaul had been lost in the Roust, and that the whole of the crew had been drowned. A similar story is told of some women in the island of Fetlar, who, when a boat's crew had perished in the bay of Funzie, were detected sitting round a well, muttering mysterious words over a wooden bowl that was supernaturally agitated. The accompaniment of a magical incantation by some process, indicative of the progress of the magical purpose that is meditated, may be found in many of the wild superstitions of Scandinavia and its colonies. While the Nornies or Destinies of Pagan times were within the recesses of a gloomy cave, dooming in a wild song the fate of the warriors who were to fall with the Earl of Orkney in an engagement on the Irish coast, they were employed on a strange loom, where human entrails furnished the materials for the warp, foemens' heads for treadles, swords dipped in gore for shuttles and darts for woofs. When the incantation was ended, the women each tore a portion of the cloth, and, mounting their horses, six rode away towards the north, and six to the south. There is also in Scandinavia an ancient rhyme, named the Quern Song, wherein two female slaves of a gigantic form sing a strange ditty, while they are employed in labouring on a quern of immense magnitude, in which they grind riches to a sea-king; but, being dissatisfied with the oppression of their master, in making them persist throughout the whole of the night in their labour, they grind against the same warrior a destructive army.

Another mode, by which the magician of Shetland obtained a power over Nature's

WITCHCRAFT.

operations, was by means of knots, the superstitious regard for them seeming to have arisen from the use to which they were from the remotest period applied as memorials of events, or as inviolable pledges of agreement, indicating that they were not to be loosened.* It has been affirmed, that the most ancient Runic characters imitated the variety of knots that were made on such occasions;† and if this be the case, we can easily account for similar magical effects being ascribed to them, as to the symbols of which they were mere substitutes.‡ The Fins were long notorious for controlling, by such means, events depending on the atmosphere, or for "untying the winds." And Brand relates a story of a witch of Shetland, who made nearly the same use of knots as Odin did of the Runæ, by which they were succeeded: for while the God, by virtue of written spells, could make a witch, when riding through the clouds, miss her aim, the Shetland sorceress, upon seeing a fowl which a-sea-eagle was carrying through the air, has taken a string, and after having cast some knots upon it, the bird of prey has let its captive fall into the ocean, from which it has been immediately recovered by a boat. Artifices of this kind were also applied to the cure of diseases; this use of them being indeed familiar to other countries. When, for instance, an old woman of Shetland has been called in to cure a sprained limb, she has tied around it a piece of woollen thread, on which was made a certain number of knots, and after muttering during the operation certain mysterious words, a cure has been soon effected. These charms were, two centuries ago, supposed to have been constructed by the Devil, from whom witches received them. Thus, in an indictment against Marion Pardon of Hillswick, it appeared in evidence, that Swene, her husband, was labouring in a peat-moss, with several other scat-holders, among whom was a poor fellow, enfeebled by disease. A Shetlander of the party, in a sneering way, asked Swene if he could not prevail upon his wife to go to her *pobe*§ the devil, and bid him *loose a knot*, that the sick man might be enabled to cast his peats.

When the Pagan magic of the North was modified by the introduction of Christianity, it was supposed that many diseases were induced by a sort of demoniacal possession that took place in different parts of the body, and that a cure was to be effected by obliging the demon to enter the body of some other animal. When a Shetland witch, therefore, had, by a compact with the prince of darkness, obtained a command over subordinate evil spirits, she could charge them to enter the mortal tenement of flesh belonging to either man or beast, and to cause affliction even unto death. Marion Pardon of Hillswick, by a power of this kind, cast fits upon Janet Robertson, but being threatened with the terror of the law, removed the disease (or rather the demon that induced it), by throwing it upon two kine that shortly afterwards expired. She also visited with sickness the wife of a neighbour, but, under fear of legal consequences, cast it upon a calf that soon afterwards ran mad and died. In another case, after inflicting illness upon a man, she cured him by putting her

---

* Hence " the true lover's knot," familiar at the present day, and the knot emblematic of friendship.

† In Hickes's Thesaurus, it is stated, "Inscriptionum Runæ in nodis sive gyris, nodorum insculptæ leguntur, propterea quod apud veteres septentrionales gentes nodus amoris, fidei, amicitiæ symbolum fuisse videtur, ut quod insolubilem pietatis et affectus nexum significavit." But when these letters were carved on wood, they sustained a considerable alteration, being rather meant to resemble sprigs that were cut from the tops of trees.—Davies' *Celtic Researches*, p. 314.

‡ Thus Odin, by the means of Runic characters, assumed the power of raising the dead to life.

§ Foster-father, or nurse's husband.

finger on his leg and then on the ground, three times to and fro: but on the rumour of the cure spreading abroad, the beldam grew angry at the exposure, and caused the disease to return. She again was earnestly entreated to restore the patient once more to a state of health,—an object that she effected, by sending him a bannock to eat prepared from her own hands, and by casting the disease on one of his cows, to whom it proved fatal.

It appears, that an exertion of the supernatural powers possessed by warlocks and witches, was often requested for both good and bad purposes. John Sutherland of Papa Stour, who lived about fifty years ago, was in the habit of procuring a fair breeze for any boats that were wind-bound. There is a tradition in the country, connected with a melancholy disaster which once befel a respectable family in Shetland, relative to a Norwegian lady, who being slighted by a young gentleman, bribed a hag to bring the direst misery to the house with whom she had been refused an alliance. The time selected for the purpose, was when the sons were about to be ferried across a voe; and in order to induce the whole of the heirs-male of the race to take the boat, a shelty that had been secured for the meditated journey of one of them, was in a mysterious manner conveyed away from his tether. The four youths, accompanied by a cousin, set sail at the close of the evening;—there was scarcely a ripple on the water, and not a noise nor a cry was heard, yet when the anxious parents, impatient of their return, instituted a search after them, they found nothing but the boat which had drifted ashore with little damage. When the dark deed of enchantment had been accomplished, the shelty that had been lost was brought back to his tether in as secret a manner as he had disappeared.

There can be little doubt, but that in a superstitious age, an individual thus consulted and treated as a common charmer, would in time become herself impressed with the same conceit, being strongly tempted to make a free surrender of her mind to this self-delusion, by the convenient power which she would find herself possessed of, under the supernatural character attributed to her. "Children cannot smile upon a witch," says an old writer, "without the hazard of a perpetual wry mouth; a very nobleman's request may be denied more safely than her petitions for butter, milk or small beer; and a great ladie's or queen's name may be less doubtfully derided." There were, however, several ways in which it was supposed that the power of the sorceress could be resisted, the chief of which was, by drawing some of her blood.* A female, upon whom Marion Pardon of Hillswick had, in her veneficial heart, cast a terrible and fearful madness, was counselled to draw blood from the witch, and this she performed by running foul upon her, and biting two of her fingers, when a recovery took place. Sometimes a magician was openly charged with the diabolical deeds which had been committed, on the principle of the text in Scripture, "Resist the devil and he will flee from you." The effect of the mystic craft would then immediately cease. Thus, when Marion Pardon had taken away the profit from certain kine, their milk was shewn to the dame, and the owner got back her profit. When another cow produced nothing but blood, the fluid was openly exposed before her eyes, and the

---

* A number of examples are given in Mr Ellis's edition of Brand's Popular Antiquities, to shew the very prevalent opinion, that drawing blood from a witch rendered her enchantments ineffectual. Thus, in the first part of Henry the IVth, act 1st, Talbot says to the Pucelle d'Orleans, "Blood I will draw on thee, thou art a witch."

beast soon grew well. In a third case, where a cow yielded nothing but a fetid matter, the runnion was not only made to look at the animal, but also to milk her, upon which a recovery ensued. But the magic of Thule was in no way so successfully combated as by the terror of the law; and in no part of Christendom has there been a more industrious search made after professors of the black art than in Orkney and Shetland. The rapacity of Earls Patrick and Robert Stewart in seizing lands from the udallers, caused them to bring to immediate justice all impious charmers, in order to obtain possession of their estates, which became due to them by forfeiture. Nor was their example unfollowed, for thirty or forty years afterwards, by those individuals who succeeded them in the government of the province. Even so late as the commencement of the last century, the witches of Shetland were, as Brand says, talked of so much anent their devilry, that he was told it was dangerous going to or living in this their abode. By the ancient laws of the country, each ranselman was directed to inquire in his quarters anent all persons using any manner of withcraft, charms, or any abominable or devilish superstitions, that they might be brought to condign punishment. Entrusted with such powers, there is no doubt that these industrious civil officers would find, in every district, some old woman, who could shew the usual manifestations of a Shetland hag,—one who was a devilish, fearful, and abominable curser,—a taker away of her neighbour's profits,—a charmer and healer of some, and a caster of sickness upon others,—who in every way lived a damnable and diabolical life, contrary to God and his commandments. Every district would display some hollow glen,

> "In which a witch did dwell, in loathy weedes,
> An wilfull want, all careless of her needes;
> So choosing solitarie to abide
> Far from all neighbours, that her devilish deedes
> And hellish arts from people she might hide,
> And hurt far off unknown whomever she envide."—SPENSER.

The task now remains of shewing the modifications that the art of magic underwent in Shetland from being blended with ceremonies, or notions appertaining to Popery or to the Reformed Religion. When Popery prevailed in these islands, the effects of witchcraft were obviated by means of crosses, benedictions, amulets, prayers, and "other godly gear." Such virtues indeed were attributed to mummery of this kind, that the true warlocks were the Catholic clergy, who, by mere priestcraft, could at any time produce the accomplishment of objects, that in days of Paganism depended on incantations, knots, or Runic characters. But when Reformation was introduced in the land, and when the rites and ceremonies of Popery were condemned as idolatrous, it was still found not very easy to shake the popular faith in the effectiveness of many of the ancient ceremonies of the Roman Church, that were employed to ensure success in fishing and during harvest. Accordingly, a description of people was greatly encouraged who performed numerous ceremonies, which had evidently a Popish origin, that were calculated to oppose the malevolence of demons and of common sorcerers,—to heal diseases or to procure good fortune in worldly affairs. The religious charmer of Shetland would mutter some words over water, in imitation of the practice of the Catholic priest, and the element was named *forespoken water;* boats were then sprinkled with it; and limbs were washed with it, for the purpose of *telling out* pains. When a beast was wounded with elf-shot, the *saining* or blessing witch would find out the hole, inscrutable to common eyes, in which the arrow entered, and would wash the place with forespoken water. By the application of this fluid were the effects combated of an evil eye, or of an evil tongue. There was a considerable advantage in exercising a profession of witchcraft thus modified, which admitted into it Christian ceremonies, inasmuch as it had for its avowed object deeds that were opposed to the designs of the devil. Nor could a collusion with Satan be suspected, so that supernatural acts might be attempted without the fear of a capital conviction of the law.

The last modification which took place of witchcraft, arose from a doctrine taught by the Reformers respecting the efficacy of the Gospel in banishing from the land all demons. "Now do I not hear," says Brand, after he had visited Shetland, " of any such appearances the devil makes in these isles, so great and many are the blessings which attend a Gospel dispensation ; the brownies, fairies, and other evil spirits that haunted and were familiar in our houses, were dismissed, and fled at the breaking out of our Reformation (if we may except but a few places not yet well reformed from Popish dregs), as the Heathen oracles were silenced at the coming of our Lord, and the going forth of his Apostles ; so that our first noble Reformers might have returned and said to their master, as the Seventy did, ' *Lord, even the devils are subject to us through thy name.*' And though this restraint put upon the devil was far later in these northern places than with us, to whom the light of a preached Gospel did more easily shine, yet now also do these northern isles enjoy the fruits of this restraint." Such was the opinion of the Reformers in the commencement of the last century ; and it differed from one that had been entertained by the Roman Church in an important particular. The Catholic divine never arrogated to himself the power of banishing the trows of Shetland from their native rocks, streams, or seas, but he conceived, that, by means of exorcisms, he could preclude them from particular sites of ground. The Reformer, however, supposed, that the light of the Gospel would, by its effulgence, penetrate into the very domiciles of unclean spirits, and expel them to unknown regions.

When a view like this gained ground, it will scarcely create surprise that the Bible should become no less useful an instrument in the hands of charmers than crosses, forespoken water, and benedictions. It was recommended, that the lonely wanderer by night among the bleak scatholds of Thule, should bear in his hands the Holy Scriptures, as a means of screening himself from the attacks of the trows or demons of the hills. The inconvenience arising from such a superstitious regard paid to the Gospel, is well illustrated in a case that came, in the year 1708, before the ministers and elders in Orkney, where notions similar to those of Shetland prevailed. William Stensgar of Southside, being afflicted with a pain in his limbs, probably rheumatic, which confined him to his bed, Catharine Taylor, a poor cripple beggar woman, in repute as a charmer, was sent for to tell out the pain. She came to the man about an hour before sunrise, and by her directions he followed her to a gateway named a *slap* or *grind;* the wife accompanying with a *stoup* of water. Here the sybil halted ; the patient laid bare his knee, and she touched it with her hands, repeat-

WITCHCRAFT.

ing at the same time the following words. "As I was going by the way, I met the Lord Jesus Christ in the likeness of another man ; he asked me what tidings I had to tell. I said I had no tidings to tell, but I am full of pains, and I can neither gang nor stand. Thou shalt go to the holy kirk, and thou shalt gang it round about, and then sit down upon thy knees and say thy prayers to the Lord, and then thou shalt be as heal as the hour when Christ was born." After this raving nonsense, which by her confession she had learned when a child from an old woman, she applied to the knee the lawful charm of the Gospel, by repeating over it the twenty-third Psalm, upon which the evil spirit that caused the disease was *telled out*, and fairly transferred into the stoup of water. She then emptied the vessel on the slap, with the malevolent intention that the disease, (or, to speak more correctly, the demon that induced it), should take possession of the first unlucky wight that might pass the stile ; and when a new habitation was thus secured for the evil spirit, the possibility of the invalid experiencing a return of the complaint would be completely obviated. While, however, the charmer was employed in concealing, by means of feal and turf, the water that had been spilt on the ground, so that no suspicion of the intention might be excited, she was detected by a neighbour, who, suspecting some devilry, forced an entrance through another part of the dike and safely passed over. But there was another man who passed through the slap before sun-rising, that was immediately afterwards overtaken with bodily indisposition. This case affords a good illustration of the *gospel* sorcery, which was a natural result of the superstitious view entertained by the early Reformers, respecting the power of the Scriptures in expelling demons. Brand was, indeed, so confounded when he visited Orkney and Shetland, at the mixture of Pagan, Popish and Gospel superstitions which prevailed, that he was totally unable to justify any of them as authorised by the doctrines of the New Light, but denounced the practice of them as a hellish art and tremendous devilry, and not the product of Nature's operation.* "God so permitting it," he adds, "to be in his holy and wise providence, for the further punishment and judicial binding of those who follow such unlawful courses, and the devil thereby engaging his slaves more in his service. Yet not always the effects desired and expected do follow, that all may know the devil is a chained one, and can do nothing without the permission of a sovereign God, who is Lord over all."

These are many of the particulars I have to offer respecting the Witchcraft of Shetland, as it has existed from the earliest period, as well as the modifications that it has undergone, from the introduction of Christianity into the country. A belief in most of the superstitions enumerated is still entertained, such as in the power of taking away profits, or causing afflictions by an evil eye or tongue ; but as the doors of justice are shut against complaints of the malevolence of warlocks or witches, who only thrive under persecution, the scarcity of them at the present day is more attributable to the little disturbance which they meet

---

* Charmers of the description reprobated by Brand over-ran England, being known by the names of *wise men, wise women, cunning* or *looming women, white witches* or *blessing witches*. An old writer has remarked, that it would be better for the land, if all witches, especially the blessing witch, might suffer death. "Men," he adds, " do commonly hate and spit at the damnifying sorcerer, as unworthie to live among them, whereas they flie unto the other in necessitie, they depend upon him as their god, and by this means thousands are carried away to their final confusion. Death, therefore, is the just and deserved portion of the good witch."

KK

with from the laws, than to the want of inducement that there may be for the imagination to endow them with the attributes of sorcery. The charmers, who still exercise their profession, find stolen goods and cure diseases. One practice familiar in former times is still known. It has been long a popular belief, that when any person is emaciated with sickness, his heart is worn away; this is attributed to the agency of trows. The patient then seeks out a cunning woman, who, with several mystic ceremonies, melts some lead, and allows it to drop through an open sieve into cold water. If an image, bearing some faint resemblance to the heart, is, after a certain number of trials, produced, it is an indication that the charm has been successful; but if no such figure appears, it is a sign that the decay of this organ is irremediable.

(For the chief authority, from which this account of the Witchcraft of Shetland is drawn up, consisting of a trial for Witchcraft, dated A.D. 1644, see Note XIII. page 280. Appended to it is a description by Miss Campbell, of the mode of casting Hearts.)

ISLAND OF FOULA.

From Vailey I set sail for Foula,—a bold island rising from the surface of western sea, at a distance of eight leagues from the mainland, and towering into the sky.

> "A place there is, where proudly rais'd there stands
> A huge aspiring rock neighb'ring the skies,
> Whose surly brow imperiously commands
> The sea his bounds, that at his proud feet lies;
> And spurns the waves that in rebellious bands
> Assault his empire and against him rise."   DANIELS.

The island, when viewed from sea, presents the appearance of five hills, most of them being of a conoid form, named the Noup, Liora Field, the Sneug, Conima Field, and the Kaim, the highest of which has been estimated at 1300 feet. On the north, a small insulated rock appeared, that had all the appearance, when viewed at a distance, of the ruined arch of a religious building. The boat lingered a short time among the banks on the east of the island to catch cod for bait used at the Haaf; and so fast did we take them, that our boat might have soon been filled.

On our passage, numbers of the Ca'ing whales appeared; and, nearer the island, there were many of the smaller seals, or *Tang-fish*, so named from being supposed to live among the *Tang*, or larger fuci that grow near the shore. The phrenologists of Paris, judging from the form and size of the cranium of the seal, have hazarded an opinion, that he is possessed of uncommon intelligence. I am confirmed in the same notion, from a different kind of observation. These animals, if taken young, are said to be easily domesticated, when they readily assume the habits of the dog; shewing attachment to particular individuals of the human species, repairing to the water in quest of fish, and returning to the roof where they have experienced kindness.

In a few hours, I arrived at Ham town, where there is a small gio, that affords a landing-place for boats. The kirk is situated a little to the south, the duty of which is weekly performed by a schoolmaster, while it is visited once a year by the minister of Waes, for the purpose of administering the sacrament.* It was formerly the custom of the inhabitants, after divine service, to repair to the church-yard, for the sake of a competition in strength,—who should throw to the greatest distance a large stone, named a *putting-stone*,—the old men standing by to tell what feats they and their ancestors had done, and to lament the feeble powers of a newer and degenerate race. In one of the valleys, the remains of a wood have been detected, and Mr Low heard the tradition, that Foula was despoiled of its sylvan honours by the Lewismen who, in one of their plundering excursions, burnt the trees, in order to prevent them from being a future shelter to the natives.

There is little doubt but that this island is the Thule which Agricola descried from Orkney; since it is often seen from the vicinity of Papa Westray. Learned Antiquaries have long indeed had no doubt of the fact, from the resemblance which they find between the words Foula and Thule.† The natives, however, formerly gave to the place the appellation of Uttrie; it is now named Fughloe, [Foula] or Fowl Island, from the numbers of the feathered tribe that make it a place of resort.

Foula was one of the last places in which the Norse language was spoken. Mr Low found it, nearly fifty years ago, much worn out. "It was evidently," he remarked, "much mixed with English. None of the natives could write the ancient language, and few could speak it. The best phrases were lost, and little more remained than the names of a few objects, and two or three remnants of songs, which an old man (William Henry of Guttorm) could repeat, though indistinctly."

The ascent from the east to the summit of the hills of Foula, is very steep; on the west they are broken by the sea into one line of precipitous cliffs. On the nearest of them, lying to the north-west of the island, the Shetlander has fancied he could perceive, amidst the sable gloom of the evening, numerous twinkling rays, emitted by a native light from a carbuncle, that has been fixed in the steep cliff. My Cicerone was, therefore, at great pains to point out the particular situation

" Of that admired mighty stone,   the Carbuncle that's named,
Which from it such a flaming light,   and radiancy ejecteth,
That in the very darkest night   the eye to it directeth."—DRAYTON.

The low lands remote from the sea are frequented by parasitic gulls, which build among the heather. The surface of the hills swarms also with plovers, Royston crows, sea-pies, or curlieus. On reaching the highest ridges of the rocks, the prospect presented on every side

---

* Mr Low, in his visit to Foula, observes, that, at the desire of the whole island, he preached once to a most attentive audience of the whole community. "These honest creatures," he adds, "in the simplicity of their hearts, are not shy to express their approbation of a public discourse, even in words, and that aloud. The common appellation to all acquaintances is *brother*.'

† In a note in the handwriting of Mr Pennant, on a page of Mr Low's Tour, I find the following remark. " This was the *Thule* of *Tacitus*, which, from its height, was easily seen in the circumnavigation of the Orknies, by the Roman fleet. Dispecta est et Thule. How nearly is the name preserved!"

is of the sublimest description. The spectator looks down from a perpendicular height of 1100 or 1200 feet, and sees below the wide Atlantic roll its tide. Dense columns of birds hover through the air, consisting of maws, kittywakes, lyres, sea-parrots, or gullemots;—the cormorants occupy the lowest portions of the cliffs, the kittywakes whiten the ledges of one distinct cliff, gulls are found on another, and lyres on a third. The welkin is darkened with their flight; nor is the sea less covered with them, as they search the waters in quest of food. But when the winter appears, the colony is fled, and the rude harmony produced by their various screams, is succeeded by a desart stillness. From the brink of this awful precipice the adventurous fowler is, by means of a rope tied round his body, let down many fathoms; he then lands on the ledges, where the various sea birds nestle, being still as regardless as his ancestors of the destruction that awaits the falling of some loose stones from a crag, or the untwisting of a cord. It was formerly said of the Foula man,—" his *gutcher* (grandfather) *guid before*, his father guid before, and he must expect to go over the Sneug too."

I ascended several of the highest points of the rocks of Foula. One of them is occupied by the Bonxie, or Scua Gull, the terror of the feathered race, but so noble minded, as to prefer waging war with birds larger than himself. The Eagle forbears to make an attack upon lambs while Scua is present; on which account he was long considered a privileged bird, the act of destroying him being visited with a severe penalty. On the summit of Liorafield is a small hole within which several barrels of lines are said to have been let down without finding a bottom. It is covered with a flag, which I had the temerity to remove, notwithstanding an ancient superstition, that he who the first time is upon the island, opens the *Liora* or vent that leads to this subterraneous abode of Trows, dies immediately afterwards. On the summit of Foula there is a view, on the south, of the distant shores of Orkney; but on the east, Hialtland is fully exposed in all its native wildness, appearing as one long range of desolate hills.

FOULA TO BRESSAY SOUND.

I found a large boat sailing to Vailey from the Haaf, and availed myself of the opportunity of taking a passage in it, but having offended the demon of Liora-field, by exposing to the light of day, the opening that led to his secret habitation within the hill, a perilous if not fatal passage across the wide channel we had to cross, followed as a matter of course. Accordingly, the wind sprung up, the waters began to swell, our heavily freighted boat shipped much water, and at length the main-sail gave way, so that after a passage of eight hours, not unattended with danger, we with difficulty arrived in port.

The approach of autumn now gave me notice to quit the islands of Shetland. The Greenland vessels were constantly arriving in the harbours to bring back the seamen whom they had taken with them early in the spring to the Northern Seas. The short nights preventing the fishers from sailing to the Haaf, they were catching, by means of handlines, ling and cod, which were allowed to remain in salt until beginning of the spring. Heavy gales were coming on, which, combining with the spray of the sea that was flung up, in some places destroyed the crops in a single night.* The shipwreck of a Russian vessel had occurred on the coast, on which occasion I observed a number of boats crews toiling with all their might at their oars, for the sake of plunder. But the most decided indication of the season was the brilliancy with which the evening was lighted up by the aurora borealis; streamers of a reddish yellow colour darting over the heavens with a tremulous and curved motion.

I soon arrived at Bressay Sound, named in Norwegian Annals Bredeyiar Sound, where the fleet of King Haco was moored for several days after sailing from Norway, in an unsuccessful expedition against Scotland. "The leader of his people," says Sturlas, "unmoored the ploughers [ships] of the ocean, and raised aloft the expanded wings [sails,] of his sky-blue doves [ships]. Our Sovereign rich in the spoils [gold,] of the sea-snake's den, viewed the retiring haven from the stern of his snorting steed [ship] adorned with ruddy gold."†

At Lerwick, to which place I returned, there is an object the most desirable to a traveller,—a comfortable inn.‡ For too often in rambling over the bleak seatholds of the country, the traveller is apt to long for the accommodation so expatiated upon by good Master Isaac Walton, "An honest ale-house, where we shall find a cleanly room, lavender in the windows, and twenty ballads stuck about the wall." He who may wish to explore the most secluded parts of Shetland, and to proceed with a true spirit of independence, will find no great difficulty in inducing the cottagers to accept of an adequate remuneration for receiving him beneath their roof. But with these free notions, he must submit to great inconvenience, chiefly arising from the want of cleanliness that stamps the character of the Shetland hovels; this want of comfort, however, will be at any time preferred, rather than be reduced to the necessity of seeking for gratuitous comfort in more commodious habitations; yet, as I have often experienced, too frequently is this reluctance subdued, by the generous invitation that has met on his lonesome way the unintroduced and weary stranger.

The hospitality of Shetland has long been recorded by the northern poets, and there still remains in the country all the practice of it that was recommended in the Havamaal of Odin. "To the guest, who enters your dwelling with frozen knees, give the warmth of your fire; and he who hath travelled over the mountains hath need of food and well-dried garments." The vicinity of Lerwick is associated with the hospitality shewn to Ronald Earl of Orkney, when, in company with Harold, his partner in the earldom, he was

---

* "When the winds blow in great force," says a describer of Shetland, "the surges rise in proportion, dashing violently against the rocks. The white salt froth which is forced up against the highest promontories, mixes with the air in circulation; is carried over lands under cultivation; falls, as it passes, on the corns; dries and hardens upon them, by which its farther growth is impeded: and the most sanguine hopes of the poor farmer destroyed. The straw even, as well as the hay, becomes unfit for any purpose in husbandry."—*Considerations on the Fisheries in the Scottish Islands, p. 17.*

† Expedition of King Haco against Scotland.—Translated by Johnson.

‡ This was kept by a very civil family of the name of Sinclair, and possesses very good accommodation. There is an opportunity of seeing in this place the conviviality of the county, which is quite as much an industrious pains-taking landlord would desire. Honest Barnaby would have been quite at home in this place, the wild scene around him bearing no faint resemblance to that of Kighley.

————————Ubi montes   minitantes, vivi fontes,
Ardui colles, aridæ valles   laeti tamen sunt sodales,
Festivantes et jucundi,   ac si domini essent mundi.

cast upon some rocks near Gulberswick. Much treasure, with which the vessel was loaded, became lost; but the Earl still preserved his good spirits, and amused himself during the night in composing sportive verses. In the morning, when a landing was effected, the doors of the inhabitants were thrown open for the accommodation of the party; and as the Earl was exceedingly wet, he was presented with the common garb of the country, which consisted, as he remarked, of a rough-skinned, thick-napped leather coat, which he wore with pleasure, as he had taken leave of his "sea-horse," and as the splendour of garments was then to him of little avail. The Earl sent twelve of his companions in misfortune to Einar of Gulberswick, but the proud udaller, over-anxious to take the lead in hospitality, sent a message, that he would not receive them, unless the Earl himself would condescend to be his guest. Ronald, however, expressed little fear of the threat being put into execution.*

I now prepared to leave Hialtland, and availed myself of a passage politely offered me in his Majesty's brig the Nimrod, by Captain Dalling. But I did not leave the country without paying a third visit to Unst, where I had discovered the chromate of iron.

This ore has, of late years, been an object of commercial importance, on account of the use to which it has been converted, in affording the means of procuring a yellow pigment for the use of the Arts. Although found in some parts of the Continent, the country from which it was most frequently obtained was America, while the expence of bringing it over was very considerable. The chrome of this substance also promises to be of much use in its application to the dying of silk, wool, linen and cotton, as is shewn in the account which has been given in the Journals of the experiments of M. J. L. Lassaigne.

My discovery of the chromate of iron took place in the autumn of 1817, and was first announced to the public through the medium of Dr Thomson's Journal, in a short notice written by Professor Jameson. The information attracted the attention not only of scientific mineralogists, but of the manufacturing chemists; and, as I had been prevented, by the lateness and inclemency of the season in which I visited Shetland, from devoting as much time to the prosecution of this discovery as the importance of it merited, I was induced, in the following year, to pay a second visit to this remote district of Britain. My wish then was to ascertain the general site of ground in which this ore occurred in the usual form of imbedded masses and veins, and to render the proprietors of the land aware of its distinctive character, and of its importance, in order that the search after it might be continued when I was absent.† In this object I was perfectly successful; and my second visit to Shetland afforded me at the same time the opportunity

---

* The jocular character of the Earl is thus shewn in the Orkneyinga Saga:
—" In e rem dein gratiam, ingentes foci, ad quos se fovebant, succeduntur; ancilla interim ingressa valde tremuit et locuta est qua non intellexere, ast Comes se ejus linguam percipere asserebat.
  Inhalas adhuc Asa,   Hututututu udi redebo?
  Atatata in aqua jacet,   Perquam frigesco; ad ignem.

† When the intelligence of my discovery of the chromate of iron had arrived in Shetland, after my first visit to that country, there were few landed proprietors who could persuade themselves that it was of the least importance, so often had they had been deceived by visitors who had come over, impressing them with false notions of the value of mines and minerals. To Mr Edmonstone of Huness, however, I successfully addressed myself, and spent some days in pointing out to this gentleman, and his servants, the character of the ore which was strewed over the hills in astonishing abundance; for, owing to the resemblance that it bore to a kind of diallage or hornblende, it was repeatedly mistaken for this substance. Accordingly, in following up these instructions, he perceived, for the first time, that a valuable bed of this ore awaited the operation of the miner, within scarcely more than a hundred yards of his own door.

CONCLUSION.

of conducting a Geological Survey of the whole of these islands. Of the great sacrifice of my time incurred in these journeys, as well as of their expence, I would say nothing :—the handsome testimonial of approbation that I have received from the Society in London for the encouragement of Arts and Commerce, leaves me nothing on this score to regret ; and, if the result of my labours should in any way conduce to the resources of Shetland, or to the knowledge of the natural history of this remote province, I would wish for nothing more, than that it should be considered as one of the effects arising from the encouragement given to the study of Mineralogy in the University of Edinburgh.

EDINBURGH,
Oct. 31, 1821.

NOTES TO ITER IV.

NOTE XII. Page 258. ANCIENT NORSE ROMANCES OF SHETLAND.

The argument of the Shetland romance given in page 258, as explained by William Henry of Guttorm, has appeared in print, for the first time, from Mr Low's MSS. I would have inserted the words which were taken down by this Tourist, but as they have already appeared in Dr Barry's History of Orkney (page 484), a reprint is scarcely demanded. I may observe, that the imperfect orthography of the poem, owing to the transcriber's ignorance of the northern languages, rendered it to Dr Percy wholly unintelligible. A gentleman, however, of Edinburgh, well versed in Danish literature, had some intention of transmitting the ballad to Copenhagen, under the impression that it would there stand a chance of being interpreted. In Dr Barry's work (page 482 and 403), may be also found a few ancient Shetland words, collected by Mr Low from Foula, as well as the Lord's Prayer in Norse, which it is unnecessary to republish.

NOTE XIII. Page 259. WITCHCRAFT OF SHETLAND.

TRIAL OF WITCHES IN SHETLAND, A.D. 1644.

Intent upon Pannel Marion Peebles alias *Pardone, spouse to Swene in Hildiswick.*

In the first, you the said Marion Peebles *alias* Pardone, is Indytit and accusit for the sinful and damnable renouncing of God, your Faith and Baptism, giving and casting of yourself, body and saul, in the hands of the Devil, following, exercising, using and practising of the fearfull and damnable craft of Witchcraft, Sorcerie, and Charming, in manner following, viz.

In the first, you are Indytit and accusit for coming in the month of

Jmvjc. and thirty years, to the house of John Banks in Turvisetter, and Janet Robertson, his spouse, with a wicked, devilish and malicious intention to cast Witchcraft and Sickness upon them ; and missing the said Janet there, for going to Sursetter, where she then was, and after cursing and scolding her, telling her that she should repent what she had done to your daughter and good-son. And for that immediately with the word, ye, by your devilish art of witchcraft, did cast sickness upon the said Janet, who, immediately upon your departure, fell in an extraordinary and unkindly sickness, and lay eight weeks, taking her shours and pains by fits, at midday and midnight, and so continued most terribly tormented ; her said sickness being castin upon her by your said devilish witchcraft, during the said space, until the said John Banks came to you and threatened you, at which time ye gaif him a gullion of silver [2s value], to hold his peace and conceal the same, promising to him that nothing should ail his wife. And thereafter, for that ye sent her ane cheese of the breadth of one loof, composed by your said devilish art of witchcraft, which ane jinke-roll, and desiring her the said Janet to eat the same, when (whereof the said Janet refused to eat,) yet immediately she grew well, but two of her kine died, the said sickness being casten upon them by your said wicked and devilish art of witchcraft.

2. *Witchcraft.*—Likeas also, you are indytit and accusit, for that by your said art of devilish witchcraft, ye did, upon the recovery of the said Janet, cast the same sickness upon Marion Banks, sister to the said John Banks, which troubled her after the same manner, tormenting her for twenty days, until that one Osla in Olnasfirth, coming to you, by direction of the said John Banks, and warned you hereof, whereupon, by your said devilish witchcraft, the said sickness was taken off the said Marion and casten upon a young cow of the said John's, which took wodrome, [*madness,*] and died within twenty-four hours, which ye cannot deny.

3. - *Item,* Ye the said Marion are indytit, for that you being very shroudly suspected, and commonly bruited as a common witch, ye coming along upon some of your said devilish and wicked intentions to unquil Edward Halcro in Overure, qr. he was dichting bear to steep for malt, you being of wicked intention, by your said devilish craft, did undo the said making of malt, and he suspecting you, after he had reproved you for minding you about him, ye said to him all would be well touching the said making, as it so fell out ; so taking upon you and acknowledging by your wordis your power in the said wicked and devilish art of witchcraft. That, after that, he being there scrowing corns, and ye persisting in your said wicked and devilish intentions to undo and provock the said Edwd. you did thereby marr and undo twa whole makings of the same bear, qlk never did good, qlk ye rank witch cannot deny.

4. *Witchcraft.*- Item, the said Marion is indytit and accusit for that in April 1641, the sd. Edwd. coming to your houss, after ye had urged him to take meat, he took resolution to go to the war [*sea-weed*] having not intention before, and going with Sueno your husband to the *gio* heid [*narrow creek with high rocks*] where they were usit to go down, he being affrayit to go down first, desyrit your husband to go before him, quha refusing to go, the raid Edwd. went, whereon he going down and stepping upon a stone which was ever a sure step before, ye the said Marion, be yor. said wicked and devilish art of witchcraft, maid the said stone to lows and fall down with him, whereby his life was in great perill, yet saved to the admiration of all the beholders. And ye being accusit for taking the said occasion and cryme upon you, anserit that it was not for his gud, but for Helen Thomson his spous gud that he was savit.

5. *Witchcraft.*—Item, ye the said Marion are indyttit and accusit for that ye by yor said wicked and devilish art of witchcraft, did cast ane terrible and fearful madnes and sickness upon ane Madda Scuddasdoughter, your awin friend, becaus she wold not byd with you, yron she continuit most terriblie tormentit, and throw the torment of the sd. disease, she was caryit manytimes to run upon her awin sister yt. keepit her, and divers so as to have devorit them in her madnes, and so continuit a zeir and half ane zeir, till she, being counsallit be   of Hildiswick, ran upon the sd. Marion and drew blood of you, within Jas. Halcros hows, biting twa of yr. fingers till they bled, whereupon the said Madda Scuddadoughter recoverit of her disease, and came to her ryt sinces, thereby manifestly

LL

shewing, and approving your sd. trade, and exercising of you, said Marion Pardone, your sd. devilish and wicked craft of witchcraft, tormenting and abusing thereby of weak Christians, Goddis people, againes quhom ye carrie evil will and malice, which ye rank witch cannot deny.

6. *Witchcraft.*—Item, ye the sd. Marion Pardown ar indyttit and accusit for that zeers syne, James Halcro in Hilldiswick having a cow that ye alledged had pushed a cow of yours, ye in revenge thereof, by yr. said devilish art of witchcraft, made the sd. James his cow, milk nothing but blood, whereas your awin cow had no harm in her milk; whereupon they suspecting you, shewit the sd. bloody milk to Marion Kilti your servant, quha desyrit of you the same bloody milk for Goddis caus to shew you, and said she houpit the cow sould be weil; quhilk having gotten, and coming therewith to your hous, and shawing it to you, thereafter the cow grew weil, thairby shewing and proving your sd. devilish practyce of the art of witchcraft.

7. *Witchcraft.*—Item, ye the said Marion are indyttit and accusit for that you having a'no 1642 zeirs, hyrit ane cow from Androw Smith, younger in Hildiswick, which ye keepit frae the bull, when she wald have taken bull, and the sd. Andro getting knowledge thereof, causit the same to be brought to the bull and bullit against your will. The next year when she calved, ye by your sd. devilish art of witchcraft, took away her proffeit and milk, sa that she milked nothing but water, quhilk stinked and tasted of sharn a long tyme, till that you comming by the sd. Andro his hous, he suspecting you, caused you to milk her and look to her, after which doing, immediately the sd. cows milk cam to its own nature,—thairby indicating and shewing your sd. devilish, and wicked, and abbominable airt and practyce of witchcraft,- and quhilk ye cannot deny.

8. *Witchcraft.*—Item, ye the said Marion ar indyttit and accusit, for that in anno , ye coming by ane pies of grass quhairin Andro Smith elder in Videfield had six kine tederit, quhairintil ye went, and out of whilk grass ye and your son, after you had lousit and taken the kyne, fell in scoulding with and abusit the said Andro, and said to him that he sould not have so many kyne to eat grass and milk the next zeir;—according to the qlk words, sa it fell out thereafter; for that by your sd. devilish art of witchcraft, the sd. hail six kyne died befoir the next half yeir, all fat and gudlike by that same order, as they were lousit by you on tether, beginning at the first cow, (quhilk was ane black cow, qlk ye lousit, qlk died 20 days before Yule, fat and tydie,) and so furth in succession the rest, by your sd. devilish witchcraft, conform to your sd. veneficial, wicked and malicious powers, qlk ye cannot deny.

9. *Witchcraft.*—Item, ye the sd. Marion ar indyttit and accusit for that yeirs syne, ye coming to the said Andro Smyth elder, and desyring him len you ane of his hors, to go to Urafirth to lead peatis, qlk he refusit to do, ye out of a wicked and malicious heart said to him that he would repent it: whereupon ye by your sd. wickeed and devilish airt of witchcraft, and for outting of your malice, and for keeping of your said devilish promeis, within aught days thereafter did kill ane of his best warke hors, and within half ane zeir thereafter other three of his sd. hors; thairby shewing baith in your words and deeds, your wicked and devilish skill concerning the practise of the fursd. devilish and abbominable airt of witchcraft, qlk ye cannot deny.

10. *Witchcraft.*—Item, you the sd. Marion ar indyttit and accusit, for that years syne, ye being suspectit to have castin sickness upon the said Andro Smith elder his oy, qrof she lay long benumed and senseless, ye coming tyme foirsd. to the hous of Overure, and they challenging and quarrelling you therfor, ye fell into cursing and swearing, and went to the dore, qr ane calf was standing in the dore besyd you, qrupon in your sd. wicked and devilish malice, be your sd. detestable craft of witchcraft, ye did cast sickness that it presentlie run mad, cracy, and died.

11. *Witchcraft.*—Item, ye the said Marion are indyttit and accusit for coming to Andro Erasmusson's house in Eshaness,   qr. he having ane cow three days calved befoir, qrupon as ye luikit, ye immediately be airt and devilrie cast sickness, that she immediatlie crap togidder, that no lyf was looked for her; till they sent for you, and causit you lay your hand upon her, qrupon scho then immediatlie recoverit, and was weil,—thereby

manifestlie and cleirlie shewing your forsd. wicked, devilish and detestabil lyf, carridge, trade and practise of the forsd. abominable airt and craft of witchcraft, qlk ye cannot deny.

12. *Witchcraft.*—Likeas ye the sd. Marion to cullour and extenuat your sd. craft, alledging that ye wantit the profit of your kyne, qlk was not true, but onlie to tak occasion, by your sd. wicked and devilish airt of the profit of the said Andro his kyne, came to his hous in July therefter, and efter cursing his wyf, quha shawed you the milk of her kyne, desirit her to caus Usla Sinclair, her servant woman, to go with you to kerne, qlk she did. Qrby, and by your sd. wicked and devilish airt, you touk away with you the profeit of the sd. Andro his kyne until the space of throttein dayes; till the sd. Andro his wyf went to your hous, and shewit you the milk and butter, and maid publication yrof to the nybours, and immediatlie thereafter gat back her profeit of baith her milk and butter;—qrby manifestly appears, and is shawen, your guiltines in taking the samen be your sd. wicked and detestabil aert of witchcraft, and your restoring again of the samen upon a challenge, qlk ye cannot deny. Item, ye ar indyttit and accusit for that   zeirs syne, ye cam to Thomas in Urabister, and desyrit a quoyach cow of his of four zeir old to hyre, qlk was with calf then, whereof he maid you half a grant, but not the full, untill he could advyse with his Mrs, the gud wyf of Urafirth, quha would not consent; and becaus ye gat her not, ye outscoldit him and wer verie angrie. And in revenge of his sd. refusal, immediatelie yrafter ye cas secknes upon the sd. cow, qlk being at the hill with otheris of his kyne, scho tuik a wodroam or madnes and cam scouring hame frae the rest to the byre dere, brak up the saim and went in, having her head thrawin backward to her back, that 4 people could not get it back, and thereby dyed throw the sh. diseas, cassin on her by your sd. airt, working and witchcraft, qlk ye cannot deny.

14. *Witchcraft.*—Lykeas ye not being in your devilish and wicked mynd eneugh revenget and satisfyit, ye be the same your craft. devilrie, and witchcraft, within six weeks yrefter, cast the lyke secknes upon ane uther cow of the sd. Thomas his kyne, whereby scho also died mad and in woddram, and for the qlk you are also indyttit, accusit, and cannot deny the samin.

15. *Witchcraft.*—Item, ye the sd. Marion are indyttit and accusit for that in anno 1634, at Michelmes, when the cornes were taking in, the sd. Thomas in Urabister having aught piere of hors and mairs gaing on the riggs of Olnais firth, ye cam furth with a staff to ding awa his hors, qn. ye fell and hurt your knee, whereupon ye, to revenge yourself, and to assyth your wicked and malicious heart and mynd, did, by your foirsd. airt of witchcraft and devilrie, caus that within aught dayis thereafter his best hors died, and thereafter before Candelmes uther sex hors and mares.

At Scalloway, the 15th March, 1645 zeirs.

We the Moderator and remanent Brethren of the Presb. of Zetland, being convened day and place forsaid, and having examined the above wreattin process, doe find and declare the poyntis former market in the margine [*now marked in Italics*]: being lawli prowing to be witchcraft, and yrfor the pairtie guiltie wortdy of death be the law of God and the law of the kingdome, and requyris you judges to put them to the knawledge of ane assye, and minister justice upon them accordinglie, as ye wil be ansrable to God, his Maijestie and Counsel, and to discharge of your deutie heeranent.

NICOL WHYTE, *Moderator.*
W. ROBERT MURRAY, *Clk.*

Fytts.—Item, ye the said Marion Peebles *alias* Pardoun, ar indyttit and accusit for that at Candlemiss or thereby 1643, on ane Sunday, ye coming into the hous of James Halcro in Hildiswick, where Andro Broun then wis for the time, and falling into contest, and fletting with him about linching ane boat, ye, being enraged, set your venefical malice against him, and cursit him with many wicked and execrable words, and by your damnable and venefical heart wishit and cravit ill may so befall him; whereupon by your develish airt and craft of witchcraft ye bewitched him, and cast sickness upon him immediatly that he fell in a deadlie sickness and diseas.—That upon Munday next hereafter, he did contract sa vehement and deadlie diseas and sickness, tormentit thereby fra the croun of his head to the sole of his fute, that there was no lyff expectit of him. Quhairfor his nybers, knawing your detestable brute of witchcraft, and your pouir at your said practising, and that on whomsoever your cursed charm fell, sum notable and extraordinar mischieff and evile followit to yame, they did advys him to send for you, to shaw that there wis na lyff for him, and that they all suspectit you for casting the samin upon him. Qupairupon, after many dinyellis to cum and see him, at last you cam to him, quhen shewing you his diseas and sickness, togidder with the racking pain thereof, imputit by him and utheris to be your act and doing, Andro thaerfor pray it you to lay your hand upon him, which you wold not do, nor be na intreattie nither of him nor of your nybures moved thereto, till that they all that were in the hous, being wearied of your refusal, went furth grivet, and prayit you for Goddis cause to lay your hand upon him ; and then at last, being movit thereto, using your said venefical and damnabil charms and witchcraft, ye did uncover his leg, and pat your finger thereon, and on the ground three several tymes, to and fra ; qrby immediatlie, by your said airt of witchcraft and charms, he fell, and said his pein and diseas was desolvit frae the crown of his head to the sole of his fute ; at qlk tyme he was before her tueth sa heavyly diseased frae top to toe, through all his body, with swelling in his handes, lykwise armis, leges and knees, that he was unable to move or turn himself in the bed ; but after your said tutch, he became able to sit up, and turn himself in the bed, and within twa dayes, was fullie recoverit. and went furth. Quhilk sudden recoverie, togidder with your forme and manner of charming, and cureing of be your said tutch and charmes being spread abroad amang your nybers, and the same cuming to your ears, about 14 days after his recoverie, ye said to your nybbers, emgrace on them that had bewitched you, that wald not witch you oer the bankes [*high rocky shore*] ; quhairupon immediatlie again he fell again in the sd. sicknes wors than befoir, and paynet away with sic extremetie of sickness, that he sent to you againe, desyring meat out of your hand ; and after long intreatie, ye wald not cum to him with it, least your witchcraft and charmes again sould cum to lyt, but sent wt. Swene your husband, ane bannock,* after long stryving betwixt the sd. Swene and you, qlk of you sould give the samin to him ; qlk he having eaten, he again recoverit presentlie thereafter, and the sd. sicknes was cassin be you upon ane cow, pertaining also to Andro, qlk then died. Qlk haill premis wer wrought and done be your sd. detestable and devilish airt of witchcraft and charming, qlk ye cannot deny.

Item, ye the sd. Marion, ar indyttit and accusit for that, you bearing ane deadlie and veneficall malice in your heart agains the sd. umquill Edward Halcro in Overure, (as in your former dettayes and accusationis persisting in,) and incrissing your malice and divelish intentiones of your wicked heart, and taking occasion to renew and bring your wicked intention by your sd. wicked airt of witchcraft, to work his ruyine and death,—(being set on edge be a speitch spoken he him to the sd. Swene your husband, when he was castin [*cuting*] peates to him in Voir [*seed time*] last year, as the sd. Andro Brown also was castin peats to him, having callit to your sd. husband, and bade him go to you, to desyre you to go to your polbe [*nurse's husband*] the devill, and bid him loose ane knot, that the sd. Andro Brown myt be able, being then verie waik, to cast out his bank of peates :)—qurpon ye and the sd. Swene being angrie, awaitting your occasion to practise your said abominable airt and craft of witchcraft, to destroy and put down the sd. Edward Halcro, and having covenantit and conversit with the devill to bring the saim to pass, (as ane declaration of umquill Jvenit Fraser, witch, whom disyrit the devill to move her to assist you doth prove, qlk the both hefore and after her conviction did testiffie,) ye be your sd. wicked, detestable, abhominable and develish airt of witchcraft, being transformed in the lyknes of an pellack quhaill, (at the [counsel of the sd. Swene,] and be your consent and wish, the devill changing your spirit, qlk fled in the same quhaill ;) and the said Edward being at sey with Malcolm Smyth, sone unto Helen Cloustin, his spous, and Nicol Smyth, sone to Grissel Bruce in Gluis, and   Finland, servant to the sd. Edward, all four in ane fishing-boat coming frae the sey at the north bankis of Hildiswick, on ane fair morning, the   day of

---

* Marginal Note in the handwriting of the Moderator, "then confessit, she sent the Bannock."

last bypast, ye did cum under the said boat and overturnit her with ease, and drowned and devoirit thame in ye sey, right at the shore, when there wis na danger utherwayis, nor hazard to have cassin thame away, it being sik fair widder, as said is. Lykwais when the said umquill Edward wis fund with the said umquill   , and you and the said Swino your husband wir sent for, and brought to see thame, and to lay your hands on thame   dayis after said death and away casting, quhaire their bluid was evanished and desolved from every natural cours or caus to shie and run, the said umquill Edward bled at the collir bain or craig bane, and the said   in the hand and fingers, gushing out bluid thereat to the great admiration of the beholders and revelation of the judgment of the Almytie. And by which lyk occasionis and miraculous works of God, made manifest in murders, and the murderers, whereby be many frequent occasiones brought to light, and the murderers be the sd. proof brought to judgment, convict and condemned, not onlie in this kingdom, also this countrie, but lykwayis in maist forrin Christiane kingdomis; and be so manie frequent precedentis and practising of and tuitching murderis and murdereris notourllie known, so that the foirsaid murder and witchcraft of the sadis persons, with the rest of their companions, through your said husbands deed, art, part, rad and counsall, is manifest and cleir to not onlie through and by the foirsaid precedentis of your malice, wicked and malishis practises, by witchcraft, confessionis and declarations of the said umquill Janet Fraser, witch, revealed to her as said is, and quha wis desyrit by him to concur and assist with you to the doing thereof; but lykwais be the declaration and revelation of the justice and judgmentis of God, through the said issueing of bluid from the bodies, qrby booth you and your said husband are found takin, and proven in the art of your said witchcrait and murder; and speciallie when the said Marion Peebles *alias* Pardoun, now an pannel, quhilk ye booth rank witch and murderir, cannot deny.

Lykeas ye the said Marion, indyttit and accusit as ane common rank witch, charmer and deceaver, and quaha wer all your dayes, then lx. years and more, been so report and halden, bearing yourself sa,   consulting, riving with the devill in his caus, who did change lyknis appearing to you severallie; for that ye being cuming fra Breckon to Hildeswick, in the month of   last, quhen you wir to be apprehendit and sent in for the foirsayid crymes to suffer, the devill there in the way, did converse and appear to you, both in your going to and frae Brecken and Hildiswick, in the lyknes of twa corbies, ane on every side of you, clos at your sides, going and happing alongis the way with you to Hildiswick, and stayid where you went, not leaving you three quarters of a myle, till Robert Ramsay overtuik you, when they came full flyght to the sey, and the   corn land and hills; he then did challenge you anent the saidis corbies, of the cause of thair so far accompanying you, sa neir and sa far way, it not being the natuir of wyld fuillis to follow sa far, and keep pace sa neir approaching ony man or woman. Ye then did cast a glos upon it, saying they smellit bread on you, quhilk made them, (to quhom ye sayd ye was casting bread) to come,—quhilk wis onlie a lie maid by you, conceeling. At your returne they continuit with you, and conversit *ut supra*, als far back agane as scoir and threttein. As lykways, you have not onlie behavid yourself as sayd is, as ane common rank witch, alwayis giving yourself to charmis, and never knowing the tew God, and quhom the truly sentifyed Chryst ar, not sa much as to learne the Lordis Prayer, nor to repeat the samen in all your lyfetime, but ar reprobit from God; has given yourself, boith saul and bodie, to serving the Devill, and bund up in him, that you will not muster power, nor will cast off the Devill, sa mutch as to follow learning to repeat the Lordis Prayer amangist Goddis ministers and children, but ar, and has been all your dayis ane wicked, devilish, fearful and abhominable curser; quhaver ye ever cursed, ane them ye disendit and wishit evil to, everie evil sicknes, herme and death followit thereupon, throw your   diabolical tongue, witchcraft and cursing. And has ever behavit yourself as ane common witch and charmer, taker away of your nyber's profeits of their roumes, landes, cornes, grass, butter, key, sheip, and wul, and a charmer and healer of sum, and caster of sicknesses upon uthers, and everie way living a damnable, wicked and diabolical lyff, contrarie to God and his commandments. Quhilk you cannot deny, and quhairfoir you the said Marion ought and sould undergo the tryal of ane assyse, and being convictit and adjudged thairfoir to the death, and your hail landis, if

any be, ye have foirfattit, and your moveabil goods escheat and inbrought to his Majesty's use, conforme to the lawis and daylie practise of this realme.*
The Brethren considering the premises *ut supra* in the former sheets of paper.

                                                              NICOL. WHYTE, *Moderator.*
                               (Signed)   W. ROBERT MURRAY, *Clk.*
Provin.

Curia Justiciar. vicecomitatus de Zetland, tento apud Scalloway Banks, in castro ibidem, per venerabiles viros Magistrum Jacobum Mouat de Ollaberrie, Johannem Stewart de Bigtoun, et Patricum Umphray de Sand, Vicecomitatus ac Justiciar Deputatus, die vigesimo primo Martis 1644.

Curia tenta et legitima affirmata.

The quhilk day compearit James Gray, Pror-fiscal, and producit the dittay of witchcraft given agains Marion Pardon and Margaret Guthramdaughter witches, pannels, and desyrit they sould be accusit, and the said ditty put to the trial of an assyze; whereupon the Judges Deputes ordained them to be called, upon which the Pror-fiscal askit instruments of Court.

ASSYZE.

Jas. Mouat of Hamne Voe.	Manis Finlayson in Burroland.
Olla Manson of Hesbrough.	Manis Swainson in Tongine.
Andro Manson of Mangister.	Willm. Tullocht in Skelberrie.
Thos. Manson in Braure.	Olla Williamson in Glus.
Laurene Gresvillsone in Tanwick.	John Ornsone, *senior* in Enisfirth.

Jas. Gryersone in Setter.
Olla Gunner in Sullom.
Jas. Andrewsone in Uzea.
Andrew Smyt, younger in Hildswicke.

The Assyze being recavit, sworn and admittit; and, after reading the dittay, and examination of the pennelles thereupon, and having recavit the depositiunes of divers famous witnesses, quhilk wer sworne tutching the dittays, proving them, as lykwayes in consideration of their confessions, and instances markit and set downe in and upon the said dittayis. They passing out of judgment, and reconsidering the saidis dittayis, togidder with the saidis depositiones of witnesses, having namit Olla Mansone of Hesburgh chancellar; and after examining the hail poyntis and consultation of the delusions and confessiones of the said Marion, fyllis hir, that the hail poyntis of dittay are agains her, boith general and special, except thelt of Thomas of Urabister not provin, and anent Edward Halero's malt, quherein they rest clauseure, and

They all in one voice ffyllis her of the haill poyntis of dittay producit, and remittis sentens to the Judges, and dome to the dempster. In witnes qrof subscribit be the chancellar.

                                         (Signed)   OLLAW MAGNASSONE.

Continuis sentence to the morow xxij Martii 1644.

The Judges adjudges and decerns the pannells to be taken brought hence to the place of execution to the Hill of Berrie, and there wyryt at ane stak, and brunt in ashes, betwix and 2 aftirnoone, qlk Andro of Offir, dempster, gave for dome.

Respecting the foregoing Trial of Witches, the original document was in the possession of a

---

* " Proven also Mart. Qn thay war waking er, scho speirit qr her husband wis, qn answeting her speiring gains her husband, scho assertit he lay tutching her hand, and would not suffer her to confess."—The Note is in the handwriting of the Moderator.

gentleman of Shetland, lately deceased. It is to be regretted that the transcript made from it is in some degree an imperfect one; but I have rather preferred printing it as it has been received, than make any change that is not authorised by the original, which I have not the means of consulting. The possession of the transcript I obtained through the kindness of Mr Ross, late Collector of the Customs in Lerwick.

The custom of Casting Hearts, alluded to in page 274, is so well related by Miss Campbell of Lerwick, in the Notes to her recent Novel entitled Harley Radington, illustrative of Shetland manners, that I shall beg leave to transcribe the passage.

"When people are afflicted with consumptive complaints in Zeatland, they image that the heart of the person so affected has been wasted away by the enchantment of the fairies, or witchcraft of some other evil beings.* Old women, and sometimes men, profess to cure this disease. The patient must undergo the following curious and very ridiculous operation: —He is directed to sit upon the bottom of a large cooking pot, turned upon its mouth; a large pewter dish is placed, or held upon his head; upon the dish a bason or bowl is set nearly full of cold water; into this water the operator pours some melted lead though the teeth of a common dressing comb. A large key is also employed in this operation. All this is performed with many strange incantations and gesticulations. If the lead falls into a shapeless lump, they declare that the heart and the lungs of the patient are completely washed away, that they will have infinite trouble, and perhaps, after all, will not be able to bring back the heart and lungs to their natural and healthful form. The lead is again melted, and run into the water through the teeth of the comb; it most likely assumes some shape, which the operator assures the spectators is the exact form of the patient's heart in its diseased state. The lead is repeatedly melted, and poured through the comb into the water; every time it is asserted to be more and more like the natural heart and lungs, and the bewitchment, of course, is rendered weaker and weaker. The patient undergoes this three times, with some days between each operation. When the last cast of the lead is over, the operator shews it round, and points out how exactly every part of the heart and the lungs are restored to their natural and proper shape; if the patient dies (perhaps his death is hurried on by the fatigue and agitation occasioned by this mummery), his death is ascribed to some oversight in the strict performance of all the relative parts of this casting of the heart. The moon must be at a certain age, and it must be performed at a certain turning of the tide and hour of the night; numberless other things must be attended to. The operator will take anything they please to give, if it should be the half of all their goods and chattels, but he must not touch money. He appoints, however, a particular place, where a Danish coin, worth fivepence, current in Zealand, is to be laid, (as many as they like—the more the better, no doubt); this money is for the fairies, who come, it is asserted, and take it away; but the poor honest operator must not, and will not finger it, otherwise his trouble would come to nought, and the spell which bound the patient would be firmer than ever. This operation of casting the heart is performed to this day in some parts of the Zetland Isles, and implicit belief placed in this efficacy. The patient must wear the lead, which has been used, in his bosom, for some time after the operation."

ADDITIONS TO ITER IV.†

In a pamphlet, entitled, *Considerations on the Fisheries in the Scotch Islands*, there are

---

* I found Dyspepsia to be the most frequent disorder attributed to a decay of the heart.—S. H.
† Having finished my journey through the Isles of Shetland, I have to acknowledge the attentions and civilities I received from several gentlemen not before mentioned, among whom are Mr Scott, *jun.* of Sands, Mr Ross of Weisdale, and Mr Moncrieff of Selie Voe.

many curious detached circumstances relative to the fisheries of Shetland, as they were conducted several years ago, a few of which I shall extract.

Description of the Haaf about fifty years ago, when succouring vessels were employed in guarding crews.

"The various articles for the grand fishery being provided, the natives push in a body, all round the islands, on the same day, which is commonly the 1st of June, and a kind of annual jubilee. They soon reached the Haaf:"—"There they immediately set to work, and persevere with the most unremitting diligence during the season, which only lasts six weeks; for when the sun declines to the south, the nights grow dark, and the succouring vessels frequently lose sight of the boats under their care. These boats left to themselves, strive to push for the shore, amidst the greatest danger, especially when they are stationed on the west of the Shetlands, about 15 or 16 leagues out at sea; and often miserably perish within sight of the shore, where the wives and children of the poor fishers are the melancholy witnesses of their sad catastrophe, without being able to afford them any assistance."

"Many adventurers from the south have for several years past fished on these coasts with uncommon success, and greatly improved this important branch of trade. They arrive on the coast in small vessels of 60 or 20 tons; and after purchasing their boats in the country, and hiring their fishers by the month or season maintenance included; they put three boats, commonly with five men in each, under the care of one vessel; the most experienced man in every boat is made patron or skipper."—"They proceed to what distance these skippers direct, towing their boats with proper ropes, placed in such a manner, that they do not run foul of one another, at any time during the passage. The first day the men in each boat assist in beating the lines, and have them all ready for the night's fishing. When they are about to throw their lines, the vessels bring to, and the boats are manned; they then put off together from the vessel, rowing different ways from each other, on a certain point of the compass, with which each boat is supplied; and when they come to the designed spot, they cast their first buoy. While the boats are fishing, the succouring vessels run around them, telling them the hour of the night, keeping close to the fishers, and cheering them to support their spirits in this dangerous and fatiguing business. About an hour after sunrise, they begin to take in the lines, and when that is done, they return to the ships, where they throw their fish on board, and moor their boats properly astern, at necessary intervals. The different crews, after having refreshed themselves, and taken some rest, return to their fish about noon, and vie with each other who shall cure them the best."

APPENDIX.

In this Appendix, I shall insert a few articles I have omitted treating of.

Bressay.—In page 109, it might have been stated, that Bressay was the ancient property of the Hendersons of Gardie, the eldest branch of an early Scandinavian family, descended from a grand Fowde, sent to Shetland by the King of Denmark in the 15th century, whose commission was, until a late date, carefully preserved. Their names ceased to be regular patronymics about a century and a half ago. At that time their estate, which was the largest in the country, was divided, according to the laws of udal succession, among six sons. The Island of Bressay became the property of the late Thomas Mouat, Esq. of Garth, by marriage with the niece and heiress of the late James Henderson, Esq. of Gardie. It is now in possession of his nephew William Mouat, Esq.

Coal-fish.—In page 78, the particular manner in which the fishing of the *Gadus carbonarius* is conducted, was not described. But in a pamphlet published A.D. 1787, entitled Considerations on the Fisheries in the Scottish Islands, it is particularly mentioned, and I understand that it is conducted in the same manner at the present day. The coal-fish are taken in the Rousts of Sumburgh and Scaw.

"The yawl contains three and sometimes four men, for the cole-fishery. Each of the boats is rowed by two men; the others are placed one at the stern and another at the head, with floating lines thrown out on the tide-side; the hook being baited with the whitest part of the belly of the cole, cut nearest to the size of a herring. The rowers direct the boat as close to the edge of the broken water as they can with safety; for were they to fall into the tide, they must perish, as no assistance could be given them. They exert their utmost strength on this occasion, to keep the hook always on the surface, whilst the fishers fix their eyes on the bait, as the more the water is raised by the force of the tide, the more successful the fishing proves, as the deceit is better concealed. Whenever the coles come to the surface of the water, they are then in quest of herrings, and if the fishers find any in their stomachs, they deem it a treasure, and apply small pieces of it over the other bait. When the tide is run and the fish follows, he drags for it, by putting to the line a lead or *sinker*, which is commonly a pound and a half weight; this being let down into the water to the depth of twenty fathoms or more, he hauls it up with all quickness possible. Thus the deception takes place most powerfully, and the fish aiming at the herring in motion, and seemingly running away, is the more easily taken. This species always plunges deeper into the water, in proportion as the tide wears weak."

Whales.—In page 172, it might have been observed with regard to any whale being driven ashore, that, according to the old laws of Shetland, it was not a droit of Admiralty, unless it was too large to be drawn by four oxen.

Sheep-Pastures.—In page 185, I was apprehensive of having too strongly reprobated the practice of rooing sheep, which is much abused, from the neglect of selecting a proper time for the operation, (if, indeed, any time be justifiable for its adoption,) when the wool is not naturally loosened. I find, however, that Mr Low, in his Fauna Orcadensis, is infinitely more decisive than myself in protesting against the practice. He calls the penns, in which the rooing is performed, a place of execution, where the wool is torn, not shorn, off the backs of the sheep,—"an operation," he adds, "that brings the whole blood into their skin, and is not only disgusting, but, if the season proves harsh, is the cause of great destruction." Miss Campbell, the writer whom I have lately quoted, observes, that "the wool is not cut off with sheers, but pulled up by the roots, and the animal is left quite naked; that, too, in the month of May, when the weather is often extremely cold and stormy in Zetland. It is supposed that the wool gets coarse from being cut, and this barbarous practice is continued for the sake of preserving wool very fine."

Regent's Fishing Bank, page 250.—I have received a few additional particulars respecting this bank, from a young man, Arthur Halcro, employed in fishing upon it this year, who attended me through the various parts of Shetland, when I visited the country. He states, that forty vessels were this summer employed on the bank, who met with the greatest success, whenever the weather was favourable. The depth of water on it, he considers to be from 46 to 70 fathoms; and he supposes it to terminate in a point from which Foula lies E. by S.

Population.—In Shetland this is a curious investigation, but it requires so many data before we can account for the variations it has exhibited, that I would rather decline the task of entering upon the subject at all, than treat of it most imperfectly. The number of inhabitants was estimated in the year 1755 at 15,210; in the year 1793 at 20,186; and in 1810 at 23,000. Mr Sheriff, in the latter period, conceived, that the cultivated land did not exceed 25,000, or 50 square miles: that the population was equal to any part of the British Empire where great towns did not prevail, and that there were not fewer than 460 persons upon each square mark of land that is cultivated; the Scathold adding little to wealth and support.

Ancient Music of Shetland.—In page 253 and 259 allusion was made to the Day-Dawn and to the Foula Reel, two Shetland airs, the first of them being very ancient. By the kindness of Mr Henderson of Bardister, I have procured a copy of these melodies, as they have been set by Miss Kemp of Edinburgh, a teacher of acknowledged musical taste and abilities, to whom I feel particularly obliged for this favour. A native Shetland song, to the tune of the Foula Reel, first appeared among an ingenious collection of poems, written by Miss Chalmers of Lerwick, and it is copied from thence in page 259.

The Day Dawn.

AN ANCIENT SCANDINAVIAN AIR PRESERVED IN SHETLAND, SET BY MISS KEMP OF EDINBURGH.

The Foula Reel.

A POPULAR NATIVE SHETLAND AIR, SET BY MISS KEMP OF EDINBURGH.

INDEX.

Aithsvoe, 182.
Agricultural Society, 202, and Preface.
Armada, Spanish, shipwreck of, on the Shetland coast, 4, 29, 196.

Baa, 260.
Bailiff, ancient, of Shetland, 100, 101.
Bailiasta, Kirk of, 157.
Balta Sound, 163.
Bigsetter Voe, 201.
Black cattle, 168, 177.
Bland, 177, 252.
Bledoe, 207.
Boats, 0, 222.
Boatmen, 197.
Booths, 169.
Bothwell, Earl of, anecdote of, 112.
Boumacks of Orkney, 136.
Bressay and Bressay Sound, 109, 111.
Broonies, 207.
Brownie (a domestic trow,) 205 to 207.
Buidy, 207.
Buill, 184.
Buill, Head of, 125.
Burgh, Barons of, 114.
Burghs, ancient, 86, 107, 149, 156, 171, 195, &c.
Burra Voe, in Yell, 169.
Burroland, 89.
Busta, 181.
Bysmer, 209.

Ca'ing-whale, see Delphinus deductor.
Canage, 135.
Carbuncle, superstition relating to, 275.
Carmelan, (vessel so named), shipwreck of, 117.
Cassies, or straw-baskets, 179.
Casualties of superiority, 134.
Catfirth, 113.
Christianity, introduction of, 162, 236.
Chromate of Iron, 164, 278, and Preface.
Chapels, old, 198, 203, 236.
Cliff-Hills, 71.
Coal-fish, 78, 289. (See also Sillocks and Piltocks.)
Cod Fishery, 230, 251, 290. (See also Ling Fishery.)
Colafiord Voe, 218.
Coningsburg, 91.
Cornwaters, 259.
Costume of the Natives, 9, 24, 82, 188.
Cottages, 21, 243.
Crucifield, 160.
Cullswick, 195.

Cupping, mode of, 244.

Day-dawn, an ancient air, 253.
Deaths and Funerals, customs and superstitions relating to, 248, 249.
Delphinus deductor, or ca'ing whale, 165, 172.
Dependants or Retainers introduced by Lord Robert Steuart, 75.
———— of Scotland, bound by an obligation of manrent, 140.
Dikes, 168, 203.
Doreholm, 234.
Dunrossness, 8, 13.

Eagleshaw, 238.
Eshaness, 234.
Eswick, 114.

Fair Isle, 4, 27.
Feideland, 220.
Festivities, 252.
Fetlar, Island of, 148.
Fevers, ravages of, 243.
Fishing Station, description of, 221.
Fitfiel-Head, 8, 70.
Fits prevalent during divine service, 158.
Fladibister, 92.
Floke, (a pirate,) anecdote of, 201.
Food, 207.
Foude or Fowde, 100, 101.
Foula Reel, 291.
Fortified sites of ground, 72, 79, 116, 149, 156.
Foula, Island of, 274.
Frau-a-Stack, 250.
Funzie, 150.

Garthsness, 72.
Gio, definition of, 73.
Girlsta, Lake of, 201.
Godsends, 197.
Grassum, 43, 132.
Grutness Voe, 12.
Gue, 259.
Guisards, 257.
Gulberswick, 278.

Haaf, 221, 288.
Habitations, ancient and modern. (See also Cottages), 167, 241, 246.
Had-dogs, 184.
Hamburgh Traders, 169, 217.

INDEX.

Harvest, 204, 276.
Hascosea, 109.
Hawk-hens, 134, 176.
Helga Water, 232.
Helyer, 170.
Hermaness, 158.
Herring-Fishery, 214.
Hillswick, 228.
Hoga, 199.
Hospitality, general remarks on, 277.

Infield, 202.
Iron-mica, 71.
—— pyrites, 72.
Jurisdiction of Shetland, history of, 99, 143. (See also History of Udallers.)
Juggs, 171.

Kelp, 169, 207.
Kirk-Holm, 196.
Kirn-Milk, 177, 207.
Kiverins, 188.
Kleber, 244.
Klibbar, 179.
Knots, superstitions of, 269.

Lagman. (See Lawman and Foude.)
Latitude of Shetland, 1.
Land-maill, 43.
Language, 11, 224, 275.
Lawman, 102. (See also Foude.)
Law-book, ancient, 102.
Lawright-man, 39, 101.
Lawtings, 99, 149, 160.
Lewismen, 79, 275.
Lerwick, 107.
Light-house (Sumburgh,) 77, 141.
Lines, fishing. (See Ling and Cod Fisheries.)
Ling-fishery, 216, 220, 225, 226, 229, 288.
Lits or Dyes, 188.
Lodges, Fishermens', 221.
Longevity, 244.
Longitude of Shetland, 1.
Lubba, 183.
Luggie's Knoll, 111.
Lunna, 114.

Maiseys, 180.
Magnus, St,, 236.
Maurent. (See Dependants.)
Manure, 201.
Mark of Land, 35, 131. (See History of the Udallers.)
Marriages, 247, 253.
Mavis Grind, 216.
Medicines, ancient, 244.
Medina Sidonia, Duke of, anecdote of. (See Armada.)
Meikle Roe, 214.
Meiths, 221.
Mill, 205.
Moggies livered and cropping, 232.
Molucca beans, 151.
Mouness Castle, 164.
Mousa, 86.
Music, 258.

Natives, physiognomy of, 23.
Navir, Grind of, 236.
Noss, 109.

Opgester, and custom of opgesterie, 128.
Otters, 242.
Ox and sheep silver, (or penny), 48, 112.
Outfield, 202.

Outskerries, 116.

Papa Stour, 249.
Parishes, regulations of, 239.
Pastures, 204.
Patronymics, 247.
Peat, 178
Piltocks, 25.
Plough, 200.
Poor, (Parochial Regulations), 240.
Population, 290.
Poultry-fowls, 135.
Putting-stone, 275.

Quarf, 199.
Quendal, 12, 19, 69.
Quern, 205.

Radmen, 103.
Raiths, 221.
Ranselmen, 39, 100, 143, 239.
Regent's Fishing Bank, 230, 290.
Rental, ancient, 133.
Rivlins, 24.
Roads, 106.
Roeness Voe and Hill, 225.
Roer Water, 218.
Roman Antiquities, 13, 30, 148, 156.
Romances, ancient Norse, 258, 280.
Ronans, 198.
Rooms, 167.
Rousts, 77, 156, 163, 289.
Rueing, 185, 290.
Runic Inscriptions, 237, 248.

Sandlodge (Mines), 90, 142.
Sandness, 264.
Sand Voe, (Northmavine), 224.
Sandwick, 81.
Saxavord, 159.
Saxe's Kettle, 164.
Scalloway, 93.
—— Bay of, 196.
Scat. 36.
Seatholds, 37, 70, 199.
Scraada, holes of, 235.
Sena Gull, 276.
Scudler, 257.
Seals, 166, 251, 261, 274.
Seas, superstitions of, 260.
Seater, 177.
Sepulchral remains, 69, 166, 182, 218, 237, 238, 248.
Sheep, 70, 182, 209, 290.
Shell-fish found in Sumburgh, 81.
Shelty, 70, 157, 179.
Shetland, history of, dark period, 13.—Subdued by Harold, 34. - Becomes pledged to Scotland, 42. (See History of the Udallers.)
Shynd-bill, 122.
Shoopiltee, 254, 261.
Sillocks, 25, 31, 182, 250.
Sinclairs, of House Island, 198.
—————— Orkney, (Four brothers), 115.
—————— Strom, 201.
Skeo, 169, 207.
Skerry Fight, 118.
Spade, 179, 200.
Sperre, Malis, feud of, 199.
Steepled Chapels, 198.
Steinbartes, 83, 141.
Stenness, 235.
Stock-fish, 170, 207.
Stone-Axes. (See Steinbartes.)
Stewarts, Earl Robert, 74. (See also History of the Udallers.)

—— Patrick, 93. Ditto.
Strom, Lake of, 202.
Sumburgh, 73.
Swire, 70, 177.
Sword-dance, 252.

Tait, David Gilbert, 151.
Tangwick, 234.
Teinds, 137, 227.
Temples, Scandinavian, 159.
Tenants, kindly, 132.
Tenures, Feudal, illustrations of, 132.
—— Udal, 119.
—— Fishing, 226.
Thule, 275.
Tingwall, 98.
Toasts, 208.
Torsk or Tusk fish, 116, 252.
Towns, 167.
Town-mails, 177.
Tows, 222.
Trees, 178.
Trades, 208.
Trolhouland, 189.
Trows, 189.
————, Sea, 160, 264.
Tuskar, 179.

Vailey, 264.
Variola, mode of treating, by John Williamson, 238.
Ve Skerries, 262.
Vementry, 241.
Villians, of Ure, 235.
Visseeks, 259.
Vivda, 170, 207.
Voe, 73.
Volcanic Products, 159.
Vord Hills, 159, 226, 241, &c.

Udal Lands, origin and definition of 36, 37, and 115.
—— Tenures, nature of, 119 to 121.
—— Laws, origin and diversity of, 121 to 131, and 145.
—— Laws, perfectly distinct from Feudal conditions, 131, 132.
Udallers, history of. Mode of adjusting a mark of land, 35 to 37. What part of their lands were liable to scat, and their mode of paying it, 37. Oppressed by the mother country of Norway, 38. Shetland constituted into a Fowdrie, 38. Relations of Udallers to the Earl of Orkney, 39. Burdens of tithes, umboths and wattle, 40. Origin of laws of udal succession, 40. Lands during the Norwegian Government never feudalised, 41. The Earldom of Orkney, including Shetland, accrues to Henry Sinclair of Scotland, 42. Orkney and Shetland become pledged to the Scottish Crown, with a stipulation that their ancient laws should be preserved inviolate, 42.—Feudality first introduced into Shetland in its mildest form, 43.—Udallers distinguish themselves from feudal tenants by the name of Rothmen or Roythmen, 44.—New Scottish settlers endeavour to set aside the old laws of udal succession, and introduce newer ones, more favourable to primogeniture, 44, 145.—Udallers under Sir Ja. Sinclair, resist the invasion of their udal rights, by defeating the Earl of Caithness, 45.—Lord Robert Steuart becomes feuar of Orkney and Shetland, 45.—The Crown creates a number of feudal vassals, 45.—Grant to Lord Robert Steuart revoked in favour of the Earl of Boswell, who was created Duke of Orkney, 46.—Probable intentions of Scotland never to part with Orkney and Shetland, 46.—Lord Robert Stewart, reinstated as feuar of

Orkney and Shetland, who exchanges his Abbey of Holyrood for the temporal estates of the Bishopric of Orkney, 47.—Oppressions of the udallers under him, in his endeavours to wrest from them their estates, 47, 48.—Lord Robert deposed, and imprisoned for his persecutions, 48.—Reinstated in his possessions, with the additional powers of Justiciar; also created Earl of Orkney and Lord of Zetland, and after a temporary exclusion from the possession of the Bishopric, restored to it, 49.—Again disposed, 50.—Earldom granted to Lord Chancellor of Scotland and the Lord Justice-Clerk, 50.—Lord Robert Steuart reinstated, who assumes the power, in consequence of his new grant, of overruling the decrees of Court with regard to udal lands, and of confiscating estates, 50, 52.—Patrick Steuart, son to Robert, is invested with the Earldom, who exercises powers of the most illegal kind in his designs on udal lands, 52, 53. Deposed, 53.—His estates not immediately declared to be forfeited and for what reason, 54, 55.—Orkney and Shetland again annexed to the Crown, and arrangements in consequence, 55.—Granted to Farmers, 56.—Altered state of udal tenures after the forfeiture of Earl Patrick, 56, 57.—Tyrannies of the Tacksmen to whom Orkney and Shetland were let, 57.—Encroachments on the possessions of the udallers by the new settlers, 59.—Earl of Morton acquires possession of the Crown estates of Orkney and Shetland, on the plea of a mortgage, and usurps a direct superiority over udal lands, 60.—Orkney and Shetland seized upon by Cromwell, 60.—Agin restored, on plea of a mortgage, to the Morton family, 61.—Douglass of Spynie, Fuctor of the Crown rents, feudalises nearly all the udal lands, and adds to the distresses of the udallers, 61.—Denmark fails in obtaining an acknowledgment that Orkney and Shetland were held in pledge to this power, 62.—Orkney and Shetland re-annexed to the Crown, by the cancelling of the claims of the Morton Family, 64.—Orkney and Shetland let out to Tacksmen, 65.—State of Bishops' rents, 66. Earl of Morton reinstated, with new powers, 66.—He obtains a discharge of the reversion, but is deprived of the jurisdiction of the islands, 66. Sells his interest in the islands to Sir Lawrence Dundas, 66.—Effects arising from the ancient injuries which Orkney and Shetland have sustained, 67.—Termination of a law-suit brought by Sir Lawrence Dundas, relative to the landed tenures of Shetland, 138.
Unicorn Rock, 112.
Urns, ancient sepulchral, 166, 182.
Uyea Sound, (Unst), 165.

Wadmel, 35, 187.
Water, superstitions respecting, 164, 232, 272.
Wattle, 48, 134.
Weapons of War, ancient, 85, 141.
Weights and Measures, 133, 209.
Whales, 261, 290. See also Delphinus Deductor.
Whalsey, 116.
Whiteness, 201.
Witchcraft, history of, 265, 280.
Wool, 187.
Wrecks, 245, 265, 277.

Yaggers, 214, 265.
Yawls. See boats.
Yelaburn, 164.
Yell, 169.
Yell Sound, 172.

www.ingramcontent.com/pod-product-compliance
Lightning Source LLC
Chambersburg PA
CBHW022057230426
43672CB00008B/1200